JOHN OF THE CROSS AND THE COGNITIVE VALUE OF MYSTICISM

The New Synthese Historical Library
Texts and Studies in the History of Philosophy

VOLUME 37

Series Editor:

NORMAN KRETZMANN, *Cornell University*

Associate Editors:

DANIEL ELLIOT GARBER, *University of Chicago*
SIMO KNUUTTILA, *University of Helsinki*
RICHARD SORABJI, *University of London*

Editorial Consultants:

JAN A. AERTSEN, *Free University, Amsterdam*
ROGER ARIEW, *Virginia Polytechnic Institute*
E. JENNIFER ASHWORTH, *University of Waterloo*
MICHAEL AYERS, *Wadham College, Oxford*
GAIL FINE, *Cornell University*
R. J. HANKINSON, *University of Texas*
JAAKKO HINTIKKA, *Boston University, Finnish Academy*
PAUL HOFFMAN, *Massachusetts Institute of Technology*
DAVID KONSTAN, *Brown University*
RICHARD H. KRAUT, *University of Illinois, Chicago*
ALAIN DE LIBERA, *École Pratique des Hautes Études, Sorbonne*
DAVID FATE NORTON, *McGill University*
LUCA OBERTELLO, *Università degli Studi di Genova*
ELEONORE STUMP, *Virginia Polytechnic Institute*
ALLEN WOOD, *Cornell University*

The titles published in this series are listed at the end of this volume.

JOHN OF THE CROSS AND THE COGNITIVE VALUE OF MYSTICISM

An Analysis of Sanjuanist Teaching and
its Philosophical Implications for
Contemporary Discussions of Mystical Experience

by

STEVEN PAYNE, OCD

DeSales School of Theology, Washington, U.S.A.

KLUWER ACADEMIC PUBLISHERS
DORDRECHT / BOSTON / LONDON

Library of Congress Cataloging in Publication Data

Payne, Steven, 1950-
  St. John of the Cross and the cognitive value of mysticism : an
analysis of Sanjuanist teaching and its philosophical implications
for contemporary discussions of mystical experience / by Steven
Payne.
       p.   cm. -- (The New synthese historical library ; 37)
  "Began as a doctoral dissertation ... at Cornell University"-
-Introd.
  Includes bibliographical references.
  ISBN 0-7923-0707-0 (alk. paper)
  1. Mysticism. 2. John of the Cross, Saint, 1542-1591.
3. Mysticism--Catholic Church. 4. Knowledge, Theory of (Religion)
5. God--Knowableness. 6. Catholic Church--Doctrines. I. Title.
II. Title: Saint John of the Cross and the cognitive value of
mysticism.   III. Series.
BV5083.P38 1990
248.2'2'092--dc20   90-31968

ISBN 0-7923-0707-0

Published by Kluwer Academic Publishers,
P.O. Box 17, 3300 AA Dordrecht, The Netherlands.

Kluwer Academic Publishers incorporates
the publishing programmes of
D. Reidel, Martinus Nijhoff, Dr W. Junk and MTP Press.

Sold and distributed in the U.S.A. and Canada
by Kluwer Academic Publishers,
101 Philip Drive, Norwell, MA 02061, U.S.A.

In all other countries, sold and distributed
by Kluwer Academic Publishers Group,
P.O. Box 322, 3300 AH Dordrecht, The Netherlands.

Printed on acid-free paper

All Rights Reserved
© 1990 by Kluwer Academic Publishers
No part of the material protected by this copyright notice may be reproduced or
utilized in any form or by any means, electronic or mechanical,
including photocopying, recording or by any information storage and
retrieval system, without written permission from the copyright owner.

Printed in the Netherlands

TABLE OF CONTENTS

ABBREVIATIONS	vii
INTRODUCTION	ix
CHAPTER ONE / John of the Cross	1
1.1. Preliminary Remarks	1
1.2. The Man	4
1.3. The Texts	10
CHAPTER TWO / The Doctrine of St. John of the Cross: The Structure of the Human Person	16
2.1. The Sensory Part of the Soul	18
2.1.1. The Body	18
2.1.2. The Exterior Senses	19
2.1.3. The Interior Senses	20
2.2. The "Spiritual Part" of the Soul	23
2.2.1. The Intellect	24
2.2.2. The Will	33
2.2.3. The Memory	38
2.2.4. "Spiritual Senses" and "The Substance of the Soul"	41
CHAPTER THREE / The Doctrine of St. John of the Cross: The Dynamics of Spiritual Development	50
3.1. The Starting Point: Human Existence as "Fallen"	51
3.2. The Stages and Means of Spiritual Growth	55
3.2.1. Beginners and the Passive Night of Sense	61
3.2.2. Proficients, the Passive Night of Spirit, and Spiritual Espousal	66
3.2.3. "Perfect" Souls, Spiritual Marriage, and the Unitive Way	78
3.3. The Goal of Religious Development	82
CHAPTER FOUR / Some Transitional Observations on the Nature of Christian Mysticism and the Data to Be Explained	91
4.1. Toward a More Adequate Characterization of Christian Mysticism	92
4.2. The Data to Be Explained	116

CHAPTER FIVE / Some Objections Considered 126
5.1 Objections Based on the Problem of Inter-Subjective Agreement 129
    5.1.1. Disagreement Between Mystics and Non-Mystics 130
    5.1.2. Disagreement Among Mystics Themselves 137
    5.1.3. The Role of the Mystics' Prior Beliefs in Shaping Their Experiences 146
5.2. Objections Based on the Issue of Testability 153
5.3. Other Objections 164

CHAPTER SIX / Mysticism and the Explanatory Mode of Inference 174
6.1. Explanations and the Explanatory Mode of Inference 176
6.2. Competing Explanations of Mysticism 184
    6.2.1. The Hypothesis that Mysticism is a Cognitive Mode of Experience 184
    6.2.2. Reductive Psychoanalytical Accounts of Mysticism 188
    6.2.3. Reductive Psychological Accounts of Mysticism 198
    6.2.4. Reductive Physiological Accounts of Mysticism 204
    6.2.5. Reductive Sociological or Anthropological Accounts of Mysticism 206
6.3. The Reasonableness of Accepting Mysticism as a Cognitive Mode of Experience 209

CHAPTER SEVEN / Conclusions 215

BIBLIOGRAPHY 220

INDEX OF NAMES 235

INDEX OF SUBJECTS 239

ABBREVIATIONS

Throughout this study I rely on the Spanish edition of the works of St. John of the Cross found in Lucinio Ruano, OCD, ed., *Vida y Obras de San Juan de la Cruz*, with a Biography of St. John of the Cross by Crisogóno de Jesús Sacramentado, OCD, rev. and enl. by Matías del Niño de Jesús, OCD, 7th ed. (Madrid: Biblioteca de Autores Cristianos, 1973), hereafter cited as *Vida y Obras*. Unless otherwise noted, all English translations of John's writings are taken from *The Collected Works of St. John of the Cross,* trans. Kieran Kavanaugh, OCD and Otilio Rodriguez, OCD, 2d ed. (Washington, DC: ICS Publications, 1979); occasionally I will add the original Spanish text in parentheses or brackets to help clarify the meaning of certain passages.

Some of John's major works are divided into numbered books, chapters, and subsections or paragraphs. To simplify the process of citation, I will use the following scheme of abbreviation:

A .... The Ascent of Mount Carmel (Subida del Monte Carmelo)
N .... The Dark Night (Noche oscura)
C .... The Spiritual Canticle (Cántico espiritual)
F .... The Living Flame of Love (Llama de amor viva)
Precautions... The Precautions (Cautelas)
Counsels....... Counsels to a Religious on How to Reach Perfection
               (Cuatro avisos a un religioso para alcanzar la perfección)

Large Roman numerals will be used to distinguish the books of the *Ascent* and *Night* commentaries; arabic numerals indicate the chapter (in the *Ascent* and *Night*) or stanza (in the *Canticle* and *Flame*), while lower case roman numerals refer to the paragraph or subsection according to the enumeration found in *Vida y Obras* and *Collected Works* (though not necessarily in other editions). Both the *Canticle* and *Flame* commentaries occur in an earlier and later version, known as A and B respectively. I will generally cite the B redactions of these works unless otherwise noted, for reasons explained below.

Thus, for example, "A II, 8, v" means that the passage in question will be found in book two of *The Ascent of Mount Carmel*, in the fifth subsection of chapter eight; "C 39, vi; xiv" directs the reader to the sixth and fourteenth subsections of the commentary on stanza thirty-nine of the B redaction of *The Spiritual Canticle*. For the remaining minor works (letters, poems, maxims and so on), since the *Vida y Obras* and *Collected Works* do not always agree in the organization of this material, I will indicate where particular passages can be found in both editions. In addition, I will give the date and addressee of quoted letters when this is known, and will refer to John's poems by their opening line in Spanish.

INTRODUCTION

Among Anglo-American philosophers, interest in mysticism has typically been limited to the question of whether or not mystical and religious experiences provide evidence for, or knowledge of, the existence and nature of God. Most authors conclude that they do not, because such experiences lack certain qualities needed in order to be counted as cognitive. In this study I examine some current philosophical opinions about mysticism and objections to its epistemic significance in the context of a detailed study of the writings of a single mystical author, the Spanish Carmelite Saint John of the Cross (1542-1591). I argue that from his works one can draw a coherent theory of what takes place in the *Christian* mystical life, and will indicate how acceptance of this theory might be defended as rational through a type of inference often referred to as the "Argument to the Best Explanation." In this way I hope to show that mysticism still has a significant bearing on the justification of religious faith even if it cannot be used to "prove" the existence of God.

The nature and advantages of my own somewhat unusual approach to mysticism can perhaps best be explained by contrasting it with the way other authors have dealt with the subject. One of the most striking developments in recent decades has been the growing fascination with mysticism, meditation, and the experiential aspects of religion. In many circles, interest in such topics has become not merely acceptable but highly fashionable. The works of popular psychologists and sociologists such as Jung, Maslow, Ornstein, and Berger have lent a new aura of intellectual respectability to the study of religious experience. Now, for example, scientists may unselfconsciously measure the heartbeat and brainwave patterns of meditating monks without feeling any need to justify research which a generation ago would have been considered unscientific, pointless, and bizarre.

Frequently the new interest in religious experience goes hand in hand with a noticeable shift or decline in the role assigned to abstract reason and proof in the religious sphere. Not too many decades ago, "encounter" theologians such as John Baillie and H. H. Farmer were already insisting that "our knowledge of God rests rather on the revelation of His personal Presence as Father, Son, and Holy Spirit" (Baillie 1959, p. 132; cf., Farmer 1942; and Hepburn 1968, pp. 24-59). More recently, Edward Schillebeeckx has declared that "Christianity is not a message which has to be believed, but an experience of faith which becomes a message"

(Schillebeeckx 1982, p. 50), while Dermot Lane, in an introduction to contemporary theological trends, writes that:

> The question of God today is not a question about proving the existence or nonexistence of a being we call "God." If it were simply a matter of proving the existence of God, then we could proceed to assemble the best proofs and present them to the world at large, and all would be well....
> The question of God for us today in the twentieth century, as distinct from any other century, is about the possibility of experiencing God in the world....The mystery of God is not some kind of theorem to be proved; it is rather an experience to be lived. (Lane 1981, p. 2).

Others likewise speak of a "Copernican revolution" in theology, a "turn to the subject" which stresses the grounding of theological statements in personal experience, particularly the so-called "limit-situations" of human existence.[1] Even within the Roman Catholic tradition, it is not at all uncommon today to find authors arguing that the only way truly to know God, to be sure of God's reality, is by experience. Mystics are regarded as individuals who have been preeminently successful in this endeavor. In more popular works there is sometimes a strong anti-philosophical, even anti-intellectual bias to this position; religious experience is commonly thought of as a more reliable and personal foundation for belief, freed from the "shackles of logic" and the "arid mind-games of professional academics."

Yet in spite of such developments—sometimes even in reaction against them—modern philosophers of the analytic tradition have tended to adopt a far more negative attitude toward mysticism and religious experience, giving the topic only rather scant and superficial attention. Those with a more jaundiced view of religion generally suspect that believers have rallied to the standard of "direct experience" only because the older rational defenses have been shown to be inadequate. To these philosophers it seems either that mysticism and religious experience are being brought forward to fill the supporting role for which the traditional "proofs" are no longer available, or else that appeal to such phenomena represents the final admission that religious belief has no rational basis whatsoever.

Thus introductory texts in philosophy of religion typically contain a critical examination of the ontological, cosmological, and teleological arguments; only afterwards, for the sake of completeness, is religious experience considered, to see if it can provide any rational support for belief in God. Most discussions presume that the central question is whether or not the occurrence of certain unusual mental states can provide evidence for the existence of the sort of being which Christians worship and Christian mystics claim to encounter. If the conclusions reached are negative, mysticism and religious experience are set aside as of no further philosophical interest.

In this way, mysticism gets treated almost exclusively in the context of the "Argument from Religious Experience," generally considered to be among the least promising of the traditional arguments for the existence of God. Of the many objections raised against counting religious experiences as a "way of knowing," the most common concern the related issues of testability and inter-subjective agreement. Some philosophers deny the cognitive value of mystical experiences on the grounds that they are not publicly accessible in the way that ordinary perceptions are, or because the claims to which they give rise cannot be corroborated by standard checking procedures. Others argue that such phenomena cannot support belief in the Christian God because the mystics themselves make incompatible assertions about what they experience; mystics of the West claim that they encounter a loving personal being, while many Eastern mystics reject this description. The implication seems to be either that the experiences themselves are different, or else that the same kind of experience lends itself equally well to theistic and non-theistic interpretations. In either case, any defense of a particular religious system based on the universal consensus of the mystics seems to be undermined.

These and other objections will be studied in greater detail in a later chapter. However, even if one agrees with the negative conclusions which many authors have reached, the limitations of this approach are surely clear. First of all, in attempting to deal comprehensively with the whole range of religious experience in the space of an article or a few paragraphs, it is almost impossible to avoid a certain superficiality and oversimplification of the complex phenomena involved. Most Anglo-American philosophers have no extensive first-hand acquaintance with the literature of mysticism, and rely on other philosophers and commentators for the characterization of a specific transitory subjective state which they call "*the* mystical experience," thereby failing to note that the mystics themselves describe a rich variety of experiences with differing cognitive values.

To put the problem another way, these contemporary philosophical discussions typically rest upon unexamined and sometimes conflicting notions of what mysticism is all about, notions which can be distinguished by the different answers they would imply to questions like the following:

1. Is the central issue the epistemic value of individual experiences or is it a matter of evaluating a whole mode of experience?

2. Can mystical experiences be sharply distinguished and treated in isolation from other religious experiences (e.g., numinous experiences)?

3. Are mystical experiences altogether ineffable, or can one to some extent describe them? Are the mystic's statements intelligible to the non-mystic?

4. Are mystical experiences mere "feeling-states" (like pains, etc.), or are they more like ostensible perceptions?

5. Do all human beings have a latent capacity for mystical experiences, or does the mystic instead have a kind of "sixth sense" which the non-mystic lacks?

6. Are mystical experiences everywhere the same, or do they differ in intensity, duration, emotional tone, and even subjective content? Is the disagreement among mystics of different cultures attributable to different experiences, or is it rather a matter of different interpretations of the same experience?

7. Is the "felt character" of the Christian mystic's experience theistic or non-theistic? Is it merely an experience of absolute unity which the Christian *takes to be* an experience of God?

Some authors, for example, assume that mystical experiences are supposed to be *totally* ineffable, and will therefore argue that "mystical intuition is not a genuinely cognitive state" because the mystic "is unable to produce any intelligible propositions at all" (Ayer 1946, pp. 118-119). Others, however, maintain that we *do* understand what mystics are talking about and for that very reason are able to see that the experiences they describe are non-cognitive. Thus critics who start from incompatible notions of the nature of mysticism may end up arguing at cross-purposes. Even when this does not happen, if the philosopher's understanding of the subject is inadequate, he may find himself refuting claims which the mystics do not actually make. Such discussions, however interesting, are likely to strike the informed reader as beside the point.

A second serious limitation of standard philosophical critiques of religious experience is that they generally rest on the assumption that it is unreasonable to accept such experiences as veridical unless one has first found a valid inductive or deductive argument for the existence of God. Such an assumption, however, seems dubious at best. Certainly no analogous principle holds in the area of ordinary perceptions; it is reasonable for me to believe that I am now seeing a desk, or that the temperature at the center of the sun is several million degrees Kelvin, though I have no idea how I would prove such things to a skeptical friend.

There are, in fact, a variety of ways in which one can defend the reasonableness of a particular belief. One common method is to argue that the belief is in some sense better able to account for the relevant facts than alternative hypotheses. When formalized, this mode of reasoning is sometimes called "explanatory inference" or the "argument to the best explanation." Philosophers of science have recently devoted some attention to the way in which this kind of inference is used in the scientific field, and Peter Achinstein (1971) has argued that it is a distinct mode of reasoning which does not presuppose the possibility of using induction to arrive at the same conclusion.

The present study will attempt to show how one might go about justifying belief in the cognitive value of mystical and religious experience by means of an "explanatory inference." The advantage of this approach, in my view, is that it relies on a mode of reasoning which we all commonly use and which the mystics themselves seem to employ in their own defense. It is my impression that many Christian mystics believe that they have encountered God at least partly because no other explanation of their total experience appears nearly as plausible to them.

For a formal reconstruction of an explanatory inference, as we will later see, one must specify not only the hypothesis one is considering, but also the facts or evidence it is meant to "explain." In the case of mysticism we could in principle proceed in an *a priori* fashion, establishing a typology of explanatory inferences based on different conceptions of the character of religious experiences and the claims made by mystics in attempting to give some account of themselves. We could indicate, for example, what an argument to the best explanation might look like if one assumes that mystical experiences are strange transitory "feeling-states" of absolute undifferentiated unity, and one further supposes that the Christian mystic's claim that he is experiencing *God* is intended (at least in part) to explain the origin and character of such experiences. Other explanatory inferences could be constructed based on alternative notions of what the experiences are like and what hypotheses are offered to account for them. One could then evaluate the strengths and weaknesses of the different arguments given the assumptions made in each case.

Such an approach, however, would prove extremely cumbersome, and would still leave us with the question of which assumptions about mystical phenomena are correct, and which particular explanatory inference therefore seems to have the best chance of success. For our purposes it will be more helpful to focus on the works of a major mystical author whose writings are generally recognized as presenting a reasonably reliable and systematic account of the mystical life. The author I have chosen is St. John of the Cross, who is one of the most careful and methodical mystical theologians of the Christian tradition. John has been named "Doctor of the Church," and even outside the confines of Roman Catholicism "is usually accepted as the greatest theologian of Christian mysticism in meeting the problem of providing a systematic description of the mystical state and experience" (Whitson 1966, p. 22). I therefore feel that St. John of the Cross's doctrine can safely be taken as a standard example of orthodox Western mystical theology, accepted as such by a large mainstream segment of the Christian tradition (which is perhaps not true of Eckhart's popular writings, for example). Although he was a consummate poet, John's prose works are clear, measured, and full of interesting conceptual distinctions; Sanjuanist teaching therefore seems far more amenable to philosophical scrutiny than the more impressionistic outpourings of other Christian mystics.[2]

I believe, in short, that John's writings contain a fairly accurate description of the full range of experiences associated with mysticism (or at least one major strand of Christian mysticism). John himself also tries to give reasons for the character and pattern of these experiences, in terms of the activity and motives of God. I will argue that, with appropriate updating, one can derive from his works certain claims or hypotheses which can in some sense be regarded as providing as good an explanation of the mystical data as any of the competing naturalistic alternatives.

It is important to be as clear as possible about the purpose of this project. No "proof" of the existence of God will be proposed; rather, I hope to show that, give certain reasonable convictions about the nature of mystical phenomena and the relative inadequacy of naturalistic explanations of them, convictions which need not be based on prior religious beliefs, a person may be justified in regarding mystical consciousness as a cognitive mode of experience, and even perhaps as a way of knowing God. I likewise do not mean to claim that John's is the only viable theistic account, or that it is vague enough to cover every sort of experience or state which is popularly called "mystical." It is quite possible that a similar project could be undertaken with the mystical writings of other authors, even those from other religious traditions. And while granting that there are sometimes striking affinities between the teachings of John of the Cross and those of a Hakuin or Rumi, for example, I will not try to prove that they were all saying the same thing or describing identical experiences; as I will argue below, the cognitive value of mysticism is not totally undermined by lack of complete consensus among mystics. Yet precisely because John is so widely recognized as an authority on the subject in both the East and the West, we can assume that many have found in his writings an accurate account of the spiritual life, and that therefore John's descriptions may be presumed to be generally faithful to the facts.

Finally, I am not expecting to convince agnostics or atheists that Christian mystics really are experiencing God. Explanatory inferences here are not nearly as neat or conclusive as the traditional arguments for the existence of God. Whether one decides that a certain hypothesis accounts for the data better than other alternatives and is therefore plausible will depend on a number of factors, such as what one takes the data to be, what criteria one uses for evaluating the adequacy of an explanation and the weight one assigns to each, etc. These are areas where reasonable individuals can arrive at different conclusions. Thus if someone believes that the mystical life is significantly different from what John claims, or does not attribute any special significance to some of the features he describes, then that person may not find John's explanation particularly convincing. I do think that one can rationally hold that the facts are more or less as John indicates. However, I am primarily interested in sketching out the logic of an "explanatory inference" in support of the cognitive value of mysticism. Readers can come to their own conclusions about what it is reasonable to believe here, once they understand the issues involved.

Though the exact nature of my project may still remain somewhat unclear, the obscurity should gradually diminish as we proceed through the different sections of this essay. Chapter 1 contains a brief introduction to the life, writings, and influence of St. John of the Cross, in order to provide the background information needed for the detailed exposition of his teaching in the second and third chapters. Chapter 2 explains John's epistemological views as well as his notion of the "structure of the the soul." In Chapter 3 I outline his theory of spiritual dynamics, focussing especially on what he takes to be the principal developmental stages of the mystical life and the experiences associated with each.

These findings are consolidated in a transitional fourth chapter, where they are employed in criticizing certain popular accounts of the nature and common features of mystic states, and in developing a short summary of important mystical data, for use in later sections of this study. The discussion becomes more strictly philosophical in the fifth chapter, as we begin to lay the groundwork for the "explanatory inference." Now obviously one would not be able to conclude that it is reasonable to regard mystical consciousness as a cognitive mode of experience if in fact there were already conclusive arguments to the contrary. But many philosophers believe that they can provide such arguments. In Chapter 5, therefore, I deal with some of the traditional objections raised against the cognitive value of mystical states, showing that most of these objections rest on assumptions about the nature of mysticism which, given what we have already learned from John's writings in previous chapters, seem highly dubious.

The sixth chapter presents in outline form the complete inference, indicating how one might attempt to argue that the hypothesis that mystical experiences are cognitive explains the phenomena in question better than some of the major reductive accounts which have been offered, accounts which deal with mysticism in terms of psychological regression, "deautomatization," neurochemical activity in the brain, social needs and pressures, and so on. The final chapter summarizes the conclusions reached, indicating some possible directions for further research.

This book began as a doctoral dissertation in philosophy at Cornell University. Part of Chapter 4 is drawn from my article, 'The Christian Character of Christian Mystical Experiences,' originally published in *Religious Studies* 20 (1984) by Cambridge University Press. Subsequently, a number of significant studies have appeared on the evidential value of mysticism and religious experience. Limitations of time and space do not permit me to discuss all of these new works in detail here, though I hope to do so in the future. In general, however, their findings seem fundamentally compatible with, and supportive of, positions defended in the following pages.

I am particularly indebted to Professors Allen Wood, Norman Kretzmann, and Norman Malcolm, the original members of my dissertation committee, for their generous assistance; and to Professors Carl Ginet and James O'Donnell who served in various roles after Professor Malcolm's retirement. Through brief conversations and correspondence, Professors William Rowe, William Wainwright, Nelson Pike, C. B. Martin and Donald Henson also provided valuable advice and bibliographical leads during my initial research. Over a number of years, discussions with Discalced Carmelites and Sanjuanist scholars such as Kieran Kavanaugh, Otilio Rodriguez, Eulogio Pacho, Federico Ruiz, Kevin Culligan, and Michael Dodd have helped to clarify obscure points in the teaching of St. John of the Cross. Though none of the above are responsible for its shortcomings, all of them have made this study far better than it would otherwise have been. Thanks are also due to D. Reidel and Kluwer Academic Publishers for their boundless patience at my slow pace; to the Discalced Carmelites of the Washington Province, who supported me in this project; and to my family for their continual encouragement. In gratitude, I dedicate this work to all those who helped me bring it to completion.

NOTES

[1] See, for example, Baum 1970; and Tracy 1975, pp. 91-118. This is not to say, however, that these authors would all characterize the relationship between human experience and theological claims in the same way.

[2] The adjective "Sanjuanist" is widely used in the literature when speaking of what pertains to John of the Cross, and will appear frequently in subsequent pages.

ACKNOWLEDGMENTS

Peter Achinstein, *Law and Explanation*, © 1971 (Clarendon Press, Oxford, England) used with permission;
W. T. Stace, *Mysticism and Philosophy*, © 1960 (Macmillan Press, Ltd., London) used with permission;
The Collected Works of St. John of the Cross, translated by Kieran Kavanaugh and Otilio Rodriguez, © 1979 (ICS Publications, 2131 Lincoln Road, NE, Washington, DC 20002) used with permission;
The Collected Works of St. Teresa of Avila, vols. 1-3, translated by Kieran Kavanaugh and Otilio Rodriguez, © 1976-1987 (ICS Publications, 2131 Lincoln Road, NE, Washington, DC 20002) used with permission.

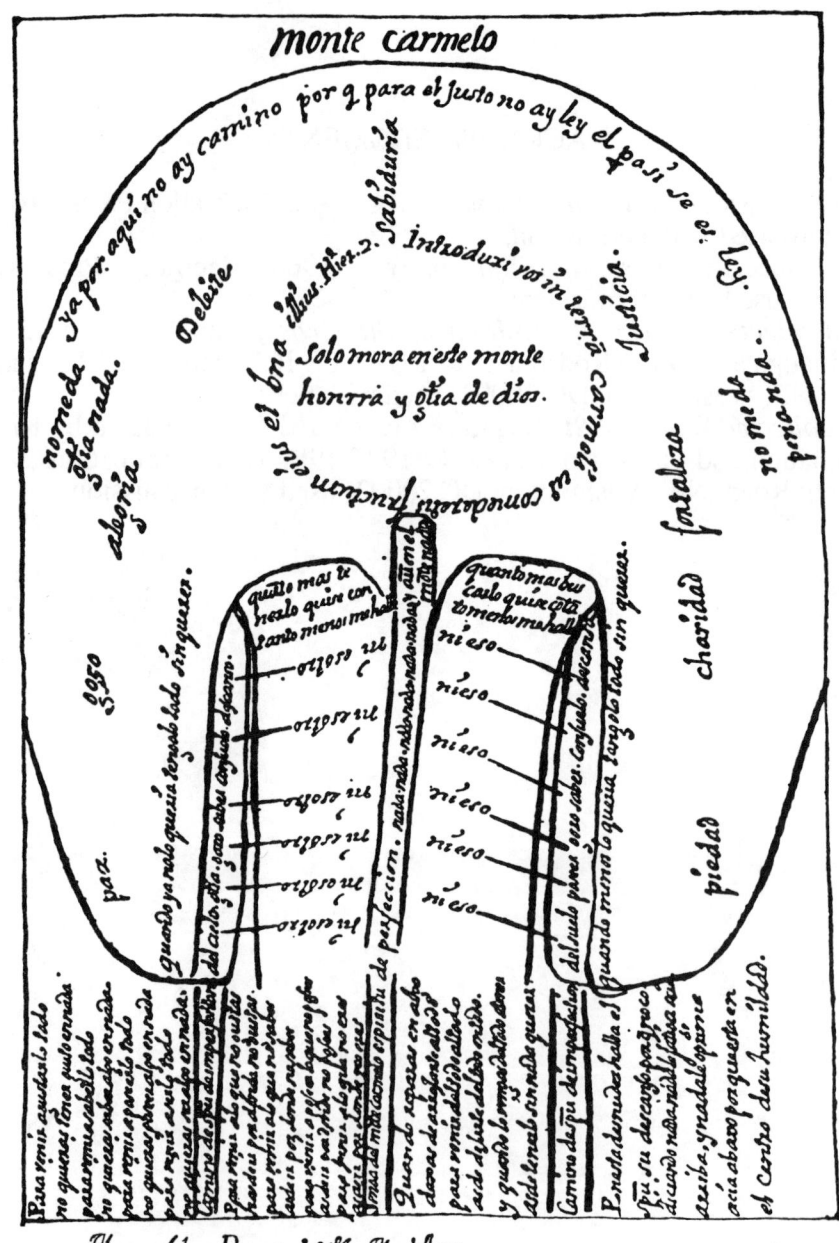

Sketch of Mount Carmel by Saint John of the Cross

(Courtesy of ICS Publications)

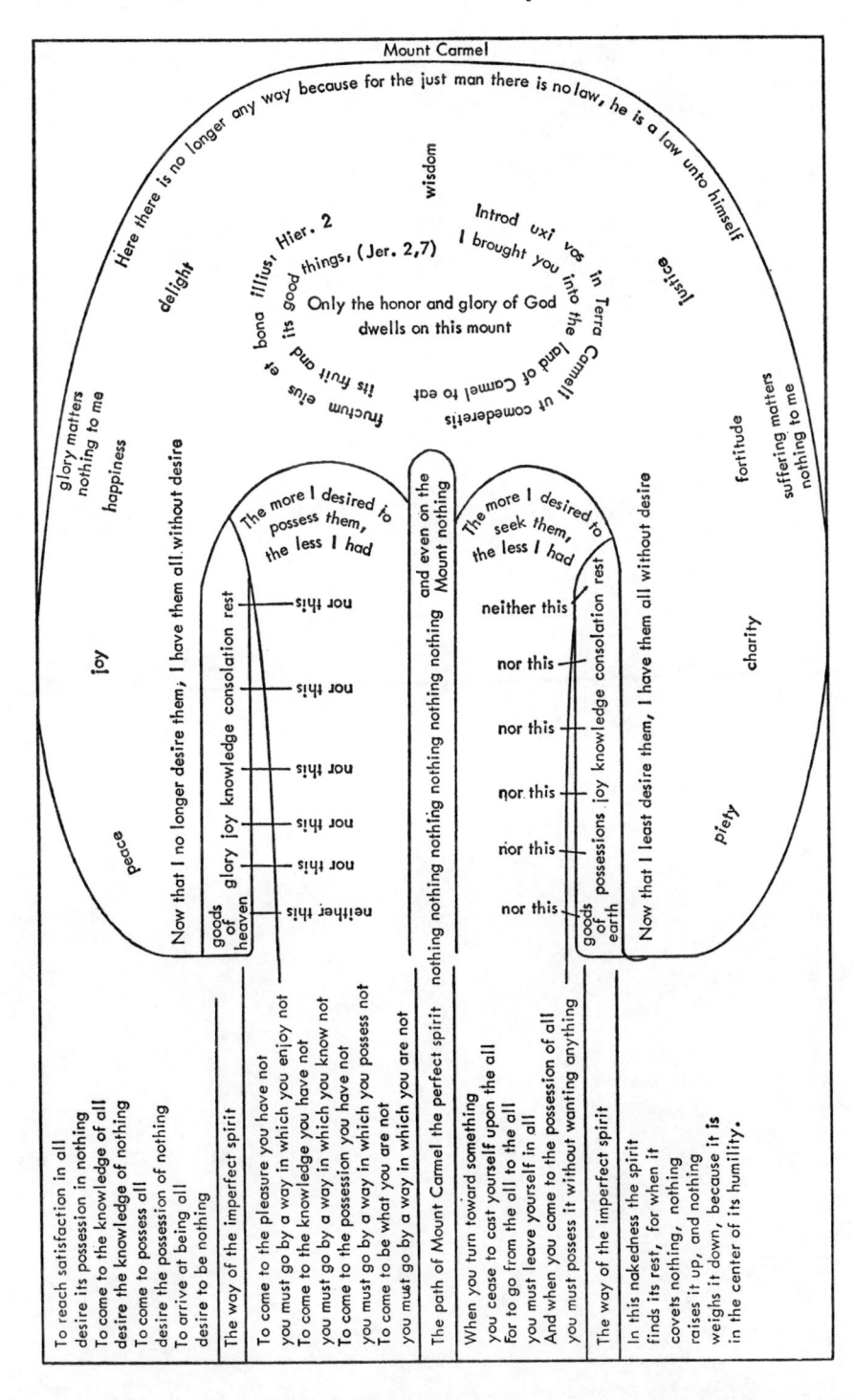

ENGLISH TRANSLATION OF TERMS USED IN ST. JOHN'S ORIGINAL DRAWING.

Mount Carmel

Here there is no longer any way because for the just man there is no law, he is a law unto himself

delight · wisdom · justice

Introd uxi vos in Terra Carmeli ut comederetis fructum eius et bona illius, Hier. 2

(Jer. 2,7) I brought you into the land of Carmel to eat its fruit and its good things,

Only the honor and glory of God dwells on this mount

glory matters nothing to me · happiness · suffering matters nothing to me

peace · joy · fortitude

Now that I no longer desire them, I have them all without desire

The more I desired to possess them, the less I had — and even on the Mount nothing — The more I desired to seek them, the less I had

goods of heaven: glory joy knowledge consolation rest
— neither this
— nor this
— nor this
— nor this
— nor this

nothing nothing nothing nothing nothing nothing

neither this —
nor this —
nor this —
nor this —
nor this —
goods of earth: possessions joy knowledge consolation rest

Now that I least desire them, I have them all without desire

charity · piety

The path of Mount Carmel the perfect spirit

To reach satisfaction in all
desire its possession in nothing
To come to the knowledge of all
desire the knowledge of nothing
To come to possess all
desire the possession of nothing
To arrive at being all
desire to be nothing

The way of the imperfect spirit

To come to the pleasure you have not
you must go by a way in which you enjoy not
To come to the knowledge you have not
you must go by a way in which you know not
To come to the possession you have not
you must go by a way in which you possess not
To come to be what you are not
you must go by a way in which you are not

The path of Mount Carmel the perfect spirit

When you turn toward something
you cease to cast yourself upon the all
For to go from the all to the all
you must leave yourself in all
And when you come to the possession of all
you must possess it without wanting anything

The way of the imperfect spirit

In this nakedness the spirit
finds its rest, for when it
covets nothing, nothing
raises it up, and nothing
weighs it down, because it is
in the center of its humility.

CHAPTER ONE

JOHN OF THE CROSS

1.1. Preliminary Remarks

In recent years, one finds the name of St. John of the Cross appearing everywhere from the "Entertainment" section of *Newsweek* (Ansen with Huck 1982) to the opening page of Carlos Casteneda's *Tales of Power* (Casteneda 1974; cf. de Mille 1977, ch. 9). Modern authors are likewise fond of ringing the changes on the title of his most famous work, *The Dark Night of the Soul*. This classic text provides the starting point for Daniel Berrigan's personal reflections in *The Dark Night of Resistance* (1971). A study of D. H. Lawrence is entitled *The Dark Night of the Body* (1964). Tom Wolfe describes the effects of the American space program on the astronauts as 'The Dark Night of the Ego' (1973). Even Douglas Adams (author of *The Hitchhiker's Guide to the Galaxy*) calls his latest Dirk Gently mystery *The Long Dark Tea-Time of the Soul* (1988).[1]

It was not always thus. Only a century ago the writings of St. John of the Cross were virtually unknown outside of Spain and the Carmelite Order. In the popular imagination, his stark, ascetic figure was almost totally overshadowed by the warm and colorful personality of his contemporary and fellow reformer, St. Teresa of Avila. It was only after more careful editions of his works began to be published in the early 1900s that scholarly interest picked up. Jean Baruzi's monumental *Saint Jean de la Croix et le Problème de l'Expérience Mystique* (1924), gave enormous impetus to the study of this Spanish Carmelite, not only because it was a solid and impressive piece of intellectual labor, but also because Baruzi's more controversial claims could be answered only by careful analysis of the texts. Shortly thereafter, in 1926, John was declared "Doctor of the Universal Church" by Pius XI, an act which constituted, at least in the minds of many Catholic authors, the definitive approval of Sanjuanist doctrine.[2]

Anglo-American interest in St. John of the Cross likewise developed slowly. Although as early as the seventeenth and eighteenth centuries there were individual authors (e.g., Augustine Baker, Richard Crashaw, William Law, and Francis Rous) who were familiar with his thought, John's initial impact on the English-speaking world was generally indirect, through the influence exerted by the Carmelite school on later currents of European spirituality.[3]

The name of St. John of the Cross was finally introduced to a broader segment of the British reading public in 1856 with the publication of Robert A. Vaughan's popular *Hours With the Mystics*. Although Underhill aptly describes this work as a "rather supercilious survey of the mystics" (1955, p. 150), it was in fact one of the earliest studies of the history of mysticism to appear in English, and devoted considerable space to a discussion of the Sanjuanist teachings. Unfortunately, Vaughan's evaluation of St. John, like that of so many later commentators, was deeply colored by his distaste for "Romanism." He describes John's mysticism as "unnatural" and quietistic, and attributes to him the promotion of a "doctrine of blind obedience to ecclesiastical superiors" by means of which Rome was attempting to enslave the world. Yet Vaughan admits to a certain "melancholy admiration" for John, whom he considers a "consummate ascetic" and a "genuine," though "miserably mistaken," mystic (1893, vol. 2, pp. 149-152, 183-197).

In 1863, Canon Dalton published a short anthology of Sanjuanist writings entitled *The Spirit of St. John of the Cross*, but it was not until the following year that the first English translation of the *Complete Works* appeared (John of the Cross 1864; cf. Fitzgerald 1948). Finally, after a further interval of three decades, several important studies of mysticism were published around the turn of the century, in all of which John was given a position of some prominence. Dean Inge, in the Bampton Lectures of 1899 (published the same year under the title *Christian Mysticism*), points to St. Teresa and St. John of the Cross as the foremost examples of Spanish Counter-Reformation devotional mysticism, but accuses the latter of having a "one-sided and defective grasp of Christian truth" (1956, pp. 223, 230). Repeating many of Vaughan's objections (cf. Peers 1944, p. 125), Inge is particularly critical of John's "terrible view of life and duty," his "nihilism and acosmism," and his "complete subservience to Church tradition and authority," though Inge too admires the heroism with which John pursued his goal (1956, pp. 228-230).

The following year, the Canadian psychiatrist R. M. Bucke listed "Juan Yepes" among those who had almost certainly attained the state of "Cosmic Consciousness" (1900, pp. 118-127). Bucke may have given too much credence to the hagiographical embellishments found in earlier biographies of the Spanish saint, but the quotations he selects seem to indicate a broad familiarity with John's works.

Bucke's book was read with interest by William James, whose classic study, *The Varieties of Religious Experience*, was published in 1902. James's reaction to John of the Cross, while not as negative as Inge's, is nevertheless not altogether sanguine.

The Roman Church has, in its incomparable fashion, collected all the motives towards asceticism together, and so codified them that any one wishing to pursue Christian perfection may find a practical system mapped out for him in any one of a number of ready-made manuals....But whenever a procedure is codified, the more delicate spirit of it evaporates, and if we wish the undiluted ascetic spirit—the passion of self-contempt wreaking itself on the poor flesh, the divine irrationality of devotion making a sacrificial gift of all it has (its sensibilities, namely) to the object of its adoration—we must go to autobiographies, or other individual documents.

St. John of the Cross, a Spanish mystic who flourished—or rather who existed, for there was little that suggested flourishing about him—in the sixteenth century, will supply a passage suitable for our purpose. (James 1936, pp. 298-299; cf. Culligan 1972)

However, like Vaughan and Inge before him, James seems to have been unfamiliar with John's *Spiritual Canticle* and *Living Flame of Love;* he takes all of his quotations from the *Ascent* and *Dark Night of the Soul*, where the Sanjuanist doctrine receives its starkest expression.

In any case, John's importance as a major figure in the history of mysticism was now sufficiently established, and subsequent studies in this century generally afforded him a place of special prominence. And yet, partly due to the enduring influence of the opinions of the authors just mentioned, the writings of John of the Cross have continued to provoke strong reactions, both positive and negative. On the one hand are those who characterize John as "the most precise and analytical of all the writers on the mystical life" (Happold 1970, p. 94), a "theologian of the highest calibre, bringing to his works a mind of scintillating clarity, drawing logical distinctions with a nicety and sureness of touch which bespeak the scholar at every turn of phrase" (Dicken 1963, p. 30). Surprisingly, even the Marxist Garaudy has claimed that "for us Marxists, the greatest representatives of human love are the Spanish mystics, Saint Teresa and Saint John of the Cross" (Garaudy 1966, pp. 157-158).[4]

At the other extreme, however, are those who continue to view John primarily as the "horrible ascetic," "terrible, dry-eyed and bleeding" (cf. Peers 1944, pp. 160-161; Idem 1946, pp. 25-26), whose mysticism is "basically anticognitive" (Werblowsky 1966, p. 180).[5] Stace and others add that John is "no first-class intellect," and "not intellectually comparable to the German mystics, Eckhart and Ruysbroeck" (Stace 1960a, p. 222; Idem 1960b, p.185).

Where does the truth lie? In order to determine the validity of the various criticisms and interpretations of St. John of the Cross, or to evaluate the philosophical significance of his teaching, one needs at least a brief and reasonably systematic exposition of John's key doctrines. But before providing such an analysis, I will first say something about the man himself, not only because the biographical data may be unfamiliar to the reader, but also because some information about his life, the period in which he lived, and the audience he was addressing is necessary for an accurate reading of the Sanjuanist texts.

1.2. The Man

Anyone interested today in studying the life of St. John of the Cross is faced with several major obstacles. First, unlike St. Teresa, John left no autobiography, and his surviving works contain few explicit references to himself and his activities. Moreover, not only were the earliest testimonies concerning his life and virtues (e.g., the depositions given in the processes of beatification and canonization) "heavily influenced by a cultural view of sanctity common to the sixteenth and seventeenth century ideas prevalent in Spain" (Hardy 1978b, p. 507; cf. Hardy 1978a, pp. 313-323), but also the first biographies, written more than thirty years after John's death, were partly polemical works published in the midst of a great ideological struggle within the Discalced Carmelite group over the nature of its vocation. Thus the traditional image of John as the harsh ascetic is to some extent more the product of the ruling party's effort to present a saint in conformity with their own picture of the ideal Carmelite than it is the product of a disinterested concern for the truth (cf. Moriones 1968; Idem 1972). One might say that the "search for the historical Juan de la Cruz" is almost as complex and difficult as the "quest for the historical Jesus." It is only within the last several decades that a more balanced and accurate portrait of the Saint has begun to emerge.[6] Yet although a great deal of the investigation remains to be done, the following points seem well-established.

Juan de Yepes y Álvarez was born in Fontiveros, Spain in 1543 and raised by his widowed mother in circumstances of dire poverty. From 1559 to 1563, while working in the Plague Hospital of Medina del Campo, John was able to attend classes at the city's new Jesuit College, where he received his basic training in Greek, Latin and rhetoric. At the age of 20 he entered the Carmelite Order, taking the religious name of Juan de Santo Matía. After his novitiate year, John was sent to the Carmelite College of San Andrés in Salamanca. According to the Carmelite *Constitutions* in effect at the time, all colleges of the Order were required to teach courses on the doctrine of the Carmelites Michael of Bologna and John Baconthorpe; the Spanish Carmelites seem to have been particularly interested in the latter, "whereas the teaching of Michael of Bologna was practically confined to the publication of his works" (Crisógono 1958, p. 35; cf. Idem 1973, pp. 58-60). Though there are no unambiguous indications of Baconthorpe's influence on St. John, it seems unlikely that the young student would have escaped all exposure to his thought. Baconthorpe was a subtle and eclectic scholar who did not hesitate to disagree with Aquinas on many important issues; it is sometimes suggested that acquaintance with his works may have helped John avoid any slavish adherence to Thomistic doctrines (cf. Crisógono 1929, vol. 1: chs. 2-3; Idem 1932; Alberto 1947, pp. 39-48; Maurer 1967, 'John Baconthorp,' *New Catholic Encyclopedia*, vol. 7, pp.1029-1030).

During these same years John attended classes at the University of Salamanca, which at that time rivalled Paris and Oxford as one of the great schools of Europe. For three years (1564-1565, 1565-1566, 1566-1567) John followed the Arts course at the University, and then returned again, after ordination in July of 1567, for a fourth year of studies as a theologian.

Although we do not know precisely which courses John attended, historians have provided much helpful information about the academic life at the University in the years during which John was enrolled. The faculty, first of all, included such illustrious scholars as Luis de León, Juan de Guevara, Mancio de Corpus Christi, Enrique Hernández, Gregorio Gallo and his successor, Gaspar de Grajal, as well as many others of equal stature. Despite what has sometimes been supposed, the work of these professors was not confined to the dogmatic propounding of a monolithic orthodox scholastic system. Though the influence of Aristotle and Aquinas were strong, the intellectual atmosphere was remarkably open and exciting. Academic positions included, besides a Chair of St. Thomas, Chairs of Scotus and Durandus.

The statutes prescribed the reading and explanation of these doctors in their respective chairs, but left the liberty to impose them or not to the professor.
...All systems were discussed, all opinions could be held. There were no limits beyond that of faith....When nominalism began to be the burning question in the universities of the centre of Europe, the cloisters of Salamanca had Masters brought from Paris to explain the new doctrines and four new Chairs were established—two for the nominalists and two for the realists.... In another field, that of pure philology and literature, the presence and the work of El Brocense and Fray Luis de León are the best proof of the rejuvenated atmosphere of humanism which was breathed in the Salamanca lecture halls. (Crisógono 1958, pp. 33-35)

Thus, for example, there was a lively struggle at the University over the interpretation of Scripture, between "the 'scholastics,' tenacious partisans of fidelity to the Biblical tradition of the preceding centuries," and "the 'scripturists,' who sought the literal sense of Scripture through a development of scientific methods and the study of language" (Kavanaugh 1979, p. 18). Gaspar de Grajal, St. John's probable teacher, was a prominent "scripturist," and according to some experts, John's own approach to Scripture, along with his willingness to cite Biblical passages in the vernacular, suggest that his sympathies lay with the Scripturist group (Ibid.).
We may say, then, that John's university studies helped provide him with the intellectual framework for his later writings in mystical theology, and may have given him the opportunity to pursue his interest in the topic.[7] It is clear, at any rate, that he had contact with some of the best minds of his day, and was exposed to a broad spectrum of opinions on a variety of issues. Moreover, John evidently distinguished himself in his schoolwork, for he was appointed "Prefect of Studies" at San Andrés. "This office, con-

ferred only on the most outstanding of students, obliged him to teach class daily, defend public theses, and assist the Regent Master in resolving those objections that were raised" (Ibid.). Thus John's contemporaries considered him a learned and first-rate scholar, and throughout his life the Carmelite saint had extensive contacts with academic communities.

In 1568, under the direction of St. Teresa of Avila, John helped found the first house of friars of her Discalced Carmelite Reform, and changed his religious name to "John of the Cross" as a sign of this new commitment. The Reform spread quickly, and for the rest of his life John found himself frequently occupied with the organizational demands of the new group.

From April of 1571 through May of 1572, John served as the first Rector of the first college of the Discalced Reform in Alcalá de Henares. After this Teresa arranged to have him sent as confessor to the convent of the Encarnación in Avila, where she was then prioress; for the next five years, John focussed his efforts on the spiritual direction of the nuns, and began writing them maxims, "notes and other papers with holy thoughts for their spiritual profit" (Crisógono 1958, p. 221; cf. Eulogio 1969, pp. 75-98). It was during this period as well that he enjoyed about two years of close personal contact with St. Teresa herself, who was then at the summit of her mystical life.

Meanwhile, opposition to the Teresian movement was growing, and John became an unwitting pawn in the struggle between the Calced and Discalced groups; on December 2, 1577, he was taken forcibly from his cell at the Encarnación, and remained incarcerated in the Carmelite monastery of Toledo until his dramatic nocturnal escape nine months later. After this, he was elected prior of the monastery of El Calvario (from November of 1578 to June of 1579), rector of the first Andalusian college of the Reform in Baeza (1579-1581), and prior of the monastery of Los Mártires in Granada (1582-1588); throughout this time he continued to serve as spiritual director to various communities of Carmelite sisters, and for the last three years at Granada he was appointed Vicar-Provincial for Andalusia, which required him to visit all of the monasteries and convents of the Reform in that region of Spain.

In June, 1588 John was elected prior of the monastery in Segovia, the new administrative seat of government of the Discalced group. Three years later, however, John once again suffered the consequences of a fierce ideological struggle among the Carmelites, but this time within the Discalced group itself. The two key figures in the battle were the good-hearted but apparently somewhat imprudent Jerome Gracián, who had been Teresa's confidant and first provincial of the newly-formed Discalced Carmelite province, and his successor, Nicolás Doria, a man of implacable will whose primary administrative goal was the enforcement of "strict observance." The details of this dispute are still controverted; it has been characterized as a conflict between fervor and laxism (according to the partisans of Doria), or between a legalistic and a more humane, charismatic approach to the Teresian ideal (according to Gracián's sympathizers), though either extreme of interpretation seems to involve a great deal of oversimplification.[8]

In any case, at the Madrid Chapter of 1591 John apparently spoke out against the measures which Doria planned to take against Gracián and the nuns who had opposed his efforts to submit them to tighter organizational control. As a consequence, he was stripped of all offices and sent into exile in Andalusia. He died shortly after midnight on the morning of December 14, 1591, at the small Carmelite monastery of Ubeda. He was forty-nine years old.

All of John's major works were written after his escape from Toledo. During his nine months in prison he had composed several poems, including a substantial portion of the 'Spiritual Canticle'; these and other verses later served as the material for the spiritual conferences he gave to the Carmelite nuns and friars of Andalusia. Out of these grew the great commentaries, the first drafts of which were all written at approximately the same time, after his thoughts were already fully formed. Thus Crisógono explains that:

At first, as he had done in Avila, he wrote isolated sentences as notes for the nuns of Beas, whose confessor and director he was; then came the small but valuable treatise of the *Cautelas*—spiritual counsels; afterwards partial commentaries on certain strophes of the *Spiritual Canticle* and pages and even chapters of the *Ascent of Mount Carmel*. His major works, then, were a gradual development. They were preceded by small fragments which developed into chapters. It should be remarked, however, that these first writings already have a definite character about them. When the author gave shape to the greatest of his works—the *Ascent of Mount Carmel*—they were to pass into it textually, without emendation or redrafting. It can be seen that his system was already mature. There were no hesitations; his ideas were definite, deduced from a principle. (Crisógono 1958, pp. 222-223; cf. Kavanaugh 1979, pp. 33-34; Ruiz Salvador 1968, pp. 157-269; Eulogio 1969)

Naturally, this makes it easier to analyze St. John's doctrine, since it is all of a piece. Yet even though we will be concentrating here on his prose, it is worth remembering that for St. John of the Cross the *poems* represent the primary expression of his mystical experience; the commentaries are merely limited attempts to draw out a few of the riches contained in the verses. Thus he writes to Ana de Jesús at the beginning of his commentary on the 'Spiritual Canticle':

...I do not plan to expound these stanzas in all the breadth and fullness that the fruitful spirit of love conveys to them. It would be foolish to think that expressions of love arising from mystical understanding, like these stanzas, are fully explainable....

Who can describe the understanding He gives to loving souls in whom He dwells?... Certainly no one can! Not even those who receive these communications. As a result these persons let something of their experiences overflow in figures and similes, and from the abundance of their spirit pour out secrets and mysteries rather than rational explanations....

...I only wish to shed some general light on [the stanzas], since Your Reverence has desired this of me. I believe such an explanation will be more suitable. It is better to explain the utterances of love in their broadest sense so that each one may derive profit from them according to the mode and capacity of his spirit, rather than narrow them down to a meaning unadaptable to every palate. As a result, though we give some explanation of these stanzas, there is no reason to be bound to this explanation. (C Prologue, i-ii)

Scholars have had much more difficulty saying anything definite about the *sources* of John's doctrine. We know that John wrote quickly, in the midst of many pressing concerns. One of John's closest companions testified that John composed the *Living Flame of Love* "in fifteen days while here busily occupied with many other things besides" (cf. Kavanaugh 1979, p. 575). Evidence suggests that John often wrote with only the Bible at his side, relying on his memory for the infrequent quotations from philosophers and theologians.[9] He had neither the time nor the inclination for carefully footnoting his authorities, some of whom in any case might have seemed suspect to the Inquisition. Moreover, John had so thoroughly absorbed the thought of his predecessors that he might not himself have known the exact origin of the particular expressions and analogies he used, many of which had already become commonplace in medieval mystical literature.

Certainly Scripture and personal experience form the most important bases of his doctrine. John had a wealth of empirical data about the spiritual life available to him, from his activity as a spiritual director and from his own mystical experience. Particularly important was his long-term association with St. Teresa, and he looked on his writings as in some sense complementary to hers (see C 13, vii). One can see as well that John's theological opinions developed through constant dialogue with and meditation upon Biblical texts. He does not pretend that his own teaching can be found there in all its detail, nor does he look for "proof texts" to support his claims. Rather, Scripture serves as the authentic touchstone for his doctrine; he uses Biblical texts to illustrate his points, and he is willing to disavow any opinion which might be incompatible with Scripture or the teachings of the Church.[10]

John wrote at the request of those he directed, and with them in mind. In the Prologue to the *Ascent* he states:

My main intention is not to address everyone, but only some of the persons of our holy Order of the Primitive Observance of Mount Carmel, both friars and nuns, whom God favors by putting them on the path leading up this mount, since they are the ones who asked me to write this work. (A Prologue, ix)

This does not mean that John's is a cloistered spirituality, suitable only for a religious elite; after all, in the same Prologue John insists that he is offering "solid and substantial doctrine as appropriate for one kind of person as for another (*así para los unos como para los otros*) if they wish to achieve the nakedness of spirit here described" (A Prologue, viii--my translation), and his most sublime commentary, the *Living Flame*, was composed for Ana de Peñalosa, a laywoman. It means rather that John is addressing the small group which is willing to take what he says to heart. His teaching is "for the few" only because there are so few who are willing to accept his challenge to wholehearted conversion. John admits that his doctrine, while "good and very necessary," will not appeal to "the kind of spiritual people who like to approach God along sweet and satisfying paths" (Ibid.).

The nature of his audience, therefore, suggests an additional reason for John's apparent unconcern with careful references to previous authors, or with the incidental details of the scholastic theories he uses; many of those for whom he was writing were poorly educated by today's standards, and would not have been able to follow complicated philosophical or theological arguments. Thus he writes, again to Ana de Jesús:

> I hope that, although some scholastic theology is used here in reference to the soul's interior converse with God, it will not prove vain to speak in such a manner to the pure of spirit. Even though Your Reverence lacks training in scholastic theology by which the divine truths are understood, you are not wanting in mystical theology which is known through love and by which one not only knows but at the same time experiences. (C Prologue, iii)[11]

John is, of course, an intelligent author, who consistently tries to present the theoretical underpinnings of his system, but he is primarily interested in providing sound spiritual advice for his readers. We can understand, then, why he seldom bothers to check his non-Scriptural quotations or to correct minor inconsistencies and repetitions in his texts, and how he could leave the *Ascent* and *Dark Night* unfinished.[12] John was, to be sure, a careful writer, and at the end of his life we see him revising some of his commentaries; yet the defects we have just mentioned seemed relatively unimportant given the purposes for which he wrote. John's interests were primarily practical rather than theoretical, and the development of his ideas, especially in the *Canticle* and *Flame*, is often more organic than deductive.

All of this will prove helpful for the interpretation of the Sanjuanist texts. Since John does not offer us scholastic treatises, we will not expect to be able to subject his works to the same exacting line-by-line analysis which proves so fruitful in the study of such theologians as Aquinas and Scotus. The clues to John's philosophical and theological principles are often scattered throughout his writings. Moreover, a number of important terms (e.g., 'faith,' 'appetites,' 'union,' 'espousal') have several interrelated meanings for John of the Cross, so that individual passages have to be read in context and in the light of other remarks.

John wrote for an audience whose Christian faith he could take for granted; none of those he directed would have denied the possibility of genuine encounters with God. Therefore, we cannot expect to find in John a direct answer to contemporary philosophical doubts about the epistemic value of mystical experiences; many of the modern philosophical issues surrounding mysticism would not have been within his intellectual horizon. Nevertheless, there is much in John's writings that is of philosophical interest. As I hope to show, one can derive from John's system certain principles which provide a framework for developing helpful approaches to recent questions about the significance of mysticism. John has a certain theory of what is going on in mysticism which, when suitably updated, can serve as a reasonably adequate "explanatory model" of the phenomena involved.

John wrote during the Spanish "Golden Age," when the influence of Erasmus was still felt strongly on the Iberian Peninsula. Montaigne, Cervantes, and Suarez were John's contemporaries; at the time of his death, Hobbes and Bacon were already alive, Gassendi and Descartes soon to be born. European thought was at a turning point. But this was likewise the era of the Counter-Reformation, a period of intense, militant religious fervor which often took bizarre and fanatical forms. It was as if the Spaniards believed they could stem the rising tide of "Lutheranism" by the sheer force of their devotion. Reliable statistics suggest that one out of every eight people in Spain was a member of some religious order; religious visionaries, ascetics, and stigmatics were the popular idols of the day. The Inquisition thus had grounds for their fear that this intense religious enthusiasm would become perverted and slide over into every form of rank superstition. But its activities had a far worse effect than the dangers it sought to avert; there was a gradual suppression of creative thought. In their efforts to insure orthodoxy, Spanish thinkers embraced the teachings of Suarez, who had succeeded "in embalming Scholasticism in its perfect and most luminous form.... In Spain his death marked the end of philosophical speculation for centuries, and his Thomism reigned unchallenged" (McInnes 1967, 'Spanish Philosophy,' *Encyclopedia of Philosophy,* vol. 7, p.514). By the middle of the seventeenth century, then, Spain had effectively cut itself off from the mainstream of European intellectual life. St. John of the Cross, in other words, wrote during what was perhaps the most creative period of Spanish history.

1.3. The Texts

Before presenting the thought of St. John of the Cross, it is necessary to say something about the traditional controversies regarding the integrity and authenticity of the texts usually attributed to him. Of John's total literary output, the three major treatises (i.e., the *Ascent-Night, Canticle,* and *Flame*),[13] a few opuscules, some maxims, about two dozen poems, and fragments from roughly thirty letters are all that remain. Of course it is not easy to determine how much more John actually wrote.[14] The most regrettable loss, though, is surely the disappearance of much of his correspondence; not one of his many letters to St. Teresa, for example, has survived. We know from a characteristic incident reported by his biographers that John once destroyed a packet of Teresa's letters when he felt he was becoming too "attached" to them. Moreover, during the final exile one of Doria's administrative assistants mounted a campaign to smear John's reputation and collect evidence for which he could be expelled from the Order; some of the nuns, fearing that his letters to them would be misinterpreted, burned whole sackfuls of his writings.

To make matters worse, we possess almost nothing in the Saint's own hand besides some of the letters and maxims. John's works were not published until twenty-seven years after his death; in the meantime, his writings were copied and recopied (often carelessly), and distributed all over Spain, reaching as far as Portugal, France, and Italy. The *editio princeps* itself (1618) was not a particularly admirable piece of work; the *Spiritual Canticle* was omitted, and the editors made substantial changes in the text, unable to resist the urge to "correct" and "clarify" what John had written. Finally, more than a century later, careful research led to the unsettling discovery that there were in fact two distinct versions (called the 'A' and 'B' redactions) of both the *Spiritual Canticle* and the *Living Flame*; in both cases, the B redaction contained significant textual changes and additional material. The B redaction of the *Canticle*, in particular, has been the source of much controversy, and several commentators, following Chevallier and Baruzi, have disputed its authenticity.[15]

It is perhaps not surprising, then, that some authors have described John's works as "like a field full of ruins" (Cognet 1959, p. 44), and believe that there was a deliberate effort to destroy or distort the original manuscripts in order to make John appear as orthodox as possible. Of course, the villain in this imagined scenario is the Spanish Inquisition; it was "the menaces and pressure of the theologians and ecclesiastical authorities" (Stace 1960a, p. 232) which prevented John and Teresa from saying what they "really wanted to say," or provoked others to alter their doctrine. Cognet (1959, p. 44), for example, suggests that John destroyed his own writings for reasons of prudence, and Inge asserts that:

> Persecution, when applied with sufficient ruthlessness, seldom fails of its immediate object. It took only about twelve years to destroy Protestantism in Spain; and the Holy Office was equally successful in binding Mysticism hand and foot. And so we must not expect to find in St. Teresa or St. Juan any of the characteristic independence of mysticism.... Faith presented them with no problems; all such questions had been settled once for all by Holy Church. (Inge 1956, pp. 217-218)

As we shall later see, such claims have played an important role in philosophical discussions of mysticism; authors who believe that mystical expe riences are all alike and inherently monistic or pantheistic argue that Christian mystics mistakenly describe their experiences in dualistic terms primarily under the influence of Church teaching.

But while it is possible that John might have "destroyed the manuscripts copied with his own hand, fearing that they might come to be venerated for reasons other than the value of their teaching" (Peers 1953, vol. 1, p. xlvi)—such an act would have been in keeping with his self-effacing character—it seems altogether implausible to suppose that John was easily swayed by others or that he would have suppressed his ideas out of a concern for his own safety. John was nothing if not brave and forthright in his convictions; we have already seen his readiness to face death at the hands of his captors rather than renounce the Reform, and his constant and courageous denunciation of the despotic policies of the Discalced leadership, even when he knew this would lead to his persecution. John does, of course, submit his views to the judgment of the Church, but only because he considers the latter a reliable guide to religious truth, not because he fears ecclesiastical punishments.[16] There is little evidence in the texts, furthermore, of any vacillation or hesitation about the doctrine he sets forth.

The effects of the Inquisition on John's authorship, then, are not as clear as they might at first appear. Rather than supposing that he was intimidated into modifying or suppressing his real opinions, one could argue with equal justification that he was consequently motivated to express himself with greater precision and care so as to avoid any possible misunderstanding.

As for later Carmelite editors, there clearly were some attempts to modify John's statements in certain editions (e.g., the *editio princeps*). But few scholars today would agree with Baruzi's claim that B redactions of the *Canticle* and *Flame* are themselves the products of such attempts, or that the final portions of the *Ascent* and *Dark Night* were too controversial to be allowed to survive. As it turns out, the manuscript evidence for the authenticity of the B redactions is quite good.[17] Nor are there substantial doctrinal changes, as is sometimes claimed, between the A and B versions of the *Canticle*. The alterations are rather in the direction of a more consistent presentation of the stages of the spiritual life, and a more careful distinction between what is attainable in this life and what is reserved for the next.[18] Such changes are of the sort one might expect from a conscientious author who revised his hastily written treatises in order to express himself more clearly. There seems to be nothing added in the B redactions for which a parallel cannot be found elsewhere in John's writings (cf. Thompson 1977, pp. 45-54).

In this study, then, I will simply take it for granted that the B redactions of the *Canticle* and *Flame* are authentic, and represent John's final word on the subjects addressed in these treatises. I am also confident that, despite the fragmentary nature of some of the texts, there is sufficient material in what has survived to enable us to reconstruct John's theological system. Since there is as yet no definitive critical edition of John's works, I will rely on the seventh edition of the Spanish text given in the "Biblioteca de Autores Cristianos" series, which is unquestionably reliable enough for our purposes. Finally, I will use the B redactions of the *Canticle* and *Flame* and will ignore variant readings unless otherwise noted.

NOTES

[1] See also the brief comments on the popularity of this "dark night" terminology in *The Long Dark Night of the Soul: The American Intellectual Left and the Vietnam War* (Vogelgesang 1984).

[2] See Lucien-Marie de Saint-Joseph v.d., 'Jean de la Croix (Saint),' *Dictionnaire de Spiritualité*, Tome VIII, cols. 408-447. Baruzi's book contains a useful bibliographical sketch of works on John of the Cross prior to his own; see Baruzi 1924, pp. 713-749. Modern European thinkers such as Bergson and Blondel also had a high regard for John's writings. See, for example, Chevalier 1959, pp. 33, 100, 155, 211-212, 249, 264-265, 276-280; and Blondel 1925, pp. 2-63.

[3] In *Holy Wisdom*, Dom Baker (1575-1641) appeals to St. John in support of his own teaching (Baker 1876). Yet Baker seems "to have been familiar only with the *Ascent* of St. John," according to David Knowles (1961, p. 175). For the poet Crashaw, see Gosse 1883, where the author says that Crashaw had "read the passionate canticles of St. John of the Cross" (p. 153). Désirée Hirst asserts that the great Anglican spiritual writer William Law (1686-1761) had read the works of both Teresa and John (Hirst 1964, p. 271). For Francis Rous (1579-1669), see Bouyer 1969, pp. 136-139. Both Fénelon and Madame Guyon had read John of the Cross, and the former appealed to the Mystical Doctor in his own defense against Bossuet (see Sanson 1953). Later philosophers such as Maine de Biran had some limited exposure to Sanjuanist ideas through Fénelon, especially his widely-read *Maximes des saints;* Leibniz may have learned of John through his correspondence with Poiret (see Baruzi 1924, p. 452; Forest 1942, p. 34). For the influence of John of the Cross on other French spiritual writers, see Le Brun v.d., 'France: VI. Le Grand Siècle de la Spiritualité Française et ses Lendemains,' *Dictionnaire de Spiritualité*, Tome V, cols. 921-923. For the influence of the Carmelite school on currents of spirituality in France and the Lowlands, see Orcibal 1959, and Baruzi 1924, pp. 732-737.

[4] For a recent analysis of the *Ascent of Mount Carmel* from the perspective of dialectical materialism, see Ballestero 1977.

[5] See Peers 1946, pp. 20-25 and Peers 1944, pp. 122-123 for a brief summary of the negative influence of Vaughan, Inge and James on later interpreters of St. John of the Cross.

[6] The biographical information here is drawn from the two best modern biographies of John: Fr. Bruno's *St. John of the Cross* (1932) and Crisógono's 'Vida de San Juan de la Cruz,' in *Vida y Obras*. For an English version of an earlier edition of this latter work, see Crisógono de Jesús, OCD, *The Life of St. John of the Cross* (London: Longmans, Green & Co., 1958). For some important and recently-discovered manuscripts relating to the history of the Teresian Reform, and thus touching upon the circumstances of John's life, see the ongoing series *Documenta Primigenia* (1973-), edited by the Institutum Historicum Teresianum.

[7] Quiroga's biography of St. John (the first, published in 1628) claimed that during his student days John made a special study of mystical authors, "in particular of St. Denis and St. Gregory," and had then written a discourse contrasting the illuminist errors of his time with the authentic spiritual tradition of the Fathers. However, Eulogio Pacho, the foremost authority on the history of the Sanjuanist texts, finds Quiroga's claim doubtful, although be believes John may have studied mystical theology during this period (see Eulogio 1969, pp. 56-59).

[8] For further information about the personalities of Doria and Gracián, and the impact of the Doria-Gracián dispute on John's final days, see Hippolyte de Sainte-Famille, O.C.D. 1946; Bruno 1942, pp. 119-121, 279-281, 283-286; Rohrbach 1966, pp. 179-182, 205-217, 221-227; Silverio's *Historia del Carmen Descalzo,* vol. 6 (1937); and the very readable, though somewhat unreliable biography by Brenan (1973, pp. 19-20, 59). See also Teresa's comments on Doria and Gracián in her *Book of Foundations,* chs. 23 and 30.

[9] The authors John explicitly names include Aristotle, Boethius, Pseudo-Dionysius the Areopagite, Augustine, Gregory the Great, Thomas Aquinas, Bernard, St. Teresa and the poet Boscán. However, even these few citations are sometimes to pseudonymous works (e.g., *De Decem Gradibus Amoris Secundum Bernardum* and *De Beatitudine,* both falsely attributed to Aquinas, and also the Pseudo-Augustinian *Soliliquorum animae ad Deum,* not to be confused with the authentic *Soliloquies* of Augustine). In addition to these authors, it is likely that John had read the Northern mystics, especially Tauler and Ruysbroeck, as well as the Victorines and certain Spanish spiritual writers, such as Bernardino de Laredo and (perhaps) Francisco de Osuna. For the literary sources of John's doctrine, see Crisógono 1929, vol. 1, pp. 21-53; A Benedictine of Stanbrook Abbey 1954; and Orcibal 1966.

[10] See A Prologue, ii; C Prologue, iv; F Prologue, i. Of course, John's interpretation of Scripture does not always meet modern critical standards; he is nevertheless seldom as fanciful in his exegesis as many of the spiritual writers who preceded him. Moreover, there seems to be nothing crucial to his teaching which depends for its sole justification on a dubious interpretation of Scripture. For further discussion of these issues, see Ahern 1952; Baruzi 1947, "Saint Jean de la Croix," *Histoire Générale des Religions,* vol. 4, pp. 188-191, 517-518; Morel 1960, vol. 1, pp. 198-205; Nieto 1979, pp. 41-56; Vilnet 1949; and Vilnet v.d., 'Écriture Saint et Vie Spirituelle, Part III: L'Écriture et les mystiques,' *Dictionnaire de Spiritualité,* Tome IV, Part 1, cols. 248-253.

[11] Note that, for John, the expression 'mystical theology' means, not the academic discipline, but rather contemplation or the experimental knowledge of God; see A II, 8, vi; N II, 5, i; 12, v; 17, ii; vi; 20, vi; C 27, v; 39, xii.

[12] The *Ascent* commentary ends abruptly in mid-sentence. When John revised the *Canticle* stanzas with their commentaries, he did not bother to correct many of the cross-references in the text, so that, in the second redaction, the reader is frequently referred to the wrong chapter; see the examples cited by Baruzi 1924, pp. 28-29, from the seventeenth and twenty-fourth strophes of *Canticle* B. The cross-references in the *Ascent-Night* are not always correct either; see A II, i; 5, i.

[13] I speak of *three* treatises because modern scholars insist that the *Ascent* and *Night* together form a single work, both parts of which are incomplete. See Juan de Jesús María, OCD 1943, pp. 27-83; Ruiz Salvador 1968, pp. 194-199.

[14] Besides the college essay on mysticism mentioned in footnote 7, John is alleged to have written some pastoral poems during his novitiate, as well as some minor treatises, such as *Qualities of a Solitary Bird* and *The Miracles of the Images of Guadalcázar* (see

Crisógono in *Vida y Obras* 1973, pp. 248-257). Except for the last mentioned opuscule, however, Eulogio argues that these writings either never existed or else are not distinct from the works which have survived (Eulogio 1969, pp. 44-69, 414-416, 422-464). We also know of another opuscule, now lost, of which St. Teresa offers a humorous critique in her famous *Vejamen*.

15 The second redaction of the *Canticle* contains an additional stanza and is "a quarter as long again as the first" (see Peers in *The Complete Works of St. John of the Cross* 1953, vol. 2, p. 11). Moreover, the other stanzas with their commentaries are rearranged to make the doctrinal exposition clearer. Chevallier has claimed that there are actually *six* distinct manuscript versions of the *Canticle,* but scholars today generally agree that there are two principal redactions, with an intermediate version sometimes designated A'. For the main figures in the arguments against the authenticity of *Canticle* B, see Chevallier 1922; Idem 1930; Krynen 1948; Vilnet 1949; and Duvivier 1971. The evidence in favor of the authenticity of *Canticle* B and the refutation of the various objections are best summed up by Eulogio de la Virgen del Carmen 1969; Idem 1967; Idem 1976. A useful summary of the case for authenticity can also be found in Thompson 1977, pp. 33-59.

16 See A Prologue, ii; II, 27, iv; C Prologue, iv; F Prologue, i. Brenan mentions some interesting testimonies to the effect that John was delated to the Inquisition several times during his own life and nearly arrested (Brenan 1973, pp. 77-78). The evidence for this, however, is rather slender, since many of the files of the Inquisition have since disappeared.

17 The best manuscript of *Canticle* B, known as the Codex of Jaén, can be traced back to Ana de Jesús, for whom the commentary was originally written, and shows signs of dependence on the version of the text given in the Codex of Sanlúcar de Barrameda; this latter manuscript, moreover, contains *Canticle* A with interlinear comments and corrections apparently in the Saint's own hand, many of these referring to points developed at greater length in the second version (see Thompson 1977, pp. 33-43).

18 In commenting on the first version of the poem, John ran into some important difficulties, because he understood certain later stanzas to refer to disturbances and distractions which were supposed to have ceased after one reached the state of the spiritual life already described in the earlier stanzas. A rearrangement of the stanzas allowed him to treat the different stages in their proper order (see Eulogio de la Virgen del Carmen 1958, pp. 307-337; Idem 1960, pp. 312-351).

CHAPTER TWO

THE DOCTRINE OF ST. JOHN OF THE CROSS: THE STRUCTURE OF THE HUMAN PERSON

As the opening words of his *Precautions* suggest, all of John's works were written to teach his readers how to attain "union with God" in a short time (see also *Counsels*, i & x, and the heading of the *Ascent*). The three major treatises (*Ascent-Night, Canticle*, and *Flame*), composed as commentaries on mystical poems, describe the various experiences and obstacles which one encounters on the way to this goal. If today the teaching of John of the Cross (and that of his companion, St. Teresa) is "regarded by most continental scholars as the point of reference to which all other writings [in the field of mystical theology] must be brought" (Dicken 1963, p. 5), it is largely because he was more successful than any of his predecessors in giving a complete and systematic account of mystical phenomena, and in clearly distinguishing the principal phases of spiritual development.

John's doctrine rests upon a two-fold analysis of the fundamental *structure* of the human subject and of the *dynamics* involved in advancing toward "union with God." (Indeed, the latter is significantly shaped by the former; as one would expect, John's estimation of the possible scope and character of spiritual development depends upon his convictions about the fundamental capacities and make-up of human nature.) Accordingly, my own discussion will be divided into the same two parts; the present chapter will sketch the broad outlines of Sanjuanist epistemology, while the next will deal with what John presents as the typical stages in mystical prayer. Throughout, my purpose is neither to defend John's philosophical assumptions nor to enter into traditional disputes about the nature of knowledge or the organization of the human soul, but simply to provide the background information required for the correct interpretation of John's claims about mysticism.

But while John's "dynamic view of man is derived primarily from [his] personal experience" (Culligan 1979, p. 110), his account of the structure of the soul draws heavily upon the scholastic theories and terminology of his day; as a result, the modern reader is faced with certain hermeneutical problems. For example, some commentators have tried to read John as if he were a contemporary author, without realizing that key terms such as "union," "knowledge," "experience" and "the soul" may have had a different meaning for him than they do for us today. This has led to serious misrepresentations of his thought. To make matters worse, there is no one place where John sets forth his basic philosophical and psychological principles in an organized way; one is forced, therefore, to sift through the writings for clues to the presuppositions underlying his teaching.

In addition, even those familiar with scholasticism have often erred by assuming too readily that John was fundamentally a Thomist.[1] More recent studies have shown that John disagreed with Aquinas on a number of substantive issues. And although his basic intellectual framework was undeniably scholastic, John was an original thinker who was not afraid to modify received views in order to deal with the spiritual life more clearly and accurately.

The medieval psychological theories with which John of the Cross was familiar offered an account of human cognitive and volitional abilities. Since John believed that mystical experiences, at their best, involve "both knowledge and love" (see **A** II, 13, iv; **N** II, 12, ii-vii; 13, i-iii; **F** 3, xxxii-xlix), he naturally borrowed from such theories in describing the process of spiritual growth. This does not mean that his teaching rises or falls with the scholastic principles he employs; one senses that John would have been just as willing to use more modern psychological theories had he known them and felt he could thereby better express his own views. It does mean, however, that one must understand some of the general features of the earlier theories in order to explain John position accurately.

In the first place, then, one of the most common complaints agains St. John is that his thought is pervaded by an outmoded neo-platonic dualism (cf. Bendick 1972; Maio 1973; Herrera 1968; Idem 1977; Mallory 1977). Critics note, for instance, that he several times compares the body to a "prison" (see **A** I, 3, iii; 15, i; II, 8, iv: **C** 18, i), and insists repeatedly that one's "natural abilities" must be "annihilated" in order to reach supernatural union with God (see **A** II, 2, i-viii; 5, iv; 7, v-ix; **N** II, 9, ii-iii; 14, i). Yet although there certainly are passages which by modern standards suggest an unuly negative attitude toward the body and material creation, the charge seems ultimately anachronistic and unfair. Whatever misgivings John has about the human person's physical nature are based on the belief that the body somehow impedes the complete experience of God, a view he shares with other scholastic authors, including St. Thomas.[2] Moreover, when the "body-as-prison" remarks are read in context, they turn out to illustrate other philosophical and theological points, and do not prove that John identified the subject with his immaterial soul.[3] St. John of the Cross does admit a fundamental division in human nature, yet not, as one might expect, between body and soul, but instead between sense and spirit. The soul, John says, has both a "sensory" and a "spiritual" dimension; the "sensory part" of the soul includes the body and the senses (exterior and interior), while the "spiritual part" includes the three spiritual faculties of intellect, memory, and will.[4] Thus the word "soul" (*alma*), John's most common term for the human subject, ordinarily refers to the total person, but places the accent on his "interiority and spirituality"; that is to say, for John the human subject's physical nature is also included in the meaning of "soul," even though he considers the body to be of secondary importance.

The sense/spirit dichotomy plays a crucial role in the Sanjuanist system. It forms the basis for John's interpretation of the Pauline distinction between the "animal" and the "spiritual" (or the "old" and the "new") man (see A II, 19, xi; III, 26, iv; N II, 3, iii; F 2, xxxiii-xxxiv; 3, lxxiv-lxxv). Similarly, the all-important transition in the spiritual life from active meditation to contemplative prayer is described as a transfer of operations from the sensory to the spiritual level (see N I, 10, i; 11, i; F 3, xxxii). John also refers to the sensory part of the soul (*parte sensitiva*) as the exterior (*exterior*) and lower (*inferior*) part, and to the other as the interior (*interior*), higher (*superior*) and rational (*racional*) part (see A I, 13, x; II, 2, ii; N I, 4, ii; C 18, i-viii). Most of the time John seems to use this notion of the two "parts" or "levels" of the soul primarily to speak about two basic and opposing orientations of the individual, either toward God or toward the satisfaction of selfish inclinations.

All of these points will be explained more fully in the following analysis of the structure of the soul according to St. John. It is important to remember, however, that beneath the complex divisions into various faculties, passions, appetites, and so on, there is the fundamental *unity* of the human person. Although John of the Cross does not entirely avoid the danger of hypostatizing the soul's powers, he repeatedly emphasizes in his more careful statements that the different parts of the soul form only one "suppositum" or subject (see N I, 4, ii; II, 1, i; 3, i; F 1, x). And every aspect of the individual, from the physical body to the higher faculties of memory, intellect, and will, shares in the benefits toward which John directs his readers.

2.1. The Sensory Part of the Soul

2.1.1. THE BODY

As mentioned before, the body is not a central concern in John's thought. Yet he believes it affects a person's religious development in at least three ways. The first, and perhaps least significant, is that taking pride in one's "beauty, grace, elegance, bodily constitution, and all other corporal endowments" (A III, 21, i) can inhibit spiritual growth; St. John of the Cross scarcely touches on this problem, however, since he assumes that most of his readers have matured at least beyond the most blatant forms of vanity over one's physical appearance.

Second, there is a sense in which "the corruptible body weighs down the soul" (a paraphrase of Wisdom 9:15, which John quotes in N II, 1, ii; C 19, i; 39, xiv; F 2, xiii). This is true not only because the soul, while united to the body, knows only through material phantasms and consequently is not naturally capable of direct knowledge of God (see below), but also because humanity's physical nature was "weakened" and "corrupted" by Adam's fall (see especially C 23, ii-vi). Thus, according to John, even when God begins to give himself to the soul supernaturally, the body, in its initial debilitated condition, suffers intensely, and is not capable of bearing very strong "communications." In some of the most powerful religious experiences the person's natural life seems to be temporarily suspended, to prevent what the "spiritual part" receives from overflowing into the sensory part, with devastating effects on the body.[5] Until the body is sufficiently strengthened through the purifications wrought in the Dark Nights, devout individuals may "suffer many infirmities, injuries, and weaknesses of stomach," undergoing "raptures and trances and the dislocation of bones" (N II, 1, ii—my translation). In other words, many of the extraordinary phenomena associated with mysticism in the popular imagination are, in John's view, merely its accidental accompaniments, the product of human limitations.

Third, as a person grows in the spiritual life the body is also strengthened, so that raptures, ecstasies, and so on gradually cease. In fact the goal of the "ascent" is a condition in which all aspects of the human subject, including the body, are brought into harmonious relationship with one another, a condition which John compares with that of Adam in Paradise (see N II, 24, i-iii; C 23, i-v; 26, xiv; CA 31, ix; 37, vi). Though there are certain periods of religious development in which the individual seems to be regressing or becoming more "fragmented," the overall movement is toward complete psycho-physical integration. Once this integration is largely achieved, one's capacity for "divine communications" is increased; intense mystical experiences are no longer so disruptive, and even the body can share in the joy and good effects they convey (see A III, 26, v: C 28, ii-x; F 2, x-xiv; 3, vii).

To sum up, then, John's attitude toward the body is by no means purely negative. Human corporeality is a source of certain difficulties in the spiritual life. John's solution, however, is not to reject the body, but rather to bring it into harmony with the other constituents of human nature. In this way, the person as an integrated whole is able to participate in mystical "union" with the divine.

2.1.2. THE EXTERIOR SENSES

The exterior senses are the familiar ones of sight, hearing, taste, touch, and smell. They correspond to, but are not identical with, the bodily organs of sense. The first three assume special importance in John's writings insofar as they provide helpful analogies for certain kinds of religious experiences—the "visions," "locutions," and "substantial touches" which we will discuss later.

John accepts the scholastic dictum that "there is nothing in the intellect which is not first in the senses"; he believes that all our natural knowledge of the world is ultimately derived from sensory experience.

> ...As the philosophers say, the soul is like a smooth *tabula rasa* on which nothing is written (*pintada*) when God infuses it into the body, and except for what it comes to know through the senses, nothing is communicated to it from any other source. (A I, 3, iii— my translation)

Thus John adopts an empiricist position regarding the human subject's unaided cognitive abilities; in this respect, at least, he parts company with Platonists.

Finally, John writes at great length about the "sensory appetites," which he sometimes describes as residing in the sensory part of the soul. It is clear, however, that these appetites are not independent substances or agencies, but rather the attraction which the subject feels toward what satisfies the senses.[6] As this concerns human affectivity, we will have more to say about it in the section on the will.

2.1.3. THE INTERIOR SENSES

Following Aristotle, most scholastic thinkers maintained not only that all knowledge derives ultimately from sensation, but also that knowing involves the reception by the intellect of a "form" or "species" of the thing known.[7] This "intelligible species" has to have the same mode of existence as the intellect itself. But the latter is immaterial, and thus has no direct access to sensibles. Consequently, in order for the necessary immaterial form to be produced from the information provided by the senses, a certain intermediate process of "abstraction" must take place. Besides the five external senses, then, these philosophers argued for the existence of a number of "internal" senses, to explain, among other things, how sensation can give rise to knowledge.

Now the scholastics themselves did not agree on the number or function of the different internal senses. Baconthorpe, following Al-Ghazali, held that there were six: the central sense (*sensus communis*), the estimative sense, the cogitative sense, memory, imagination, and phantasy (see Alberto 1947, p. 42; Bord 1971, p. 82). Aquinas and Averröes accepted only four: the imagination or phantasy, the estimative sense (called the "cogitative sense" in human beings), the memory, and the central sense (see Bord 1971; *Summa Theologiae* I, 78, 1).[8] John of the Cross, however, seems to reduce the number even further, to:

...two interior corporal senses, the imagination and the phantasy. They are of service to one another in due order, because the one is discursive by imagining (*discurre imaginando*), and the other forms the image, or that which is imagined, by means of phantasms (*forma la imaginación o lo imaginado fantaseando*). For our discussion there will be no need of distinguishing between them. This should be remembered if we do not mention them both explicitly. All that these senses, then, can receive and construct are called imaginations and phantasms (*imaginaciones y fantasías*), which are the forms represented to these senses by material images and figures (*imagen y figura de cuerpo*). (A II, 12, iii—my translation, following Bord)

In one place (**C** 18, vii) John includes *memory* among the interior senses, but this is apparently only a slip, since elsewhere he continually insists that the memory is a spiritual faculty; in fact, the whole structure of Books II and III of the *Ascent* is based on this assumption (see also, e.g., **F** 3, xviii-xxii). Finally, he mentions the *central sense* only once, but calls it, oddly enough, "the central sense of the phantasy" (*sentido común de la fantasía*) which serves as a "receptable and archives" for the forms of the objects of the external senses (**F** 3, lxix—my translation; cf. **FA** 3, lxix). There is no reference at all to an "estimative" or "cogitative" sense.

For years commentators have puzzled over John's enigmatic remarks about the interior senses, trying to reconcile them with the Thomistic position. More recently, however, André Bord has argued convincingly that John developed an original position of his own, perhaps drawing directly or indirectly on Avicenna. Avicenna held for the existence of five internal senses, but believed that the phantasy was the same as the "sensus communis," and thus functioned as a kind of central clearing house and archives for the "forms" received from the five external senses (Bord 1971, p. 82). John accepts the identification of the phantasy with a central sense which acts as a "storehouse." He drops all of the other interior senses, however, except for the imagination, to which he assigns a discursive function. This leaves him, then, with the intriguingly simple and creative notion of a twofold inner sense comprised of phantasy and imagination, which, for practical purposes, can be treated as a single "central sense" (Ibid., p. 83); here, as Bord points out, John comes near to the basic scheme Aristotle presents in *De Anima*, Book III. We can make his conception clearer by looking more closely at how the phantasy and imagination function in the Sanjuanist system.

For St. John, then, the phantasy collects the impressions of external objects received through sight, hearing, taste, touch, and smell, and stores these in the form of figures and likenesses which the scholastics call "phantasms" or "sensible species" (see **A** II, 16, ii; 24, v; III, 13, vii; **F** 3, lxix). These "phantasms" are quasi-material representations of sensible objects (individual trees, horses, and so on), and thus pertain to the organic order. By illuminating these particular images the active intellect produces an "intelligible species" (the concept "horse" or "tree," for example) in the passive intellect, which results in knowledge. This will be explained in more detail in the section on the intellect. In any case, it should be clear why John avoids saying that the phantasms are preserved by the memory; since the latter is, according to the Spanish Carmelite, a purely spiritual faculty, it cannot be directly informed by sensible species. Storing the images elsewhere enables the memory to belong to the higher part of the soul.

John also discusses images which do not arise through the normal processes of perception. God and the angels, he says, sometimes act directly on the external or internal senses, especially at certain times in the spiritual life (see **A** II, 11, i-vi; 16, i-iv; III, 4, i; 7, i; 10, i; 37, i; **N** II, 2, iii). In this way, for example, it might seem to a devout individual that she is actually seeing the mother of Jesus in the flesh (a corporal vision), or an image of Mary might be introduced directly into her phantasy without any employment of the external senses (an imaginative vision). In either case, however they may be produced, the phantasy stores the forms of these communications as well.

The imagination, on the other hand, is the mind's ability to construct new and more complex images from the materials contained in the phantasy. Thus we are capable of conjuring up mental pictures of mountains of gold or palaces of pearls, to use John's examples (**A** II, 12, iv); yet these new likenesses never go beyond the recombination of what is provided by the senses (see **A** II, 8, v; 12, iii-v; III, 24, i). Besides this, the imagination is responsible for the discursive flow of mental impressions, such as occurs in daydreaming; it is by nature inclined to come and go, to wander freely (see **A** II, 12, iii; 13, iii; 14, v; **N** I, 8, iii; 9, viii; **F** 3, xxxii).

The phantasy and imagination work together in close connection with the memory. It is apparently through the mediation of the memory that the imagination receives the materials from the phantasy for constructing new images and stringing them together into an imagistic line of thought. Moreover, the new "forms and figures" are placed back into the phantasy for preservation, once more through the cooperation of the spiritual faculty of memory. We notice again the integral unity of the human person in St. John's psychological theory, since here neither the sensory nor the spiritual powers seem able to function properly without each other's assistance (see **A** II, 8, v; 16, ii; and Bord 1971, pp. 84-85).

Finally, these two interior senses play a crucial role in the religious exercise known in the Roman Catholic tradition as meditation. John himself describes meditation as:

> ...a discursive act using forms, figures, and images, imagined and fashioned by these senses; for example, the imagining of Christ crucified, or at the pillar, or at another station (*paso*); or of God seated with great majesty upon a throne, or the imagining and considering of glory as a beautiful light, etc.... (**A** II, 12, iii—my translation)

In other words, for John and his contemporaries the term "meditation" refers to a discursive form of prayer, involving extensive use of mental imagery.[9] Those engaged in this practice may, for example, try to picture their favorite saints, or place themselves imaginatively in some Biblical scene, thereby evoking the appropriate religious sentiments and perhaps drawing certain edifying conclusions. Here, as John notes, the imagination draws upon what is preserved in the phantasy and produces a succession of inspiring mental representations (see A II, 12, iii-viii; 13, i-vi; 14, i-iv; N I, 8, iii; 9, viii; F 3, xxxii).

Now despite what is sometimes claimed, John does not reject meditation out of hand, and admits that it is valuable for spiritual beginners; it provides them, for example, with some small knowledge of God, and, through the attraction exercised by the sensual imagery involved, raises the appetites to higher things (see A II, 13, i-v; 14, i-ii; 17, iii-vii; N I, 8, iii). Nevertheless, meditation suffers from the same limitations present in all thought using "forms and figures." The mind knows only through advertence to phantasms, and these in turn are only representations of actual or possible sensible objects. Since God is immaterial, God cannot be represented properly by a sensible species; as a result, we are not naturally capable of direct knowledge of God's essence (see A II, 12, iv-v; III, 12, i-iii). At best we can only attain a very remote knowledge of the Creator through reflection upon material creation. Moreover, as long as the mind is preoccupied with its forms and images, it is not free to receive the imageless communication which God is ready to impart in contemplation (see A II, 16, vii-xii; III, 11, i-iii). At a certain point in the spiritual life, then, meditation must be left behind, to make way for this higher form of prayer, as we shall see below.

2.2. The "Spiritual Part" of the Soul

As noted earlier, John's major break with Thomism is his inclusion of the memory among the spiritual powers of the soul. Yet it is easy to see why a three-fold division of these faculties would have appealed to him. By accepting it, he aligned himself with Augustine and the whole Augustinian tradition, which included some of the best mystical authors of earlier generations (e.g., Bonaventure, Ruysbroeck, Catherine of Siena, Bernardino de Laredo [author of *The Ascent of Mount Sion*], and even Teresa of Avila herself). Moreover, the tripartite scheme offers a much neater framework for explaining how the higher part of the soul is perfected by the three theological virtues of faith, hope, and charity. Finally, though he has little to say about it, John would presumably have appreciated the possibility of finding an image of the Trinity in the triad of intellect, memory, and will.[10]

The following section of this chapter contains a brief analysis of what John has to say about the three spiritual faculties, focussing especially on the role each plays in contemplative experience. I will also consider some of his enigmatic remarks on the "substance of the soul" and the "spiritual sense." As we will see, although John finds it fairly easy, when discussing ordinary experience, to indicate which operations belong to which faculties, such distinctions become less clear when he is dealing with mystical experiences, apparently because in the higher stages of religious development the intellect, memory, and will work in unison.

2.2.1. THE INTELLECT

Among the spiritual faculties, the intellect enjoys a certain priority for John of the Cross, inasmuch as the memory and will "depend upon the intellect in their operations" (A I, 8, ii; cf. A III, 1, i; 16, i; vi), so that the memory recalls what has *already* been understood by the intellect and stored by the phantasy, while the will is attracted to what has *already* come to be known through perception. As a result, when John treats of these powers, the greatest attention is usually devoted to the intellect; thus, for example, the entire second book of the *Ascent* is an exhaustive, and often exhausting, analysis of "all the natural and supernatural apprehensions of the intellect" (A II, 10, i), while an equivalent amount of space in Book III is devoted to the other two spiritual faculties combined.

I have already noted John's assertion that all our natural knowledge is derived from sense experience. When spelled out in scholastic terms, this means that the external senses receive impressions of sensible objects, on the basis of which mental representations, known as "phantasms," are formed. But these phantasms are particular, quasi-material images, lacking in universal application. As Copleston puts it:

Through sensation we can apprehend only particular men or trees, for example, and the interior images or phantasms of men or trees are always particular. Even if we have a composite image of man, not representing any one actual man distinctly but representing many confusedly, it is still particular, since the images or parts of the images of particular actual men coalesce to form an image which may be 'generic' in respect of actual particular men but which is itself none the less particular, the image of a particular imagined man.... The image of a man must be either of a man who has or of a man who has not some hair on his head. If the former, it does not in that respect represent bald men; if the latter, it does not in that respect represent men who are not bald.... (Copleston 1950, vol. 2, p. 389)

In order to arrive at universal concepts, then, a further process of "abstraction" is required. Speaking metaphorically, John says that the intellect comes to the interior sense of imagination and phantasy "as if to a port or place of provision, in order to give and to receive" (A II, 16, iv— my translation), and adds that the role of the intellect is "to form the intelli gible species (*inteligencias*) and remove from them the iron of species and phantasms (*del hierro de las especies y fantasias*)" (A II, 8, v).[11] St. John of the Cross does not indicate in detail how this process is carried out, but seems to favor an explanation along Thomistic lines. Aquinas, following Aristotle, argues that in the soul's "intellectual part, there is something active and something passive" (*S.T.* I, 79, 3 ad 1).[12] The passive intellect is simply the mind's capacity for knowledge, including its receptivity to the concepts of external material objects.[13] But while these singular objects are actually sensible, they are only potentially intelligible. Consequently, the "active intellect" is required to "reduce" the possible intellect "from potency to act"—that is, from the *capacity* to know to an *act* of knowledge—"by abstraction of the species from material conditions" (*S.T.* I, 79, 3; cf. *De Veritate* X, 6); similarly, John himself speaks of the "the intellect which philosophers call 'active,' whose work is in the forms, phantasms, and apprehensions of the corporal faculties" (C 39, xii—my translation), and cites the scholastic principle, "Ab obiecto et potentia paritur notitia" (A II, 3, ii).

Thus, for example, by "illuminating" a particular mental image of a human being, the active intellect "renders visible the intelligible aspect of the phantasm," and produces in the possible intellect the universal concept of "rational animal"; this is a concept of the human being's essence, and therefore covers all men and women, "bald or not, white or black, tall or short" (Copleston 1950, vol. 2, p. 389).[14]

According to this account, then, ordinary cognition of the most basic kind occurs when the passive intellect is "informed" by the "intelligible species" (i.e., concepts) of sensible things, species generated or "abstracted" by the active intellect from the corresponding phantasms. The key to this epistemic theory is the notion that the subjects somehow "participate" in the objects of their cognition, that the mind in its own way *becomes* whatever it knows. The relationship between the intelligible species and the passive intellect is in some respects like that between form and matter, an analogy which Aquinas and his followers take very seriously.

Thus a young black cat is a cat because of its substantial form, and it is young and black because of its accidental forms, say size and black color. In the process of cognition these forms, while existing physically, or ontologically, in the extramental object, enter the knowing subject and become, intentionally, his own forms. They do not become the forms of that subject physically, since this would make the subject become ontologically whatever he knows—e.g., a man would thus become a young black cat. But the forms become intentionally his, and he becomes intentionally whatever he knows.

This phenomenon is referred to as the intentional presence of the object in the knowing subject. Intentional is here not opposed to real, but rather to physical.... Both the union of substance and accident and that of form and matter result in a third reality differing from its two components. The intentional union, however, is more intimate. Through it the faculty becomes the other, as other, while still remaining itself; through it the subject knows the other as other. (Donceel 1967, *New Catholic Encyclopedia* vol. 8, p.231)

And so, for example, if I correctly recognize the animal before me as a cat, then the form which, in the animal, makes it to be a cat, is also present in my mind as the intelligible species by which I understand.[15] Such species or concepts are not themselves the primary objects of our knowledge but instead the *means* by which material objects are known. For Thomas and his followers, "the proper object of the human intellect, which is united to a body, is a quiddity or nature existing in corporeal matter" (*S.T.* I, 84, 7), and the cognitive act in which an object is apprehended by means of its substantial rather than its accidental form—that is, where the informing "species" is of the things's *nature*—may be described as knowledge of a thing's "essence" or "quiddity." Thus I have essential knowledge of a human being when, from a specific phantasm of a man, I abstract the universal concept "rational animal"; I understand the individual person as an instantiation of a universal nature, and know him in terms of what makes him to be the kind of being he is.

This, then, is the general structure of the Thomistic theory of knowledge. For some contemporary readers, it will seem hard to understand, much less to accept. Here it is unnecessary to defend the theory or to consider the many variants of the basic account which were developed by other scholastic philosophers. John of the Cross shows little interest in working out the details of his own position, and gives few indications of the responses he would have made to the more obvious questions and objections raised against Thomistic epistemology (cf. Preller 1967, pp. 37-73; Kenny 1976, pp. 273-296; Sheehan 1976, pp. 307-321; Boler 1982, p.472). Nevertheless, it is important to have at least a rough grasp of how such theories work, since many of John's explanations of mystical experience were shaped by a theory of knowledge much like the one we have just sketched. Although John's epistemological views will require some further elaboration when we come to consider the effect of the appetites on the spiritual faculties, we are already in a better position to make sense of some of John's puzzling claims about our knowledge of God and creatures.

For example, throughout the *Ascent* John repeatedly emphasizes that "the intellect cannot profit from its natural knowledge" because "everything that the intellect can understand...is most unlike and disproportioned to God" (A II, 8, iv-v; see also A II, 3, ii-iv; 4, iv; 8, ii-vi; 12, iv-v; 16, iii-ix; III, 12, i). He therefore says that the intellect must be "blinded" and "stripped" of its natural knowledge. It is hardly surprising, then, that John's mysticism has been described as "basically anti-cognitive and irrational" (Werblowsky 1966, p. 180). Elsewhere, however, John acknowledges that a "remote knowledge" of God *is* possible in this life (see A II, 8, iii; C 4, i-iii; 5, i-iv; 6, v-vi; 14 & 15, xxv-xxvii). These apparently conflicting statements become more intelligible when we compare them with what Aquinas says about our knowledge of God.

As Thomas indicates, one of the most important consequences of our natural ordering toward knowledge of sensibles through the forms abstracted from phantasms is that we can have no "essential" knowledge of God or spiritual substances while united to the body. Because they are not material, such substances cannot be sensed; hence no phantasm of them can be constructed from which the active intellect could produce concepts of their essence.[16] The soul knows naturally "only what has a form in matter, or what can be known by such a form" (*S.T.* I, 12, 11). Yet because God is the cause of created things, it is possible to attain some knowledge of Him "by comparison with sensible bodies of which there are phantasms"; in particular, we know God "as cause, by way of excess and by way of remotion" (*S.T.* I, 84, 7 ad 3).

...Because [sensible things] are His effects and depend on their cause, we can be led from them so far as to know of God *whether He exists*, and know of Him what must necessarily belong to Him, as the first cause of all things, exceeding all things caused by Him.

Hence we know...His relationship with creatures so far as to be the cause of them all; also that creatures differ from Him, inasmuch as He is not in any way part of what is caused by Him; and that creatures are not removed from Him by reason of any defect on His part, but because He superexceeds them all. (*S.T.* I, 12, 12)

In other words, according to Aquinas, we can at least know that God exists (by reflection upon the "Five Ways," for example); we can likewise know in what respects God differs from creatures by "denying of God anything that belongs to the contingent as such" (the famous *via negativa* or *via remotionis*), and we can attribute "to God in an eminent degree everything that can be considered a perfection pure and simple" (the doctrine of analogy) (Wallace 1977, pp. 131-132). Thus we can know that there is a God, who is not only immaterial and immutable, but also just, wise, powerful, and so on. This may not be "essential" knowledge of God, but it is at least within our natural capabilities, since it makes use of ordinary sensible species.

John of the Cross generally speaks of "clear and distinct ideas" (*noticias*) rather than "intelligible species," but his general position seems more or less the same as the one we have just outlined. He argues, for example, that:

...all distinct ideas and images (*todas las noticias e imágenes distintas*), natural or supernatural, that can be the objects of a person's faculties, are incomparable and unproportioned to God's being. God does not fall under...genus and species, whereas, according to theologians, creatures do. And the soul is not capable of receiving clearly and distinctly in this life what does not fall under...genus and species. (A III, 12, i)

At the same time, however, John does apparently recognize the possibility of some limited natural knowledge of God. He does not talk at any length about inferring God's existence from that of the world, but he does speak of the *beauty* and *harmony* of creatures as pointing to their Creator (see **C** 4, i-iii; 5, i-iv; 36, v-viii; and the fourth of the *Romances*, which begins "—Hagase, pues—dixo el Padre—"). Likewise, John's insistence that "the soul must journey by knowing God through what He is not, rather than through what He is" (**A** III, 2, iii) echoes Aquinas's own expression of the *via negativa*, that while we are unable to apprehend the divine substance "by knowing *what it is*" yet "we are able to have some knowlege of it by knowing *what it is not*" (*C.G.* I, 14, 2).[17] Finally, John claims that God possesses eminently the perfections found in creatures (see, e.g., **A** III, 21, ii; **C** 14 & 15, v; **F** 3, xiii-xv; 4, v).

But if St. John of the Cross admits, however grudgingly, that we are naturally capable of some distant knowledge of God, why does he stress that such knowledge "cannot profit" the soul? Why does he say that, in order to arrive at mystical union, the faculties in general, and the intellect in particular, must be "cleansed and emptied of everything relating to sense (*todo lo que puede caer en el sentido*), divested and liberated of everything clearly apprehensible (*todo lo que puede caer con claridad en el entendimiento*)" (**A** II, 9 i), because "nothing which the imagination can imagine and the intellect receive and comprehend (*entender*) in this life is or can be a proximate means to union with God" (**A** II, 8, iv—my translation; see also **A** II, 4, ii-vi; 5, vii-viii; 8, i-vii; 12, ii-v; 16, vi-xii; III, 12, i-iii)? The implication seems to be that union has a noetic dimension and involves the intellect in an important way; otherwise it would scarcely matter whether the mind was entertaining concepts and images of material things or not.

In fact, John's insistence on divesting the intellect of "particular knowledge" is demanded, at least in part, by the epistemological theory he adopts. One important implication of the Thomistic account of knowledge is that "one's attention cannot be given to many things at once, unless they are related to one another in such a way that they can be taken as one" (*De Veritate* XIII, 3; see also Ibid. XVIII, 4 ad 8), as when, for example, we consider head, hands and feet as parts of a whole human body, or think of three pieces of furniture within the larger setting of a particular room.

The reason for this is that it is impossible for one and the same subject to be perfected at the same time by many forms of one genus and diverse species, just as it is impossible for one and the same body at the same time to have different colors or different shapes. Now all intelligible species belong to one genus, because they are perfections of one intellectual faculty: although the things which the species represent belong to different genera. Therefore it is impssible for one and the same intellect to be perfected at the same time by different intelligible species so as actually to understand different things. (*S.T.* I, 85, 4)[18]

John's first biographer reports that the young Carmelite read this passage from the *Summa* as a student, and was delighted to discover the principle that the intellect is incapable of receiving many forms at once (see Orcibal 1963, p. 235). Although Quiroga may have been mistaken about John's source for this scholastic commonplace, he at least recognized its importance in Sanjuanist thought. The emphasis on emptying the intellect of "clear and distinct concepts" is based on the assumption that, in mystical union, God takes on the role played by the active intellect in ordinary knowledge, and "informs" the possible intellect directly, producing an obscure apprehension or "knowledge" of the Divine. And just as a piece of clay cannot be molded into a new shape (e.g., that of a statue) until the old shape (e.g., that of a bowl) is destroyed, so too the possible intellect cannot receive the divine "form" conveyed in mystical experience until the "forms and intelligible species" of creatures are expelled.

This explanation of mystical experiences in terms of the action of God on the possible or passive intellect has a long and venerable history, going back to the Greeks and their early commentators (see Merlan 1969, which traces the historical roots in Plato and Aristotle of what Merlan calls "mysticism of reason or simply rationalistic mysticism" [p. 2]). Modern research suggests that John's immediate source may have been the Pseudo-Taulerian *Institutions* (see Orcibal 1963, pp. 263-279). Aquinas likewise often describes essential knowledge of God in similar terms when discussing rapture, or the knowledge of angels, the blessed, and Adam in the state of innocence.[19] He notes, for example, that:

...When any created intellect sees the essence of God, the essence of God itself becomes the intelligible form of the intellect. Hence it is necessary that some supernatural disposition should be added to the intellect in order that it may be raised up to such a great and sublime height. (*S.T.* I, 12, 5)

St. John of the Cross writes that while "the intellect by its own power extends itself only to natural knowledge," it "has a potency for the supernatural whenever Our Lord wishes to raise it to a supernatural act" (A II, 3, i—my translation). In several places he says explicitly that God communicates knowledge directly to the passive intellect in contemplation (see A II, 32, iv; C 14 & 15, xiv-xv; 39, xii; cf. N II, 13, iii), and innumerable other statements clearly take this view of the intellect's role in contemplation for granted (see the early chapters of A II, as well as A III, 5, iii; 12, i). For example, John can speak of the soul becoming "deiform" in contemplation, and being raised "from the natural to the divine," because in a way this is precisely what his epistemological theory implies; the relationship between God and the possible intellect is like that between form and matter, so that at the moment of this obscure contemplation, the mind is, in a certain sense, divinized (see A III, 2, viii-ix; N II, 4, ii; 13, xi; C 26, x-xvii; 39, iv; F 2, xxxiii-xxxiv). The "substantial knowledge" thereby produced in the possible intellect is "loving," because it arouses an intense desire for God.[20] John also describes it repeatedly as "obscure" and "general," because, like its object and cause, it is "unmodified by the boundaries of form, species, and image" (**A** II, 16, vii; cf. **A** II, 14, viii-xii; 15, iii; 24, iv; **C** 12, ii; **F** 3, xlix-li). But as we have seen, the knowledge and ideas produced by our natural cognitive powers are "clear," "distinct," and "particular," involving advertence to phantasms and the specific concepts of creatures. St. John of the Cross maintains, therefore, that the intellect cannot be simultaneously "informed" by natural knowledge and the "substantial knowledge" given in contemplation. Thus the claim that natural knowledge "cannot profit the soul" simply means that while the intellect is single-mindedly preoccupied with creatures it is unreceptive to the "obscure knowledge" of God; on the other hand, during the time God operates directly on the possible intellect, all other thoughts are banished (see **A** II, 14, xi-xii; 15, iii; 16, xi; **C** 16, xi; 26, xiv-xvii).

In light of the preceding discussion, we are already able to draw some important preliminary conclusions about the Sanjuanist view of mysticism. First of all, for John of the Cross the "secret wisdom" of contemplation is received *passively*. This means, of course, that it cannot be acquired solely by the unaided ascetical effort to suppress all particular thoughts and desires, but requires the intervention of God.[21] It also means that, despite what Stace claims, the mental state of the recipient is not simply identical with what is left of consciousness after "emptying the mind of all empirical contents" (1960a, p. 102). Admittedly, John does say that "when a person has finished purifying and voiding himself of all forms and apprehensible images," and "as soon as natural things are driven out of the enamored soul, the divine are naturally and supernaturally infused, since there can be no void in nature" (**A** II, 15, iv). But the process is "automatic" only in the sense that God ordinarily wills to give himself to anyone who does not resist by clinging to "particular knowledge." On the other hand, John is perfectly familiar with the pathological conditions of torpor and confusion brought on by physical or psychological disturbances, in which the mind remains blank, unable to focus on anything clearly; he sharply distinguishes such states from authentic contemplation (see, e.g., **A** II, 13, vi; 14, vi-vii; **N** I, 9, i-ix). For St. John of the Cross, then, the "secret wisdom" has a positive content. What mystics experience during moments of intense union is not just "pure awareness" or the absence of particular images and concepts, but the *presence* of a new "loving knowledge" which absorbs their attention and drives out all other thoughts.

In the second place, as we have already noted, John clearly holds that the contemplative and mystical states he discusses have a *noetic* dimension. This is obviously part of the reason for describing them in terms of "knowledge" and of God's operation on the passive intellect in a way analogous to the role of the agent intellect in ordinary knowledge and perception. Unfortunately, certain commentators have been misled by some of John's remarks on "substantial union" and the recondite character of the divine communication, and have argued that, according to St. John, mystical union is not a conscious experience at all (see Werblowsky 1966, p. 182; Gibbs 1976, pp. 541-549). What puzzles these authors are statements where John seems to say that the locus of mystical union is the "substance" of the soul *rather* than the intellect (see, e.g., A II 24, iv; 32, i-iii; F 3, lxix), and by passages suggesting that at certain stages of the spiritual life, contemplation is "secret and hidden from the very one who receives it" (N I, 9, vi). John's notion of the "substance of the soul" will be discussed more thoroughly below. In general, however, such texts must obviously be interpreted in light of everything else John says. Thus the assertion that "this general knowledge" is "sometimes so subtle and delicate that the soul...does not perceive or feel it" (A II, 14, viii—my translation) follows an earlier comment that "at the beginning of this state the loving knowledge is *almost* unnoticeable" (A II, 13, vii—emphasis mine), and is in turn followed by the observation that the person in this state is said to do nothing "not because he fails to understand, but because he understands by dint of no effort other than the reception of what is bestowed" (A II, 15, ii). In other words, John does not mean to deny that the contemplative is aware of the divine communication at some level; he is simply saying that this "substantial knowledge" is so new and unfamiliar that initially it may not be recognized for what it is, because it is not understood and perceived in the ordinary way. John stresses the "obscurity" of this "substantial knowledge" only when he is contrasting it with the "clarity" of natural knowledge or the Beatific Vision. Yet (invoking the Aristotelian principle that "the clearer and more obvious divine things are in themselves, the darker and more hidden they are to the soul naturally") John also notes that, from an objective point of view, mystical knowledge is actually *clearer* and *more lucid* than the product of our natural cognitive abilities, because the God who acts upon the passive intellect is himself supremely intelligible (see A II, 3, vi; 8, vi; 14, xiii; N II, 5, iii; cf. von Balthasar 1986, vol. 3, pp. 133-144).

In the third place, the "natural knowledge" which mystical union precludes is "occurrent" rather than "habitual." In other words, when John says that those united with God in contemplation are divested of all "particular concepts" and "distinct knowledge," he does not mean that they lose their understanding of mathematics, for example, or their ability to swim, to distinguish colors, or to do philosophy. John does not advocate an inhuman suppression of our natural cognitive powers, nor the pursuit of ignorance or amnesia. His point is rather that during the period of intense mystical union itself, mystics "cannot actually advert to any other thing" (C 26, xvii—my translation), because their intellects are being informed by God and are therefore not receptive to being actually informed by the species of creatures. Put in more contemporary terms, this means that during such moments mystics are unable to exercise their ordinary concepts of material objects.[22] But they retain their "acquired knowledge," and are free to utilize it again once the effect of this union passes (see **C** 26, xvi).

Fourth, it is clear that John is not an opponent of rationality in any simple and straightforward sense. Despite Inge's accusation that he demands "the sacrifice of reason" (1956, p. 229), John compares right reason to the temple of God (**A** I, 9, vi), and insists repeatedly that the person desiring union with God must be guided by reason (see especially *Sayings of Light and Love* 19, 34, 41, 42, 43 in *Collected Works* ["Dichos de Luz y Amor" 19, 36, 43, 44, 45 in *Vida y Obras*]; **A** I, 8, iii; II, 21, iv; 22, ix; xi; xv). According to St. John of the Cross, God:

...is ever desirous that man insofar as possible take advantage of his own reasoning powers. All matters must be regulated by reason save those of faith, which though not contrary to reason transcend it. (A II, 22, xiii)

Thus John does not require the annihilation of reason, but only the recognition that what the mystic receives in contemplation cannot be attained by our unaided rational powers.

Finally, some of John's statments on the "ineffability" of God and mystical communications seem to be associated with the theory of knowledge we have been examining. Consider, for example, the following passages:

Because this interior wisdom is so simple, general, and spiritual that it did not enter the intellect enveloped...in any species or image subject to sense, it follows that the sense and imagination (*el sentido e imaginativa*) are unable...to imagine it in order to say something about it..., although the soul is clearly aware that it understands and tastes this delightful and wondrous wisdom. It is like one who sees something he has never seen before, nor has he seen anything like it; although he might understand and experience it (*gustase*), he would not be able to give it a name or say what it is no matter how hard he tried.... How much less could one describe something that has not entered through the senses! (**N** II, 17, iii—my translation)

Since this is pure contemplation, the soul sees clearly that it cannot say anything about it, except to speak in certain general terms, of the abundance of delight and blessing....

This divine knowledge of God never deals with particular things, because it concerns the First Principle. Consequently, it cannot be expressed in particular terms, unless a truth about something less than God is seen together with it. (A II, 26, iii-v—my translation)

Throughout his writings, John characterizes many things as "indescribable," including the harm caused by inordinate appetites (**A** I, 9, iv), and the sufferings of the passive night of the spirit (**N** II, 6, ii; 7, ii); he also offers many reasons why mystical knowledge cannot be adequately expressed in words. I will have more to say about John's general treatment of ineffability in the fourth chapter.

In passages such as those quoted above, however, John seems to be relying "upon a theory of meaning not utterly unlike that which the British Empiricists came to hold; if no sense experience, then no idea and no meaningful name" (Kellenberger 1979, p. 310). In particular, John appears to believe that one has not really *described* an X (or described it *adequately*) unless one applies a "name" to it, a name associated with a sensible impression or intelligible species of X (or something resembling it), which enables the hearer to form a corresponding "concept" (i.e., intelligible species) of X (see **A** II, 3, ii-iii, for example). Mystical communications will not be "describable" in this narrow sense because they do not involve any "nameable" species through which they could be understood. But this does not imply that such experiences cannot be "described" in the broader and more ordinary sense. John admits that we can make meaningful statements about these communications; he explicitly says in one of the quotations above that they can be described "in certain general terms." Thus, whatever one may think of the theory of language and description John invokes, it is clear that John has not here committed himself to any of the more extreme and paradoxical versions of the claim that mystical experiences are "ineffable."

2.2.2. THE WILL

The spiritual faculty of the will (*voluntad*) is given special prominence in the Sanjuanist system, and there are places where John even analyzes union with God in terms of the conformity of the divine and human wills (see **A** I, 5, iii; **N** II, 11, iii; **C** 38, iii-iv; **F** 3, xxiv; cf. Juan de Jesús María 1955, pp. 3-103). Such passages have led certain commentators to suspect John of a kind of spiritual "voluntarism" (see Trethowan 1975b, pp. 87-89; Idem 1975a, p. 18; Cupitt 1981, p. 139). As we saw in the preceding pages, however, St. John of the Cross by no means neglects the noetic dimension of contemplative and mystical experiences. In reality, John sees the two faculties of intellect and will as inseparably linked in the spiritual life, since "it is impossible to attain to the perfect love of God without the perfect vision of God" (**C** 38, v).[23]

John's teaching on the will and human affectivity is an important and difficult topic, which deserves extensive treatment in its own right. However, John himself indicates that "the same doctrine that serves for the one faculty will evidently apply to the others also" (**A** III, 34, i), because of their close interrelationship. Therefore, it is unnecessary to repeat points already made in dealing with the role of the intellect, and the discussion here can be brief.

I noted above that in scholastic philosophy, "appetite in the strict sense...designates the capacity of a thing to seek its *good*...; when used more broadly it includes the actual seeking as well" (Wallace 1977, p. 74). Thus St. Thomas and the scholastics attribute appetite "to all beings, from God, who has Will, to primary matter, which has an appetite for substantial form" (Stock 1967, *New Catholic Encyclopedia* vol. 1, p. 703). In the case of human beings, there are, besides the natural appetites, certain other appetites elicted by cognitive acts. These "elicited appetites" are distinguished by the kind of knowledge which evokes them. For the scholastics, since "knowledge...is divided into sense knowledge and intellectual knowledge," the "appetites are correspondingly divided into sensitive appetite and will, the appetite that follows on intellection" (Wallace 1977, p. 74). Thus the human volitional powers depend upon our cognitive abilities, since the will inclines toward and away from the goods or evils intellectually presented. In particular, it is the will alone which seeks purely rational and spiritual goods as such, since these are not within the scope of the sensory appetites.

As far as I know, John nowhere describes the will as an "appetite," a term he usually uses in reference to what the scholastics call the "sensory appetites."[24] Nevertheless, many of his statements suggest a theory of volition similar to the one just outlined. Thus he seems to have an analogous view of the relationship between intellect and will. In *Ascent* I, 8, ii, for example, he notes that the memory and will "depend upon the intellect in their operations." In several places he repeats the principle that "in the natural operations and acts of the soul, ...the will does not love except what the intellect understands distinctly" (**F** 3, xlix; cf. **C** 26, viii). At the same time, John also observes that "the intellect and other faculties cannot admit or deny anything without the intervention of the will" (**A** III, 34, i). There is, in other words, a reciprocal influence of the will upon the intellect; human beings may voluntarily focus their thoughts and attention on a particular object of their desire.

Yet there is more to human affectivity than the will alone. In describing the other components of our conative side, John of the Cross employs a rich array of expressions whose meanings often seem to overlap. He speaks, for example, of "longings" (*ansias*), "desires" (*deseos*), "hunger" (*hambre*), "concupiscence" (*concupiscencia*), "affections" (*afecciones*), "seeking" (*querer*) and so on (see Ruiz 1968, pp. 581-585; Culligan 1979, pp. 119-125; and the appropriate entries in Luis de San José 1948). For our purposes, however, the most important terms are "appetites" (*apetitos*) and "passions" (*pasiones*), terms which John borrowed from the scholastics but sometimes used in a different way.

The word *apetito* has no exact equivalent in English, and some commentators suggest that it has at least six different meanings in John's writings (Guillet 1971, p. 27). Nevertheless, as I noted above, John uses it most often in describing the tendency of each human faculty to seek its own pleasure (*gustos*) and satisfaction (*satisfacción*), and particularly a person's attraction toward what satisfies the senses; thus he says in one place that the sensory part of the soul is "the house of all the appetites" (**A** I, 15, ii).[25] The appetites in this sense are morally neutral, and in fact have a role to play in mystical union when they are properly directed and kept within appropriate bounds. When John begins to talk about "emptying" (*vaciarse*) the soul of its appetites in the first book of the *Ascent*, he makes it clear that he is referring to "inordinate" and "voluntary" appetites (see especially **A** I, 9, ii-iv; 11, ii-iii; 12, iii-vi). Often, however, John simply neglects to add these qualifying adjectives, so that the term "appetite" itself comes to designate an unruly attraction toward pleasure to which one gives assent.

In certain passages John enumerates four "passions" of the soul (joy, hope, sorrow, fear), appealing to Boethius in defense of this division (see **A** II, 21, viii; III, 16, vi; cf. **A** Prologue vii; I, 13, v; III, 16, i-vi; **N** I, 13, xv; **C** 20 & 21, iv; ix-x; 26, xviii). Elsewhere, however, he uses "passions" more broadly, to refer to what we would today call the emotions. In either case, the passions seem to be the affective impact on the soul of the appetites' movement toward clearly apprehended goods (or away from perceived evils). The last twenty-nine chapters of the *Ascent*, for example, deal with all of the different forms of "active joy," which "occurs when a person understands distinctly and clearly the object of its joy" (**A** III, 17, i). Elsewhere John writes that:

....all pleasures, joys, and affections are ever caused in the soul by means of the desire and will for things which appear good, suitable, and delightful, being in a person's opinion satisfying and precious. And accordingly the appetite of the will inclines toward these things, hopes for them, rejoices in their possession, fears their loss, and grieves upon losing them. (Letter #12 in *Collected Works*; #13 in *Vida y Obras*)

For the most part, John treats the sensory appetites and passions as a block, without distinguishing them carefully, since the "four passions are so brother-like that where one goes actually the others go virtually" (**A** III, 16, v; cf. **A** I, 6, i; 12, iii-v). He is more interested in how the desires and emotions as a whole affect the will.

In the first place, John believes that human beings can exert control over their attraction toward sensible pleasure and satisfaction; the "power of the soul," which "comprises the faculties, passions, and appetites," is "ruled by the will" (**A** III, 16, ii). This means that a person can choose to forgo sensible pleasure for the sake of a higher good. At the same time, however, desires and emotions may be so strong that they cloud the mind and fix one's attention on the desired object; human beings may follow inclinations they would otherwise reject, simply because they are unwilling to endure the pain which this rejection would cause them (see, e.g., **A** I, 8, i-vii; 12, v; **C** 16, iv-vii; **F** 3, lxx-lxxv). Thus John observes that when the emotions dominate, "the entire soul, will, and other faculties also go wherever one of these passions goes, and live as its prisoners" (**A** III, 16, vi—my translation). In other words, unruly appetites and passions may limit an individual's freedom.

John of the Cross applies this account of volition and affectivity to the question of union with God. Because the will is a spiritual faculty, it somehow participates directly in mystical union. In fact, John believes that the ultimate good toward which the will tends is God himself, and it achieves complete satisfaction in the loving possession of Him (see **A** II, 6, i-iv; III, 16, i-iii; **N** II, 13, xi; 21, xi; **C** 2, vii; 6, ii; 38, ii-v; **F** 3, lxxviii-lxxx). However, as noted above, the will by its own power can only seek those goods which are the object of the intellect's clear knowledge. But since the intellect cannot naturally attain "essential knowledge" of God, the will in turn is not naturally capable of seeking God as God is.[26] Therefore, in order to reach union with God, the will must receive an "obscure love" corresponding to the "obscure knowledge" communicated to the intellect; the person then loves intensely, but without a clear understanding of the divine object of her love (see, for example, **A** II, 14, xii; 24, ix; **N** I, 10, vi; 11, i; II, 5, i; 12, ii; v-vii; 13, ii; 16, xiv; **C** 13, xi; 26, v-viii).

Unfortunately, when the emotions and desires are centered on finite goals, the will is less free for union with God in love, not only because the person's affective energies are scattered, but also presumably because the intellect is kept busy with "particular knowledge" and is therefore unreceptive to divine communications. John argues that inordinate appetites cause both positive and privative damage; they not only "weary, torment, darken, defile, and weaken" a person, but also "deprive him of God's Spirit" (**A** I, 6, i). It is in the explanation of this "privative harm," rather than in his discussion of the intellect, that John most often invokes the principle that "two contraries cannot coexist in the same subject." He writes, for example, that:

> Darkness, an attachment to creatures, and light, which is God, are contraries and bear no likeness toward each other.... Consequently, the light of divine union cannot be established in the soul until these affections are eradicated. (**A** I, 4, ii; see also **A** I, 6, i-iv; **N** II, 5, iv; 9, ii)

According to John, moreover, "love effects a likeness" between lover and beloved, so that "he who loves a creature...is as low as that creature, and in some way even lower, because love not only equates, but even subjects the lover to the loved object" (**A** I, 4, iii). In order for the will to reach union with God, then, the old "form" of attachment to creatures must be expelled by an infusion of the new "form" of divine love, which unifies a person's affective abilities and directs them toward God (see, e.g., **A** I, 4, iii; 5, ii; vii; 6, ii; 14, ii; **N** I, 11, i; II, 4, i-ii; 8, ii-iv; 9, i-iii; 11, i-iv; 13, xi; **C** 28, i-iv; the poem 'Por todo la hermosura'; *Maxims on Love* #19 in *Collected Works* [*Puntos de Amor* #97 in *Vida y Obras*]). Finally, John of the Cross holds that this "obscure love" is produced by the very same communication which imparts "obscure knowledge" to the intellect; God touches both faculties in a single act, though at first the effects may be felt more strongly in one or the other (see **A** II, 24, viii; 32, iii; **N** II, 12, v-vii; 13, i-v; **C** 26, v-ix; 27, v; **F** 1, xvii).[27]

Whatever one may think, then, of John's account of the will and the scholastic theories on which it is based,[28] they suggest three points worth noting about the Sanjuanist understanding of mysticism. First, John sees *love* as an essential ingredient in higher mystical states. Because mystics of other cultures do not always describe their experiences as "loving," some philosophers have tried to use the presence or absence of this quality as a criterion for distinguishing fundamentally different types of mystical experiences (cf. Zaehner 1961; Idem 1970; Wainwright 1981, pp. 31-41). Others, however, maintain that mysticism is everywhere the same, and therefore argue that this affective tone is merely an accidental feature of mystical experiences, or simply the emotional repercussion produced in certain kinds of mystics (see Stace 1960b, pp. 130-132; Smart 1965, pp. 75-87). Without attempting to settle the issue here, I would at least suggest that John's statements tend to favor the former position. When St. John of the Cross attempts to describe what the mystic receives, he is unsure whether to call it "knowledge," or "love," or both at once. In fact, as the *Canticle* clearly demonstrates, he views the whole spiritual life as a developing love-relationship between divine and human partners. For St. John, then, the affective tone of mystical and contemplative experiences is at least as important as their noetic quality; indeed, he would find no meaning in such states if the quality of love were lacking.

Second, John's overall evaluation of human affectivity is fundamentally positive. This is not to deny that St. John was influenced by the spiritual theology of his day, which often tended to adopt an unduly negative attitude toward human nature. His severe remarks on the harm caused by the appetites and the need to strip the will "of all the cravings and satisfactions of the old man" so that its activities may "become divine" (**A** I, 5, vii) have convinced some commentators that John favors the annihilation of all human emotions and desires (see Bendick 1972, pp. 283-285; Mallory 1977, pp. 5-13, 16-22; Paton 1962, pp. 88-89, 94-95).[29] In his more careful statements, however, John makes it clear that he does not want to *destroy* the appetites and passions, but only to reform and redirect them. In several places, as noted earlier, he explicitly says that he is concerned with the "voluntary" and "inordinate" appetites. Elsewhere John apparently tries to modify his more extreme expressions in order to avoid misleading the reader; a sentence in *Ascent* I, 3, i, for example, begins with the words: "When the appetites are extinguished (*apagado*), or, to express it better, mortified (*mortificado*)" (my translation). Finally, John repeatedly recommends that a person striving for perfection "employ all the faculties, appetites, operations, and emotions of his soul in God" (**A** III, 16, i), and says that the soul which reaches divine union finds "a place in God where she can satisfy her appetites and faculties" (**C** 35, iv). Such statements would obviously make no sense if all human desires and emotions were eliminated. For St. John of the Cross, then, human affectivity is of value, because of the role it plays in mystical union with God (see Payne 1978, pp. 126-136; cf. Baruzi 1924, pp. 413-438).

Finally, whatever importance John attributes to the will and passions, he is certainly no proponent of irrational religious emotionalism. John is very clear on how misleading feelings can be in the spiritual life. He maintains, moreover, that all of the faculties and appetites must be "ordered according to reason" before a person can attain union with God (see **A** I, 8, i-iii; 9, vi; III, 16, ii; 26, v-vi; 29, ii; **N** I, 6, vi; **C** 20 & 21, iv; **F** III, lxxii-lxxv).[30] The final goal of the mystical life is a state in which all of one's powers and abilities work in harmonious order.

2.2.3. THE MEMORY

In his recent study, *Mémoire et Espérance chez Jean de la Croix* (Paris, 1971), André Bord shows that St. John's theory of memory (*memoria*) is perhaps his most original contribution to philosophical psychology. Bord has provided a convincing interpretation of certain enigmatic and apparently inconsistent passages in the Sanjuanist writings which have baffled previous generations of commentators. Because Bord's reconstruction of John's theory of memory seems both plausible and well-argued, I will simply summarize those of his conclusions which have the greatest bearing on the present discussion.

Scholastic accounts of memory attempt to explain the human being's ability to reflect on objects not present to the senses, and to recall previously acquired concepts and knowledge, in terms of a general epistemological theory like the one outlined above. Thomas Aquinas, for example, considered it unnecessary to postulate the existence of a separate spiritual faculty to account for this ability. According to the Angelic Doctor, the *imagination* is all that is required to retain phantasms; as for the intelligible species, these are preserved by the intellect itself. Thus he writes that "memory as belonging to the mind is not a power distinct from the possible intellect," although "there is a distinction between memory and possible intellect according to orientation to different things" (*De Veritate* X, 3 ad 1; see also Ibid. X, 2; and *S.T.* I, 79, 6 & 7).

St. John of the Cross aligns himself with the Augustinian tradition by classifying memory as a distinct spiritual power, but he diverges somewhat from both Thomas and Augustine in the function he assigns to this faculty. For St. John, memory is, first of all, an ability to recall the past, to retrieve what one has already learned and experienced. Thus John indicates that this faculty is able to remember (*acordar*), to forget (*olvidar*), to consider (*pensar, considerar*), or to set aside and withdraw from (*vaciar, enajenar*) its corresponding objects (see Bord 1971, pp. 76-78, as well as **A** III, 3, v; 7, ii; 9, iv; 13, i; 14, i; **F** 3, xxi). He likewise notes that memories can be aroused either voluntarily or involuntarily, through the influence of the unconscious, the will, the devil, or God (see, for example, **A** III, 4, i-ii; 8, iii; 10, i; 13, vi; **N** I, 4, iv; II, 7, i; 9, vii; **C** 16, iv; 35, v; **F** 1, xvii).

In the second place, John also uses the term "memory" for the *product* of the power of recollection, i.e., for the *present act* of remembering. Memory in this sense might be described as a field of awareness which particular memories enter and leave, and is thus an aspect of consciousness itself. Here it is difficult to make any sharp distinction between intellect and memory. In fact, John continually speaks of the "forms, figures, and knowledge" (*formas y figuras y noticias*) of the memory. Moreoever, in dealing with the active purification of the memory in Book III of the *Ascent*, he divides its apprehensions according to the categories used earlier in discussing the intellect, and repeatedly refers the reader to his previous remarks (see, for example, **A** III, 1, i-ii; 2, xv; 13, iii; 14, ii). John of the Cross evidently believes that the same phantasms and intelligible species are involved in both remembering and in knowing or perceiving. In other words, from the point of view of the subject, the main difference between an actual perception of a tree and a present recollection of that perception is that the external senses are not involved in the latter experience; in both cases, however, the person entertains the same concept.

Thus John sees memory and intellect as subject to similar natural limitations and in need of a similar purification. Like the intellect, memory can become obsessively preoccupied with certain thoughts and ideas, especially when these arouse strong feelings and desires.

> The soul is incapable of truly acquiring control of the passions and the restriction of the inordinate appetites without forgetting and withdrawing from the sources of these emotions. Disturbances never arise in the soul unless through the apprehensions of the memory. When all things are forgotten, nothing disturbs the peace or stirs the appetites. As the saying goes: What the eye doesn't see, the heart doesn't want. (A III, 5, i; see also A III, 3, iii-vi; 4, ii; 5, ii-iii; 6, iii-iv; 10, ii)

But because the memory is a spiritual faculty, it also participates directly in the union of the soul with God. In order to attain this goal, the memory must be emptied "of all forms that are not God" (A III, 2, iv).

> For as we mentioned in the night of the intellect, God cannot be contained (*no cae debajo*) in any form or distinct knowledge.... Since...the memory cannot at the same time be united with God and with forms and distinct knowledge, and since God has no form or image comprehensible to the memory, the memory is without form, figure, or phantasy when united to God.... (Ibid.; see also A III, 2, ii; viii; 3, vi; 5, iii; 11, ii)

Since this teaching is essentially the same as that given for the other spiritual faculties, there is no need to dwell upon it here. It does, however, point to a third and extremely important feature of the Sanjuanist theory of the memory: namely, that is is not a "receptacle" or "archives." Unlike Aquinas and Augustine, John apparently does not hold that a person's ideas and knowledge are stored in the memory. Otherwise, he could not consistently claim that emptying this faculty of its apprehensions does not harm, but actually perfects, the "acquired knowledge of the sciences" (**C** 26, xvi). Instead, John seems to suggest that there are two "receptacles" which the memory draws upon: the *phantasy* and "the *soul itself*" (see Bord 1971, pp. 81-96; see also **A** III, 7, i; 13, vi-viii; 14, i-ii). These preserve one's knowledge and ideas even when the soul is absorbed in union with God.

The interior sense of the *phantasy* has already been discussed in an earlier section. Here we are only concerned with its relationship to the memory. Bord argues that John identifies the phantasy with the "central sense" of medieval psychological theories; in other words, the phantasy receives and stores the phantasms produced by natural sensation (or supernatural intervention). Out of these, the discursive power of imagination, through the cooperation of the memory, is able to construct new "forms and images" and to deposit them back in the phantasy (see **A** II, 8, v). Likewise, the memory assists the intellect in selecting the phantasms required for its consideration and judgment (see **A** II, 16, ii). Thus the memories of natural or supernatural knowledge (*noticias*) involving sensible species are preserved by the phantasy.

However, other kinds of knowledge, especially the purely spiritual "touches of union with God," involve no particular "corporal image and form"; these apprehensions are remembered "intellectually and spiritually through the form impressed on the soul (which is also a spiritual or formal form, idea, or image)," because the phantasy, "being...corporal, ...has no capacity for spiritual forms" (**A** III, 14, i-ii).[31] Thus the *soul itself* serves as a receptacle for these purely spiritual "forms," and the soul "is aware that it has them within itself as an image in a mirror" (**A** III, 13, vii). Bord argues that this receptacle is identical with the "central sense of the soul" (*sentido común del alma*) mentioned in *Flame* 3, lxix, which John describes as the soul's "power and capacity for experiencing, possessing, and tasting" the objects of the spiritual faculties (see Bord 1971, pp. 90-91).[32] If Bord is right, then there is a close parallel between the two "receptacles" of the Sanjuanist theory; the interior "central sense" (or phantasy) of the corporal part, and the "central sense" of the soul, would be the two archives upon which the memory draws.

In any case, we can see that when John talks of purifying, purging, and emptying the memory, he is not implying that his readers should strive to forget everything they know and remember. His point is rather that memory, as an aspect of consciousness itself, "should be left free and disencumbered and unattached to any earthly or heavenly consideration" (A III, 2, i) so that it may be receptive to the divine communication. When the memory is filled with thoughts of creatures, it is not "free for the Incomprehensible Who is God"; and while mystics are absorbed in union with God, they forget everything else, because they are "unable to advert to more than one thing" (A III, 5, iii; see also A III, 2, viii-xiv; 15, i). For John, it is the theological virtue of *hope* which accomplishes the necessary purgation of the memory, and leaves it free for God.

Thus we reach the same conclusion regarding the memory as we did with the intellect and the will. According to St. John of the Cross, the ordinary operations of the spiritual faculties are not to be *destroyed*, but only to be set aside when a higher, mystical communication supervenes.

2.2.4. "SPIRITUAL SENSES" AND "THE SUBSTANCE OF THE SOUL"

John of the Cross frequently describes mystical union in terms of God's action on "the substance of the soul," and some of his remarks also suggest that contemplatives are equipped with a certain capacity, analogous to the powers of physical sensation, by which they are able to perceive spiritual realities. Many careful readers have therefore wondered what role the notions of "the substance of the soul" and the "spiritual sense (or senses)" play in Sanjuanist thought. Since this question has a direct bearing on John's conception of the nature of mysticism, let us end the present discussion of the "structure of the soul" with some brief observations on these obscure notions.

In *Night* II, 24, ii, St. John refers to the "sensory and spiritual parts" of the soul, "with their *senses*, faculties, and passions" (emphasis mine). Elsewhere he speaks of "the eyes of the soul," "spiritual hearing," and "substantial touches of union" (see, for example, A II, 11, vii; 16, xii; 23, ii; 32, ii-iv; N II, 23, xi-xii; 24, iii; C 10, iv-ix; 14 & 15, xv; 32, viii; F 2, xxi-xxii). In distinguishing different kinds of purely spiritual, intellectual apprehensions, John first notes that they "can all be titled visions of the soul," but goes on to add that:

> Since these apprehensions reach the soul in ways similar to those of the other senses, we can, properly and specifically speaking, apply the term vision to whatever the intellect receives in a manner resembling sight.... A locution signifies whatever is received in a way similar to that of hearing. And we apply the term spiritual feelings to whatever is perceived after the manner of the other senses, such as the supernaturally enjoyable experience of a sweet spiritual fragrance, savor, or delight. (A II, 23, iii)

Finally, as I noted above, John also mentions a "central sense of the soul" in a crucial passage from the *Living Flame* commentary:

By the sense of the soul (*sentido de el alma*) is here understood the strength and virtue which the substance of the soul has for perceiving (*sentir*) and enjoying (*gozar*) the objects of the spiritual faculties, through which it tastes the wisdom, love, and communication of God. Hence...the soul calls these three faculties (memory, intellect, and will) deep caverns of sense, because in and through them the soul profoundly perceives (*siente*) and enjoys (*gusta*) the grandeurs of God's wisdom and excellence.... All these things are received and seated in this sense of the soul, which, as I say, is the virtue and capacity which the soul has for perceiving, possessing, and enjoying (*sentillo, poseello y gustallo*) everything. And the caverns of the faculties administer them to it, just as the corporal senses aid the central sense of the phantasy (*sentido común de la fantasía*) with the forms of their objects, and this central sense is the receptacle and archives for them. Therefore this central sense of the soul, which has become the receptacle and archives for the grandeurs of God, is illuminated and enriched according to what it attains of this lofty and glorious possession. (F 1, lxix—my translation)

It is hardly surprising, therefore, that some theologians appeal to St. John in support of the notion that there are "spiritual senses" whose nature and structure mirrors that of the corporal senses.[33] But to interpret John's remarks correctly, we must first look more closely at what he means by "the substance of the soul," since (at least in this quotation) he seems to associate the soul's "sense" with its "substance."

The terms "substance" and "substantial" have a variety of related meanings in the works of St. John of the Cross. I have already noted John's use of the expression "substantial knowledge," and pointed out that he tends to treat "substantial" and "essential" as synonyms. In general, John uses "substance" for the inner reality of a thing or person. He apparently believes that every "nature" in some way has a corresponding "substance," and so occasionally speaks of the "sensory and spiritual substance of the soul" (see N II, 6, iv; F 2, xxii). Most often, however, "the substance of the soul" refers to the innermost "depths" or "center" of the subject, "where neither the center of the senses nor the devil can reach" (F 1, ix; see also A II, 24, iv; 26, v-vi; 31, ii; 32, iii-iv; N II, 9, iii; 13, iii; 23, xi-xii; C 14 & 15, xii-xviii; 19, v; 22, v; 25, viii; 39, viii; F 1, ix; xiv; xvii-xx; 2, viii-x; xvii; xxi; xxxiv; 4, iv-xv). It is thus the point of contact between the human and divine.[34]

In certain places John mentions the soul's substance and faculties *together* in a way which seems to suggest that the substance, *rather* than the memory, intellect, and will, is the proper locus of mystical experiences. He says, for example, that in the state of spiritual marriage "the faculties are not always in actual union, although the substance is" (C 26, xi; see also A II, 32, ii-v; F 2, xxi; xxxiv). In the above quotation from the *Living Flame*, the "central sense of the soul" (which presumably serves the same function for the "spiritual senses" as the corporal "central sense" does for the five external senses) is identified with the capacity of "the substance of the soul" for "perceiving and enjoying the objects of the spiritual faculties" (F 3, lxix).

Some have concluded, therefore, that John postulates "the existence of some additional faculty in the soul, quite distinct from either the higher or lower natural faculties, by which the highest divine communications are received" (Dicken 1963, p. 372). Others, however, are quick to point out the difficulties raised by such a notion. Thus one critic argues that "the attempt to draw an analogy between the *sensus communis* and an alleged faculty in the 'substance of the soul,' ...for receiving contemplation from the three spiritual faculties, is simply absurd," because "memory and will are not in any way faculties of perception" nor "functions of a single spiritual quasi-organ" (Gibbs 1976, p. 544). Another problem is that mystical union in the substance *alone* would apparently fall outside the realm of conscious experience altogether, since it involves none of the natural faculties. Likewise the notion of the "spiritual senses" analogous to the physical senses only seems to complicate John's psychological theory needlessly, and offers little help in explaining the apparent similarities between mystical experiences and sense perceptions. However, John's remarks can be interpreted in a way which avoids some of these difficulties. Dicken, for example, suggests that "the substance of the soul...is perhaps best rendered as 'the totality of the higher faculties of the soul'" (Dicken, 1963, p. 33; see also pp. 368-374). This proposal is somewhat misleading, since it would render John's references to "the substance and faculties of the soul" inexplicably redundant. Nevertheless, Dicken correctly perceives that the Sanjuanist "substance of the soul" is not some fourth independent component of the rational part, nor a bare substrate in which the faculties inhere as accidents. John of the Cross was not particularly interested in scholastic disputes about the relationship between the soul and its faculties.[35] His approach is more practical and concrete. For John, the "substance" is simply "that capacity or faculty in one's psychological makeup for experiencing fruition, delight, and joy; or sadness, anguish, and desolation, etc." (Kavanaugh 1979, p. 572).[36] Similarly, the "(central) sense of the soul" is the person's ability to perceive and retain what is communicated to the faculties. In effect, the two expressions refer to the same reality.[37]

Why, then, does John occasionally speak of the faculties *and* substance of the soul? Part of the reason is that he sometimes identifies the memory, intellect, and will with their *natural* operations (Orcibal 1966, pp. 147-151, 186-196). Thus, when he describes "toques de sustancias desnudas" which redound to the faculties, he is not suggesting that these experiences involve an immediate contact between property-less divine and human substances. Rather, "substantial touches" are general communications "without form, figure, or concept," which are experienced passively in the person's most profound depths, and which overflow in more intense and specific effects upon the different faculties; sometimes, for example, these "touches" will produce a sense of deeper "insight," and at other times will arouse a more fervent love (see, for example, C 26, xi, and F 1).[38] The expression "substance of the soul" gives John a way of distinguishing the central experience of union from ordinary experiences, as well as from less important supernatural experiences involving particular faculties. Thus the distinction between faculties and substance amounts to a distinction between the natural abilities of the intellect, memory, and will, and the capacity of the totality of the faculties to "be moved by God in such a way that the soul 'feels' or 'sees' *his* substance" (Dicken 1963, p. 369, where the author clarifies the somewhat misleading remark cited above). John seems to be saying, in other words, that mystical union involves the whole person, and occurs at a level of the subject prior to the separation into distinct powers and acts.[39]

The Sanjuanist notions of "spiritual sense" and "the substance of the soul" are admittedly obscure. I believe, however, that the interpretation offered here manages to avoid some of the difficulties mentioned above. Consequently, we may now turn our attention to John's views on the process of spiritual development, the second part of his twofold analysis of the human person.

NOTES

[1] This is especially true of earlier Catholic authors, though the tendency is still evident even in more recent studies (e.g., Wilhelmsen 1985). For older works which minimize the differences between Aquinas and John of the Cross at the expense of fidelity to the Sanjuanist texts, see, for example, Frost 1937; Garrigou-Lagrange 1958; Marcelo del Niño Jesus 1930; Maritain 1959; Merton 1951; McCann 1955. Maritain tries to resolve the apparent disagreements between St. Thomas and John of the Cross by claiming that Aquinas wrote from a "speculative" point of view, whereas John's analysis was "practical," distinguishing the powers of the soul "not according to their essential ontological articulations, but according to the subject's principal concrete modes of activity with respect to his ends" (Maritain 1959, p. 330). Merton and McCann simply follow Maritain here. For a critique of this solution, and a defense of the real differences between Aquinas and John, see Morel 1960, vol. 2, pp. 27-33; Ruiz Salvador 1968, pp. 287-292; Bord 1971, pp. 300-305.

[2] Aquinas says that the vision of God cannot be experienced naturally in this life, because the soul united to the body knows only through advertence to phantasms, which cannot serve as "created likenesses" of any spiritual substances (see, for example, Aquinas *Summa Theologiae* I, 89, 1; Idem *In De Anima* XVI; Idem *Summa Contra Gentiles* 3, 47 and below).

[3] The image, as used in A I, 15, i and C 18, i (a passage not found in the first redaction of the commentary) describes the relationship between individuals and their unruly desires; compare A I, 7, ii; III, 16, vi. In A I, 3, iii (and possibly also in II, 8, iv) the prison metaphor illustrates an empiricist theory of knowledge, and reminds the reader of Locke's remark that the internal and external senses "are the windows by which light is let into this *dark room*. For methinks the *understanding* is not much unlike a closet wholly shut from light, with only some little opening left, to let in external visible resemblances, or *ideas* of things without." See Locke *Essay Concerning Human Understanding* II, 11, par.

17 (Yolton edition vol. 1, p. 129), and also Copleston 1952, p. 72. Thus John's use of the image does not necessarily commit him to dualism.

[4] I am therefore rejecting Dicken's claim that "for St. John of the Cross a human being may be regarded schematically as a tri-partite and as it were stratified entity," where the three strata are the body and the sensory and spiritual parts of the soul (Dicken 1963, pp. 328-331). John's usage is not always consistent, but in C 28, iv he says explicitly that "the sensory part includes the body," and clearly implies as much in C 13, ii-vi and F 2, xxii. Admittedly, there are numerous places where John speaks of "the soul *and* the body," or seems to distinguish them; see, for example, A II, 11, vi; 24, i; 26, viii; C 8, ii-iii; 28, viii; F 2, xxxi. But the point here is rather that in most places where John uses the term "soul" the modern reader can substitute "person" or "self" without damaging the meaning of what John says. See Ruiz Salvador 1968, pp. 300-301; and Burrell 1967, pp. 404.

The term "spirit" likewise has a number of interrelated meanings for John, including at least the following: 1) the superior part of the soul; 2) the substantial value of things, as opposed to the "rind" (*corteza*) of sense (see, e.g., A II, 17, vi; III, 13, iv); 3) the spiritual person in his operations and way of life; and 4) the Holy Spirit. For further discussion of the meaning of "spirit" in John's works, see Sanson 1953, especially pp. 27, 335-337; and Eulogio de la Virgen del Carmen 1961, p. 61.

[5] Thus some of these experiences seem to occur in a state of semi-detachment from the body; see A II, 24, ii-iii; N II, 1, ii; C 13, ii-vii; F 1, xxvii; 4, xi-xii. It is worth noting that when John says that certain experiences cannot be enjoyed in this life, he often means, not that one has to die first, but rather that such experiences occur before physical death only through an extraordinary intervention of God, in which "the natural functions of the soul toward the body are supplied by His favor" (A II, 24, iii). In *Quaestiones Disputatae de Veritate* XIII, 3, St. Thomas Aquinas similarly observes that "a man living in this mortal body cannot see God through His essence, unless he is made unconscious of the bodily senses." (Here and in subsequent quotations from this text I am using the three volume translation of *De Veritate* found in *Truth*, translated by Mulligan, McGlynn and Schmidt [1952-1954]; this particular passage is found on p. 194 of the second volume.)

[6] Scholastic thinkers use the term "appetite" to refer to the inclination of a thing toward the good, toward an object suitable to itself. They likewise distinguish natural from elicited appetites; the latter are aroused by cognitive acts. Since, in their view, knowledge itself can be fundamentally divided into sense knowledge and intellectual knowledge, the appetites can also be divided into the sensory appetites and the will (which is the appetite of the intellectual part of human nature). Thus "a sensitive appetite is a capacity to be aroused by a concrete object perceived through the senses"; it "belongs to the sensory part" of the soul inasmuch as it does not depend for its existence and operation on the intellect, but only on those aspects of human nature that we have in common with other animals (see Stock 1967, 'Appetite,' *New Catholic Encyclopedia*, vol. 1, pp. 703-706). John sometimes refers to the sensory appetites collectively as "sensuality" (*sensualidad*); see A I, 14, ii; 15, ii: III, 26, iv; N Explanation, ii. At other times the term "sensuality" refers to the whole sensory part of the soul, with its inordinate movements; see C 18, ii-viii.

[7] See Aristotle *De Anima* 3.429a10-432a14. Athough Aquinas distinguished intention from intelligible species, later scholastic philosophers tend to use the two terms, as well as form and concept, interchangeably.

[8] Aquinas, in other words, does not distinguish between imagination and phantasy, and maintains that what is called the estimative power in animals is termed the cogitative power in human beings, because this power takes on new functions when connected with the intellect.

[9] The practice of meditation was highly developed and systematized in John's day, and received its classic expression in the *Spiritual Exercises* of Ignatius of Loyola. Those unfamiliar with the Roman Catholic tradition may find it odd to refer to such pious ratiocination as *prayer*, and indeed there are theologians who would argue that only the expressions of devotion and love which the process produces are prayer in the strict sense. However, in this work I will follow the more common practice of applying the phrase "discursive mental prayer" to this activity as a whole (see Bouyer 1961, pp. 68-75; Fenton 1938, 211-218).

[10] In only one place does John seem to echo Augustine in associating each member of the Trinity with a different spiritual faculty; compare F I, 15 with Augustine's *De Trinitate* XXI, 40-41. The former passage seems to have been added in the second redaction of the *Flame* commentary (see Bord 1971).

[11] Notice that the passage from A II, 16, iv speaks of *the* interior sense of imagination and phantasy, thus supporting Bord's claim that for John there is only a single interior sense; also, the word which I translate "port" (*puerto*) appears as *puerta* (i.e., door or gateway) in some manuscripts. In the second quotation, I am assuming that *inteligencias* refers to the intelligible species of the scholastic theory, and *especies* refers to the sensible species.

[12] Here and elsewhere in this book, "*S.T.*" is used as an abbreviation for the title of the *Summa Theologiae*; moreover, all quotations of this work are taken from the three volume translation by the Fathers of the English Dominican Province (1947-1948), unless otherwise noted. Compare also Aristotle *De Anima* III, 4-5; Aquinas *S.T.* I, 79, 3-4; Idem *De Anima* III-V; Idem *De Veritate* X, 6. Thomas prefers to call the receptive power of the intellect "possible" rather than "passive," because some philosophers use the latter expression for "the act of a corporeal organ" (*S.T.* I, 79, 2 ad 2). John follows other authors, however, in using the two expressions interchangeably.

[13] Anthony Kenny describes the possible intellect as "the power to exercise the dispositions acquired by the use of the agent intellect," and "the collection of concepts and beliefs that [a person] possesses" (see Kenny 1976, pp. 279-280). This description seems too restrictive, however, since both Aquinas and St. John hold that God can directly infuse knowledge into the possible intellect without the intervention of the active intellect, especially in the Beatific Vision.

[14] Strictly speaking, the effect of the active on the possible intellect is known as the "species impressa," to which the possible intellect reacts by producing the "species expressa" or "verbum mentis," which is the full-blown concept. Thomistic philosophers likewise argue over whether it is better to say that the active intellect "abstracts" the idea from the phantasm, or merely interacts with the latter. Finally, these thinkers distinguish the "first act" of the intellect (i.e., the simple apprehension of a thing's essence or quiddity, which we are describing here) from its "second act" of judgment, in which something is affirmed or denied of something else. See Copleston 1955, pp. 181-184; Owens 1982, pp. 452-453; and Knudsen 1982, pp. 481-482.

[15] This is a slight oversimplification. I am assuming that the concept in question is the universal concept of a cat's essence. If, on the other hand, I identify the creature as a cat

simply because of its color or shape, the species in question corresponds only to the accidental properties of the feline.

[16] See articles 2, 3, 11 and 12 of Aquinas *S.T.* I, 12, and article 2 of *S.T.* I, 28; Idem *De Anima* XVI; Idem *De Veritate* 10, 11. Even our own souls, on this account, are known to us only through their activities, and not essentially. The phantasms and intelligible species which, in their primary intentionality, enable us to know sensible objects, also have a second-order function in self-knowledge, when we perceive how they are involved in the intellectual act (see, for example, *S.T.* I, 87, 1; Idem *De Veritate* 10, 8).

[17] "*C.G.*" is used in this study to refer to the *Summa Contra Gentiles*, and I will be quoting from the five volume Pegis translation (1955-1957) unless otherwise noted. Compare A I, 4, v; II, 8, v; 26, xviii; and Aquinas *S.T.* I, 3, Introduction; Idem *De Veritate* X, 11 ad 5. Of course, both authors owe a great deal to the *via negativa* of Pseudo-Dionysius here. Moreover, when John speaks of advancing by "unknowing," he also means that we should even let go of the "remote knowledge" of God when contemplative prayer supervenes (as we shall see below).

[18] In light of such statements, I must disagree with Kenny's claim that "what St. Thomas means by the information of the receptive intellect by an idea is not the episodic exercise of a concept...but rather the acquisition of the...long term capacity to think thoughts of a certain kind" (Kenny 1976, p. 281). When Aquinas says that the intellect cannot be informed by two intelligible species at once, he is talking about the *episodic* exercise of concepts, not about long-term capacities.

[19] Aquinas holds that Adam in the state of innocence did *not* enjoy the direct vision of God. (See also Aquinas *S.T.* I, 12, 2 & 9; I, 94, 1; *De Veritate* VIII, 1; X, 11; XIII, 2-4; XVIII, 1. Compare Q. 92, art. 1 of the Supplement to the *Summa Theologiae*, compiled by Rainaldo de Piperno from St. Thomas's commentary on the Fourth Book of the *Sentences* of Peter Lombard.) Aquinas's account of rapture is in most respects quite similar to John's description of the intellect's role in the higher stages of contemplation; both agree that a certain vision of God's essence is possible before death through a miraculous elevation of the human being's powers, which "abstracts" the person from all sensory knowledge and activity. The main difference between the two authors seems to be that Thomas limits the experience to a mere handful of chosen souls—perhaps only Moses and St. Paul—and insists that it takes place through a "created medium" of supernatural light or grace; John is less clear on this question of a "created medium," and apparently holds that such experiences, though rare, occur more often than the Angelic Doctor allows, and perhaps are enjoyed in a limited way by those who reach Spiritual Marriage (as we shall see below).

[20] For the expression "substantial knowledge," see especially C 14, xiv; 39, xii. It should be noted that John sometimes uses the terms "substantial" and "essential" as synonyms; see, for example, A II, 5, iii; C 19, v. For the use of the expression "loving knowledge" (*noticia amorosa*), see A II, 13, vii; 14, ii; xii; 15, i; N II, 10, i; 12, iv; F 3, ix; xxiv; xliii.

[21] On the "passivity" of the soul in the reception of this contemplative knowledge, see, for example, A II, 15, ii; 32, iv; F 3, xxxiii-xxxiv. Although John frequently advises his readers to divest themselves of all particular desires and concepts, he is careful to note that he is really talking about the mortification of the *voluntary* appetites (see A I, 11-13). The whole of the *Night* commentary is based on the assumption that individuals cannot achieve the purity needed for mystical union by their own efforts. In other words, what John requires is simply that the person *cooperate* with the process, and *let go* of particular

thoughts and desires when the "obscure knowledge" supervenes; this is part of what faith implies for John.

[22] Notice that the kinds of concepts excluded here are those defined by the scholastic theory of knowledge sketched earlier. This does not necessarily mean that mystical union is completely "a-conceptual" according to our modern notion of concept. In other words, during such periods the mystic would presumably be unable to imagine or think about cats, horses, trees and so on, but perhaps might still be able to recognize the "substantial knowledge" as subtle and loving, and its object as good and holy.

[23] Actually, John adopts no clear position on the question of whether intellect or will is the primary faculty, since both have an indispensible role to play in union with God, and since this union occurs at a level of the person where such distinctions are less important. One reason for his attention to the will is suggested by the rest of the passage here quoted: "...just as the ultimate reason for everything is love (which is seated in the will), whose property is to give and not to receive, whereas the property of the intellect (which is the subject of essential glory) lies in receiving and not giving," so John, as spokesman for the enamored soul, "does not put first the glory she will receive from God, but rather puts first the surrender of herself to Him through true love, without concern for her own profit" (C 38, v).

[24] John does sometimes speak of the "spiritual appetites," the "appetites of the spiritual part," or the "appetite of the will"; see, for example, N II, 11, iii; C 28, viii; 40, i; Letter #12 in *Collected Works* (Letter #13 in *Vida y Obras*).

[25] In C 20 & 21, iv, John says that there are "two natural powers, the irascible and the concupiscible," but it is unclear whether this corresponds to the traditional scholastic division of the appetites; in any case, John makes almost no use of the distinction (cf. A III, 29, ii-iv; C 20 & 21, vi).

[26] It might be argued that if human beings are capable of some limited natural knowledge of God, then they are also capable of some limited natural love of God. John would probably admit this, but argue that this love is inevitably as restricted as the particular forms and concepts on which it depends (see, for example, what John says in A III, 12, i-iii).

[27] John seems to be saying that in the earlier stages of the spiritual life, a person may have a deeper experience of the grandeur of God without any sensible feelings of greater affection, or may experience sudden impulses of love for God without any corresponding sense of knowing God more deeply; but this difference in effects is due to the state of the soul rather than the nature of the divine communication.

[28] One problem with such theories is that the will is conceived rather narrowly, and the appetites and passions are "normally considered only insofar as they may diminish freedom," with little recognition of the complexity of their relationship to human volition (Burrell 1967, p. 406). Another problem is that such accounts tend to hypostatize the faculties and appetites, as if they were independent agents battling for control of the soul. (It becomes difficult to explain coherently, for example, how the will can "exclude" certain thoughts from the intellect, since the will is not a cognitive faculty, and depends on the intellect to know what is being excluded.)

[29] It is worth noting that Teresa herself was dismayed by some of John's extreme statements. In the "Vejamen," which contains a humorous critique of one of his writings, she observes, "Seeking God would be very costly if we could not do so until we were dead to the world. The Magdalene was not dead to the world when she found him, nor was the Samaritan woman or the Canaanite woman....God deliver me from people so spiritual

that they want to turn everything into perfect contemplation, no matter what." (*Collected Works of St. Teresa*, vol. 3, pp. 360-361).

30 Note that Kavanaugh and Rodriguez do not always use the word "reason" in their translation of these passages.

31 John also says that some supernatural *imaginative* apprehensions leave a form impressed upon the soul (see A III, 7, i). I assume, however, that what is impressed in this case is not the imaginative form itself but its spiritual effect (see Bord 1971, p. 88).

32 I have followed Kavanaugh's translation of F 3, lxix except that I have continued my earlier custom of translating *sentido común* as "central sense" rathen than "common sense," because the latter expression has a different meaning in ordinary English usage.

33 Poulain, for example, argues at length that there are five spiritual senses, and cites John in connection with the notion of spiritual touch (see Poulain 1911, pp. 88-113).

34 When referring to this most intimate and spiritual part of human nature, John speaks of the "center" (*centro*), "substance" (*sustancia*), and "depths" (*fondo*) of the soul; the last term in particular recalls the "Fundus" or "Grund" of the Northern mystics (see, for example, F 2, viii; 3, lxviii; 4, iii-v; xiv). For a masterful explanation of John's use of these terms, see Sanson 1953a, pp. 70-82). In F 1, xii, John writes that "the soul's center is God," since the soul tends toward God with all its strength as a stone tends toward its "center" in the earth.

35 Some authors maintain that John follows Thomas in affirming a *real distinction* between the soul and its faculties (see Crisógono 1929, vol. 1, pp. 78-79; Frost 1937, pp. 124-125; Gibbs 1976, p. 545). Perhaps this claim might be argued for John's treatment of the *natural* operations of the faculties. However, as Orcibal notes, when John is discussing mystical union he seems to adopt "the theory of a virtual distinction, which may be called Augustinian," and is best illustrated by "the neo-platonic image of rays which cease to exist when they lose contact with the sun" (Orcibal 1966, pp. 188-189).

36 In a continuation of this same passage, Kavanaugh gives a slightly different explanation of John's occasional references to the "sensory substance": "And since these experiences are possible in the sensory as well as in the spiritual part of the soul, John speaks sometimes of the sensitive substance, and sometimes of the spiritual substance."

37 See again the quotation from F 3, lxix above, and Dicken 1963, p. 371. Further evidence is John's occasional substitution of "substance" for "memory" in discussions of the faculties. According to Bord, the explanation is that John sometimes replaces "memory" with a reference to one of its receptacles, and equates the "substance" with the "central sense of the soul" (see Bord 1971, pp. 91-95).

38 John sometimes speaks of "substantial touches in the will," which is further evidence that the "substance" is not totally distinct from the faculties as such (see A II, 32, ii-iii).

39 Compare Stein 1960, pp. 115-119. For other contemporary approaches to the notion of the "substance of the soul" see, for example, Dupré 1980, pp. 459-462; and Bernardo María de la Cruz 1967, pp. 174-186.

CHAPTER THREE

THE DOCTRINE OF ST. JOHN OF THE CROSS: THE DYNAMICS OF SPIRITUAL DEVELOPMENT

Though St. John of the Cross draws upon the philosophical account of the soul outlined in the last chapter, he show little inclination to work out its finer details, and is clearly more interested in offering spiritual guidance than in settling philosophical disputes. For the most part, John invokes his notion of the soul's structure only in order to clarify his explanation of the journey toward divine union, and he willingly modifies principles of scholastic psychology for the same reason. Any review of the Sanjuanist system would therefore be radically incomplete without a summary of John's teaching on the process of spiritual growth, especially since this teaching represents his most influential contribution to Western mystical theology.

Like most theories of psychological and spiritual development, John's teaching includes an account of: 1) the *initial state* of the person undergoing change; 2) the *means* of growth and the successive *stages* by which it is achieved; and 3) the *goal* of the developmental process. In fact, John divides his own discussion along these lines when he suggests three reasons for calling the journey toward divine union a "night." (Note in passing that these three "reasons" are *not* different temporal phases of the spiritual life, as has sometimes been thought.)

> The first has to do with the point of departure, because the individual must deprive himself of his appetite for worldly possessions. This denial and privation is like a night for all his senses. The second reason refers to the means or the road along which a person travels to this union. Now this road is faith, and for the intellect faith is also like a dark night. The third reason pertains to the point of arrival, namely, God. And God is also like a dark night to man in this life....
>
> ...To provide further enlightenment about all this, we shall discuss each of these causes of night separately. (A I, 2, i-v)

My own presentation of John's theory will likewise be divided into three main sections. The first will deal with his account of the individual's psychological and spiritual condition prior to undertaking a life of prayer and self-denial. In the second, I will identify and describe the successive stages of spiritual progress according to the Sanjuanist scheme. The final section of this chapter will summarize John's conception of the goal of religious development, the complete transformation of the soul in God.

3.1. The Starting Point: Human Existence as "Fallen"

While John maintains that the soul must set aside its natural activity during contemplation in order to receive the divine communication, he also believes that there is nothing in human nature as such which prevents this from occurring. As originally constituted, all of our natural powers are meant to cooperate harmoniously in the experience of God and creatures. Thus John writes that:

In the state of innocence all that our first parents saw, spoke of, and ate in the garden of paradise served them for more abundant delight in contemplation, since the sensory part of their souls was truly subjected and ordered to reason. (A III, 26, v; see also N II, 24, ii-iii; C 26, xiv-xvi)

In other words, the arduousness of the spiritual journey and the infrequency of the higher mystical experiences are not due to our *essential human structure*, but rather to our *existential condition* of psychological disequilibrium and alienation from God. John of the Cross interprets this condition theologically as the result of "original sin," inherited from Adam, and sees the disorder of the appetites and passions as the most devastating aspect of this "fallen" state.[1] Because this disorder impedes the reception of God's communications, he identifies the mortification of the appetites as the "starting point" and *sine qua non* of the journey toward divine union (see A I, 2, i-ii).

In my earlier treatment of the intellect, memory and will, I indicated how inappropriate desires and emotions can hinder mystical union by occupying the spiritual faculties with particular goods and concepts. But for St. John of the Cross the negative consequences are not limited to the purely spiritual level; in this "fallen" state, a person's natural abilities are impaired as well. Here modern readers can readily agree with John's diagnosis of the psychological and moral harm caused by the disorder of the appetites, even if they reject his theological explanation of its origin. John maintains that the unruly appetites "weary, torment, darken, defile, and weaken" the soul, and describes the various forms of damage in great detail (see especially chapters 6 through 10 of *Ascent* I). On the level of affectivity, the lack of integration among competing drives and emotions leaves an individual restless, distracted, anxious, depressed, enervated, and torn by conflicting desires. On the intellectual level, inordinate appetites cloud the mind and turn reason into rationalization.[2] Thus John writes that "in detachment from things" one "acquires a clearer knowledge of them," because "the senses cannot grasp or attain to more than the accident, whereas the spirit purged of the clouds and appearances (*especie*) of accident penetrates the truth and value of things" (A III, 20, ii); at least part of what he is claiming is that the "fallen" man's vision of the world will be systematically distorted by his tendency to view all creatures solely in terms of their accidental relationships to his changing moods and feelings. In fact, John maintains that inordinate appetites cause so much harm even in the secular arena that the ascetical program he recommends can be justified on the basis of its "resulting temporal advantages, prescinding from the spiritual ones" (Ibid.; see also A III, 4, ii; 6, iii; 23, iii-vi; 26, v-vi).

This characterization of the state of a person before undertaking the journey toward God may be exaggerated in certain respects, but the experiences described are familiar enough; we all know what it is to be unable to think clearly and perceive accurately because of some emotional upheaval. For John, the spiritual life involves movement from a condition in which such experiences predominate and impede divine communications, to a condition in which all desires and energies are integrated and directed toward union with God; spiritual growth goes hand-in-hand with moral and psychological growth.

Since John believes that the soul can be united to God in many different ways, he distinguishes the goal of spiritual growth from other kinds of "union." He notes, for example, that:

...God sustains every soul and dwells in it substantially, even though it may be that of the greatest sinner in the world. This union between God and the creature always exists. By it He conserves their being.... Consequently, in discussing union with God, we are not discussing the substantial union which is always existing, but the union and transformation of the soul in God. This union...we find...only where there is a likeness of love. We will call it "the union of likeness," and the former "the essential or substantial union." The union of likeness is supernatural, the other natural. The supernatural union exists when God's will and the soul's are in conformity....(A II, 5, iii)

The same point is developed at greater length in a key passage from *Canticle B*.[3]

...It should be known that God's presence can be of three kinds: The first is His presence by essence. In this way He is present not only in the holiest souls, but also in sinners and in all other creatures. For with this presence He gives them life and being.... The second is His presence by grace, in which He abides in the soul, pleased and satisfied with it. Not all have this presence of God; those who fall into mortal sin can lose it.... The third is His presence by spiritual affection,...by which He refreshes, delights, and gladdens [souls].

Since it is certain that at least in the first way God is ever present in the soul, she does not ask Him to be present in her, but that He...reveal His hidden presence.... Yet insofar as this soul is full of fervor and tender love of God, we should understand that this presence she asks the Beloved to reveal refers chiefly to a certain affective presence which the Beloved accords her. (C 11, iii-iv)

A comparison of these two quotations helps to clarify John's terminology. Evidently "the essential or substantial union" mentioned in the first is the same as the "presence by essence" mentioned in the second; here these expressions point to a kind of causal proximity between God and the various finite beings, including the soul, which God creates and maintains in existence.[4] There also appears to be a close relationship between "the union of likeness" and "the presence by grace." Neither seems necessarily to entail a clear and explicit *awareness* of God. Moreover, even though individuals receive grace before their wills are totally conformed to the divine will, the *degree* of grace will presumably be proportionate to the degree of conformity. By contrast, the "affective presence" of God apparently involves a vivid impression of God's nearness, or of absorption in the divine, accompanied by such emotions as joy, love, awe or dread; most of those states which modern writers would label as "mystical or religious experiences" would be included under this heading.

Readers are sometimes surprised that, in certain passages, St. John of the Cross seems to give priority to the "union of wills," which need not be "mystical" in the ordinary sense at all (see especially A II, 5, iii-viii). However, this position becomes more understandable when one recalls that John considers mere feelings by themselves to be an unreliable indicator of closeness to God, that "the union of wills" is wrought by the primary Christian virtue of charity, and that God's "presence by grace" provides the basis for all the other forms of "affective presence" (see, for example, A I, 11, ii-iii; III, 16, i-iii; C 1, iii-iv; 31, i-ii). Nevertheless, the ideal, in John's view, would be for a person to enjoy all three kinds of "presence" at once.

How, then, are these different modes of union or presence related to each other? Obviously, John does not believe that God's "affective presence" and "presence by grace" are simply *reducible* to God's "substantial presence." Thus he stresses that the "union of likeness" between the divine and human wills is "supernatural" and "not always existing" (A II, 5, iii); moreover, he shows no inclination to interpret mystical experience as a purely *natural* intuition of God's sustaining presence.

On the other hand, some Catholic commentators, hoping perhaps to defend the Mystical Doctor against any suspicion of ontologism, have insisted that "the merely natural union...has nothing to do with St. John of the Cross's union of the soul with God" (Eulogio de San Juan de la Cruz 1963, p. 67). The danger with this claim is that it tends to make the divine "presence by grace or affection" depend upon some extrinsic addition to the soul which is unrelated to God's ontological presence as Creator. One is then easily misled into thinking of the soul as a kind of receptacle into which certain quantities of grace are "poured," with the degree of mystical or moral union corresponding to the amount of grace present.

In reality, John's own position seems to be that there is a fundamental *continuity* between the different kinds of union, and that mystical experiences and the "conformity of wills" represent a further "unveiling" or manifestation of the deity who is already there as Creator. Thus, in the above quotation from the *Canticle*, he writes that since "God is ever present in the soul, she does not ask him to be present in her, but that He...reveal His hidden presence" (**C** 11, iv; see also **A** II, 5, iv; **C** 1, viii-x; **F** 4, vii). Elsewhere John suggests that God's "substantial presence" automatically overflows into a complete transformation of the soul once the obstacle of inordinate appetites is removed.

A ray of sunlight shining upon a smudgy window is unable to illumine that window completely and transform it into its own light.... The extent of illumination is not dependent upon the ray of sunlight but upon the window. If the window is totally clean and pure, the sunlight will so transform and illumine it that to all appearances the window will be identical with the ray of sunlight and shine just as the sun's ray.... The soul upon which the divine light of God's being is ever shining, or better, in which it is always dwelling by nature, is like this window....

A man makes room for God by wiping away all the smudges and smears of creatures, by uniting his will perfectly to God's.... (**A** II, 5, vi-vii)

In other words, John is claiming that although the Creator is always mysteriously near and available to everyone, the psychological and spiritual disorder of our fallen state all but drowns out any awareness of this presence. On the other hand, as we advance in the spiritual life and become more fully integrated, our consciousness of the ever-present God deepens, and eventually blossoms into mystical union.[5] As John puts it, the divine is "*naturally* and supernaturally infused" into the soul once the "impediments and veils" are removed (**A** II, 15, iv—emphasis mine). Nevertheless, the gratuity of the "supernatural" modes of presence or union is preserved, since one cannot attain the requisite mortification of the appetites solely through one's own efforts.[6]

In short, the aim of the Sanjuanist spiritual program, contrary to one popular opinion, is not to warp or destroy human nature, but to bring it to fulfillment. In fact, John would hold, it is their immaturity and lack of psychological and moral health which typically prevent human beings from experiencing God more profoundly. Mystical experiences are ultimately grounded in an ontological relationship to God which everyone enjoys; they are not the exclusive prerogative of a handful of gifted souls, from which the rest of us are forever barred. On the contrary, John believes that all can attain some experience of the divine if they cooperate with God's purifying activity, a process one should willingly undergo if only for the sake of the resulting psychological benefits. Few reach mystical union with God only because few are willing to endure the rigors of the journey.

3.2. The Stages and Means of Spiritual Growth

St. John of the Cross is undoubtedly "best-known" for "his description of the dark night of the soul," but he develops this theme against the background of the more traditional three-fold division of the spiritual life into the "Purgative Way" of *beginners*, the "Illuminative Way" of *proficients*, and the "Unitive Way" of the *perfect* (Smart 1967a, 'John of the Cross,' *Encyclopedia of Philosophy* vol. 4, p. 286; see also Ibid. 1967c, 'Mysticism, History of,' vol. 5, p. 426; Larkin 1967, 'Ways, The Three Spiritual,' *New Catholic Encyclopedia* vol. 14, pp. 835-836). Thus, as will be explained below, the "passive night of sense" is John's name for the frequently difficult transition from the beginner's focus on meditation and active self-discipline to the more contemplative prayer of the "Illuminative Way," whereas the "passive night of the spirit" represents the final purification needed by those progressing in contemplation in order to reach the most "perfect" union with God attainable in this life (i.e., that permanent mystical union which he also calls "spiritual marriage"). Nevertheless, although the general shape of the Sanjuanist spiritual itinerary is relatively clear, there has been some disagreement over its details, due to certain characteristics of John's literary style and manner of presentation. Before systematically outlining his teaching on the stages of spiritual growth, then, I will briefly mention five features of John's prose treatises which can easily disorient the unwary reader.

In the first place, St. John of the Cross often gives an idealized and somewhat oversimplified description of each stage of development for the sake of a more lucid and systematic presentation. For example, in some places he seems to suggest that one's spiritual progress is *exactly* proportionate to one's degree of moral and psychological progress. It would be a mistake, however, to accept such suggestions without reservation. As other statements show, John is well aware that matters are not so neat and simple in real life; though these three areas are intimately linked, emotionally immature people sometimes enjoy "higher" or more spectacular religious experiences than their better adjusted companions (see, for example, A II, 22, xix; N II, 2, iii-iv; and the "Censure and Opinion on the Spirit and the Attitude in Prayer of a Discalced Carmelite Nun").[7] Again, John writes that those who reach the "unitive way" are "like the angels who judge perfectly the things that give sorrow, without the feeling of sorrow" (C 20 & 21, x; cf. C 20 & 21, xi-xvi; 24, v). Yet, even if such individuals are no longer subject to the same emotional turmoil as beginners, it is certainly an exaggeration to claim that they *never* experience sorrow or grief. In fact, John's final letters (see, for example, the letter of August 19, 1591 to Doña Ana de Peñalosa [#28 in both *Collected Works* and *Vida y Obras*]) reveal his own suffering and depression long after he had presumably attained the state of "spiritual marriage." (Similarly, St. Teresa's more autobiographical writings clearly show that she experienced emotional highs and lows even after attaining the same mystical state.)

Second, in order to identify a particular phase of the spiritual life more clearly, John of the Cross often describes "the most that God communicates to a soul at this time"; this does not mean, however, that God always imparts everything mentioned to all who reach the state in question, "or that He does so in the same manner and measure of knowledge and feeling" (**C** 14 & 15, ii). For instance, even though contemplatives are more prone to trances and imaginative visions at a certain stage of their development, it is at least theoretically possible for someone to traverse the entire path to mystical union without ever undergoing such experiences (see **A** II, 17, ii-vii). John recognizes that "God leads each one along different paths" (**F** 3, lix), adapting himself to an individual's specific strengths and weaknesses. It is therefore an error to suppose, as some have, that one can easily determine whether a person has reached a given stage of the spiritual life simply on the basis of the occurrence or non-occurrence of some particular phenomenon which John associates with that stage.

In the third place, the presentation of each stage varies to some extent according to the perspective from which John is writing and what he wants to teach the reader at a given moment. This is especially true, for example, in his treatment of "proficients," who have successfully negotiated the passive night of sense but have not yet passed through the passive night of spirit; John stresses the holiness and virtue of proficients when he is contrasting them with beginners, but points out their vices and defects when explaining the need for a further purgation (compare **N** I, 12-13 with **N** II, 1, ii and 2, i-v). Similarly, readers will understand the *Dark Night* better if they realize that the poem and commentary are written from the viewpoint of someone who "has already reached the state of perfection—that is, union with God through love" (**N**, Prologue); no one actually *undergoing* the passive night of the spirit is likely to call it a "glad night" (*noche dichosa*), or to be so optimistic about its eventual outcome.

A fourth source of difficulty is the arrangement of material *within* the *Canticle* and *Ascent-Night*. In the second redaction of the *Spiritual Canticle*, John reorganizes his poem and thereby redistributes the commentary among the different stages of the spiritual life. For example, stanzas which *Canticle A* 27, iii assigns to the state of spiritual espousal are associated in *Canticle B* 22, ii with spiritual marriage, and vice versa. As noted in the first chapter, recent studies have demonstrated that most of the changes are simply the result of John's efforts to present the successive phases more consistently, and in proper chronological order; nevertheless, the differences between the two redactions have produced some confusion about the nature and distinguishing characteristics of each stage, and have even led some commentators to deny the authenticity of the later version.

The organization of the *Ascent-Night* poses problems of another sort, which require more extensive treatment. At the beginning of the first book of the *Ascent*, after quoting the opening lines of 'En una noche oscura,' John writes:

...One should know that the soul must ordinarily pass through two principal kinds of night (which spiritual persons call purgations or purifications of the soul) in order to reach the state of perfection.
...The first night or purgation, to which this stanza refers and which will be under discussion in the first section of this book, concerns the sensory part of the soul. The second night, to which the second stanza refers, concerns the spiritual part. We shall deal with this second night, insofar as it is active, in the second and third sections of the book. In the fourth section we shall discuss the night insofar as it is passive.
The first night is the lot of beginners, at the time God commences to introduce them into the state of contemplation.... The second night or purification takes place in those who are already proficient, at the time God desires to lead them into the state of divine union. (A I, 1, i-iii; compare A Prologue, vi; I, 13, i; 14, i; II, 1, i-iii; 2, iii; III, 1, iii; N Prologue; I, 14, i-vi)

In this quotation, John identifies two chronologically successive "nights," corresponding to the two fundamental aspects of human nature, the sensory and the spiritual. Both nights, in turn, have an active and a passive part. John is also dividing the spiritual life into three consecutive "states," separated by the two "nights." The "night of sense" represents the transition from the condition of *beginners* to that of *proficients* (or contemplatives), while the "night of spirit" is the final purification before attaining that union with God which John elsewhere describes as the state of the *perfect* (see N I, 1, i; II, 1, ii).

Certain passages add further refinements to this basic scheme. In some places, for example, John associates the three stages with the "three ways" of traditional Christian spirituality, as noted above; thus the "purgative way" corresponds to the state of beginners, the "illuminative way" to that of proficients, and the "unitive way" to the perfect (see N I, 9, vi; 14, i; C Theme, ii). Other statements indicate that it is the onset of the *passive* nights in particular which signals the change from one state to another (see especially A I, 13, i; II, 13, i; 15, i; N I, 7, v; 8, i-ii; 9, vii; II, 1, ii). The active nights of sense and spirit, insofar as they can be associated with a particular phase of spiritual development, seem to have special relevance for beginners and proficients, respectively. Thus, since the active night of sense involves the mortification of inordinate voluntary sensory appetites, it represents the *sine qua non* for anyone beginning a life of prayer (see A I, 4, i); proficients, on the other hand, are more prone to visions, revelations, locutions, and so on, and therefore need especially to undertake the active night of spirit, in which they strive to detach their spiritual faculties from all that is not God (see A II, 16, iii; N II, 1, i; 2, iii).[8]

A comparison of the quotation on the previous page (from *Ascent* I, 1, i-iii) with the present state of the Sanjuanist texts reveals how John organizes his exposition of these "nights." He deals with the "active night of sense" in Book I of the *Ascent*, and the "active night of spirit" in Books II and III. As already indicated, Books II and III are further subdivided into treatises on the active purification of the intellect, memory and will through the theological virtues of faith, hope and charity, respectively. The work known today as *The Dark Night* corresponds to the proposed "fourth section" of the *Ascent*, in which the author promises to "discuss the night insofar as it is passive" (A I, 1, ii). Book I of the *Night* covers the "passive night of sense," while Book II treats the "passive night of the spirit."

In other words, John does not deal with the different stages and nights in their proper chronological order. The explanation for this odd arrangement may be found in the second chapter of *Ascent* I. There John presents his "three reasons for calling this journey toward union with God a night" (i.e., the privation of the appetites, faith, and the divine communication, which are respectively the starting point, means, and goal of this journey), and says that he will discuss each in turn (see above, p. 50). Evidently these "three reasons" had a decisive influence on the organization of the *Ascent-Night*, since he then proceeds to consider the total purification of the appetites in Book I of the *Ascent*, the need for a faith "not exclusive of charity" (A I, 2, iii) in Books II and III, and the dark, painful communications of God in the *Night*. As noted above, however, these "three reasons" are not consecutive *phases* of religious development, but different *aspects* of the entire journey; God is always offering Himself to the soul in one way or another, while faith and the complete mortification of the appetites are the tasks of a lifetime.[9]

As the following chart indicates, then, each major division of the *Ascent-Night* is devoted to a combination of topics which do not entirely coincide:

Divisions of *Ascent-Night*	The Nights	The Three Reasons for Calling the Journey a Night
Ascent I	Active Night of Sense	Privation of the Appetites
Ascent II & III	Active Night of Spirit	Journey in Faith
Night I	Passive Night of Sense	Communication of God
Night II	Passive Night of Spirit	

Moreover, in the *Ascent* John seems to subordinate the consideration of particular stages of prayer to the discussion of the first two "reasons" as they apply generally to the entire spiritual life. The *Night*, however, deals with the third reason (i.e., the communication of God) principally in terms of how it is experienced during the passive nights (cf. Juan de Jesús María 1943, pp. 52-63).

Not surprisingly, many commentators have misinterpreted the *Ascent-Night* because they failed to grasp the distinction between the "three reasons" and the successive nights. According to Orville Clark, for example, John teaches that "the soul must pass through three dark nights or purgations": the "night of sense," the "night of spirit," and the "night of faith" (Clark 1972, pp. 244-245). Thus Clark mistakenly transforms the second "reason" into a final stage of the spiritual life. Dean Inge is even more badly muddled; following Vaughan, he claims that John distinguishes three successive stages: the night of sense, the night of faith, and the night of memory and will (Inge 1956, pp. 224-227). Other authors criticize John for making impossible demands on beginners, as if he claimed that the appetites must be completely mortified before one even begins to experience the initial stirrings of contemplation. In reality, the severest statements in the first book of the *Ascent* usually concern what is required before reaching the *end* of the journey toward God, and John recognizes that the greatest part of the necessary purification is accomplished in the *passive* nights; beginners need only make a sincere effort to respond to God's grace and control their immoderate desires (see, for example, A I, 13, i; N I, 8, iii-iv; 13, i-xv; II, 3, i-iii). In short, a correct notion of the structure of the *Ascent-Night* will help readers to avoid serious misunderstandings of Sanjuanist doctrine.

The final problem to mention here is that there is no single scheme of stages which clearly dominates all of John's works. This fifth source of difficulty is already suggested by earlier remarks. The *Ascent-Night* and *Flame* rely heavily on the imagery of light and darkness, and the former divides the journey toward union according to the successive nights of sense and spirit, as we have seen. The *Canticle*, on the other hand, generally eschews talk of active and passive nights, and instead describes the spiritual life in terms of a developing relationship between two lovers, dividing the process into four stages: the "trials and bitterness of mortification and...meditation," the "paths and straits of love," "spiritual espousal," and "spiritual marriage" (C 22, iii). How these stages correspond to the phases outlined in the *Ascent-Night* is never explained in any detail. Fortunately, both the *Canticle* and *Flame* occasionally mention the traditional "three ways" and "three states"; by using these references and carefully comparing the descriptions of each stage which John identifies, scholars have been able to discover with some success how these different schema fit into a single overarching vision of the process of spiritual development. Zabalza, for example, argues plausibly that "mortification and meditation" are the lot of beginners, that contemplatives experience the "paths and straits of love," and that "spiritual espousal" corresponds to the final period of the passive night of the spirit, ending when the soul enters the "unitive way" of "spiritual marriage" (see Zabalza 1963 pp. 11, 140). If this position is basically correct, then the different systems John uses for distinguishing major phases of the spiritual life may be correlated roughly as follows:

Three States	Three Ways	Nights	Bridal Imagery
Beginners	Purgative	Active Night of Sense	Mortification
Proficients	Illuminative	Passive Night of Sense	Paths and Straits of Love
		Interlude (Active Night of Spirit)	
		Passive Night of Spirit	
			Espousal
The Perfect	Unitive		Marriage

I realize that certain details of this diagram can be criticized. Scholars disagree, for example, on whether the passive night of sense pertains to beginners or proficients, and whether espousal belongs to the illuminative or unitive way.[10] Since these questions have little direct bearing upon the present discussion, however, they need not be settled here. After all, beneath all of the divisions there is fundamentally only *one* night, a single process by which the soul is gradually divested of everything that can impede union with God. John himself recognizes that schematic divisions always represent a certain impoverishment of the complexity and continuity of lived experience; nevertheless, they are useful for organizing one's discussion of the dynamics of spiritual growth.

In the following pages, therefore, the exposition of John's views on the stages of religious development will be presented in three blocks, corresponding to the traditional three "stages" or "ways." Though John simply borrowed this threefold division from his predecessors, it provides a convenient framework within which his more original contributions may be better situated. The first section, then, will include a discussion of beginners and the passive night of sense. The second deals with proficients and the passive night of spirit, ending with some words on spiritual espousal. In the third section I will explain John's notion of "spiritual marriage" and the unitive way.

3.2.1. BEGINNERS AND THE PASSIVE NIGHT OF SENSE

St. John of the Cross gives relatively little attention to the early stages of prayer, partly because he believes that there is already an abundant literature on the topic (see N I, 8, ii). As a result, his teaching on beginners may be summarized rather briefly.

I have already described the spiritual, psychological, and moral disorder which marks the human being's "fallen" condition. Spiritual *beginners*, for John, are all who have taken the first steps toward surmounting these limitations and advancing toward God, especially the "twice-born," who have been "resolutely converted to His service" from a prior religious existence which was mediocre at best (N I, 1, ii).[11] The salient feature of the beginner's spiritual practices is a certain preoccupation with sensible consolations (*gustos*); the chief task of the soul in this "purgative way" is to "[exercise] herself both in the trials and the bitterness of mortification and in meditation on spiritual things" (C 22, iii).[12]

After an initial "conversion," the beginner usually goes through a phase of great religious enthusiasm; this "first fervor" phenomenon is familiar to most spiritual writers and psychologists of religion.

> The soul finds its joy (*deleite*)..., in spending lengthy periods at prayer, perhaps even entire nights; its penances are pleasures (*gustos*); its fasts, happiness (*contentos*); and the sacraments and spiritual conversations are its consolations (*consuelos*). (N I, 1, iii)

Christian beginners, especially those of Roman Catholic background, often find enormous satisfaction in elaborate meditations on truths of the faith or imagined Biblical scenes, from which they draw edifying conclusions and appropriate religious sentiments. Though John repeatedly warns his readers about the limitations of such discursive meditation and the danger of seeking sensible consolations in prayer, he admits that both are necessary at this early stage of spiritual growth. Beginners are still largely under the sway of their appetites, and since God desires to raise them to union "with order, gently, and according to the mode of the soul," he "must begin by touching the low state and extreme of the senses" (A II, 17, iii). The enjoyment found in spiritual exercises helps to draw beginners away from their desire for grosser pleasures. Thus John writes that:

> ...for beginners it is permissible and even fitting to find some sensible gratification and satisfaction in the use of images, oratories, and other visible objects of devotion so that with this pleasure they may renounce worldly things from whose taste they are not yet weaned or detached. This is what we do with a child when we desire to take something

away from him; we give him another thing to play with so that he will not begin to cry when left empty-handed. (**A** III, 39, i; compare **A** I, 14, ii-iii; II, 12, v; **N** I, 1, i-ii; 8, iii; **F** 3, xxxii)

Similarly, discursive prayer diverts one's attention from inappropriate desirable objects by filling the mind with pious considerations. Though such considerations "are not a proximate means toward union for proficients, they are a remote means for beginners" (**A** II, 13, i), because the latter acquire "some knowledge and love of God" through meditation and become habitually oriented toward the divine (**A** II, 14, ii). John therefore recommends that beginners continue meditating as long as they are able to do so and derive some pleasure from it (see **A** II, 13, iii; 14, i; 17, vii).

Nevertheless, this "purgative way" is a state of spiritual immaturity which must eventually be transcended. In the opening chapters of the *Night*, St. John of the Cross offers a masterful critique of the imperfections of beginners, which stem principally from the continued strength of their sensory appetites, and their consequent tendency to make sensible pleasure the sole criterion of spiritual value. John notes, for example, that beginners:

...frequently believe that what is not their will, or that which brings them no satisfaction, is not God's will, and, on the other hand, that if they are satisfied, God is too. They measure God by themselves and not themselves by God.... (**N** I, 7, iii)

Such souls may take a strange delight in unreasonable fasts and mortifications, which John describes as the "penance of beasts" (**N** I, 6, ii), while at the same time neglecting the "rough way of the cross," which consists in adapting themselves to God's will (**N** I, 6, i-vii; see also **A** II, 7, v-xii). The satisfaction they find in their spiritual exercises will lead them to harbor a certain pride and complacency, imagining that they are great servants and favorites of God, and looking down on those who do not enjoy the same kind of religious fervor (see **N** I, 2, i-vi; 5, ii; 7, i; 12, ii). They likewise easily assume that any disapproval of their spirituality arises out of ignorance or a "lack of holiness" (**N** I, 2, iii).

The same defects are found in the *prayer* of beginners; "one minute they are meditating upon one subject and the next upon another, always in search of some gratification in the things of God" (**N** I, 6, vi). The clear images and concepts of their discursive prayer impede the reception of the "substantial knowledge" of God (as noted in the previous chapter). Besides this, however, beginners easily fall into the further error of supposing that those ideas and considerations which generate the most pleasure are the most spiritual and most closely resemble the divine.

It is extremely easy to judge the being and height of God less worthily and sublimely than is suitable to His incomprehensibility. Though a person may not form an explicit idea (*aunque la razón y juicio no haga expreso concepto*) that God is similar to these ap prehensions, nevertheless the very esteem for them...produces in the soul an esteem and opinion of God less elevated than that given in the teaching of faith: that He is incomparable, incomprehensible, etc. (A III, 12, i)

Finally, the prayers of beginners are sometimes accompanied by a degree of sexual arousal, which shows that the satisfaction they find in spiritual exercises is not yet far removed from natural sensuality and eroticism (see N I, 4, i-viii). Since some psychologists have tried to work out a reductive account of mystical experiences in terms of repressed or sublimated sexual energy, it is worth noting that John ascribes unhealthy manifestations of sexuality to the earlier stages of prayer; in the later stage of spiritual marriage, however, sexuality is apparently integrated with the other components of the human personality.

In chapter 13 of *Ascent* I John gives beginners certain counsels for conquering their appetites and overcoming their imperfections. First, he says, you must "have a habitual desire to imitate Christ in all your deeds by bringing your life into conformity with His" (A I, 13, iii). Next he lists the famous maxims which begin:

Endeavor to be inclined always:
    not to the easiest, but to the most difficult;
    not to the most delightful, but to the harshest;
    not to the most gratifying, but to the less pleasant;....(A I, 13, vi)

as well as the verses from his 'Drawing of the Mount,' which open with the lines:

To reach satisfaction in all (*todo*)
desire its possession in nothing (*nada*).
To come to possess all
desire the possession of nothing.
To arrive at being all
desire to be nothing.
To come to the knowledge of all
desire the knowledge of nothing....(A I, 13, xi)

As Morel rightly notes, these startling directives are not meant to encourage a morbid attachment to suffering for its own sake, which would be just as harmful as the excessive attachment to pleasure.[13] Instead, John wants to aid individuals in the "purgative way" in restoring the proper equilibrium to their lives, so that their actions are no longer determined by the pursuit of pleasure and avoidance of pain, but begin to be guided by reason and the divine will.

By trying to follow this advice, the beginner enters the "active night of sense." Yet the beginner's efforts, though necessary, are not sufficient to effect a total cure, for "until a soul is placed by God in the passive purgation of that dark night..., it cannot purify itself completely from these imperfections" (**N** I, 3, iii), partly because even the efforts at reform are often motivated by a desire for further gratification. Consequently, after a short period, God introduces the beginner into the "passive night of sense," which is marked by a frustrating inability to meditate and the disturbing loss of satisfaction in spiritual practices (see **A** Prologue, iii; II, 12, vi; 13, i; 14, iv; **N** I, 8, iv; **F** 3, xxxii).[14]

> ...It is at the time they are going about their spiritual exercises with delight and satisfaction, when in their opinion the sun of divine favor is shining most brightly on them, that God darkens all this light and closes the door and spring of the sweet spiritual water they were tasting.... God now leaves them in such darkness that they do not know which way to turn in their discursive imaginings; they cannot advance a step in meditation, as they used to do.... He leaves them in such dryness that they not only fail to receive satisfaction and pleasure from their spiritual exercises and works, as they formerly did, but also find these exercises distasteful and bitter.... This change is a surprise to them because everything seems to be functioning in reverse. (**N** I, 8, iii)

As a result, individuals who experience this "ligature of the senses," as it is sometimes called (cf. Dicken 1963, pp. 163-164), will frequently "fatigue and overwork themselves, thinking they are failing because of their negligences or sins" (**N** I, 10, ii). In reality, the difficulties accompanying this shift to the state of proficients are simply the inevitable consequences of their hard work as beginners. Eventually, the continued effort to squeeze fresh insights and feelings from the same discursive reflections reaches the point of diminishing returns. The soul has already attained all it can from meditation; now its efforts at prayer quickly lead to a state of quiet solicitude for God without complicated mental activity, which was the goal of meditation in the first place (see **A** II, 12, vi-viii; 14, i-iv; 15, i-ii; **F** 3, xliv). Thus the individual is beginning to outgrow childish enthusiasm. As in the relationship between two human lovers, the person is passing beyond early infatuation to a deeper and more peaceful love, requiring fewer words and acts (compare Tyrell 1980).

This passive night of sense by which one advances to the "illuminative way" is "the most critical point of all in spiritual development," because it represents the transition to a predominantly contemplative mode of prayer (Dicken 1963, p. 164). In John's view, all later phases of the mystical life are simply a further unfolding of what begins here. However, though this state is "common" (**N** I, 8, i) and is perhaps the most clearly defined stage of the religious growth-process, many persons manage the shift only with great difficulty "because they do not want or know how to advance, or because they receive no direction on breaking away from the methods of beginners" (**A** Prologue, iii). For this reason, John presents "three signs" for determining whether an individual is in the passive night of sense and should discontinue meditation.

The first is the realization that one cannot make discursive meditation nor receive satisfaction from it as before....
The second sign is an awareness of a disinclination to fix the imagination or sense faculties (*sentido*) upon any particular objects, exterior or interior....
The third and surest sign is that a person likes to remain alone in loving awareness of God, without particular considerations, in peace and quiet and repose.... (A II, 13, ii-iv)[15]

The first sign alone is insufficient, according to John, since the inability to meditate could be due to spiritual laxity or some physical or psychological disorder. The disinclination to fix one's attention on other objects indicates that the cause is not simply dissipation, while the "loving awareness" suggests that this darkness is not simply a natural "stupefaction" produced by a certain "humor in the heart or brain" (A II, 13, vi).

John's discussion of these three signs, presented in a slightly different form in chapter 9 of *Night* I, reveals some important features of his understanding of contemplative experience. First, he clearly recognizes the role that purely natural causes can play in producing analogous states; his comments give no "impression of psychological naiveté" (Horsburgh 1972, p. 65).[16] Second, contrary to a common philosophical criticism of mystical authors, John does admit certain kinds of "testing procedures," here and elsewhere, for distinguishing authentic from inauthentic experiences of the divine (as we will see in more detail in the fifth chapter). Third, the emphasis on the element of "loving awareness" shows that, even in its earliest stages, contemplation has a noetic component, and is not simply the absence of particular thoughts and images. John does admit that "this state of loving knowledge is almost unnoticeable" at first, particularly when one "does not permit himself any quietude, but strives after the other more sensory experience" (A II, 13, vii). Thus individuals entering this passive night who persist in trying to meditate may be inclined to claim that they are only experiencing a "painful concern and solicitude" for God (N I, 9, iii—my translation).[17] Nevertheless, if they give up such effort and remain calm, they will become increasingly aware of the presence of a "general, loving knowledge of God" (A II, 13, vii; see also A II, 14, viii; 15, i-v; N I, 9, iv-vii; 10, iv-vi; 11, i-ii; F 3, xxxiii-xxxvi).[18]

Finally, the loss of sensual gratification in spiritual exercises helps the soul to overcome the beginner's faults described above. Interestingly enough, John claims that "the first and chief benefit that this dry and dark night of contemplation causes is the knowledge of self and of one's own misery," and that the other benefits "flow from self-knowledge as from their font" (N I, 12, ii). As a result of the difficulty now encountered in prayer and the practice of virtue, the soul in this state becomes painfully aware of her weaknesses, and is no longer able to maintain such a high opinion of herself (see N I, 2, vi-viii; 10, i-iii; 11, ii; 12, ii-vii; 13, viii). From this self-knowledge proceeds "knowledge of [God's] grandeur and majesty," since "as the philosophers say, one extreme is clearly known by the other" (N I, 12, iv-v). The person therefore "communes with God more respectfully and courteously" (Ibid., iii). In addition, his new-found humility produces a greater "love of neighbor, for he will esteem them and not judge them as he did before, when he was aware that he enjoyed an intense fervor while others did not" (Ibid., viii). According to John, then, the "ligature of the senses" gives individuals a deeper knowledge of God, themselves, and others. (These statements are particularly interesting, because they suggest that not all of the mystic's claims to "knowledge of God" are based on experience in the same way; here such knowledge is *derived* from self-knowledge. Thus it is a mistake to assume, as many philosophers do, that *all* mystical knowledge claims are comparable to more ordinary claims to know a sensible object one has ostensibly perceived.)

Further benefits of this dry purgation include a "withering" of the appetites, spiritual sobriety, greater constancy in virtue, and a habitual remembrance of God (see N I, 13, ii-xv). Now that the soul has undergone an initial "accomodation of the senses to the spirit" (N II, 2, i), and consequently has begun to receive a certain "general loving knowledge," she advances into the "illuminative way" of contemplatives.

3.2.2. PROFICIENTS, THE PASSIVE NIGHT OF THE SPIRIT, AND SPIRITUAL ESPOUSAL

According to St. John of the Cross, the soul which traverses the first "passive night" to become a contemplative does not ordinarily move immediately to the final preparations for permanent union with God, despite its remaining imperfections.

Instead, after having emerged from the state of beginners, it usually spends many years exercising itself in the state of proficients. In this new state, as one liberated from a cramped prison cell, the soul goes about the things of God with more abundant interior delight than it did in the beginning.... Its imagination and faculties are no longer bound to discursive meditation..., as was their custom. The soul readily finds in its spirit, without the work of meditation, a very serene, loving contemplation and spiritual delight. Nonetheless, since the purgation of the soul is not complete..., certain needs, aridities, darknesses and conflicts are felt. These are sometimes far more intense than those of the past and are like omens or messengers of the coming night of the spirit. (N II, 1, i)

Between the two "passive nights," then, there is often an interval of relative peace and contentment, broken from time to time by moments of intense religious ecstasy or pain. The passive night of sense has already produced a certain reallocation of the individual's cognitive resources through the partial subjugation of the inordinate appetites. Now proficients become more and more attuned to a whole realm of experience previously impeded by their preoccupation with the sources of sensory pleasure. They develop a clearer and more objective perception of the world around them. Likewise, the contemplative mode of consciousness, which began as little more than a vague and poorly-defined "awareness" or "sense of presence," continues to intensify, eventually blossoming into the transitory experiences of mystical absorption which John calls "touches of union" (see, for example, A II, 24, iv; 26, v-x; 32, ii-iv; III, 2, v-vi; N II, 23, xi-xii; 24, iii; C 14 & 15, xiv-xvi).[19] At times, perceptual and contemplative elements combine in "the living contemplation and knowledge of creatures" (C 6, i), whose beauty offers a certain "trace" of God and seems haltingly to disclose an "admirable immensity" underlying them (C 7, i).[20]

This is also the period when the extraordinary phenomena popularly associated with mysticism are most likely to occur. John mentions, for example, that proficients are subject to "raptures and transports" (N II, 1, ii), and "frequently behold imaginative and spiritual visions" (N II, 2, iii) or "apprehend certain extraordinary words, sometimes from the envisioned persons" (A II, 11, i); they may likewise acquire prophetic knowledge of "the thoughts of others, or their interior state" (A II, 26, xiv), "the number of days they have to live, or the trials they will have to endure, or something that will befall a particular person or kingdom, etc." (A II, 27, ii). Such phenomena, which so fascinated John's contemporaries, are exhaustively analyzed in Books II and III of the *Ascent*, and described more poetically elsewhere. While his analysis cannot be reviewed here in detail, the following points are worth noting.

First of all, John's etiological classification of these different experiences is based upon the scholastic psychological theories outlined earlier. He believes that the same kinds of apprehensions which arise naturally through perceptions and reflection can also be produced *involuntarily* through the intervention of God, angels, devils, or unconscious forces at various stages of the cognitive process; his systematic treatment of these extraordinary apprehensions in *Ascent* II is organized according to the point at which the intervention occurs, from "supernatural knowledge which reaches the intellect by way of the exterior senses" (A II, 11, i), to "imaginative visions," in which the imagination and phantasy receive sensible species without the aid of the five bodily senses (A II, 16, i-ii), to purely spiritual "visions, revelations, locutions, and spiritual feelings," which are "imparted to the intellect without the intervention of the exterior or interior bodily senses" (A II, 23, i).[21] This approach works relatively well for the analysis of less spiritual experiences, since corporal visions, voices, and so on are easily distinguished from one another on the basis of the sense involved. However, John obviously has greater difficulty fitting more elevated apprehensions into his classificatory scheme. For example, though some purely intellectual apprehensions bear a certain analogy to sight and thus may be called "visions," those ostensibly involving a direct awareness of the divine without the mediation of forms and concepts are not "visions" in any *distinctive* sense, but instead simply an aspect of union itself; the same holds true for locutions, revelations, and spiritual feelings, which is presumably why John says that these four kinds of apprehensions "can *all* be titled visions of the soul" (A II, 23, ii—emphasis mine). Thus St. John of the Cross seems uncertain whether to call the highest spiritual communications "visions of incorporeal substances," "revelations of naked truths about God," "substantial locutions," "divine touches," or "spiritual feelings"; all of these expressions ultimately refer to union with God, which is not among the more particular apprehensions from which the person must be detached (see A II, 24, i-iv; 26, i-x; 27, i-ii; 31, i-ii; 32, i-iii; cf. Panakal 1969, p. 72; Payne 1990).

Second, though John obviously does believe that God and other incorporeal substances can act directly upon the senses and intellect, he recognizes that not everything which appears to be of supernatural origin actually is so. He notes, for example, that the spiritual person's seemingly miraculous ability to read souls is often simply the result of heightened sensitivity to "exterior indications (even though extremely slight) such as words, gestures, and other signs" (A II, 26, xiv). Again, as he writes elsewhere:

Some intellects are so lively and subtle that, while recollected in meditation, they reason naturally and easily about some concepts, and form locutions and propositions very vividly, and consequently think that these locutions are from God. But that notion is false, for an intellect, freed from the operation of the senses, has the capacity to do this and even more with its own natural light and without any other supernatural help. Such an occurrence is frequent. (A II, 29, viii)

Moreover, according to St. John of the Cross, even those extraordinary phenomena which surpass the proficient's natural ability may be nothing more than the secondary effects of a more interior divine communication. Thus John maintains that "raptures and transports" are merely the physical repercussions of an intense infusion of contemplation, which ordinarily cease once the proficient's weak sensory nature is purified in the passive night of the spirit (see (N II, 1, ii; 2, v; C 13, ii-vii; 14 & 15, xvii-xix). In fact, it would seem a reasonable extension of his position to suggest that corporal and imaginative visions and voices are, in general, "a kind of overflow and echo of a much more intimate and spiritual process," the "radiation and reflex of contemplation in the sphere of the senses."[22]

This helps to explain, in the third place, why St. John of the Cross shows so little enthusiasm for the paranormal, despite his extensive treatment of occult phenomena. As we have seen, the proficient's experiences vary enormously in nature and value, depending on their intensity, source, and degree of interiority. John maintains, in general, that the more spiritual and interior the experience, the more it benefits the soul, other things being equal, though he notes that some "exterior corporal visions" of divine origin are "more effective" than imaginative visions which are weaker or have another cause (A II, 16, iii).[23] Furthermore, St. John repeatedly indicates that there are criteria for distinguishing authentic from inauthentic experiences, principally in terms of their content and effects; those from God, for example, usually "infuse knowledge and love, or sweetness" in the soul (A II, 16, x), and are never incompatible with orthodoxy (see, e.g., A II, 16, iii-v; xiv; 17, vii; 18, vii; 24, v-vii; 26, v-vii; xvii-xviii; 27, iii-vi; 29, xi; 30, iii-iv; III, 13, vii-ix). Nevertheless, he does not spell out these criteria in much detail, since he feels it is a waste of time trying to determine which experiences are from God. He holds, on the contrary, that a person must remain detached from all such apprehensions, for those of divine origin achieve their intended effect regardless of whether or not one pays attention to them (see A II, 11, v-viii; 16, v; x-xiv; 17, vii; 21, iv; 24, viii; 26, xviii; 30, v; III, 8, v; 13, i; 31, ii). What matters, according to John, is not the particular words, images, and ideas in which the divine communication is "clothed," but the obscure contemplative love and knowledge produced in the soul. Unlike many of his contemporaries, John sees little intrinsic spiritual value in extraordinary phenomena as such, and discusses them at length only to warn his readers against becoming distracted by visions, voices, and ecstasies.

To sum up, then, John of the Cross teaches that after individuals pass beyond a predominantly discursive form of prayer, they begin to enjoy an ever deepening contemplative awareness of the divine, variously described in the Sanjuanist writings as "secret wisdom," "mystical theology," "a secret, peaceful, loving inflow of God," or "the language of God in the soul" (see, e.g., A II, 8, viii; N I, 10, vi; II, 5, i-iii; 17, i-viii; 18, v; C 27, v; 39, xii; F 3, xxxii-xxxvii).[24] Though this contemplation involves as "obscure knowledge" unmarked by particular concepts and images, during its more intense phases it may give rise to detailed visionary experiences or cause the proficient to undergo trances and raptures. In addition, the occasional "needs, aridities, darknesses, and conflicts" felt during these periods are in part simply a natural depressive reaction to the passing of such stronger transitory communications; contemplatives may fear that God has abandoned them, or become restless and impatient at the return to their normal state.[25]

In short, even though proficients in the "illuminative way" have made significant progress, they are not yet physically and psychologically strong enough to receive more "vigorous spiritual communications" (N II, 1, ii), and continue to retain "the imperfect affections and habits still remaining like roots in the spirit" (N II, 2, i). Moreover,

> These proficients also have the so-called *hebetudo mentis*, the natural dullness everyone contracts through sin, and a distracted and inattentive spirit....
> This is the stage in which the devil induces many into believing vain visions and false prophecies. He strives to make them presume that God and the saints speak with them;

and frequently they believe their phantasy. It is here that the devil customarily fills them with presumption and pride. Drawn by vanity and arrogance, they will allow themselves to be seen in exterior acts of apparent holiness, such as raptures and other exhibitions. They become audacious with God.... They fall into these miseries by being too secure in their surrender to these apprehensions and spiritual feelings; and this, just when they were beginning to make progress along the way. (N II, 2, ii-iii)

The conduct required of someone at this stage is to "walk in faith," without clinging possessively to natural knowledge or the marvelous religious experiences one receives. John of the Cross calls this effort "the active spiritual night, because a person does what lies in his own power to enter this night," by "emptying and purifying" the intellect, memory and will "of all that is not God" through the theological virtues of faith, hope and charity, respectively (A II, 6, vi; cf. A I, 1, ii; II, 6, i-viii; III, 1, i; 16, i).

John's teaching on this "active night of the spirit" (called "active" because the individual feels more in control than in the "passive night," though John is well aware that the virtues are divine gifts and not simply the product of human effort) is found primarily in Books II and III of the *Ascent*, and can be easily summarized. In general, as he examines all of the natural and supernatural apprehensions of the faculties in turn, John repeatedly warns the proficient to "reject" and "pay no attention to" any distinct apprehension, remaining instead in the "darkness" of faith, hope, and charity, which are the only proximate means to union with God (see, for example, A II, 6, i; 8, ii-v; 9, i; 13, i; 16, x; 19, xiv; 24, iv-viii). But because these admonitions are formulated in such strong (not to say exaggerated) terms, some commentators have mistakenly thought that they embody a purely negative conception of the theological virtues. For a clearer understanding of John's directives, then, it will be helpful to describe briefly his notion of faith and its relationship to the intellect, from which his views on hope and charity can be inferred by analogy.

One source of confusion for John's readers is that the term "faith" (*fe*) has a variety of interrelated meanings in the Sanjuanist writings. At the most basic level, St. John of the Cross obviously presupposes the scholastic teaching that faith is the virtue by which we assent to revealed propositions on the authority of the revealer, God. Thus he defines faith as "a certain and obscure habit" by which we "believe divinely revealed truths which transcend every natural light and infinitely exceed all human understanding" (A II, 3, i), and speaks of the "articles" and "truths" of faith (see, e.g., A II, 1, i; 9, i; 27, i-iv; C 12, iii-vi; and also Delaye 1975, p. 9). In addition, John sometimes identifies faith with the *act* or *object* of this assent, or with its *effects*, especially the "obscurity" it causes; he insists, for example, that faith is a "dark night" for the soul, and writes that:

...God is the substance and the concept of faith, and faith is the secret and the mystery. And when that which faith covers and hides from us is revealed...then the substance and mysteries of the secrets will be uncovered to the soul. (C 1, x; see also A I, 2, i; II, 1, i-iii; 2, i-iii; 3, iii; 4, i-ii; 6, i-ii; 9, i; 22, v-vii; C 1, xi; 12, iv-vi)

Finally, John often uses "faith" to designate an openness and surrender to God, "an integral attitude involving the whole person."[26] In this broadest sense of the term, faith goes beyond notional assent to include the other virtues as well.

Particularly in *Ascent* II, which deals with both the "active night of the spirit" and the second "reason" (i.e., faith) for calling the journey toward God a "night," John seems to set up a radical opposition between faith and knowledge. There he asserts that faith "not only fails to produce knowledge and science (*noticias y sciencia*), but also...deprives and blinds [the intellect] of any other knowledge and science" (A II, 3, iv—my translation). He likewise advises the contemplative to "lean on dark faith" and to "rest on nothing of what he understands, tastes, feels, or imagines" (A II, 4, ii), insisting that "a person should be undesirous of knowing the truths of faith clearly, that he may thereby conserve...the merit of faith" (A II, 17, v; see also A II, 1, iii; 2, ii; 3, i-v; 4, iii-vii; 6, ii; 27, iv-v; III, 31, viii).

In light of such remarks, several authors have naturally assumed that John's notion of faith is basically anti-cognitive, and that he advocates a blind acceptance of church teachings without attaching any specific meaning to them. Some simply maintain, for example, that "according to the doctrine of St. John of the Cross," the "articles and propositions of the creed" certainly do not "reveal God as He is," because "God is infinite" and "every concept, word, or image is finite" (Ferraro 1971, p. 253). Others, more extreme, claim that faith, for John, "does not impart any knowledge whatsoever," but is simply "the nakedness of the soul bereft of knowledge" (Werblowsky 1966, p. 179; compare Inge 1956, pp. 229-230).

However, the view thus attributed to St. John of the Cross often seems confused at best, and is hard to reconcile with other Sanjuanist texts. It makes little sense, after all, to describe faith as an "assent" if there is nothing definite to which one is assenting. Moreover, John's frequent assertion that faith "informs," "teaches," and "illuminates" the soul is incompatible with a purely negative conception of this virtue, for if faith were merely a "bare assent" for the sole purpose of emptying the mind, it would not matter whether the articles of faith to which one assented were true or false; they would not *inform*, but only provide the occasion for an exercise in mental asceticism. Most important of all, if John actually regarded the Scriptures, creeds, and dogmas as mere ciphers conveying nothing of God and God's works, he could scarcely hold, as he clearly does, that an individual's knowledge of the "mysteries of the faith" grows and develops as one advances in the spiritual life; those in the unitive way, for instance, could not identify what they receive as a deeper experience of the Trinity or Incarnation, unless they already had some grasp of what these doctrines mean (see **A** II, 26, ii-v; **C** Prologue, i; 1, x-xi; 7, iii; 23, i; 36, iii-xiii; 37, i-viii; 39, iii-xiii; and below).

In short, a careful and comprehensive reading of John's remarks reveals a notion of faith entirely in accord with what we have said so far about Sanjuanist teaching. St. John of the Cross does not require the annihilation of reason or the inhuman suppression of one's natural cognitive abilities, even in the religious sphere; as noted earlier, he maintains that the merest beginner gains at least some knowledge of God through meditation on Christian truths. If John puts such strong emphasis on the "darkness" and "emptiness" of faith, it is largely because of the continuity he sees between this virtue and the "general knowledge" passively imparted to the soul. In fact, John describes faith and contemplation in almost identical terms, and seems to suggest that the "general knowledge" received in contemplation is a certain outgrowth or "illumination" of the divine truths already infused in the soul through her assent to the "articles of faith." Thus, in explaining the words of the Bride in *Canticle* 12, he writes that:

...Her faith is so enlightened that it gives her a glimpse of some clear divine reflections of the height of her God. As a result she does not know what to do other than turn to this very faith, which contains and hides the image and beauty of her Beloved....
...With burning desire she exclaims...: O faith of Christ, my Spouse, would that you might show me clearly now the truths of my Beloved, which you have infused in my soul and which are covered with obscurity and darkness (for faith, as the theologians say, is an obscure habit), in such a way that, what you communicate to me in inexplicit and obscure knowledge, you would show suddenly, clearly, and perfectly, changing it into a manifestation of glory! (**C** 12, i-ii; see also **A** II, 10, iv; 29, vii; III, 7, ii; **C** 1, x-xi; 12, iii-vi; **F** 3, lxxx; and Delaye 1975, pp. 7-8)

Faith is a "dark night," then, inasmuch as it involves a receptivity to that "obscure general knowledge" which drives all distinct thoughts and images from the mind during moments of intense contemplation. The "articles of faith" are attempts to articulate the object of this "general knowledge" in finite terms and symbols. Naturally our initial acceptance of these articles will require a certain conceptualization of their content. John is not saying that these particular concepts are false, but only that they are limited, and can become an obstacle if one clings to them and remains closed to the deeper understanding given in contemplation.

Therefore, when John advises proficients to enter the "active night of spirit" by "stripping" themselves of all distinct apprehensions through faith, hope, and charity, he is not encouraging a mindless assent to Christian teaching, but only reminding proficients not to become so fixated upon their favorite religious ideas that they fail to advance. Unfortunately, contemplatives are easily distracted by the particular concepts and images in which their extraordinary experiences are "clothed"; this attachment to visions, voices, and so on, leads to the spiritual pride and presumption described above. John of the Cross notes that "no proficient, however strenuous his efforts, will avoid many of these natural affections and imperfect habits" (N II, 2, iv). In fact, the contemplative's faults are "more incurable" than those of beginners precisely because he considers them "more spiritual than before" (N II, 2, iv—my translation).[27] In order to reach permanent union with God, the soul must undergo the final purification of the second "passive night."

According to John, then, after individuals have endured the sufferings of the "passive night of sense," they usually enjoy a long period of relative tranquility and satisfaction, during which they begin to become accustomed to their new contemplative mode of experience. However, the alternating raptures and aridities show that all is not well, and that the proficient is still troubled by unresolved conflicts and deeply-rooted faults. Eventually this inner struggle reaches a crisis point, and the person is plunged into the horrors of the "passive night of the spirit," in which God:

...leaves the intellect in darkness, the will in aridity, the memory in emptiness, and the affections in supreme affliction, bitterness, and anguish, by depriving the soul of the feeling and satisfaction it previously obtained from spiritual blessings. (N II, 3, iii)[28]

Readers of St. John of the Cross have been particularly fascinated with his teaching on the "passive night of the spirit," and there have been frequent attempts to relate it to modern developments in philosophy and theology. Though such attempts are often illuminating, it is important to remember that, first and foremost, John is describing an existential process, not expounding a metaphysical or epistemological theory; classifying him too quickly as a quasi-Hegelian or "death-of-God" theologian can lead to a biased and one-sided reading of his texts.[29]

The second book of the *Night* describes in frightening detail the trials of this terrible purgation, which go far beyond anything previously experienced. At this time "a person feels so unclean and wretched that it seems God is against him and that he is against God" (N II, 5, v). He considers himself "forsaken and despised by creatures, particularly by his friends" (N II, 6, iii), and:

...feels very vividly indeed the shadow of death, the sighs of death, and the sorrows of hell, all of which reflect the feeling of God's absence, of being chastened and rejected by Him, and of being unworthy of Him, as well as the object of His anger. The soul experiences all this and even more, since it seems that his affliction will last forever. (N II, 6, ii)[30]

To make matters worse, someone in this state is unable to "raise his mind and affection" to God, and has "so little strength and fervor that [he] thinks God does not hear" his entreaties; "consequently, a person can neither pray vocally nor be attentive to spiritual matters, nor still less attend to temporal affairs and business" (N II, 8, i). He "suspects that he is lost" and sometimes "dissolves in tears," though "such relief is less frequent" (N II, 9, vii). His situation seems almost hopeless.

As John explains, this second "passive night" is needed to complete the work of the first, which had only trimmed the "branches" of the person's imperfections, without "pulling up roots" (N II, 2, i). The passive night of sense produced a certain "accommodation of the senses to the spirit" (Ibid.), so that both parts could be jointly purified in the passive night of the spirit.

> The real purgation of the senses begins with the spirit. Hence the night of the senses we explained should be called a certain reformation and bridling of the appetite rather than a purgation. The reason is that all the imperfections and disorders of the sensory part are rooted in the spirit and from it receive their strength. All good and evil habits reside in the spirit and until these habits are purged, the senses cannot be completely purified of their rebellions and vices. (N II, 3, i; see also N II, 2, v; 3, ii-iii; 9, ii-vi; 11, i-iv; 14, i-iii; F 1, xxv)

Paradoxically, the ultimate cause of all these sufferings, the feelings of rejection and the sense of God's absence, is actually a more intense "inflow of God into the soul, which purges it of its habitual ignorances and imperfections, natural and spiritual, and which the contemplatives call infused contemplation or mystical theology" (N II, 5, i; see also N II, 1, i; 5, ii-vii; 6, i-v; 8, ii-iv; C 12, ix; 13, i; F 1, xix-xxiii). Anticipating certain ideas of modern psychoanalytic theory, John compares the work of this purgative contemplation to the effect of fire upon a damp log; just as the heat of the flame must drive all moisture to the surface before the wood can become wholly enkindled, so also the "loving flame of contemplation" shines upon the secret recesses of the soul, throwing all of its hidden conflicts and failings into sharp relief, so that they may be recognized and resolved.

> This divine purge stirs up all the foul and vicious humors of which the soul was never before aware; never did it realize that there was so much evil in itself, since these humors were so deeply rooted. And now that they may be expelled and annihilated they are brought to light and seen clearly through the illumination of this dark light of divine contemplation. Although the soul is no worse than before, neither in itself nor in its relationship with God, it feels undoubtedly so bad as to be not only unworthy that God should see it but deserving of His abhorrence.... (N II, 10, ii; see also A I, 11, vi; II, 8, ii; N II, 10, i-ix; F 1, xix-xxiii)

Thus the infused contemplation causes a person to "faint and suffer with self-knowledge," giving him "a very clear picture of himself" (F 1, xix-xx). The soul becomes far more profoundly aware of her limitations, and realizes as never before her own nothingness in the face of God's majesty. As one might expect, Rudolf Otto and others have pointed to John's discussion of this state as a classic description of numinous experiences, in which an individual is confronted with the radical holiness and "Other-ness" of the divine (see Otto 1958, p. 106; though the English edition attributes the three Sanjuanist passages cited to the *Ascent*, they are actually taken from N II, 5, vi; 6, iv; and 6, i respectively).

Some further points about the passive night of the spirit are worth noting here. First, since this final purification involves a fundamental dismantling and re-integration of the former personality structure, it is hardly surprising that those in this state should suffer terribly, and that all their instincts should rise up in revolt at the violent death of the "old man." This also helps to explain, for example, why John will say at one moment that someone undergoing these trials "feels that he is against God" (N II, 5, v), and assert shortly thereafter that the same person "knows that he loves God and that he would give a thousand lives for Him" (N II, 7, vii). Such apparently contradictory statements describe the contradictory feelings of the individual whose "soul becomes a battlefield in which these two contraries" of dark contemplation and remaining faults "combat one another"; he may alternately identify himself with either of the opposing forces in this struggle (see also N II, 5, v; 7, iv-vi; 9, viii-ix; F 1, xxii-xxiii).

Second, though John of the Cross has little to say about the temptations against or the doubts about God's existence that may assail a soul at this time, it seems reasonable to suppose, as some spiritual writers suggest, that the "*feeling of not having any faith*" and the "feeling that religion is not true" are the modern counterparts of the fear of rejection and condemnation by God which John describes (Chapman 1959, p. 47). After all, this passive night painfully disabuses individuals of comfortable illusions about themselves and God; one discovers that there is literally nothing exactly corresponding to his familiar notion of the deity, and that the divine is something (or Someone) far more mysterious than one had ever imagined (cf. Sanchez de Murillo 1976, pp. 278-279; and Payne 1979, pp. 210-211). In John's sixteenth century Spanish milieu, where no one seriously questioned the existence of God, contemplatives experienced the disorientation of this passive night primarily as a threat to their own self-esteem; today, when the existence of God is no longer generally taken for granted, the same upheaval may challenge a person's belief in a loving Creator. At any rate, those Christian mystics who have undergone such spiritual trials cannot easily be accused of having a naive, untested faith.

Third, John of the Cross stresses the fundamental continuity of this passive purgation with the religious experiences of the stages preceding and following it; the same "divine communication" is involved throughout, from the "first stirrings" of contemplation in the passive night of sense to the heights of mystical union, though its effects vary with the state of the soul.[31] John notes, for example, that the "light of contemplation" which now "produces such painful and disagreeable effects" is "the same light to which the soul must be united and in which it will find all its blessings in the state of perfection" toward which it is advancing (N II, 9, x; see also N

II, 5, ii-iii; 7, iv-vii; 9, i-xi; 10, iii-v; 12, i-iv; 13, x; **F** 1, xxii-xxvi). In a sense, the soul's trials are due less to the action of God than to "the qualities it possesses which are contrary to this light," because "there is nothing in contemplation or the divine inflow which of itself can give pain" (**N** II, 9, xi); "when the imperfections are gone, the soul's suffering terminates, and joy remains" (**N** II, 10, v). This teaching has some important consequences for our understanding of religious experiences. It suggests, for example, that what an individual experiences in the most advanced and intense mystical states is already present in the "loving awareness" of initial contemplation, albeit in a brief, inchoate, and barely perceptible form. It also raises the question of whether there is as clear a distinction between numinous and mystical experiences as certain authors would have us believe.[32] Moreover, insofar as Christian mystics notice a continuity between the passive night of the spirit and the unitive way, and insofar as it seems to them that they are lovingly united in the latter with the same reality which they earlier experienced as "wholly Other," their use of dualistic (and even theistic) language in describing their experience will not be entirely unwarranted.

Finally, John claims that the passive night of the spirit not only leads to great holiness but also produces a high degree of moral integrity and psychological integration, and even increases a person's physical stamina (see, e.g., **N** II, 11, iii-iv; 24, ii-iii; **C** 20 & 21, iv). The Mystical Doctor is not the only spiritual writer to make this claim, and it is one which is to some extent open to empirical testing (cf. Murphy and Donovan 1988). If it is true, then it becomes more difficult to dismiss mysticism as the product of emotional instability or wish-fulfillment; at least it is clear that the sufferings of the passive night of the spirit are nothing that the contemplative would have anticipated or desired.

To sum up, then, the second "passive night" humbles the proficient, provides a clearer knowledge of one's own absolute dependence on God, and restores the proper relationship between the different components of human nature, so that the whole person may take part in the permanent union of spiritual marriage. According to St. John of the Cross, the duration of this painful purgation will depend upon its force and the "degree of union" for which one is destined, though "if it is to be truly efficacious, it will last for some years, no matter how intense it may be" (**N** II, 7, iii-iv). Eventually, however, as contemplatives become increasingly purified, they begin to enjoy a foretaste of what awaits them in spiritual marriage. From time to time, they experience an overpowering impulse of love for God in the will, or a powerful communication of mystical knowledge to the intellect, or both at once.

> This enkindling of love and the union of these two faculties, the intellect and the will, is something immensely rich and delightful for the soul, because it is a certain touch of the divinity and already the beginning of the perfection of the union of love for which the

soul hopes. Thus one does not receive this touch of so sublime an experience and love of God without having suffered many trials and a great part of the purgation. But so extensive a purgation is not required for other inferior and more common touches. (N II, 12, vi; see also N II, 7, iv-vi; 9, iii; 10, vi-ix; 11, ii-v; 13, i-v; x; 23, i-xiv; 24, iv)

Stanzas 13 to 21 of the *Canticle* deal with "spiritual espousal" (*desposorio espiritual*), the penultimate stage of spiritual development in this life. Since this state seems to correspond to the final phase of the passive night of the spirit, I will briefly outline John's teaching on "espousal" before turning to his treatment of spiritual marriage.[33]

In the first place, St. John of the Cross distinguishes the "day of betrothal" (*dia del desposorio*, mentioned explicitly in C 14 & 15, ii, and alluded to more obliquely elsewhere) from the state of espousal which it inaugurates. Evidently the former represents the initial occurrence of the sublime "touch of divinity" mentioned in the preceding block quotation, and surpasses everything previously communicated to the soul; thus John writes that in the midst of her "greater experience...of the void of God, of very heavy darkness, and of spiritual fire which dries up and purges her," God sends the soul "some of His divine rays with such strong love and glory that He stirs her completely and causes her to go out of her senses" in an ecstasy or "flight of the spirit" (C 13, i). This "visit" or "union of love" is repeated with increasing intensity and perfection in the *state* of espousal which follows, and such experiences are among the most characteristic features of this period (cf. Zabalza 1963, pp. 31-50).

In the second place, these "rapturous visits" clearly correspond to the "substantial touches" discussed earlier.[34] According to the *Canticle*, a "substantial knowledge" of God "stripped of accidents and phantasms" is imparted directly to the passive intellect during these visits (C 14 & 15, xiv); as in the *Ascent*, John also describes this communication as "an unveiling of truths about the divinity," "a revelation of the secrets of God," a purely spiritual "vision," or an obscure knowledge of "naked substance" (C 14 & 15, xv-xvi; cf. A 24, i-iv; 25, i-iii; 26, ii-viii; 27, i; 32, ii-iii; N II, 23, xi-xii; 24, iii). In other words, as explained above, the contemplative seems to receive an immediate and mysterious "loving knowledge" of the divine without the aid of the concepts and images derived from sense experience.

Third, because of the "strong and overflowing communications and glimpse of what God is in Himself," the espoused soul "tastes sublimely the wisdom of God reflected in the harmony of His creatures and works" (C 14 & 15, iv-v). The whole world seems to be "a harmonious symphony of sublime music" in which every creature, "bearing God within itself according to its capacity, magnifies God" (Ibid., xxv-xxvii). Again, though the nature of this contemplative awareness of creation is not entirely clear from John's descriptions, it seems to be a more intense form of the "contuition" of God and creatures mentioned above, and would presumably be classified as an "extrovertive mystical experience" by Stace and others.[35]

Finally, the transitory "visits" of the Beloved gradually cure the soul of her remaining weaknesses and bad habits, by setting her appetites in order and adorning her with "gifts and virtues" (C 14 & 15, ii; cf. N II, 23, xi-xii; 24, ii-iii; C 19, vi; 20 & 21, i-iv; F 3, xxiv-xxv). As a result, not only does someone in this state ordinarily enjoy a greater degree of peace and security than ever before, but also these "gifts, perfections, and riches" are sometimes "unveiled to the soul" in such a way that she feels "clothed with delight and bathed in inestimable glory," and is able to perceive the progress she has made (C 17, vi-vii).[36] Others, too, notice "an 'I-don't-know-what' (*un no sé qué*) of greatness and dignity" which generates "awe and respect" (C 17, vii).

Nevertheless, this joy and tranquility is still limited and incomplete; the soul continues to suffer occasionally "from her Beloved's withdrawals and from the disturbances and afflictions in her sensory part," since "until the state of spiritual marriage the sensory part never completely loses the dross left from bad habits, or brings its energies into subjection" (C 14 & 15, xxx). During the period of espousal a person's prayerful recollection is often disturbed by distracting images and powerful temptations stirred up from the depths of the soul.[37] Moreover, with the end of the spiritual journey in sight, the contemplative feels like "a stone which is racing toward its center"; the passing of these transitory "visits" leave her impatient and unsatisfied, filled with a "fathomless desire for union with God," and longing for the more stable possession of the divine found in spiritual marriage (C 17, i; see also C 17, ii-iii; 18, i; F 3, xviii-xxvi).[38]

3.2.3. "PERFECT" SOULS, SPIRITUAL MARRIAGE, AND THE UNITIVE WAY

According to St. John of the Cross, the disturbances which trouble the espoused soul are substantially eliminated in spiritual marriage, which takes place "in the unitive way of the perfect" following "the illuminative way of the proficients" (C Theme, ii), and is "the highest state attainable in this life" (C 12, viii; 22, iii; cf. N I, 1, i; II, 1, ii; 20, iv; F 2, xxvii).[39]

This spiritual marriage is incomparably greater than the spiritual espousal, for it is a total transformation in the Beloved in which each surrenders the entire possession of self to the other with a certain consummation of the union of love. The soul thereby becomes divine, becomes God through participation, insofar as is possible in this life.... [The bride] has set aside and forgotten all temptations, disturbances, pain, solicitude, and cares, and is tranformed in this high embrace. (C 22, iii; see also C 17, xxx; 26, iv; F Prologue, iii-iv; 3, xxiv-xxv; and Eulogio de San Juan de la Cruz 1963, pp. 105-107).

The latter part of the *Canticle* and the majority of the *Flame* are devoted to a description of this high state, though John readily admits that it is "beyond all that can be said or thought" (C 22, v—my translation).[40] Here we can only briefly sketch the main psychological, moral, and spiritual effects of spiritual marriage.

First, in this state of transformation all of a person's abilities and desires are set in order and unified, so that "this whole harmonious composite" can be employed in the love and service of God (N II, 11, iv). Thus John says that the soul which has reached spiritual marriage is no longer bothered by a wandering imagination, or by "inordinate acts" of the appetites and passions (see N II, 13, xi; 24, ii-iv; C 20 & 21, i-xix; 26, xviii-xix; 27, vi-vii; 28, ii-ix; 29, vii-xi; F 2, xxxi-xxxv). In more modern terms, this means that one has overcome neurotic "attachments" and "useless hopes, joys, sorrows, and fears" (C 26, xviii), reaching a state of emotional and psychological maturity. In theological terms, one now lives "according to the manner of the state of innocence which Adam possessed" (N II, 24, ii—my translation).

With the achievement of this psychological integration the person also attains a high degree of moral virtue. Thus John notes that:

> ...in this state the virtues are bound together, united, and fortified by each other, and fitted to the full perfection of the soul, sustaining one another in such fashion that no part remains open or weak.... Liberated now from all the disturbance of the natural passions, and...the torment and variety of temporal cares, she enjoys in security and quietude the participation of God. (C 24, v)

Once again, these solidly established virtues not only cause "habitual satisfaction and peace" in the soul, but at times "are so wont to open within her and spread their fragrance...that she is filled with the delights of God" (Ibid., vi). In other words, one kind of experience associated with the higher stages of the spiritual life is a certain transitory "activation" and "enjoyment" of these infused virtues, which the contemplative sees as mirroring the divine attributes (Ibid., iii); thus the person may feel engulfed in impulses of love, mercy, fortitude, and so on. John even goes so far as to claim that the soul which arrives at spiritual marriage is "confirmed in grace" (C 22, iii) and "ordinarily inclines and moves toward God in the first movements of its intellect, memory, will, and appetites, because of...its perfect conversion toward good" (C 27, vii), which is one of the reasons for calling persons in this state "perfect." (See also C 25, xi; 27, vi-viii; and 28, ii-viii where John clearly indicates that this "conversion toward good" involves the whole person, not just the spiritual part.) But while it may be an exaggeration to assert that such individuals are *incapable* of falling into serious sin, they are certainly far less *likely* to do so, since they no longer feel any serious attraction toward evil; they would not give up the complete satisfaction now found in God for more ephemeral pleasures. As John elsewhere says, "old lovers hardly ever fail God, for they now stand above all that would make them fail Him" (C 25, xi).

But the essential feature of spiritual marriage, which largely accounts for its psychological and moral effects, is the establishment of a certain "permanent" and "substantial" union with God, in comparison with which all other temporal and spiritual joys which might otherwise have led the soul astray now seem merely "accidental" (see **C** 20 & 21, xii-xiii). In previous stages, the contemplative alternated between moments of intense absorption in divine "visits," and other periods in which he keenly felt the "affective absence" of God. Now, however, he experiences a continual "intimate spiritual embrace" in the substance of his soul (**C** 22, v), an habitual awareness of the presence and possession of the divine which frequently flares up into a more powerful "immersion" in God (see **C** 20 & 21, i; xiv; 22, iii-vi; 40, iii; **F** 1, xv; 4, xiv-xv). Thus St. John of the Cross compares the soul to an incandescent log, "shooting out flames from itself" (**F** Prologue, iii), or to a bed in which the Beloved wakes from time to time.

It does not, however, always experience these awakenings, for when the Beloved produces them, it seems to the soul that He is awakening in its heart, where before He remained as though asleep....
...He is usually there, in this embrace with His bride, as though asleep in the substance of the soul. And it is very well aware of Him and ordinarily enjoys Him. Were He always awake within it, it would already be in glory. (**F** 4, xiv-xv; compare **C** 16, i; 24, i-ix; 39, xiv; **F** Prologue, iii-iv; 1, i-xvii; xxvii-xxviii; 3, viii-x)

Elsewhere, speaking less poetically, he observes that "even though the soul is always in this sublime state of spiritual marriage once God has placed her in it, the faculties are not always in actual union, although the substance is" (**C** 26, xi). In other words, John seems to be claiming that the person who reaches spiritual marriage acquires a continuous and delicate "awareness" of God, which at times intensifies into those experiences classically considered "mystical," but which is ordinarily enjoyed without any detriment to one's acquired knowledge or consciousness of the external world (see **C** 26, xvi).

As for the transitory experiences themselves, these seem to include all of the joyful "communications" of earlier stages, but without the raptures and ecstasies which they used to cause (see **A** III, 2, vi; **N** II, 1, ii; **C** 13, vi; 14 & 15, xxi; **F** 4, xi-xii). Sometimes the effects of such communcations last "for a long while," with the individual moving in and out of an absorption in "loving knowledge" over a period of hours or days (**C** 25, viii). John also mentions a new kind of contemplative "awakening" in which:

...the soul knows creatures through God and not God through creatures. This amounts to knowing the effects through their cause and not the cause through its effects. The latter is knowledge *a posteriori* (*conocimiento trasero*), and the former is essential knowledge. (**F** 4, v)

Here the awareness of creatures seems to be mediated by a more primordial experience of the divine knowledge and will from which they flow. While it is difficult to imagine what such an experience would be like, John evidently distinguishes it from the experience of the unity and harmony of creation mentioned in connection with spiritual espousal; it seems doubtful, therefore, that every contemplative communication of the unitive way can be classified as either an "introvertive" or an "extrovertive" mystical experience, according to Stace's criteria.[41] Indeed, John maintains that "there are many kinds of awakening which God effects in the soul, so many that we would never finish explaining them all" (F 4, iv).

Finally, some passages suggest that, even in this life, the contemplative may receive a "sublime" experience of God in "one of His attributes (His omnipotence, fortitude, goodness and sweetness, etc.)" (A II, 26, iii), as well as a certain obscure knowledge of, and participation in, the Christian mysteries of the Trinity, the Incarnation, and "the ways of the Redemption of mankind" (C 23, i).[42] Thus St. John of the Cross asserts that through its "union with the Most Blessed Trinity" the transformed soul becomes "capable of breathing in God the same spiration of love that the Father breathes in the Son and the Son in the Father, which is the Holy Spirit Himself" (C 39, iii-iv). Elsewhere, commenting on the verse "And then we will go on / To the high cavern in the rock," John writes:

The high caverns of this rock are the sublime, exalted, and deep mysteries of God's wisdom in Christ, in the hypostatic union of the human nature with the divine Word, and in the corresponding union of men with God, and the mystery of the harmony between God's justice and mercy with respect to...His judgments in the salvation of the human race....
...For one cannot reach in this life what is attainable of these mysteries of Christ without having suffered much, and without having received numerous intellectual and sensible favors from God, and without having undergone much spiritual activity; for all these favors are inferior to the wisdom of the mysteries of Christ in that they serve as preparations for the coming of this wisdom. (C 37, iii-iv)[43]

Despite the obscurity of such remarks, John says enough to suggest that the invocation of these particular mysteries is not simply the arbitrary projection of randomly chosen Christian doctrines onto otherwise neutral subjective phenomena, but is somehow rooted in the character of the experiences themselves. For example, John can say that spiritual marriage involves a further manifestation of the mystery of the Incarnation at least in part because he believes that persons in this state become "divinized" and "possess the same goods by participation that the Son possesses by nature" (C 39, vi).[44] In other words, the Christian mystic acquires a deeper knowledge of the hypostatic union by being raised to an analogous condition; through God's grace, he experiences within himself both humanity and "divinity." Moreover, through this "adoptive sonship" the soul in the unitive way receives a certain taste of Christ's relationship to the Father, and the mutual love of the Father and Son, "for it loves through the Holy Spirit, as the Father and Son love each other" (F 3, lxxxii).[45] Finally, through her own spiritual journey the soul has experienced the work of redemption and grace, and has come to realize that the same divine love which causes her own joy and that of the blessed also occasions suffering when it is resisted; thus she has a certain existential grasp of the continuity between the experiences of spiritual fulfillment and loss in this life and the next. Here we may recall John's comments on the relationship between the spiritual purgation in this life and the sufferings of those in purgatory (N II, 6, vi; 7, vii; 10, v; 12, i-iv; F 1, xxiv; 2, xxv; 3, xxii; and so on), which could easily be extended to explain the nature of hell.

As we have seen, then, John teaches that a person is originally in a state of psychological, moral, and spiritual disequilibrium, and begins to grow through discursive prayer and efforts at self-reform; if all goes well, the individual will eventually become conscious of a new, contemplative mode of awareness, which ideally will one day blossom into the experience of enjoying and possessing God in the state of spiritual marriage. With this transformation, one has reached the highest stage of development possible in this life, though "with time and practice" the "love can receive added quality...and become more intensified" (F Prologue, iii). Yet the perfect enjoyment of the divine is still somewhat impeded by the conditions of mortal existence; consequently, the person has a "gentle and delightful desire" for the beatific vision (F 1, xxvii-xxviii).

3.3. The Goal of Religious Development

It is already clear from our study that the Sanjuanist approach to mysticism differs significantly from that typically found in contemporary philosophical discussions of the topic. Most philosophers write as if the point of mysticism were the production of certain unusual subjective states. But since John understands human existence as a developing relationship of love between the individual and God, he naturally takes the goal of the mystical life to be a final consummation of the relationship in which the whole human person participates, body and soul (see C 28, ix; 40, i-v; F 1, xxvii; 2, x-xiii; xxii).

Some Sanjuanist passages deal with spiritual development within the confines of mortal existence, and therefore point to a state reached prior to death as the terminus of the process. Thus when John writes that the "third reason" for calling the journey toward union a night "pertains to the point of arrival, namely, God," he immediately adds that "God is also a dark night to man *in this life*" (A I, 2, i—emphasis mine), where the union in question takes place. The preceding discussion of spiritual marriage, "the highest state attainable in this life" (**C** 22, iii), has already treated "the goal of religious development" in this sense.

Nevertheless, though the state of spiritual marriage is already a kind of "heaven on earth," it does not yet give the soul the complete possession of the Beloved which she seeks. For this, she must take one further, final step in the spiritual journey, passing through death to eternal life with God. Thus John says that the perfect soul begs God to "consummate the spiritual marriage...perfectly by means of the beatific vision," because "however intimate may be a man's union with God, he will never have satisfaction and rest until God's glory appears..., especially since he now experiences its savor and sweetness" (**F** 1, xxvii); though this profound longing is not as painful as before,

...the sudden flashes of glory and love which appear vaguely in these touches at the door of entry into the soul, and which are unable to fit into it because of the narrowness of the earthly house, are so sublime that it would rather be a sign of little love not to try to enter into that perfection and completion of love. (Ibid., xxviii; compare **N** II, 20, v-vi; **C** 1, iv; x-xi; 8, ii-iii; 11, v-xiv; 12, viii; 36, i-xiii; 37, i-vi; 38, i-ix; 39, i-xv; 40, i; **F** 1, vi; xiv; xxvii-xxxvi)

John of the Cross shows no interest in elaborate speculations about the nature of life after death, and is surprisingly reticent about it, except to stress the superiority of beatitude to any experience of God attainable here below. But in what does this superiority consist? According to some modern scholastic theologians, the crucial difference between the mystic's experience of the divine and the vision of God in glory is that the former involves a certain "medium" while the latter does not. Maritain, for example, cites passages from John's works in defense of his view that infused love serves as the "*objectum quo*" of mystical knowledge, the *means by which* the mystic experiences God, whereas in beatitude "the Divine Essence itself will actuate our intellect immediately, without the mediation of any *species* or idea (for no idea, angelic or human, could adequately represent the Divine Essence)" (Maritain 1959, p. 310; see also pp. 261-263, 328-329). The Sanjuanist texts which appear to contradict his position Maritain tends to handle by claiming that John was not speaking scientifically or not addressing the same issue.

Of course the plausibility and significance of the claim that mystical experiences are always "mediated" will depend upon what sort of mediation one is talking about. Those who incorporate this claim in their theory of mysticism often seem to feel it is needed to preserve the uniqueness and permanence of beatitude, which would somehow be undermined if one admitted the possibility of an "unmediated" glimpse of God in this life.

This line of reasoning is not particularly convincing, though we will not pause to examine it here.[46] In the present context, it is enough to note that St. John of the Cross appears to adopt a different position on the matter.

Thus, contrary to Maritain, he teaches that God works in the "perfect" soul "without any other means (*sin otro algún medio*)" (**C** 35, vi—my translation), and that the same infused love of the Holy Spirit which purifies and illumines individuals in this life also unites them with God in glory (compare **N** II, 20, iv-vi; **C** 11, xi; 12, vii-viii; 19, iv; 26, i-iv; vii-viii; 35, ii; 36, v; 38, ii-iv; 39, iv-xv; **F** 1, xii-xvi; xxxiii-xxxv; 3, lxxxii). Though his remarks are not entirely unambiguous, they seem to suggest that what distinguishes the mystical from the beatific experience of God is not the *immediacy* but the *clarity* of the latter when contrasted with the former. John says, for example, that "in comparison with beatific knowledge," the highest contemplative knowledge received here below "is still a dark night," which will be changed after death "into the contemplation of the clear and serene vision of God in heaven" (**C** 39, xiii); elsewhere he describes the natural life of the soul in the unitive way as a "veil" so "spiritual, thin, and luminous, that it does not prevent the divinity from vaguely appearing through it" (**F** 1, xxxii).[47]

For John, in other words, the highest "touches of union" would seem to be like looking at the sun; the experience is certainly direct and immediate, but cannot be clear and continuous because of the limitations of mortal existence. In the state of glory, however, all of the soul's faculties will be permanently absorbed in the "face-to-face" contemplation of God (compare **A** II, 5, ii; **N** II, 20, iii; **C** 26, xi; **F** 4, xv). Moreover, because of her perfect vision of God, the soul will finally be able "to love God as purely and perfectly as He loves her (**C** 38, ii).

Even though there is a true union of will in [spiritual marriage], she cannot attain the excellence and power of love which she will possess in the strong union of glory. Just as the soul, according to St. Paul, will know then as she is known by God..., so she will also love God as she is loved by Him. As her intellect will be the intellect of God, her will then will be God's will, and thus her love will be God's love. (**C** 38, iii; see also **N** II, 20, v-vi; **C** 9, vii; 11, xii; 38, ii-v; **F** 1, xiv)

Finally, as we have already seen, the person who reaches beatitude enters further into "the thicket of God's wisdom and knowledge" (**C** 36, x), becoming more completely transformed in the divine attributes and mysteries (see also **C** 36, xi-xii; 37, i-viii; 39, iii-vi; **F** 3, i-xvii). In heaven such blessings are no longer given successively, but "are all contained in one essential glory" (**C** 38, i). John also says, however, that at least until the Last Judgment the angels and saints will continue to discover "so many new things" in God "that they will forever be receiving new surprises and marveling the more" (**C** 14 & 15, viii; see also **C** 7, ix; 36, x; 37, iv).

To sum up, then, St. John of the Cross holds that there is a fundamental *continuity* between the beatific vision and the "obscure knowledge" of God received in this life. Thus spiritual marriage, and indeed even the initial stirrings of contemplation, offer the soul a certain "foretaste" and "trace" of what it will know and enjoy in glory. In the discussion which follows, this will prove to be an important claim, for it means that, according to John, true contemplatives experience God *as God is*, albeit in a confused and partial way, and do not merely *infer* that they have encountered the divine from the effects produced in their souls. In other words, contemplative experiences ordinarily do have a certain perception-like quality.[48]

NOTES

[1] See especially C 23, ii-v. Sanson describes this condition as one of psychological and affective discontinuity, while Eulogio speaks of moral disequilibrium (see Sanson 1953, pp. 49-65; Eulogio 1961, pp. 38-44).

[2] See, for example, A I, 8, i-vii; 9, vi; III, 3, ii-iii; 19, iii-iv; 22, ii; 25, i-vi; F 3, lxx-lxxiv. The appetites are able to exert this negative influence upon the intellect only because of the close relationship between the sensory and spiritual parts of human nature. The devil, because he is incorporeal, lacks such appetites, and his intellect enjoys "clear natural light"; see, for example, A II, 21, vii-xii.

[3] It should be noted that the stanza from which this passage is taken does not appear in the first redaction of the *Canticle*. However, for the purposes of this study I am accepting redaction B as authentic. Moreover, I am not convinced by Baruzi's claim that this stanza is out of keeping with the rest of the poem (see Baruzi 1924, pp. 19-21).

[4] Elsewhere John uses the phrase "substantial union" for a permanent transformation of the soul in God, which is the goal of the spiritual life (see, for example, C 26, xi). He is also careful to stress, however, that the substance of the soul and God's substance always remain ontologically distinct, even in the highest mystical absorption (see, for example, C 31, i; F 2, xxxiv).

[5] Other authors who discuss John's teaching on the continuity between mystical union and the natural presence of God in the soul include Bendick 1972, pp. 287-288; Sanson 1953, pp. 65-82; Sanchez de Murillo 1976, pp. 283-286. Edith Stein points out that it is not a matter of many distinct "presences," but different modifications of the one divine presence (see Stein 1960, p. 132).

[6] Among contemporary Catholic theologians, Karl Rahner shows a similar concern with the continuity between God's natural and supernatural presence to the soul (see, for example, Rahner 1966b, pp. 165-188). Rahner would argue that even the "substantial presence" of God in the soul affects human awareness; everyone is thereby conscious transcendentally (though not thematically) of the divine as infinite mystery (see Rahner 1978, pp. 21-23, 51-71, 76-81, 170-171).

[7] Here and in subsequent paragraphs I am relying heavily on Ruiz Salvador 1968, pp. 292-293.

[8] Not all commentators agree on the number and order of the successive nights in the Sanjuanist system. Chapman argues that there are only *two* nights, and that "the active and passive are two sides of the same phenomenon," indicating respectively what the soul does and what God accomplishes in the nights of sense and spirit (see Chapman 1959, p. 80). This view has gained little acceptance among Sanjuanist scholars, however (see Dicken 1963, p. 223). By contrast, Juan de Jesús María, from whom many of the points in this section have been taken, apparently holds that there are *four* purifications which

follow in this order: the active night of sense, the passive night of sense, the active night of spirit, and the passive night of spirit (see Juan de Jesús María 1943, p. 44). This would evidently mean that beginners are in the active night of sense, while the active night of the spirit is restricted to proficients. Finally, Zabalza adds a further refinement to P. Juan's position, by maintaining that "the active night of sense and partially that of the spirit pertain to the state of beginners" (see Zabalza 1963, p. 130). These disputes need not be resolved here. In my opinion, the precise enumeration and delimitation of the different nights is less important, for John, than the recognition that the journey toward God requires a progressive and ever more intimate purification. The scheme adopted in the following pages is accurate enough for the purposes of this study.

[9] See Juan de Jesús María 1943, pp. 48-50. Oddly enough, though he cites the same article, Trueman Dicken shows some confusion about the relationship between the "three reasons" and the active and passive nights. He says at first that the "threefold division is based upon a *temporal* sequence," while the "other division is essentially a *logical* one"; this statement, however, is apparently corrected a few pages later (see Dicken 1963, pp. 225-229).

[10] Compare, for example, Crisógono 1929, 1:308-309; Emeterio del Sagrado Corazón 1959, pp. 48-49; Zabalza 1963, pp. 129-140. Federico agrees that these questions are of secondary importance (see Ruiz Salvador 1968, pp. 490-494).

[11] See also C 1, i, a passage added in redaction B to relate the early stanzas more closely to the state of beginners. The term "twice-born" is from James 1961, pp. 163ff. (see also Ruiz Salvador 1968, pp. 501-504; Zabalza 1963, p. 121; Dicken 1963, pp. 245-247).

[12] It is perhaps worth noting that in the Sanlucar codex of redaction A, the reference to meditation is inserted in the Saint's own hand (see *Cántico A* 27, iii in *Vida y Obras*).

[13] See Morel 1960, 2: 145-148. Bord makes the interesting suggestion that the verses from the "Drawing of the Mount" follow the division of the soul into faculties and substance, so that "satisfaction" corresponds to the will, "possession" to the memory, "being" to the substance of the soul, and "knowledge" to the intellect (see Bord 1971, pp. 119-121). In any case, these same verses have earned John the title of "Doctor of the Nada" (see Peers 1944, p. 124).

[14] John says that committed beginners arrive at this state "in a very short time." St. Teresa indicates that the transition can occur in as little as six months after undertaking a serious program of prayer (see Teresa's *Way of Perfection* 29, ii).

[15] Compare N I, 9, i-ix and "Maxims on Love" #40 in *Collected Works* ("Puntos de Amor" #118 in *Vida y Obras*); see also A Prologue, vi. John apparently derived his three signs from the Taulerian *Institutions* (see Orcibal 1966, pp. 124-127). For a good discussion of these three signs, see Dicken 1963, pp. 145-152.

[16] In the same place, Horsburgh writes that "the greatest mystics appear to have been eminently sane men with a handsome disrespect for the phenomena of hysteria, self-hypnosis, and the like. Nobody, for example, can read St. John of the Cross with an open mind without being checked between facile explanations." (Horsburgh 1972, p. 65)

[17] This accounts for the difference in the third sign of the *Ascent* and the corresponding sign (the second) in the *Night*. As Dicken explains, the "pain and solicitude" described in the *Night* is an inchoate form of the "loving awareness" described in the *Ascent*, and develops into the latter once the soul becomes tranquil (see Dicken 1963, 150-152).

[18] John's directive to forego discursive prayer is not unqualified, however; he notes that there are moments, especially near the beginning of the passive night, when further med-

itation is profitable, and adds that some souls are never led beyond the need for it (see A II, 15, i-v; N I, 9, ix).

[19] Today many authors would classify these "touches" as "introvertive mystical experiences" (see, for example, Stace 1960a, pp. 85-111; Stace 1960b, pp. 17-23, 185-187; Nielsen 1971, p. 49). Whether or not the contemplative states John discusses are correctly described as experiences of *God*, and fit all of the proposed criteria for "introvertive mystical experiences," is a question we will address below.

[20] John speaks of a certain "I-don't-know-what" behind the "stammering" of creatures (*Un no sé qué que quedan balbuciendo*); see C 7, i-x; 8, i. See also the entire discussion of creatures in stanzas 5 through 7 of the *Canticle*, as well as C 22, iii, which applies these verses to those who have embarked "upon the contemplative way." Though the exact nature of this contemplative experience of creatures is not entirely clear from his descriptions, it seems to resemble what some modern authors call an "intuition" (or "contuition") of God and creatures together (see Shepherd 1975, p. 29). Mascall, for example, speaks of "the common experience of people making their first retreat, that after the first day or so natural objects seem to acquire a peculiar character of transparency and vitality, so that they appear as only very thinly veiling the creative activity of God" (Mascall 1943, p. 80). At its most intense, this experience apparently corresponds to what are sometimes called "extrovertive mystical experiences" (see Stace 1960a, pp. 62-81).

[21] It is difficult to determine exactly what these experiences are like, but in a corporal vision of an angel, for example, visionaries would actually seem to see a physical form, whereas in an imaginary vision they would be aware that the experience did not involve actual seeing; a purely spiritual vision of an angel might involve clear concepts, but not sensory images. St. Teresa experienced frequent imaginative visions, which she describes in detail (see Dicken 1963, pp. 386-391).

[22] Rahner 1963, pp. 56-57; compare also A II, 29, i-v and Johnston 1971, pp. 77-80. Thus the proficient's abnormal experiences could be described in psychological terms as "hypnagogic phenomena" (involving the translation of psychic activity into "complex visual, verbal, conceptual, and activity images") or instances of "sensory translation" (involving the "experience of nonverbal, simple, concrete perceptual equivalents of psychic action"); see Deikman's 'Deautomatization and the Mystic Experience' (1980, p. 254). An intense impression of God's love, for example, might be subconsciously "translated" into a vision of Jesus saying "I love you."

[23] See also A II, 16, iii-xii; 17, i-ix; 18, iii; 21, ii; 23, iv; III, 10, i. According to John, while God reluctantly grants corporal or imaginary visions to elicit love and lead the person to higher communications, the devil produces them in order to lead the soul astray.

[24] Notice again that the expression "mystical theology" here refers to the contemplative experience of God rather than to systematic theological reflection upon that experience; note too that John never uses the noun "mysticism," preferring instead the corresponding adjective "mystical."

[25] The trials of this period would seem to include those which, according to John, sometimes characterize the passive night of sense, e.g., temptations of the flesh, a "blasphemous spirit," and scruples; see N I, 14, i-iii. Compare Dicken 1963, pp. 255-258, and Underhill 1955, pp. 226-231, 380-382.

[26] Delaye 1975, p. 10. I am following Delaye closely throughout this section. For relevant Sanjuanist passages, see, for example, A I, 2, iii; N I, 11, iv; II, 2, v; C Prologue, ii; F 3, xlvii; lxxx. Thus Mouroux says that John "reiterates the rich biblical vocabu-

lary," and that "for him, faith envelopes our spiritual life on earth" (Mouroux 1964, p. 277).

27 According to the Kavanaugh/Rodriguez translation, "proficients think that their *blessings* are more spiritual than formerly" (my emphasis). I believe, however, that mine is a better translation of this particular text, which reads, "las imperfecciones de éstos...son más incurables por tenerlas ellos por más espirituales que las primeras."

28 Once again, this phase may be described from a psychological point of view as "a period of fatigue and lassitude following a period of sustained mystical activity" (Underhill 1955, p. 382). Dicken argues that it involves a "ligature of the higher faculties" comparable to the previous ligature of the senses; just as individuals were deprived of sensible consolation in the first passive night, so now they are deprived of spiritual consolation (Dicken 1963, pp. 262-263).

29 Thus Morel's *Le Sens de l'Existence selon S. Jean de la Croix* is often described as an "Hegelianization" of Sanjuanist thought, while Baruzi is accused of assimilating John to Plotinus (see Sanchez de Murillo 1976, pp. 267-274). Leslie Dewart appeals to John in support of his proposals for a dehellenized Christian theism (Dewart 1966, pp. 58-59, 122-123); Michael Buckley relates John's "nights" to Freud's and Feuerbach's critiques of religion as projection (Buckley 1979, pp. 680-699). Comparisons between John and Nietzsche can be found in Thibon's *Nietzsche und der heilige Johannes vom Kreuz* (Thibon 1957), Morel's 'Sur Nietzsche et Jean de la Croix' (1970), and Orville Clark (Clark 1972); Clark also invokes Hegel and Heidegger. An interesting reinterpretation of John's "nights" from a moderate feminist perspective may be found in Constance FitzGerald's 'Impasse and Dark Night' (1984, pp. 93-116), frequently cited in contemporary studies of feminist spirituality.

30 Some of John's descriptions of this state clearly reflect his own spiritual and physical trials during his incarceration in Toledo; he says, for example, that the soul at this time "resembles one who is imprisoned in a dark dungeon, bound hands and feet, and able neither to move, nor see, nor feel any favor from heaven or earth" (N II, 7, iii).

31 In fact, John claims that those who undergo the passive night of the spirit are spared most of the sufferings of purgatory, since they are already purged. This suggests a certain continuity between those two purifications; even after death, the same divine love continues to draw the soul toward beatitude (see, for example, N II, 6, vi; 7, vii; 10, v; 12, i-iv; 20, v; F I, xxi-xxiv; 2, xxv).

32 Ninian Smart writes, for example, that "there is quite a difference between mystical experience and prophetic and, more generally, numinous experience" (Smart 1967c, 'Mysticism, History of,' *Encyclopedia of Philosophy* vol. 5, p. 420; see also Smart 1970, pp. 120-122, 139-140; and Smart 1958). Other authors have adopted this distinction from Smart; see, for example, Gimello's 'Mysticism and Meditation' (1978, pp. 171-172). If Smart is merely claiming that the kinds of experiences which John associates with the passive nights are different from the joyful experiences of union, then I agree; however, if he is claiming that these represent two separate and unrelated strands of experience (as he sometimes seems to suggest), then I would argue that this does not do justice to the experience of Christian mystics.

33 As noted above, the changes between redactions A and B of the *Canticle* make it more difficult to correlate "espousal" precisely with the schema of "nights" and "ways" in the *Ascent-Night*. Moreover, John sometimes uses "espousal" to refer to the state of spiritual marriage as well (see, for example, N II, 24, iii; C 23, vi; 27, iv-viii; 28, x; 30, i; F 1, xxiv). In my opinion, however, Zabalza has convincingly demonstrated the identity of

spiritual espousal with the final phase of the passive night of the spirit, though his arguments cannot be reviewed here (see Zabalza 1963, pp. 90-110).

[34] C 19, iv also speaks of "a touch of naked substances—of the soul and the divinity." Once again, John teaches that these visits only cause rapture in the beginning, before the soul has become completely purified; later they are received more gently, without bodily rigidity and the loss of sensation (see C 13, ii-vii; 14 & 15, xvi-xxi; and Zabalza 1963, pp. 39-50).

[35] Since such experiences presumably involve sense perception, and therefore (according to the scholastic account) the sensible species to which perception gives rise, it is hard to understand why John suggests that they are received "when these spiritual faculties are alone and empty of all natural forms and apprehensions" (C 14 & 15, xxvi). Perhaps, like other mystics, John is only trying to say that at such moments the contemplative experiences the world afresh, as if for the first time. Stace defines an extrovertive mystical experience as one in which a person perceives objects in the world "transfigured in such manner that the Unity shines through them," and goes on to claim that the theist automatically identifies this unity with God (Stace 1960b, pp. 15-17). While I am not entirely satisfied with this, it must be admitted that some of John's statements seem to fit Stace's characterization fairly well; for example, in an expression later modified in the final version of the *Canticle*, John says that the soul "feels that all things are God in one simple being" (CA 13 & 14, v).

[36] See also N II, 7, iv; 10, vi; 13, x; C 16, i; viii; 17, iv-x; 18, iii; 20 & 21, xiv; and Zabalza 1963, pp. 71-74, 105-110. This experience apparently gives the contemplative a new "connatural" knowledge of God, through the virtues which God imparts. This ostensible knowledge is especially interesting because it is grounded in the person's mystical experiences (which communicate these virtues) but not in the way ordinarily presumed by philosophical critics of knowledge claims based on religious experience.

[37] John attributes some of these fears and distractions to the devil (see N II, 23, iv-x; C 16, ii-vii; 20 & 21, ix). More recent spiritual writers suggest that the contemplative concentration on God in the passive night of the spirit (and hence here) allows previously repressed ideas and impulses to surface.

[38] A comparison with the *Night* suggests that, at least in some cases, the passive night of the spirit may be precipitated by the passing of such "visits," which causes the soul to suspect that her blessings are gone forever (see N II, 7, iv-vii; 10, viii-x). This shows the difficulty of determining the precise chronological relationship between the passive night of the spirit and spiritual espousal.

[39] One of the difficulties for commentators is that C 22, iii seems to claim that the "unitive way" begins with spiritual espousal. Zabalza argues convincingly, however, that espousal belongs to the illuminative way, and that therefore spiritual marriage and the unitive way are coterminous (Zabalza 1963, pp. 111-140). In any case, it is clear that espousal represents a period of transition to the final state.

[40] This passage appears in C 22, iv in Kavanaugh/Rodriguez. See also C 21 & 22, xv; 26, iv.

[41] In *Canticle* 14 & 15, v, John explicitly denies that the espoused soul's experience of creatures is comparable to seeing "creatures by means of God." See also C 39, xi; F 4, iv-vii; and Zabalza 1963, pp. 56-57.

[42] Compare A II, 27, i; C 1, vi; 7, iii-vii; 13, xi; 23, i-vi; 37, i-viii; 39, iii-vi; F Prologue, ii; 1, vi; xv; 2, i; 3, ii-xvii; lxxxii. It is worth noting that the mysteries John picks out are essentially those which Rahner describes as the three intrinsically related

"*mysteria stricte dicta*" of the Christian faith, i.e., "the Trinity, the Incarnation and the divinization of man in grace and glory" (see 'The Concept of Mystery in Catholic Theology' in Rahner 1966a, p. 65).

[43] The corresponding passages in *Canticle A* speak less reservedly about the soul in the state of spiritual marriage experiencing these deep mysteries. In redaction B, however, John is more careful to distinguish the clear vision of beatitude from the limited foretaste which a person may enjoy in spiritual marriage.

[44] See also **A** II, 5, v-vii; III, 2, viii-ix; **N** II, 6, i; 13, xi; **C** 22, iii-v; 27, vii; 36, v; 39, iii-v; **F** 1, xxvii; 2, xxxiii-xxxiv; 3, lxxviii; 'Maxims on Love' #28 ('Puntos de Amor' #106 in *Vida y Obras*). Compare Rahner's claim that "the prerogatives which accrue *intrinsically* to the human reality of Jesus through the hypostatic union are of the same essential nature as those which are also intended for other spiritual subjects through grace" (Rahner 1978, p. 200).

[45] Compare **C** 13, xi; 37, viii; 39, ii-vi; xiv; **F** 1, iii-vi; xv; 2, i-xvii; 3, lxxviii-lxxxii. Rahner praises John for offering "a true mysticism of the Trinity," in 'Remarks on the Dogmatic Treatise "De Trinitate"' (Rahner 1966c, p. 79).

[46] An excellent critique of such theories of may be found in Wainwright 1975, pp. 405-426 (reprinted in Wainwright 1981, pp. 160-184). Wainwright likewise notes that the Sanjuanist passages which Maritain cites "do not compel us to adopt" his theory, and are "equally compatible" with other accounts (Wainwright 1981, p. 174). Moreover, as I have already shown, John describes *infused contemplation* as an experience which occurs "without the mediation of any species or idea."

[47] Compare also **A** II, 3, v; 24, iv; 26, v; **N** II, 12, iv; **C** 13, x; 14 & 15, xvi; 26, iv; 39, ix-xiv; **F** 1, xiv; xxvii-xxxii; 3, x-xv; lxxviii-lxxxi. Aquinas, on the other hand, says that "the sight of the blessed is not distinguished from the sight of those in this life because the former see more perfectly and the latter less perfectly, but because the former see and the latter to not see" (see *De Veritate* XVIII, 1, and also the response to the fourth difficulty). The disagreement may be only apparent, however, since, as we saw above, Aquinas believed that certain rare individuals had been given an immediate experience of God prior to death, through the supernatural suspension of natural limitations.

[48] This is not to claim that *all* of the mystic's alleged experimental knowledge of God is non-inferential. Those in the state of spiritual marriage might say that, in addition to their "immediate awareness" of the divine, they *also* know something of God through the virtues infused in their souls.

CHAPTER FOUR

SOME TRANSITIONAL OBSERVATIONS ON THE NATURE OF CHRISTIAN MYSTICISM AND THE DATA TO BE EXPLAINED

The foregoing summary of the doctrine of St. John of the Cross is by no means complete. Nevertheless, it covers those areas of his teaching with the greatest bearing on philosophical controversies about the nature and significance of mysticism and religious experience. Now I want to treat some of these philosophical issues in a more systematic way, beginning with some further reflections on the general notion of mysticism and the phenomena with which it is associated.

As explained in the Introduction, most Anglo-American philosophers seem to have little acquaintance with classic mystical texts, and therefore tend to base their evaluations of mysticism on the facile and sometimes misleading generalizations found in the secondary literature on the subject. Here, however, we have begun with a careful study of a single mystical author, and have closely followed his own forms of thought and expression before making any attempt to specify the meaning of key terms such as "mysticism" or "union." Thus in the preceding pages I have simply adopted the Sanjuanist practice of referring to certain contemplative states as "divine communications" imparting "loving knowledge of God," without directly addressing the crucial question of whether such "highly ramified" descriptions of these experiences are justified. Though this approach has its own dangers, it appears to avoid those created by the premature and uncritical acceptance of a particular definition of mysticism which might not adequately fit the facts.

However, now that the initial survey of John's teaching is finished, some additional observations about the phenomena he describes are required to set the stage for what is to follow. For example, in order to explore the possibility of defending the cognitive value of mysticism through an "argument to the best explanation" in the sixth chapter, I will first need a clearer statement of what I regard as the facts to be explained. Moreover, this line of defense would obviously be unavailable if there were conclusive reasons *in advance* of any "explanatory inference" for rejecting mystical and religious experience as a "way of knowing." Yet many philosophers, whose views will be examined in Chapter Five, apparently think that there are such reasons. Since I will be claiming that their arguments often rest on popular but defective notions of what mysticism actually involves, I should indicate precisely where I feel such notions go astray.

The present chapter, therefore, will be divided into two parts. In the first, certain representative descriptions of the nature of mystical experience will be evaluated in the light of what we have already learned from St. John of the Cross. The second will contain a more organized summary of some of the data upon which an "argument to the best explanation" might be based.

4.1. Toward a More Adequate Characterization of Christian Mysticism

Though most of us assume that we would recognize a mystical experience if we had one or heard it recounted, the notion of mysticism itself is notoriously difficult to pin down. Many authors apparently feel that the ideal solution to this difficulty would be a general characterization of mysticism indicating the phenomenal properties shared by all mystical experiences. Moreover, certain philosophers have tried to develop lists of these "common characteristics" by comparing mystical writings from various periods and cultures, with mixed results. Before examining some of their proposals to see how well they fit the experiences John describes, I want to comment briefly on a few of the broader philosophical issues raised by the whole effort to determine the nature of mysticism in general.

One extremely important and complex issue has to do with the effects of an author's prior beliefs about mysticism upon the definition he or she proposes. Though some philosophers imply that they are merely providing a less theory-laden phenomenological description of mystical states based on a purely objective analysis of the primary sources, matters are hardly so simple, since "in selecting reports they are selecting those which contain interpretations they can believe and propagate" (Horne 1978, p. 17; compare Kennick 1962, p. 387, and Pletcher 1972, pp. 7-10). For example, partly because of their different attitudes toward Christian spirituality, Underhill regards St. Paul as a mystic "of the first rank" and draws upon his writings in developing her own account of mysticism, whereas Stace is uncertain whether Paul is a genuine mystic at all and therefore makes no significant use of his letters (see Underhill 1955, pp. 178, 367-368, 437, 455; Stace 1960a, pp. 48-49; and Stace 1960b, pp. 125-126). Here and elsewhere the conclusions drawn from the study of different reports will depend upon which reports one regards as authentic accounts of mystical experiences, and this in turn will depend upon one's previous notion of what such states must be like. It is also clear that attempts to identify the "common core" of mysticism can easily fall into a kind of vicious circularity when an author simply refuses to admit that any alleged counter-example either has a different character or counts as a genuine instance of mystical experience. This seems to be the case, for example, with some Christian writers who start from the conviction that all mystical experiences involve an awareness of God; when confronted with the testimony of those Eastern contemplatives who deliberately avoid theistic terminology in their reports (e.g., Theravada Buddhists), they are forced to argue that the latter are not true mystics or that they have systematically misinterpreted their experiences. As we begin to evaluate some standard accounts of the nature of mysticism, we will need to be especially on guard against such question-begging maneuvers in their defense.

However, despite my objections in the following pages to certain well-known attempts to list the "marks of mystical states," I do not intend to offer any alternative list of my own. In fact, though the point will not be argued here, I suspect that the deeper problem with such efforts is that mystical phenomena, like language-games, "have no one thing in common which makes us use the same word for all, —but...are *related* to one another in different ways."[1] This would certainly explain why previously proposed inventories of mysticism's identifying properties are invariably criticized either for being so narrow that they fail to cover significant strands of mysticism, or for being so broad that they include other kinds of experiences as well. In any case, it seems that for most purposes a more informal characterization which appeals to our ordinary intuitions about the meaning of "mysticism" and "mystical experience" is often sufficient, at least initially. In *Reasons and Faiths*, for example, Ninian Smart starts from the modest assertion "that a mystical experience is one which is reported by a class of persons generally referred to as 'mystics'—such men as Eckhart, St. John of the Cross, Plotinus, the Buddha, Sankara and so on," who have undertaken "a certain sort of mystical discipline."[2] Despite its vagueness, this approach at least has the advantage of not assuming in advance that mysticism is "everywhere the same." (Though Smart *believes* that it is, his initial characterization of mysticism does not necessarily *commit* him to this view.)

Nevertheless, some writers do claim to have ascertained the common features of all mystical experiences, and their accounts deserve serious and detailed consideration, especially since they are often invoked in discussions of the cognitive value of mysticism. Since not all such accounts can be evaluated here, I have chosen instead to concentrate on the influential theories of William James and W. T. Stace, for two reasons. First of all, their writings provide what are perhaps the clearest, best-known, and most widely accepted accounts of mysticism's identifying characteristics. Thus authors who draw upon James's account include Rem B. Edwards (1972, pp. 302-322), William Ernest Hocking (1928, p. 390) and Wallace I. Matson (1965, p. 20), while "Stace's typology of mystical experience" in particular "has been adopted by a number of social scientists," philosophers and theologians, with important methodological consequences (Wainwright 1981, p. 7).[3] Second, both authors include St. John of the Cross among the sources from whom they claim to have drawn their conclusions. One obvious way of testing their theories, therefore, is to check them against the Sanjuanist texts, to see if they really do seem to fit the experiences John describes, as we intend to do in the following pages.

In *The Varieties of Religious Experience*, then, James lists four characteristics which identify a state of consciousness as mystical:

1. *Ineffability.*—...The subject of it immediately says that it defies expression, that no adequate report of its contents can be given in words....
2. *Noetic quality.*—Although so similar to states of feeling, mystical states seem to those who experience them to be also states of knowledge. They are states of insight into depths of truth unplumbed by the discursive intellect...
3. *Transiency.*—Mystical experiences cannot be sustained for long. Except in rare instances, half an hour, or at most an hour or two, seem to be the limit beyond which they fade into the light of common day.... But when they recur it is recognized; and from one recurrence to another it is susceptible of continuous development in what is felt as inner richness and importance.
4. *Passivity.*—Although the oncoming of mystical states may be facilitated by preliminary voluntary operations, as by fixing the attention, or going through certain bodily performances, or in other ways which manuals of mysticism prescribe; yet when the characteristic sort of consciousness once has set in, the mystic feels as if his own will were in abeyance, and indeed sometimes as if he were grasped and held by a superior power. (James 1936, pp. 371-372)

James goes on to add that the "overcoming of all the usual barriers between the individual and the Absolute is the great mystic achievement" (Ibid., p. 410). We will return to these claims in a moment.

In *Mysticism and Philosophy*, Walter Stace draws a fundamental distinction between "two types of mystical consciousness, the extrovertive and the introvertive," which are related to one another as "two species of one genus" (Stace 1960a, p. 131). The former involves a perception of "the mutiplicity of external material objects—the sea, the sky, the houses, the trees—mystically transfigured so that the One, or the Unity, shines through" (Ibid., 61). In introvertive experiences, however, this awareness of the external world is lost; the mind is emptied of "the entire multiplicity of sensations, images, and thoughts," and the mystic experiences union with "the wholly naked One devoid of all plurality" (Ibid., p. 62).[4] Stace then identifies the key features of both states (Ibid., pp. 131-132):

Common Characteristics of Extrovertive Mystical Experiences	Common Characteristics of Introvertive Mystical Experiences
1. The Unifying Vision—all things are One	1. The Unitary Consciousness; the One, the Void; pure consciousness
2. The more concrete apprehension of the One as an inner subjectivity, or life, in all things	2. Nonspatial, nontemporal

3. Sense of objectivity or reality
4. Blessedness, peace, etc.
5. Feeling of the holy, sacred, or divine
6. Paradoxicality
7. Alleged by mystics to be ineffable

3. Sense of objectivity or reality
4. Blessedness, peace, etc.
5. Feeling of the holy, sacred, or divine
6. Paradoxicality
7. Alleged by mystics to be ineffable

According to Stace, then, both types of experience share properties 3 through 7, and both involve an apprehension of ultimate unity, which is "the very inner essence" of mysticism and forms "the nucleus round which the other more peripheral characteristics revolve" (Ibid., pp. 132-133).[5] Extrovertive and introvertive states differ only with respect to the first two properties, which concern the way in which this basic unity is experienced.

As I explained above, I want to test the accounts of James and Stace just summarized by seeing if the characteristics listed fit the states John describes. This evaluation can be somewhat simplified by noticing that there is a certain amount of overlap between the two accounts. Thus, Stace himself associates what he calls the "sense of objectivity or reality" (the third property in his lists) with the "noetic quality" mentioned by James, and the latter's mark of "ineffability" obviously corresponds to Stace's more cautiously phrased seventh feature, i.e., "alleged by mystics to be ineffable" (see Stace 1960a, pp. 44, 67-68, 70, 79, 278). Consequently, we need not discuss each characteristic separately; in addition, features which John clearly accepts or which have little bearing on the question of mysticism's cognitive value can also be handled rather briefly.

A more difficult problem is to decide which of the many psychological states treated by St. John of the Cross should be considered in checking the theories of James and Stace. In order to prove that their accounts can accommodate the data of the Sanjuanist texts, it is not enough to show that *some* of the states analyzed therein possess some or all of the features listed; in fact, for the sake of argument one may grant that the Christian mystics do sometimes enjoy experiences of the sort described by our two authors. Since Stace and James claim to be identifying the *universal* marks of mysticism, the question is rather whether *all* of the "typical and central mystical states" treated by John have *all* of these marks (Stace 1960a, p. 46). Moreover, it is necessary to focus on *clear* instances of mystical experience, since Stace hedges his bets by admitting that there are "borderline cases,...in which some but not all of the defining characteristics appear" (Ibid., p. 81). If we find John describing experiences which are clearly mystical but which lack some of the characteristics listed by James and Stace, this will indicate that their theories are inadequate or incomplete as general accounts of the nature of mysticism.

But how do we determine which states in the Sanjuanist texts should be considered clearly mystical for the purposes of this evaluation? Do we limit ourselves to the "visits" and "enkindlings" that occur during spiritual espousal and marriage? Do we also include the ecstasies of the proficient and the painful experiences of the passive night of the spirit? What about the first stirrings of contemplation at the beginning of the illuminative way? John provides little direct assistance here; as we have already seen, he never uses the expression "mystical experience," but speaks instead of "infused contemplation," "secret wisdom," "loving knowledge," "touches of union" and so on. Nor do we want to beg the question in favor of James and Stace by identifying mystical states as those which fit their theories. However, both authors cite passages from John's works which *they* regard as descriptions of mystical experiences and support for their claims. It seems fair and reasonable, therefore, to test their lists of mysticism's common features agains the kinds of experiences treated in these quotations, especially since they offer no other evidence that their theories can adequately handle the Sanjuanist data.

The section on mysticism in *The Varieties of Religious Experience* contains only two quotations from St. John of the Cross, which James clearly regards as descriptions of mystical experience. The first, taken from a general discussion of "the secrecy of dark contemplation" in *Night* II, 17, iii-vi, is presented as further corroboration of mysticism's ineffability (James 1936, pp. 398-399).[6] The second, from *Ascent* II, 26, vi-vii, deals with the "divine touches" of union, which John elsewhere associates particularly with spiritual espousal and marriage; but there is no indication that James himself means to restrict the application of the expression "mystical experience" to states occuring only in the final phases of the spiritual life (James 1936, p. 405).[7] In fact, the combination of both passages suggests that the nearest equivalent to this expression in the Sanjuanist vocabulary is the term "contemplation." That is to say, it seems that James uses "mystical experience" to cover approximately the same range of states which John would characterize as involving infused contemplation, at least in its more intense forms.

There is even stronger evidence that the same is true for Stace. The four Sanjuanist passages cited as evidence for the "universal core" hypothesis in chapter 7 of *Mysticism and Philosophy* are drawn from a section of *Ascent* II which deals, not with the most advanced spiritual illuminations, but with the first beginnings of contemplative prayer.[8] Furthermore, remarks in *Teachings of the Mystics* indicate that Stace also regards the painful contemplation of the "dark night" as a mystical state, since he argues that the suffering is largely an "emotional reaction" to an awareness of undifferentiated unity, and consequently "does not invalidate the hypothesis of the fundamental sameness of the experience everywhere" (p. 186).

In short, both James and Stace seem to suggest that their theories ought to apply to the whole range of contemplative phenomena occurring in the "illuminative" and "unitive" ways, and not merely to some small subset of these experiences. We may therefore evaluate their accounts by seeing whether the proposed lists of mysticism's defining characteristics actually fit the broad spectrum of contemplative states described in the Sanjuanist texts (e.g., the "dark contemplation" of the passive nights, the "actual union" of the substance of the soul, the "transitory unions" of substance and faculties), as we would naturally expect if these theories are true.

Before dealing with particular characteristics, however, something should be said about Stace's influential claim that there are basically "two main types of [mystical] experience, the extrovertive and the introvertive" (Stace 1960a, p. 61). Here Stace seems to have put his finger on an important distinction between mystical states which in some sense have nature or the external world as their "object," and those which do not (cf. Wainwright 1977, p. 993 and 1981, pp. 8-11, who makes a number of helpful observations on this distinction, some of which I have followed here). Thus, to use the examples mentioned earlier, there is an evident difference between those contemplative experiences in which God's "creatures and works" are perceived as a "harmonious symphony of sublime music" (C 14 & 15, xxv), and the divine "visits" and "touches" in which all sensory awareness seems to be excluded (see N II, 23, xi-xiv; C 13, i-vi). Yet it seems doubtful that *all* mystical states can be squeezed into one or the other of these categories, especially as they are presented. As noted above, for example, John indicates that those in the "unitive way" sometimes enjoy an "essential knowledge" of "creatures through God," which he distinguishes from the apprehension of "God through creatures" that Stace associates with extrovertive mysticism; yet the former experience seems seems to include some awareness of creation, which is supposedly absent in introvertive states (cf. pp. 80-81 above). Again, Stace recognizes that "there are rare cases in which the mystical consciousness is believed to become permanent, running concurrently with, and in some way fused and integrated with, the normal or common consciousness"; this is the state John refers to as "spiritual marriage" or the "unitive way."[9] But this permanent mystical consciousness is difficult to classify as "introvertive," since it is not devoid of all empirical content; nor can Stace call it "extrovertive" without undermining his claim that introvertive mysticism is higher and more "complete" (Stace 1960a, pp. 132-133). I also hope to show that some mystical states which lack ordinary empirical contents are nevertheless not merely "pure consciousness" without any content whatsoever, but have instead a phenomenally theistic character. It seems unlikely, then, that there are only two basic kinds of mystical experience. With this in mind, let us turn our attention to some of the individual features mentioned by James and Stace.

In the first place, St. John of the Cross clearly acknowledges that contemplative states (with the possible exception of those occurring in the "passive nights") have a *noetic quality* and are marked by a sense of *objectivity or reality*. This is part of the reason that John uses perceptual metaphors (e.g., vision, touch) in describing them, and constantly refers to contemplation as a "loving knowledge" or "secret wisdom" imparted to the soul (see above, pp. 30-31 and 67-68). Thus it is rather misleading for philosophers to characterize mystical experiences as subjective "feeling-states" (like depression or pain) from which the recipient merely *infers* the existence and nature of their cause.[10] Instead, an intentional character is part of mystical consciousness itself, and convinces the mystic that his or her experience has "objective reference," whether this conviction is true or not.[11]

Second, John admits the *transiency* of many mystical states. He notes, for example, that the absorption and "union of the faculties" cannot be "continuous in this life," but only in the next (C 26, xi).[12] However, this impermanence is not a universal feature of contemplative experiences, since, as Stace realizes, certain rare individuals attain a more or less continual mystical awareness (and could perhaps be expected to give clearer and more reliable descriptions of mystic states, other things being equal).

Third, St. John of the Cross would undoubtedly agree with Stace that these experiences generally involve a sense of *blessedness, peace, etc.*, and a *feeling of the holy, sacred, or divine*. This is clear from everything said in previous chapters, which we need not now review. The only possible exception would again be the painful contemplation of the passive nights, which produces suffering precisely by imparting a more intense realization of the holiness of God, though even here, John insists that "there is nothing in contemplation...which of itself can give pain," and that "the cause for not experiencing these agreeable effects" in the passive nights "is the soul's weakness and imperfection" (N II, 9, xi).

Stace also affirms in the fourth place that introvertive experiences are *nonspatial* and *nontemporal;* other authors argue that a sense of timelessness is a component of extrovertive experiences as well (see Wainwright 1977, p. 993; idem 1981, p. 10; Rowe 1978, p. 66). John himself says surprisingly little on the subject, merely noting that one is often "unaware of time" during contemplative prayer (A II, 14, xi; compare A III, 2, vi). Nevertheless, there seems to be no harm in granting that many (though not all) mystical states have these phenomenal features. They raise philosophical problems only insofar as the mystic goes on to *deny* the reality of space and time, a conclusion which is scarcely inevitable and which the Mystical Doctor never draws.[13]

The next two characteristics (paradoxicality and ineffability) both have to do with the mystic's use of language. In the fifth place, then, some of John's statements about mystical experience do clearly manifest a certain oddness and *paradoxicality*. Thus he uses striking poetic images such as "silent music," "sounding solitude," and "delightful wound" to describe various contemplative states (see C 14 & 15, xxv-xxvii; 24, vi; F 3, i-xv), and characterizes the "divine light of contemplation" as a "ray of darkness" which "illumines and purges" the soul (N II, 5, i-iii). Yet St. John takes no special delight in perplexing his readers, and carefully explains what he means by these unusual expressions.[14] Moreover, his remarks do not seem to lend any serious support to Stace's dubious explanation of mysticism's paradoxicality. The latter holds that mystical consciousness typically gives rise to a variety of paradoxes, including:

> the pantheistic paradox that God and the world are both identical and nonidentical or distinct; ...the positive-negative or plenum-vacuum paradox with its three aspects, that the One or the Universal Mind is both qualitied and unqualitied, both personal and unpersonal, both static and dynamic; ...the paradox of the dissolution of individuality wherein I cease to be individual and yet retain my individuality.... (Stace 1960a, p. 253)

He goes on to deny that these apparent inconsistencies can be explained away as the product of mere rhetorical exaggeration, misdescription, or the ambiguous use of terms, and maintains instead that they represent "outright logical contradictions" which are nevertheless "a literally correct description" of the mystic's experience (Ibid., pp. 268 and 300; see also 253-270, 298-306). This position is feasible, according to Stace, because the principles of logic are only applicable to "those experiences, realms, or worlds where there is a plurality of existences," and not "to the undifferentiated unity of the mystic" (Ibid., p. 271). His arguments in favor of this peculiar claim about the scope of logic have already been effectively criticized elsewhere, and need not be reviewed here (see Wainwright 1970, pp. 148-154; Ibid. 1981, pp. 145-154; Hepburn 1967a, *Encyclopedia of Philosophy*, Vol. 5, pp. 430-432). However, two additional criticisms of Stace's position seem in order. First, I am not convinced that mysticism typically evokes and elicits *all* of the paradoxical assertions he mentions, especially since some of them (e.g., the claim that the Absolute is impersonal) do not appear in the writings of John and other Christian mystics, at least not in any problematic form. Second, even if mystical awareness *were* simply a state of pure consciousness "empty of all content" (the negative side of the paradox) but with a positive emotional tone, it hardly follows that the experience or its description would be "self-contradictory" in a philosophically interesting sense, as Stace (1960a, pp. 256-257) apparently believes. (Notice that Stace wants to claim that the experience itself, and not merely its description, is "self-contradictory," which is a puzzling assertion at best.) As far as I can see, then, John does not, and need not, adopt Stace's questionable theory in order to explain his infrequent recourse to paradoxical expressions in characterizing contemplative states.

In the sixth place, the mystic's use of paradox is sometimes taken as partial evidence for the general *"ineffability"* of mysticism. Almost everyone who writes about mystical states agrees that they are *alleged by mystics to be ineffable*, but unfortunately there is no such agreement about the meaning and implications of this observation. Some argue, for instance, that the assertion of ineffability is self-defeating when interpreted literally, while others regard it as grounds for flatly rejecting the cognitive value of mysti cism (see, e.g., Alston 1956, pp. 506-522 and Ayer 1946, p. 119). Since the issues involved are enormously complex and are closely tied to much broader questions about the logical status of religious language in general, a comprehensive treatment of them cannot be provided here. Nevertheless, I do want to review some of John's remarks on the difficulty of describing contemplative experiences, to see how well they accord with Stace's views and whether they provide any additional reasons for thinking that mysticism is non-cognitive.

As I pointed out in the second chapter, St. John of the Cross characterizes many things *besides* contemplation as "indescribable," including the harm produced by inordinate appetites (A I, 9, iv), the anxieties of beginners (A I, 14, iii), and the torment and pain caused by the devil (N II, 23, v). He likewise suggests a number of different *reasons* for the mystic's dissatisfaction with language. At least three are combined, for example, in the following passage on the "touch...of the substance of God in the substance of the soul":

This divine touch has no bulk or volume, because the Word who grants it is alien to every mode and manner, and free from all the volume of form, figure, and accident which usually encircles and imposes boundaries or limits to the substance. This touch we are discussing is indescribable (*inefable*) insofar as it is substantial, that is from the divine substance....

...The delicateness of delight in this contact is inexpressible (*imposible decirse*). I would desire not to speak of it so as to avoid giving the impression that it is no more that what I describe. There is no way to catch in words (*no hay vocables para declarar y nombrar*) the sublime things of God which happen in the soul. (F 2, xx-xxi)

Thus John appears to be saying, in the first place, that there is a depth of delight and "delicacy" to the experience which language cannot fully convey; this is a particularly acute form of the familiar "ineffability" associated with any profound emotion (cf. N II, 7, ii; 13, i; C 20 & 21, xv). Second, he expresses a *reluctance* to speak about this state for fear of failing to do it justice and thus misleading his reader, a diffidence sometimes felt in more conventional contexts (see also F 4, xvii). Third, he seems to imply that there is a peculiar difficulty in characterizing this "touch" owing to the absence of the usual "forms and figures" found in ordinary experience. As noted in the second chapter, John apparently holds a view of linguistic meaning according to which an X is strictly and properly described only by the application of a "name" associated with a sensory "form" or intelligible species of X (or its like), which enables others to form a corresponding "concept" (i.e., intelligible species) of X; let us call this sort of characterization an "s-description" of X.[15] Such a notion seems to underlie passages like the following:

If one were to describe the color white or yellow to a man born blind,...he would not understand any better no matter how much was said, because he had never seen such colors or their likenesses...; only their names would remain with him, because he could perceive them through hearing, but not their forms and figures, since he had never seen them. (A II, 3, ii—my translation)

Contemplative states are "ineffable" in this third sense, then, because they do not involve the "nameable" forms and species needed for an "s-description" (cf. A II, 32, iii; N II, 13, i; 17, iii). I will return to this point in a moment. It should be emphasized, however, that none of the three reasons mentioned here implies that *nothing at all* can be said of mystical experiences, and in fact John elsewhere concedes that they can be discussed "in certain general terms" (A II, 26, iii—my translation).

In *Mysticism and Philosophy*, Stace notes that "James and other writers have listed 'ineffability' as one of the common characteristics of mysticism everywhere," but adds that "this word...is only the name of a problem, not something the meaning of which we understand at once"; he therefore proceeds to examine and reject previous attempts to explain "this difficulty about the use of language which the mystic feels" before offering a new hypothesis of his own (p. 278). He begins with a critique of what he calls the "emotion theory" and the "spiritual blindness theory," two "commonsense" proposals which apparently correspond to some of the Sanjuanist suggestions made above. According to the former—a version of which James seems to favor (James 1936, p. 371)—"the depth of [the mystic's] emotions accounts for his difficulties with words"; Stace grants that there is some truth to this claim, but finds it ultimately "insufficient," first, because "mystical experience is not mere emotion" but also "perceptionlike," and second, because this theory fails to recognize the special "logical difficulty" which impedes the mystic's self-expression (Stace 1960a, pp. 282-283). It is not entirely clear what sort of "logical difficulty" he has in mind, but insofar as he is simply referring to "the incommensurability of mystical consciousness with the common consciousness," his criticisms are well-taken (Ibid.).[16]

According to the second "commonsense" proposal, the "cause of ineffability" is the non-mystic's "spiritual blindness," which makes efforts to describe mystical states to him as hopeless as attempts to convey "the nature of color to a man born blind" (Ibid., p. 283). Once again, Stace poses "two fatal objections to this theory": first, "it applies equally to every kind of experience," and therefore cannot explain the distinctive "ineffability" of mystic states; and second, it wrongly places the responsibility for the "word barrier" on the hearer rather than the speaker (Ibid., pp. 283-284). The second of these objections is less compelling than Stace imagines, since defenders of the theory could simply respond that mystics encounter a "word barrier" because the common language they share with the "spiritually blind" and in which they must express themselves is not designed for the communication of spiritual insights. Moreover, given that both "commonsense theories" appear in the mystical literature, they cannot simply be dismissed out of hand as attempts by the unimaginative individual "to drag the mystical down to his own level" (Ibid., p. 281). Still, neither theory alone is altogether adequate.

Next Stace considers the suggestion that mystical experience is "unverbalizable" because it is "inherently incapable of being conceptualized" (Ibid., p. 285). According to this view, mystical language is purely symbolic, and Stace once again identifies two theories as to how it functions: the "Dionysian theory," according to which "the word X if used of God means that God is the cause of X"; and the "metaphor theory," according to which "X is a metaphor for something in the actual nature of God himself or in the mystical experience" (Ibid., p. 291; cf. Stace 1960b, pp. 133-134).[17] Against the former, Stace raises a number of familiar objections, claiming, for example, that the "Dionysian" approach leads to an infinite regress when used to explain the application of the concept "cause" to God (1960a, p. 290; 1960b, p. 134). It is not necessary to determine here whether such criticisms could be answered, since John, like many other Western mystics, shows no inclination to adopt the theory Stace calls "Dionysian." Instead, passages like the following suggest, if anything, a certain sympathy with the "metaphor theory":

Who can describe (*escrebir*) the understanding [God] gives to loving souls in whom He dwells? And who can express (*manifestar con palabras*) the experience He imparts to them? ...Certainly, no one can! Not even they who receive these communications. As a result these persons let something of their experiences overflow in figures and similes (*figuras, comparaciones y semejanzas*), and from the abundance of their spirit pour out secrets and mysteries rather than rational explanations (*que con razones lo declaran*). (C Prologue, i)

One of Stace's main objections to the "metaphor theory" is that "metaphorical language is only meaningful and justifiable if it is...translatable into literal language," or "if, at any rate, the thing or the experience for which the metaphor is supposed to be a symbol is before the mind as a presentation" (1960a, p. 293).[18] He provides no adequate defense of this dubious claim, and it seems unlikely, in general, that such criticisms are effective against more sophisticated versions of the "metaphor theory," such as one finds in some contemporary treatments of the traditional doctrine of analogy. However, this raises a number of complex issues which need not concern us here; let us turn our attention to the alternative theory he proposes.

Stace's own hypothesis is surprisingly simple, but not particularly convincing. He begins by distinguishing two questions: "whether words can be used *during* the mystical experience," and "whether they can be used *after* the experience when it is being *remembered*" (Ibid., p. 297). According to

Stace, a mystical state is ineffable in the strict sense only while it is occurring, since "within the undifferentiated unity there is no multiplicity, and therefore...no classes, no concepts, and no words"; later, however, the subject can correctly speak of it "as 'mystical,' as 'empty,' as 'void,' and so on" (Ibid.). (Obviously, Stace means that the experience, while it is going on, is "wholly unspeakable" *for the person enjoying it*; others could presumably describe the experience while it is occurring.) Of course, the mystic still finds it difficult to recount his experience accurately, but Stace attributes this difficulty to the "paradoxical" character of these states, which forces him to resort to "contradictory" statements that nevertheless express "the literal truth about his experience"; in other words, Stace believes that the mystic calls his remembered states "ineffable" because "he confuses the paradoxicality of mystical experience with ineffability" (Ibid., p. 305).

Unfortunately, this proposal seems no more satisfactory than those Stace rejects. In the first place, it relies upon a claim about the paradoxicality of mystical experience which we have already shown to be problematic; I have argued that there is no good reason for supposing that mystical consciousness is literally "self-contradictory" or has to be described in terms of logical contradictions. Second, to borrow one of his favorite objections to alternative theories, there is nothing distinctive about the kind of ineffability that Stace attributes to *occurring* mystical states, since it can likewise be ascribed to any experience which totally engages the subject's attention (e.g., the experience of being completely caught up in a piece of music, or of concentrating exclusively on parrying an opponent's thrust in a fencing match). Thus the mystic's inability to articulate his experience *while it is going on* would be primarily due to his complete psychological absorption in what he is experiencing; the question of whether or not the state is one of "undifferentiated unity" seems largely irrelevant. In short, this theory not only fails to accord with what contemplatives themselves say about their mystical apprehensions, as Stace recognizes, but also lacks the support of persuasive arguments in its defense.

Therefore, since there appear to be no good reasons for the mystic or anyone else to adopt Stace's account of ineffability, let us return to what John of the Cross says on the subject, to see whether it raises any additional doubts about the cognitive value of mysticism. I have already noted that John frequently attributes the special "ineffability" of contemplative states to the absence of any "nameable species." One obvious criticism of this view is that it employs a problematic "theory of meaning not utterly unlike that which the British Empiricists came to hold: if no sense experience, then no idea and no name" (Kellenberger 1979, p. 310). But several things may be said in reply. First, John's claim does not rise or fall with the theory of language and meaning he holds; presumably he could make the same point in a less controversial way by simply saying that, despite its perceptionlike quality, mystical consciousness is not *of* an empirical object which could be characterized in terms of its color, shape, weight, genus and species.

Second, to say that contemplative states are not "s-describable" (in the sense explained above) is not to deny that they are describable in the broader sense. John shows no hesitation in speaking of contemplation or its object as "good," "divine," "satisfying," "loving," and so on; he does not argue that such terms are inapplicable, but only that they do not fully capture the reality encountered.

This is a peculiarity of a thing that is immense: All the expressions of excellence, grandeur, and goodness are fitting (*le cuadran*), but do not explain it (*ninguno de ellos le declaran*), not even when taken together. (C 38, viii)

Finally, and most important, since John believes that contemplation involves a direct awareness of God in which all particular concepts are excluded from the mind, he sees the "ineffability" of mystical consciousness as a direct consequence of the "ineffability" of its object. For John, in other words, our ability to describe mystical states is as limited as our ability to describe God. He writes, for example, that "one can say nothing" about what transpires in spiritual marriage just as "one can say nothing about God Himself that resembles Him," for "it is God who communicates Himself with admirable glory" (C 26, iv; see also A II, 26, ii-v). At the same time, though, he obviously accepts the legitimacy of traditional talk of God, however it is to be explained. From the Sanjuanist perspective, therefore, the "ineffability" of contemplation is a product of the sublimity of the experience and the unique nature of its object, but it poses no special problems regarding the meaningfulness of the mystic's assertions which are not already raised by religious and theistic language in general. Given the confines of this present study, we can only assume for present purposes that theistic language *is* meaningful, and go on to those alleged marks of mystic states still to be considered, including passivity and the apprehension of an ultimate unity.

In the seventh place, then, James asserts that *passivity* is a universal feature of mystical experiences. This claim is difficult to evaluate, however, since "passivity" can be given so many different meanings; there is a sense in which *all* perception-like experiences could be called "passive." Stace, on the one hand, deliberately omits passivity from his lists of mysticism's defining properties, arguing that introvertive states are usually "acquired" through strenuous mental effort, and "once achieved, can as a rule be thereafter induced almost at will at least over long periods of life" (Stace 1960a, pp. 60-61). On the other hand, without denying the need for self-discipline, those Christians who regard mystical states as glimpses of God generally insist that they are always ultimately passive in order to preserve the divine autonomy and initiative, and theologians tend to work out the details of this position according to their own views on the complicated question of the relationship between nature and grace. Here I will limit myself to some reflections on the implications of the Sanjuanist texts in this regard.

In the first place, as indicated in the second chapter, John clearly holds that contemplation is in some sense "passive," in contrast to the active, discursive prayers of beginners. He also indicates that the nature of the soul's passivity changes as she advances in the spiritual life. During the so-called "passive nights," for example, the soul's principal task is simply to endure the sufferings she sustains, whereas in the state of spiritual marriage she can exert some degree of conscious control over the occurrence of transitory unions. For John the contemplative is never merely an inert block in the hands of the divine agent; even raptures and ecstasies presuppose the absence of any seriously sinful resistance to God.

However, John believes that authentic mystical experiences are never simply the product of unaided human effort. In this he seems to agree with James rather than with Stace. The latter would presumably argue in his own defense that John's views are influenced by the demands of Christian orthodoxy. While this is no doubt true, a similar claim could be made about Stace himself. He is reluctant to admit the passivity of introvertive mystical states because this would be harder to reconcile with his claim that these are simply an awareness of the Kantian "transcendental unity of apperception" after all mental contents have been removed (Ibid., p. 87; 1960b, p. 22); it is more difficult to attribute to this "pure ego" the same active role in mystic states which John and other Christian mystics attribute to God. Stace is not a careful reader of the Sanjuanist writings, and mistakenly assumes that when John says "the soul must be emptied of all these imagined forms, figures, and images," he is advocating a sustained ascetical effort to suppress "all sensations, images, thoughts, and acts of will," the result of which "can only be an undifferentiated unity" (1960a, pp. 102-103—here Stace is quoting A II, 12, iii from the Reinhardt translation). But as I have already shown, what John actually teaches is that the contemplative must willingly *let go* of particular thoughts and desires when mystical consciousness supervenes; moreover, he cautions his readers not to give up discursive meditation as long at it is still possible, since otherwise the soul would "be doing nothing and receiving nothing" (A II, 14, vi—my translation). As we shall see, John *distinguishes* contemplation from the state of "pure consciousness without content."

Stace's failure to grasp this emphasis by Christian mystics on the feeling of passivity in contemplative states is shown in his unintentionally revealing remarks on St. Teresa:

She writes that at the "highest point" of union all the faculties are lost and the subject "will neither see, nor hear, nor perceive." Possibly this refers to the emptying of the self of its empirical contents. But it is somewhat doubtful that this is what she means. The emptying oneself of sensations, thoughts, etc., is usually a deliberate process which the subject undertakes and in which he succeeds, as Eckhart says, only with the greatest difficulty. But St. Teresa writes very much as if the loss of the faculties of which she speaks were something which just happened to her as she fainted off in a trance. (Stace 1960b, pp. 177-178)

In other words, if we disregard the disparaging tone of these comments, Stace has actually put his finger on a crucial feature of Christian mysticism without even realizing it. As James asserts, contemplative experiences, at least of the sort John describes, are marked by a feeling of passivity, and a corresponding conviction that they are gratuitous, not earned. Moreover, though I cannot prove it here, the feeling of passivity seems to be more prevalent among mystics in general than Stace realizes. Eastern mystics often feel a sense of gratitude after enlightenment even when their religious tradition does not provide any appropriate object for this sentiment.

This brings us, finally, to the "apprehension of ultimate unity" which is usually regarded as the essence of mysticism and which, according to Stace, takes two major forms.[19] In the eighth place, then, Stace maintains that extrovertive states involve *the Unifying Vision* that all things are One, together with *the more concrete apprehension of the One as an inner subjectivity, or life, in all things*. John of the Cross is presumably referring to a similar kind of experience when he talks about perceiving creatures as a "harmonious composite" in which each bears "traces" of the grandeur and power of the Creator. It is difficult to draw any firm conclusions from the saint's descriptions, however, since they are infrequent and generally couched in highly metaphorical language. I will limit my own observations to the following two points. First, John's remarks provide some support for those who argue that extrovertive states also involve the apparent "transfiguration" of natural objects, a characteristic which Stace does not list (see Wainwright 1977, p. 993; idem 1981, p. 10; and also C 14 & 15, v-vii; xxv-xxvii; F 4, iv-v). Second, Stace does not take theistic descriptions of these states seriously enough. Contrary to what he implies, Stace has not shown that extrovertive experiences always involve an apprehension of a relatively neutral "Unity" in all things which the Christian mystic merely *interprets* as an awareness of God. He should at least consider the possibility that this apprehended "One" is also occasionally perceived as loving, personal, creative and so on. My own view is that while there are contemplative states in which the mystic experiences an "ultimate unity" underlying all natural objects, these may sometimes have a phenomenally theistic character.

In the ninth place, Stace asserts that "the one basic, essential, nuclear characteristic" of introvertive mysticism is *the Unitary Consciousness*, which he also calls *the One, the Void*, or a state of *pure consciousness* with "no content except itself" (Stace 1960a, pp. 110 and 86). This important claim deserves consideration at some length, since it is crucial to his analysis of mysticism as "everywhere the same" and serves as the basis for some extremely far-reaching conclusions about its cognitive value. In particular, partly by appealing to St. John of the Cross, he tries to show that the introvertive states which Christian mystics call "union with God" are actually "the bare unity of the manifold of consciousness from which the manifold itself has been obliterated," and therefore provide no support for theism (Ibid., p. 86).

Let us briefly review the stages by which Stace reaches the conclusion that "'union with God' is not an uninterpreted description of any human being's experience" but "a theistic interpretation of the undifferentiated unity" (Ibid., p. 103-104). In an early section of *Mysticism and Philosophy*, he raises the question of whether "mystical experiences are basically the same, or similar, all over the world," and concedes the problem posed for any affirmative anwer by the fact that mystics have apparently held incompatible beliefs on the basis of their experiences, and have interpreted them in mutually incompatible ways (Ibid., p. 33). To meet this challenge, Stace insists on a proper "distinction between experience and interpretation," a distinction which he claims was too often overlooked by writers such as William James and R. C. Zaehner (Ibid., p. 35). Though he admits that there is probably no such thing as "pure" experience, Stace maintains nonetheless that experience is "distinguishable though not completely separable" from its interpretation, and goes on to say that:

If a mystic speaks of the experience of "an undifferentiated distinctionless unity," this mere report or description using only classificatory words may be regarded as a low-level interpretation. But this is being more fussily precise than is usually necessary, since for all intents and purposes it is just a description. If a mystic says that he experiences a "mystical union with the Creator of the universe," this is a high-level interpretation since it includes far more intellectual addition than a mere descriptive report. It includes an assumption about the origin of the world and belief in the existence of a personal God. (Ibid., p. 37)

Stace is frequently criticized for underestimating "the complexity of the experience-interpretation relationship," and particularly for failing to recognize how the mystic's prior "beliefs shape [his] experience, just as experience shapes belief" (Moore 1973, p. 150; Katz 1978, p. 30; see also Moore 1978, pp. 108-112). While I agree with these criticisms, I want to concentrate here on the problematic notion of "levels of interpretation" introduced in the above quotation, which has more immediate bearing on the way in which Stace analyzes mystical texts.

Unfortunately, Stace does not explain in any detail how one distinguishes high-level from low-level interpretations. The quotation above indicates that an interpretation is "low-level" (and thus "for all intents and purposes...just a description") if it employs "only classificatory words" and concepts, but "high-level" if it involves "far more intellectual addition," such as assumptions about the existence of problematic entitities or the occurrence of certain states of affairs. But this is not much help without some further account of what makes expressions merely "classificatory," and here Stace's position becomes conspicuously unclear.

One might at first suppose that Stace has in mind something analogous to the "sense-datum" language proposed by certain modern philosophers, since he offers the familiar "I see a red color" as an example of a low-level interpretation of a sensory experience (p. 37). Moreover, adopting an appropriately modified "sense-datum" approach to the analysis of mystical experiences would have some obvious advantages for Stace. In particular, it would already tend to beg the question in favor of his claim that monistic descriptions of these states are relatively "low-level" in comparison with theistic accounts, for reports of "pure undifferentiated unity" contain no references to causal powers, personality, or any other properties traditionally thought to be known by inference rather than direct perception.

Yet if this were truly Stace's position, it is hard to see how he could avoid the kinds of difficulties commonly associated with sense-datum theories. For example, his view would then presumably have the counter-intuitive consequence that nearly all reports of our sensory experiences, since they generally make reference to objects and events in the world, would be high-level interpretations, whereas the occasional low-level descriptions, in terms of two-dimensional color patches, etc., would be the result of a difficult process of abstraction from the way in which we ordinarily perceive things. It therefore seems unlikely that Stace, after due consideration, would want to embrace any variant of a theory which has so few defenders today.

A more promising approach to the distinction between high-level and low-level interpretations is suggested by Stace's example of the "witness in a law court" who "is instructed to give evidence only of what he actually observes, avoiding inferences and interpretations" (Ibid., p. 32). In such a context, as Stace rightly notes, mere conjecture and idle speculation are inappropriate. At the same time, however, there is certainly no expectation that testimony should be given exclusively in sense-datum language; an eyewitness to a crime can testify that a suspect "looked powerfully built" or "behaved in a friendly manner" (rather than limiting himself to talk of buzzing noises and two-dimensional color patches) without automatically being accused of indulging in "high-level" interpretation and unwarranted inference, even if he cannot specify precisely what it was about his experiences which created the impressions he reports.

To see what bearing these remarks might have on Stace's application of the "experience-interpretation" distinction to mystic states, let us first consider more closely an imaginary case, based on his own analogy of the law court. Suppose two witnesses, A and B, both testify in a murder trial that they watched Smith shoot Jones with a Luger, but that in fact A saw only shadowy figures in the distance, while B is an expert on firearms, knows Smith and Jones well, and viewed the event at close range. Stace would presumably maintain that A's testimony involves a much higher level of interpretation than B's. But the reason for saying this cannot be that A's testimony is false, for A may *know* (perhaps on other grounds) that the shadows he saw were those of Smith shooting Jones. Nor can it be, despite what Stace seems to suggest, that A's statement includes far more existential assumptions than B's, since both make the same assertion. Moreover, if these witnesses has simply said that they *had the impression* of seeing Smith shoot Jones with a Luger, their testimony would carry no existential implications at all, for both A and B could consistently report *having such an impression* while denying that Smith, Jones and the Luger actually exist, if they suppose, for example, that the experience was an hallucination about two men long dead. Instead, at least part of the reason Stace might claim that A's testimony involves a "higher level" of interpretation would seem to be (as a first approximation) that A's statement, taken by itself, suggests that his experience somehow had a different and more specific content than it actually had, and was comparable to B's.

One might also consider here the further hypothetical case in which witness C, who has the same experience and background information as B, sincerely testifies that she "saw one individual carrying something and approaching another individual." Would this be a high-level or low-level interpretation, on Stace's account? At any rate, C, who *knows* that the individuals were Smith and Jones and that the object was a Luger, is clearly giving *less* information about the "felt character" of her experience than she could have. (I mention this case only to raise the possibility, which Stace never seriously considers, that the relatively indeterminate reports of his favorite Eastern mystics could perhaps be *omitting* some of the phenomenal features of the actual experience.)

Applying such considerations to the earlier quotations from *Mysticism and Philosophy*, then, we can agree with Stace that a mystic's claim to have experienced "mystical union with the Creator of the universe" is problematic insofar as it assumes the doctrine of creation and the existence of the Creator. But suppose that a mystic says rather that she has had an experience which *seemed* to involve mystical union with something nonsensuous, holy, personal, loving, powerful, creative and so on.[20] Such an account is one which "theistic mystics would surely find acceptable," and if accurate, recounts an experience which in other contexts it would seem natural to call simply a "feeling of mystical union with God."[21] But at the same time, a report of this kind, despite its theistic implications, does not include any dubious existential assumptions at all, since the mystic could consistently give it while denying that there is a God. Therefore, according to the standards suggested by Stace's own example of the witness in a law court, it could be counted as a low-level interpretation (or for all practical purposes, "just a description") provided that it does not imply more about the phenomenal features of the experience than was actually the case. Therefore, in order to show that *all* introvertive mystical experiences are simply "states of pure consciousness without content," Stace must first show that the theistically-flavored reports of many Christian mystics do not accurately reflect the "felt-character" of their experiences. Let us examine the arguments Stace offers in defense of this conclusion.

In the second chapter of *Mysticism and Philosophy*, Stace sets out to establish that introvertive states are essentially everywhere the same by examining select passages from the mystical writings of different traditions and attempting to separate descriptive from interpretive elements in the various accounts. He first asks the reader to consider what would happen if a person were able to empty his mind of all empirical contents; his answer is that the individual, if he did not lapse into unconsciousness, would attain a state of pure consciousness "with no content except itself," which Stace identifies with the Kantian "transcendental unity of apperception" (Ibid., p. 86). He then begins "the presentation of examples of this kind of experience" with the Upanishadic description of "pure unitary consciousness" cited above, and goes on to examine J. A. Symond's account of a type of awareness in which "nothing remained but a pure, absolute, abstract Self" (Ibid., pp. 88-93). After this, Stace turns his attention to the Christian mystics, beginning with a few quotations from Eckhart and Ruysbroeck, and suggesting that once interpretive additions are discounted, it is simply obvious that these two authors are talking about the same experience of undifferentiated unity described in the Mandukya Upanishad (see Ibid., pp. 94-100). One might dispute Stace's claim even in the cases of Eckhart and Ruysbroeck, but we need not do so here. His preference for Eckhart is in any case hardly surprising, since of all the major Christian mystics Eckhart seems most likely to substantiate his "universal core" hypothesis.

Yet Stace frankly acknowledges here a crucial difficulty for his position:

It may be alleged that although Eckhart and Ruysbroeck speak of the undifferentiated unity they are exceptions. The majority of Christian mystics do not. They speak of their experience simply as "union with God." (Ibid., p. 100)

Therefore, in order to rebut the charge that he has dealt only with those Christian mystics who support his theory, Stace proposes to make a test case of Saint Teresa of Avila, to see if her experience is the same as Eckhart's, "for it would be difficult to think of any other pair of Christian mystics who are so utterly different...in their personalities, temperaments, mental capacities, and general attitudes" (Ibid., p. 101). Presumably, if it can be shown that the experience of Teresa, who consistently speaks of "union with God" rather than "undifferentiated unity," is essentially identical to that of Eckhart (and thus to that of the Hindus), it would be reasonable to conclude that the experience of *all* Christian mystics is basically the same. In order to make the comparison, Stace decides to use Teresa's friend and collaborator, John of the Cross, as the third term, arguing that "it would be quite incredible...to suppose that St. Teresa and St. John both had experiences which they called 'union with God,' but that by this phrase they meant wholly different things" (Ibid., p. 102). He then cites four Sanjuanist passages as evidence that John:

> describes with great subtlety and wealth of detail how, in order to reach union, the mind has to suppress within itself all sensations, images, thoughts, and acts of will. It is the same process of emptying the mind of all empirical contents as we find with Eckhart, with the Upanishadic mystics, and indeed with all mystics who have been sufficiently intellectual to analyze their own mental processes.... And the only result of getting rid of all mental contents (if it does not produce unconsciousness) can only be an undifferentiated unity. (Ibid., pp. 102-103)

But if "St. John's, and presumably therefore St. Teresa's, mystical experiences were in essence the same as Eckhart's" (Ibid., p. 103), why does she never speak of "undifferentiated unity?" Stace's answer is that Teresa:

> was a woman of extremely simple Christian piety with no interest in theory, or in abstract thinking, or in philosophical distinctions and analyses, and no capacity for them.... [She] is incapable of distinguishing between experience and interpretation so that when she experiences the divisionless oneness of the mystical consciousness she jumps at once to its conventional interpretation in terms of Christian beliefs. (Ibid., pp. 103-104)

Elsewhere he adds that it was the "menaces and pressure of the theologians and ecclesiastical authorities" which prevented Western mystics in general from drifting toward monism, and induced them to develop dualistic interpretations of mystical union, even though "dualism is a flat contradiction of the nuclear common characteristic of all mystical experience, viz. that it is an ultimate unity which is 'beyond all multiplicity'" (Ibid., pp. 230-232).

From the considerations summarized here, then, Stace concludes that Christian and Hindu mystical states are essentially the same, and that both are simply experiences of undifferentiated unity. However, while this overall line of reasoning has a certain initial plausibility, a closer examination reveals that it can be challenged at nearly every turn. Thus, despite disclaimers to the contrary, Stace's whole approach manifests a decided bias toward monism, since he begins by adopting the quotation from the Mandukya Upanishad on "pure unitary consciousness" as a classic "low-level" interpretation of introvertive states, and then uses it as the standard for determining how much in other reports is purely descriptive (see especially Ibid., pp. 94-102, 194-196, 231, 259). Furthermore, Stace simply asserts, without detailed argument, that the result of the ascetical teaching he attributes to St. John of the Cross "can *only* be an undifferentiated unity" (emphasis mine) of the sort described in the Upanishads. Perhaps he would defend this assertion by appeal to the post-Kantian theory of consciousness which he seems to favor, and which may suggest to him what Christian mystical experience "really has to be." In any case, Stace apparently just *takes it for granted* that all states of awareness in which the empirical contents have been eliminated are phenomenally the same, and that the only features *essential* to a given introvertive state are those shared in common with other introvertive mystical experiences, so that anything mentioned beyond these must be either unimportant or simply an interpretive addition. But these in fact are precisely the points at issue, since Stace claims to be refuting the notion that there is a distinctive form of introvertive mystical awareness with a phenomenally theistic character (i.e., with an object experienced as personal, powerful, non-sensuous, loving and so on).[22]

Moving next to more specific and detailed criticisms, Stace's handling of the two Spanish mystics seems particularly problematic, and suggests a lack of familiarity with their writings and doctrine. In the first place, it is significant that while Stace claims to be using Teresa to test his "common core" hypothesis, he never quotes her directly; in reality, he cites only passages from John's works, which he presumably regards as easier to reconcile with his theory. Second, no one acquainted with the complexities of the Teresian and Sanjuanist vocabularies would be so confident that the two authors mean precisely the same thing by the term "union." In fact, Teresian scholars have often noted that the words *unión* and *unido* have a much broader range of meaning for Teresa than for John; the latter would never have written, for example, that "the advantage rapture has over union is great."[23] Thus, even if the *teachings* of John of the Cross and Teresa of Avila are ultimately compatible, it is a mistake to assume that they shared an identical *terminology*.

Third, the four Sanjuanist texts (i.e., A II, 12, iii; 13, iv; 14, xi; and 12, vi) which Stace cites in support of his hypothesis are taken from a section of John's *Ascent of Mount Carmel* dealing with the first stirrings of contemplation, when it is most vague and fleeting, and therefore do not necessarily prove that contemplative consciousness is *always* so indeterminate. Moreover, it is far from obvious that these texts describe "the same process of emptying the mind" found "with the Upanishadic mystics," since, according to Stace, the latter advocate a *deliberate* suppression of all mental contents, whereas John simply states that the contemplative must be willing to relinquish particular "sensations, images, thoughts, and acts of will" when the divine communication supervenes. (Nor is it clear, as I have already pointed out, that the results of such a voluntary surrender "can *only* be an undifferentiated unity.")

In the fourth place, it would be difficult to maintain that either Teresa or John were intimidated into theistic language by the ecclesiastical authorities. On the contrary, both exhibited enormous courage in writing so boldly about contemplation at a time when such themes were considered suspect. And as for Teresa's alleged intellectual limitations, while she may have had little "capacity" for the "abstract thinking" and "philosophical distinctions" involved in sophisticated sense-datum theories, both she and John were perfectly capable of making the usual distinction between experience and interpretation, familiar from law courts and ordinary life. Indeed, much of their writing is devoted to the problem of distinguishing genuine experiences of the divine from those that only *seem* to be so. At one stage in her spiritual life, for example, Teresa was plagued by fears that her contemplative experiences might be caused by the devil, even though, while they were occurring, she felt the "greatest assurance that this delight was from God"; thus (despite what Stace asserts) she obviously realized that not every experience *interpreted* as "union with God" actually *is* such.[24]

Similarly, John says at one point in his works that the advanced state of "spiritual marriage" is marked by certain sublime "awakenings" in which "it seems to the soul that God indeed moves" within, even though in fact "God is immovable" (F 4, iv-vii), thereby clearly differentiating the "felt character" of such experiences from their orthodox interpretation. Unimpressive as it may at first appear, this particular example is in fact especially telling because, for once, Stace seems to come down on the side of the orthodox interpretation; according to his characterization of introvertive mystical states, they always involve an experience of the ultimate unity as "timeless," "changeless," "eternal" and so on. In this case John's contrary assertion that God seems to "move" within cannot be attributed to the influence of orthodoxy, since John explicitly points out that the experience is different from what traditional doctrine would lead one to expect.

The evidence, in short, does not support Stace's view that, because of theological pressures or limited powers of intellectual analysis, Teresa and John gave theistic accounts of mystical consciousness which are further removed from the ideal of "pure description" than those of the Hindu mystics, and even than those of Eckhart and Ruysbroeck. As George Thomas observes:

Stace's assertion that this theistic interpretation was imposed upon Western mystics...by orthodox authorities of the Church but that Eastern mystics were free from external pressure in their monistic interpretation is unjustified. It is true that Western mystics have tended to interpret their experience in the light of beliefs derived from their own religious tradition. But Hindu monists have been influenced by their own religious tradition no less than Christian theists. (Thomas 1967, p. 102)

Moreover, as most scholars recognize, Eckhart and the Rhineland mystics were themselves heavily influenced by the Neo-Platonic conception of mystical union as a return to the characterless One. Contrary to what Stace suggests, it is Teresa rather than Eckhart who comes closest to giving the raw psychological data; precisely because she lacked the scholastic training of Eckhart and John, and wanted to describe her experiences as exactly as she could to the confessors for whom she usually wrote, her approach is typically more original and empirical, less influenced by preconceived notions of what the experiences should be like.

To sum up, then, Stace has failed to establish that all introvertive mystical experiences, including those treated by the two Carmelite authors, are states of "pure consciousness without content." In fact, the writings of John and Teresa furnish stronger positive evidence that at least some contemplative experiences are theistic, and even specifically Christian, in their implications. For example, Teresa hold that when a soul has reached the state of Spiritual Marriage:

the Most Blessed Trinity, all three Persons, through an intellectual vision, is revealed to it through a certain representation of the truth.... [These] Persons are distinct, and through an admirable knowledge the soul understands as a most profound truth that all three Persons are one substance and one power and one knowledge and one God alone. It knows in such a way that what we hold by faith, it understands, we can say, through sight—although this sight is not with the bodily eyes nor with the eyes of the soul.... (*Interior Castle*, ch. 1 par. 6 of the 7th "Dwelling Places," in Teresa 1980, p. 430)

Elsewhere Teresa indicates that she received this favor herself (see *Spiritual Testimonies*, nos. 13, 14, 29, 51, 59 and 65, in the first volume of Teresa's *Collected Works* [Teresa 1987, pp. 391-393, 400-401, 414, 425-433, 435-438]). But is she perhaps simply imposing a "high-level" interpretation upon what is essentially an awareness of undifferentiated unity, as Stace would claim? There are several clear indications that this is not the case. First, she has already frequently enjoyed "union," and insists that this is something new and different (see *Interior Castle*, ch. 1, pars. 5-6, and ch. 2, par. 2 of the 7th "Dwelling Places," in Teresa 1980, pp. 429-430, 433). Second, she was at first surprised by the occurrence of this state, assuming that it would be impossible (see *Spiritual Testimonies* no. 14, in Teresa 1987, pp. 392-393). Third, she relates that in her own experience one of the divine Persons (presumably the Son, since her writings are full of locutions from Christ) had frequently "spoken" to her, another (the "first Person") had done so only once, while the remaining Person had never done so (see *Spiritual Testimonies* no. 59, in Teresa 1987, p. 432). Whatever this means (and in some respects it accords far better with the Trinitarian theology of Karl Rahner than with that of her own day), it is difficult to see how Teresa could make such distinctions if the experience were simply one of undifferentiated unity. In short, these and other considerations strongly suggest that many of Teresa's contemplative states were *experienced as* encounters with a personal, loving, powerful triune divinity, and not just as states of "pure consciousness."

John is more circumspect in his remarks on the Trinitarian dimension of certain contemplative experiences, but the wonder is that he says anything at all about it. According to the scholastic Trinitarian theology of his day, God's actions *ad extra* proceed from the single divine being which the Father, Son and Spirit share in common, so that distinctive activities can be attributed to each of the Persons only by accommodation. Since John nonetheless indicates (albeit somewhat cautiously) that the three Persons play different roles in certain contemplative states, and that in mystical mar riage the soul experiences, through grace, a certain participation in the inner dynamics of the Trinity (see, for example, C 1, v-vi; 13, xi; 37, viii; 39, ii-vi; F Prologue ii; 1, iii-vi; xv; 2, i-xvii; 3, lxxviii-lxxxii), it seems reasonable to suppose that there is something in the phenomenal character of these states themselves which gives rise to such an interpretation, and that it is not merely superimposed upon an experience of undifferentiated unity. John also claims that in some mystical states the soul enjoys a sublime experience of God "in one of His attributes (His omnipotence, fortitude, goodness and sweetness, etc.)" (A II, 26, iii), an assertion which Christian orthodoxy certainly does not require, and one which again he would presumably be less likely to make if in fact these experiences had no content. Finally, as is evident from everything he wrote, St. John of the Cross regards it as crucial that the contemplative states he describes have a phenomenal object which is generally experienced as *personal* and *loving*.[25] Indeed, according to John the whole pattern of developing contemplative awareness is experienced as a deepening relationship of love with a divine partner. This "felt character" of contemplation and the mystical life, rather than any lack of analytical ability, is the ultimate explanation of John's non-monistic account of mystical union.

In short, it seems highly implausible to claim, as Stace does, that *all* introvertive mystical experiences are states of pure consciousness without content, even if *some* of them are. On the contrary, the evidence indicates that certain mystics, especially those who have reached the summit of spiritual development, enjoy states of contemplative awareness in which they feel themselves to be united with something which cannot be tasted, touched, smelled, seen or heard, but which seems personal, loving, powerful, creative and perhaps even triune. That is to say, they have mystical experiences which are in some sense intrinsically theistic (and even Christian) in their implications, and not merely interpreted as such. This is a conclusion with enormous ramifications, not only for the proper understanding and analysis of mysticism, but also for theologians developing a contemporary theology of God, who may need to take the testimony of Christian contemplatives more seriously.

Using the writings of St. John of the Cross and others, then, I have tried to show that while James and Stace both have certain valuable insights about the nature of mystical states, neither has provided an adequate characterization of the whole range of contemplative experience which John describes. Thus John would undoubtedly agree with James that mystical states are *passive* and have a *noetic quality* (or, in Stace's words, a *sense of objectivity*), but would deny that they are always *transitory*, and would argue that the sense in which they can be called *ineffable* does not rule out the possibility of describing them in general terms. The Sanjuanist texts likewise support Stace's contention that mystical states are generally marked by joy, *blessedness*, and *peace*, by the feeling that what is encountered is *holy*, and so on. On the other hand, they seem to disconfirm his claim that mysticism is everywhere the same, and that, when Western mystics speak of "union with God," they are merely imposing a high-level interpretation on an experience of *undifferentiated unity*. Most of the contemplative states John discusses seem instead to have an *intentional object*, which is usually perceived as *personal* and *loving*.

The importance of these observations will become clearer in the next chapter, when we begin to evaluate certain objections to mysticism's cognitive value that are based on accounts of the "common features" of mystical states similar to those of James and Stace. We may conclude the present section by simply noting once again that the fundamental difficulty facing such accounts is the vast range of experiences which fall into the "mystical" category. I have argued above, for example, that the nearest equivalent to "mystical consciousness" in the Sanjuanist vocabulary is "contemplation" (or "loving knowledge," "mystical theology," and so on). This means that proposed lists of common features will need to be sufficiently vague and general to cover all contemplative experiences from the beginnings of "infused" prayer to the heights of spiritual marriage (not to mention the mystical experiences of Eckhart, Sankara, Plotinus, Al Hallaj, the Buddha, and Richard Jefferies), and will probably be so broad that they fit other non-mystical experiences as well. Unfortunately, many philosophers have mistakenly assumed that every individual mystical state must be as indeterminate as these general accounts, and consequently conclude that such vague experiences furnish no grounds for a theistic interpretation. I have tried in this section to show that the experiences in question sometimes have a more definite content. I will argue below that if one considers the different kinds of mystical experience not merely individually but also according to their place in the overall pattern of spiritual development, a more positive assessment of their cognitive value is possible.

4.2. The Data to Be Explained

Generally speaking, one of the traits of rational people is that they will conclude that a given hypothesis or belief is plausible if it seems to them to offer as good an explanation of the evidence (or facts) in question as the alternative hypotheses that it is reasonable to consider. This form of reasoning is sometimes called "explanatory inference," and is used often in the ordinary situations of our daily lives. In the sixth chapter I hope to apply it to the evaluation of mystical experience, contending that it is reasonable to regard contemplative consciousness as a cognitive mode of experience if the supposition that it is (along with additional background information) offers no worse an explanation of the phenomena associated with mysticism than the competing reductive theories which it is reasonable to consider. There I will have more to say about the structure of this kind of argument and about how one gauges the explanatory power of different hypotheses.

I mentioned earlier that we could in principle set up a theoretical typology of "explanatory inferences" according to the different possible conceptions of the nature of mysticism and mystical claims, but that such a procedure would be extremely tedious and would still leave open the question of which conception was most accurate. To simplify matters, then, I have been assuming that the writings of St. John of the Cross are a fairly reliable guide to the phenomenal characteristics and developmental stages of mystical awareness (at least as it manifests itself in the lives of many Christian mystics), and in the exposition of his account I have tried to focus on the mystical phenomena which I later intend to use as the starting-point for my own explanatory inference. However, since the earlier presentation was so lengthy, and since not everything mentioned there is of equal relevance to my project, it may be useful to end this chapter on the nature of mysticism with a short summary of what I regard as some of the most significant evidence to be explained.

The following, therefore, is a brief list of some important assertions about mysticism which we will eventually use in constructing an "explanatory inference." Some of them are more controversial that others. Some of them likewise are more easily testable by empirical investigation. All of them, however, are based upon the Sanjuanist teachings described above.

1. The first and most important claim is simply that there *is* such a thing as mystical or contemplative consciousness, i.e., that there are certain intentional, perception-like states in which it seems to subjects that they are aware of something (or someone) ultimate which nevertheless cannot be seen, heard, tasted, touched or smelled. In some of these experiences there is evidently no awareness of the external world, whereas in others natural objects appear unified and transfigured by the underlying "ultimate" which they seem to disclose. Nearly all of those familiar with mystical literature will admit this much, even if they disagree about the other characteristics of these states or the significance of their occurrence.

2. In addition to their strongly noetic or perception-like character, these experiences typically involve a sense of blessedness, joy, satisfaction, and a feeling that what is encountered is somehow holy, divine, and supremely valuable. Among Western mystics the intentional object of such states is usually apprehended as personal, loving, creative, powerful, transcendent, and so on.

3. Given the cooperation of the subject, mystical states ordinarily grow in depth, duration, frequency, clarity, and degree of joy, peace and satisfaction, according to a consistent general pattern of successive stages and iden-

tifiable crisis points. If all goes well, the contemplative finally reaches a stable condition of more or less continual mystical awareness, punctuated by moments of more intense absorption. As these remarks suggest, the developmental process is uni-directional, and none of the major phases is usually omitted, though different individuals progress at their own pace and according to their particular needs and abilities. Thus some mystics begin their spiritual journey with discursive prayer and advance by degrees, first through a rudimentary form of contemplation and later through ecstasies and raptures, until they attain permanent mystical awareness, while others cover only a part of the path; it is virtually unheard of, however, for any mystic to proceed immediately from the stage of beginners to the unitive way, much less vice versa.

4. At least for many Christian contemplatives, the features earlier called "phenomenally theistic" are associated especially with the more advanced states of mystical consciousness, when they become much more prominent. Thus while initial contemplation is usually so ephemeral and recondite that it is "almost unnoticeable" (see A II, 13, vii), in the more constant and lucid awareness of spiritual marriage the soul has a much deeper experience of divine love, sometimes enjoys a sublime apprehension of God in one of the divine attributes or mysteries, and feels herself drawn into the inner life of the Trinity, according to the testimony of John and Teresa. The presence of these "theistic" elements seems more than just a transitory abberation in the mystical life.

5. Progress in the mystical life appears to be associated with positive developments in other areas of human existence as well, including the psychological and the moral. Of course the parallelism is not exact; some individuals achieve a high degree of psychological maturity without ever enjoying a profound mystical experience, while others reach an advanced degree of contemplation but remain emotionally stunted. Nevertheless, if John is correct, the following correlations occur with enough regularity to warrant some attempt at an explanation:

5.1. There is evidently some connection between spiritual and psychological growth when viewed over the whole course of the mystic's life. This is not to deny that there are certain phases marked by terrible emotional turmoil and even apparent regression, as in the passive nights, but these are usually related to the acquisition of a more realistic self-image and the dismantling of inadequate personality-structures in order to achieve a higher level of psychological integration (a process that occurs in psychotherapy as well). According to the testimony of John and other mystics, a person starts from a condition of emotional and psychic disequilibrium, in which his energies are dissipated and his mind clouded by conflicting desires and impulses, and gradually moves toward the stability of mystical marriage, in which these feelings and impulses are harmonized according to the divine will, and directed toward union. If John is right, then, those who reach the unitive way are less likely to be subject to the deep-seated fears and anxieties which sometimes lead people into an unconscious self-delusion about the character of their experiences; their perceptions are more objective and free of distortion.

5.2. Generally, speaking, spiritual growth is likewise associated with a certain growth in moral character. In the beginning a soul's disordered inclinations often lead her into various lapses, sometimes serious, but by the time she attains the integration of spiritual marriage she is tremendously strengthened in moral virtue and in the desire to do good; in John's words, "these old lovers hardly every fail God" (C 25, xi). If so, this makes it less plausible to suppose that those who reach the unitive way are deliberately deceiving themselves and others about the nature of their experiences for motives of pride, personal gain, etc.

5.3. Finally, spiritual growth even appears to be connected with an increase in physical well-being, at least over the long run. John indicates, for example, that the purifications of the passive nights strengthen a person in both soul and body. Part of what this means is that the psychosomatic symptoms of the individual's initial psychic disequilibrium (e.g., tiredness, distraction, sexual arousal during prayer, "weaknesses of stomach," and, later on, "raptures...and the dislocation of bones") gradually clear up as various conflicts are resolved (see N I, 4, i-ii; 7, ii; II, 1, ii). If this claim is true, then it seems less likely that the experiences of those in the unitive way are due to some pathological physical condition.

These claims are admittedly controversial, but they are to some extent open to empirical investigation, and the research which has been done seems to lend them a certain degree of support.[26]

6. The capacity for mystical experience does not appear to depend on the possession of some special "organ of mystical perception" which the majority of people lack. On the contrary, given the foregoing data and the surprising frequency of ostensibly mystical states among the general populace, it appears that the capacity or "obediential potency" for contemplative consciousness is present in all human beings, but that it is not always realized, generally because an individual is not receptive to such experiences for one reason or another. (Again, this view is supported to some degree by the empirical evidence and by the testimony of the mystics themselves, who insist that it is chiefly inordinate attachments and obsessive ratiocination which impede mystical awareness.)

7. Mystical experience is generally passive, at least in the sense that contemplatives typically feel as if they are being acted upon, or as if some supreme and unmerited insight has been granted to them. Though they can prepare for and cultivate this awareness, it is never completely under their conscious control. Thus contemplatives are often surprised and frightened by their mystical experiences when they first occur, but later struggle unsuccessfully to reproduce them during the passive night of the spirit. Moreover, according to John and Teresa, this sense of "passivity" or

"receptivity" also extends to the soul's psychological and moral development; the advanced mystic feels that the virtues and psychic integration she has come to possess were not the product of her own efforts alone, but were received from the gracious reality encountered in her contemplative states.

8. In the ordinary realm, mystics seem at least as capable as anyone else of distinguishing between reality and illusion, and they employ the same distinction in differentiating among the much broader range of experiences with which they are familiar. Moreover, if they have traversed the passive night of the spirit, they know what it is to struggle with doubt and despair. (It is therefore difficult to attribute the contemplative's confidence in the veridicality of his mystical consciousness to naiveté about the possibility of error and self-deception, or to religious credulity.)

9. Finally, the total pattern of events and experiences involved in mystical development is such that it genuinely seems, at least to the typical Christian mystic, that he or she is participating in a progressively deeper love-relationship with a good, holy, and gracious divine partner; this is not simply an alien interpretation projected onto otherwise neutral phenomena. Indeed, the mystical life seems to advance through stages similar to those observed in the human relationships of love and friendship with which the mystic is familiar; this is part of the reason why nuptial imagery is so often used to describe the process.

These nine statements, then, summarize some of the data on which I will later base my explanatory inference.[27] They are not all equally important or obvious. For example, almost everyone will grant that mystical experiences do occur, but fewer would concede that spiritual growth is positively correlated with physical well-being; this may not be a serious problem, however, since the latter claim is not as crucial as the former (even though I believe it is true). More generally, the mere fact that some of the alleged evidence is controvertible does not by itself vitiate my project. Since I am simply trying to argue that it is *reasonable* to regard mystical consciousness as a cognitive mode of experience, it is not necessary to demonstrate that all of the above claims about the facts are true. One need only show that it is *reasonable* to believe that a sufficient number of them are, and this, in my opinion, has already been established; even those who have reservations about some of the evidence-claims would presumably concede that, given what we have learned from the examination of John's doctrine and other sources, it is not *irrational* to accept them.[28]

To sum up, perhaps the most important conclusion of this chapter is that mysticism is a complex reality, and that mystical phenomena may lend support to contemplative knowledge-claims in a variety of complex ways. But before attempting to show this in greater detail by incorporating the above findings into an explanatory inference, we should first turn to a discussion of various attempts to demonstrate that mystical experiences should *not* be regarded as cognitive.

NOTES

[1] Wittgenstein 1958, p. 31e, par. 65. Though Stace himself introduces the Wittgensteinian notion of "family resemblances" into his own discussion, he apparently fails to appreciate its significance, since he goes on to argue that all paradigmatic cases of mystical experience will involve an awareness of "undifferentiated unity" (see Stace 1960a, pp. 45-47, 68, 83; idem 1960b, pp. 14-15; and Horne 1978, pp. 15-16).

[2] Smart 1958, p. 55; compare idem 1965, pp. 75-76; and idem 1978, p. 13. Of course, this informal characterization assumes some consensus about who the major mystics are and what counts as a "mystical discipline." As I have just indicated, however, one problem with this assumption is that who one considers a mystic will partially depend one's previous notion of the nature of mystical states. Smart himself distinguishes sharply between mystical and prophetic (or numinous) experiences, and therefore denies, for example, that Jeremiah was a mystic, even though John of the Cross regarded Jeremiah's religious depressions as classic illustrations of the "dark night" experience. Nevertheless, it seems to me that there is more widespread and fundamental agreement that the figures Smart mentions *are* genuine mystics than there is about the nature of mysticism itself.

[3] See also Wainwright 1977, p. 990. Among the social scientists who use Stace's account, Wainwright mentions R.E.L. Masters and Jean Houston (1966, pp. 301-313) as well as Walter N. Pahnke (1966, pp. 295-320; idem 1967, pp. 63-64; see also, for example, Raymond H. Prince 1980, pp. 338-339. Philosophers who rely on Stace's description of mystical states include Ferré (1967, p. 102) and Nielsen (1971, pp. 49-51). Ian Barbour borrows from Stace in his reflections on theological and scientific methodology (1974, pp. 79-80).

[4] Stace also observes in the same place that "the extrovertive type of mystical consciousness is...vastly less important than the introvertive, both as regards practical influence on human life and history and as regards philosophical implications" (Ibid., pp. 62-63).

[5] Stace also suggests that the extrovertive state "is an incomplete kind of experience which finds its completion and fulfillment in the introvertive kind of experience" (Ibid., p. 132; compare also Stace 1960b, pp. 14-17).

[6] Stace includes a longer version of this same text in *Teachings of the Mystics*, pp. 196-198. It is also worth noting that, immediately prior to where James begins his quotation, John indicates that he is also describing the nature of contemplation during "the darknesses and straits of the soul's purgation."

[7] On the contrary, James admits that the various spiritual stages "which we find in the Catholic books seem to me to represent nothing objectively distinct" (James 1936, p. 409).

[8] See Stace 1960a, p. 103. These four quotations are from *Ascent* II, 12, iii; 13, iv; 14, xi; and 12, vi respectively. Chapters 5, 12, 13, and 15 of *Ascent* II are anthologized in *Teachings of the Mystics*, along with chapters 5, 16, 17, and 18 of *Night* II; see pp. 187-200. (There is a misprint in the footnote on p. 199, concerning *Night* II, 5.) Stace may not always have appreciated how the experiences described in the passages he cites fit into

John's overall scheme of the spiritual life, since he was working only from Kurt Reinhardt's abridged edition of the *Ascent-Night*.

[9] Stace 1960a, p. 61; cf. idem 1960b, pp. 87-88, 96, 178. Stace is aware of St. Teresa's descriptions and personal experience of this state, but apparently not of John's since he is only familiar with the *Ascent-Night*.

[10] This point is forcefully argued against philosophers such as Schmidt by Wainwright 1973, pp. 258-259, 275-276; Idem 1981, pp. 103-107. Compare Schmidt 1961, pp. 122-136. Speaking more generally, C. B. Martin likewise characterizes the statement, "I have a direct experience of God," as "an assertion that one comes to know something, namely God, by means of one's feelings and sensations" (Martin 1959, p. 76).

[11] Stace 1960a, p. 67. Notice that Stace affirms that mystical experience is objective but, unlike Wainwright, denies that it has any *object* as such; to avoid prejudging this question, I have followed Stace's terminology here.

[12] Rem Edwards argues that this transiency seriously limits the "noetic significance" of mysticism, since "trying to know all about God on the basis of an hour of mystical experience must be akin to trying to know all about the world on the basis of an hour of sense experience" (Edwards 1972, p. 304). The analogy fails, however. In the first place, mystics seldom claim to learn "all about God"; thus John says that "one of the outstanding favors God grants briefly in this life" is an experience which reveals that "He cannot be completely understood" (C 7, ix). Second, unlike the world, God is supposed to be completely simple, so that "the soul receives the knowledge of [His] attributes in only one act of...union" (F 3, iii). Besides, not all mystical experiences *are* transient.

[13] Russell is therefore probably guilty of exaggeration when he claims that a "mark of almost all mystical metaphysics is the denial of the reality of Time" (Russell 1957, pp. 9-10). In fact, a recognition of the reality of time would seem to be *required* by the evolutionary mysticism of Teilhard de Chardin and Sri Aurobindo, for example. John's own explanation for the loss of temporal awareness is that the individual "is united with pure knowledge which is independent of time" (A II, 14, xi), an assertion which raises other sorts of problems.

[14] As Peter Moore points out in his article 'Mystical Experience, Mystical Doctrine, Mystical Technique,' while paradoxical language is fairly common in abstract, conventional accounts of mystical experience or in liturgical and theological references to the mystical object, it occurs "hardly at all" in autobiographical reports of such states (1978, pp. 103-107).

[15] See pp. 32-33 above. The "s" in "s-description" indicates that this notion is drawn from certain features of scholastic epistemology and involves intentional species. Other texts which seem to suggest this third sense of "ineffability" include A II, 26, iii-v; N II, 17, iii-v; C 26, iv.

[16] On the other hand, if Stace is criticizing the emotion theory for failing to capture the allegedly "self-contradictory" character of mystical consciousness, then his objection is less compelling, since, as I have tried to show, it is not at all clear that mystical states *are* "self-contradictory" in Stace's sense.

[17] Stace calls the former theory "Dionysian" because he believes it is the view set forth by Pseudo-Dionysius the Areopagite in *The Divine Names*; we need not decide here whether this belief is correct. In the same places, Stace criticizes another theory sometimes attributed to Pseudo-Dionysius: the view that negative, but not positive, terms can be applied to God.

[18] One typical way of handling such objections is to argue that every human being already has some dim awareness of the reality the mystic is attempting to express, and that the latter's metaphors help to evoke that awareness more strongly and explicitly.

[19] James also calls the feeling of "oneness" with the Absolute "the everlasting and triumphant mystical tradition, hardly altered by differences of clime or creed," though he does not include it among the four marks of mystic states (see James 1936, p. 410).

[20] Of course, mystics may have difficulty explaining to the non-mystic exactly what phenomenal characteristics of a given mystical state make it seem to be an experience of something holy rather than demonic, personal rather than impersonal, loving rather than malevolent, and so on. But that hardly proves that a description in these terms is unwarranted, any more than a witness's testimony is discredited because she cannot say precisely what features of her experience inclined her to claim, for example, that a suspect's behavior seemed natural and friendly rather than formal or cleverly feigned.

[21] Wainwright 1977, p. 1004. Wainwright is actually criticizing Ninian Smart's claim that "phenomenologically, mysticism is everywhere the same," and that theistic accounts of mystical states are "highly ramified" and should therefore be considered interpretations rather than descriptions. Smart originally defended this position in 'Interpretation and Mystical Experience' (1965, pp. 75-87), an abbreviated version of which was later published under the title 'Mystical Experience' in *Art, Mind and Religiou* (Smart 1967b, pp. 133-143.). Nelson Pike offers analogous criticisms of Smart's thesis in his 'Comments' on the latter paper, in the same volume (Pike 1967, pp. 144-150).

[22] It is also worth noting that even *if* Stace succeeded in proving that mystical experiences are "everywhere the same," this would not by itself show that they are all states of "pure consciousness without content." Theoretically one could just as easily stand his whole line of reasoning on its head, by using theistic accounts as the touchstone, and arguing that since John, Teresa, Eckhart and Ruysbroeck all speak of "union with God," and since the Mandukya Upanishad is "clearly" referring to the same kind of experience, the states treated in the Upanishads must also be phenomenally theistic, even though, for various cultural and historical reasons, they are not described in such terms.

[23] Teresa, *The Book of Her Life*, ch. 20, par. 1 (Teresa 1987, p. 172). Teresa's views on this kind of "union" had undergone considerable development be the time she wrote the *Interior Castle*, where she associates it with the fifth of the seven progressively more exalted spiritual "dwelling places." All of this is explained in detail in Dicken, 1983, pp. 407-429.

[24] Teresa, *The Book of Her Life*, ch. 23, par. 2 (Teresa 1987, p. 201). For a recent philosophical discussion of Teresa's concerns about demonic deception see Mavrodes, 'Real v. Deceptive Mystical Experiences,' (1978, pp. 235-258).

[25] Other attributes John mentions as sometimes mystically "experienced" include God's wisdom, mercy and charity, all of which suggest a personal and loving tone to such states (see A II, 26, iv; C 14 & 15, xii-xv; 37, ii-vii; F 3, ii-xvii).

[26] One problem with attempting to test whether mystics grow in psychological and moral maturity as they advance in the spiritual life is that the outcome will depend in part on the concept of maturity one adopts. Thus for someone convinced that quasi-perceptions of spiritual realities are a symptom of mental and emotional instability, the contemplative's mystical experiences will themselves provide conclusive evidence that he or she is not psychologically mature. Determining the validity of claims 5.1, 5.2 and 5.3, then, is not solely a matter of empirical investigation. Nevertheless, in recent years some studies

have been carried out using less question-begging criteria of psychological adjustment, with interesting results. I will mention only a few here.

In a "survey of ultimate values" conducted by the National Opinion Research Center, a representative group of 1,500 American adults were asked the following question, which the researchers felt reflected the core of mystical experience: "Have you ever felt very close to a powerful spiritual force that seemed to lift you out of yourself?" About forty percent reported having had such an experience at least once. Those claiming to have had these experiences often were "disproportionately male, disproportionately black, disproportionately college-educated, disproportionately above the $10,000-a-year income level, and disproportionately Protestant"; the researchers likewise note that they "did administer the brief Psychological Well-Being Scale developed by Prof. Norman Bradburn," and that "the relationship between frequent ecstatic experiences and psychological well-being was .40, the highest correlation, according to Bradburn, he has ever observed with his scale" (see Greeley & McCready 1975, pp. 15-16). The survey is treated in greater detail, with some references to earlier research, in McCready 1974, pp. 55-70; see also Greeley 1974, pp. 11-12. According to a preliminary report of findings in a similar survey conducted in England, "at least a third of British adults claim to have had a direct mystical" or spiritual experience ('Mystic Moods Move British,' *Boston Pilot* 17 June 1977, p. 5). See also, e.g., Hood 1975 and Hay and Morisy 1978.

In an unrelated study, Marilyn May Mallory administered a battery of psychological tests to 54 Dutch and Flemish Carmelites, and concludes from the results that "the degree of prayer development is related to a complex of co-determinants: a high degree of happy emotionality, a low degree of anxiety, extraversion, social and religious dependency, normal ego strength, and stability." She goes on to say that these "psychological traits suggest that what Eysenck calls a 'strong nervous system' is a necessary prerequisite to mystical/contemplative development" (Mallory 1977, pp. 23-69 and 299).

Admittedly the methodology of these studies is not entirely beyond criticism. For example, the aforementioned survey question posed by Greeley and McCready would presumably elicit affirmative responses for other experiences besides the strictly mystical, as Wainwright points out (1978, pp. 399-400). For a detailed critique of Mallory's study, see Payne 1978, pp. 130-132. Nevertheless, the limitations of these studies do not completely discredit their findings, which deserve to be investigated further. For a very useful review of recent scientific research on meditation and contemplative practices, together with a comprehensive bibliography of the relevant literature from the past fifty years, see Murphy and Donovan 1988.

[27] For the sake of simplicity, I will sometimes symbolize the different components of the total evidence by the letter "E" together with a subscript indicating the number of the statement in which the component is mentioned. Thus "E_1" refers to the evidence that mystical experiences occur, while "$E_{5.3}$" refers to the evidence that spiritual development is correlated with physical well-being (see the sixth chapter).

[28] Of course, as I will explain more fully in chapter six, beliefs are rational or irrational relative to a given situation. That is to say, it might be reasonable for person A, with his knowledge and convictions, to accept proposition P, and unreasonable for person B, with different knowledge and convictions, to accept it. For example, it was presumably reasonable for Charlemagne to believe that the earth is flat, but such a belief would be unreasonable for Carl Sagan. Therefore, when I assert that it is *reasonable* to accept a sufficient number of my evidence-claims, I mean reasonable for someone acquainted with roughly the same data which we have discussed in preceding pages, who is thus in roughly the

same epistemic position as the author. It seems to me that those who do not accept these claims could still concede that it is reasonable (or at least not clearly irrational) for someone in these circumstances to accept them.

CHAPTER FIVE

SOME OBJECTIONS CONSIDERED

In the next chapter I hope to show that the facts about mysticism outlined above (if indeed they *are* the facts) are explained at least as well by the hypothesis (H_1) that contemplative consciousness is a cognitive mode of experience as by other competing hypotheses that it is reasonable to consider. However, those who have followed the discussion this far are likely to feel that, even if the above claims about the nature of mystical phenomena are true, they represent only a part of the total picture, since many philosophers believe they can provide equally good grounds for *doubting* the cognitive value of mystical states, or of religious experiences in general.[1] Thus, in response to the suggestion that "the best explanation" of mystical states is "the existence of God," Bertrand Russell comments:

...that the whole argument from our own mental states to something outside us, is a very tricky affair. Even where we all admit its validity, we only feel justified in doing so, I think, because of the consensus of mankind. If there's a crowd in a room and there's a clock in a room, they all can see the clock. The fact that they can all see it tends to make them think that it's not an hallucination: whereas these religious experiences do tend to be very private. (Russell & Copleston 1964, p. 179)

Again, C. B. Martin holds that there are no legitimate tests and checking procedures for determining which mystical states are authentic, and that therefore "the mystic's possession of these experiences" cannot be "in itself a way of knowing the existence or nature" of their external cause (Martin 1959, p. 86; cf. pp.72-74, 88-94). Antony Flew adds "that religious experiences are enormously varied, ostensibly authenticating innumerable beliefs many of which are in contradiction with one another or even themselves; and,...that their character seems to depend on the interests, background, and expectations of those who have them rather than upon anything separate and autonomous" (Flew 1966, p. 189). Such examples seem to suggest that, regardless of the data listed in the previous chapter, there are other facts about mystical phenomena which make it *unreasonable* to regard contemplative consciousness as a cognitive mode of experience. In other words, if the observations made by authors such as Russell, Martin, and Flew are sound, my project of constructing a successful explanatory inference is doomed to failure.

In this chapter, therefore, I want to review some of the major objections to the cognitive value of religious experiences in general, and mystical consciousness in particular. Before examining certain standard lines of criticism in detail, however, some initial clarifications are in order.

First, there is a difference, in my usage, between a cognitive experience and a cognitive *mode* of experience. For the purposes of the present discussion an experience will be counted as cognitive only if it is perception-like and veridical, i.e., only if the experience is intentional and "the relevant properties of the intentional object (the object in the mind) correspond to the relevant properties of an actual object (an object which exists independently of one's consciousness of it at the moment of the experience)" (Polkowski 1971, p. 4).[2] Those who favor a causal theory of perception would add that a cognitive experience must be caused by its object in the appropriate way (see Swinburne 1979, pp. 247-248). (Notice that I am not claiming that the conditions mentioned here are *sufficient* for cognitivity, but only that they are *necessary*). Thus an alcoholic vision of pink elephants would not be cognitive in this sense, despite its perception-like character, because it is non-veridical. On the other hand, a *mode* of experience will by counted as cognitive only if a sufficient proportion of the states of that type satisfy the conditions for cognitivity, so that such experiences can generally serve as a reliable way of knowing about that which caused the experience and corresponds to its intentional object (cf. Wainwright 1973a, pp. 258-259, 269-270; idem 1981, pp. 83-84, 96-100).[3] The important point here, however, is that to assert that a *mode* of experience is cognitive is not necessarily to claim that each individual experience of this kind is cognitive. Thus ordinary sensory experience is a cognitive mode of experience, even though some ostensible perceptions are non-veridical. I will be assuming, therefore, that one may consistently hold that contemplative consciousness is a cognitive mode of experience while admitting that *some* mystical states may not be cognitive in the sense outlined here.

In the second place, it is worth noting that we ordinarily accept ostensible perceptions as cognitive unless we have positive reasons for not doing so; that is to say, we take how things *seem* as at least prima facie evidence of how they actually are. Swinburne calls this the "principle of credulity," and argues that without it we would have difficulty avoiding skepticism about sensory experience (Swinburne 1979, pp. 254-271; cf. Broad 1953, p. 197; Polkowski 1971, pp. 71-72; Hick 1977, p. 54). More will be said later about this principle and the special considerations which limit its application; here I want to suggest only that if it truly seems to mystics that are encountering something nonsensuous, personal, loving, powerful, and so on, this constitutes at least a prima facie reason for believing that they are, even if we should later decide on the basis of the total evidence that this belief is mistaken.

Third, to explain the usage here of such terms as "rational" and "reasonable," I am assuming throughout that reasonable individuals sharing the same knowledge can sometimes rationally arrive at contrary conclusions on certain issues (e.g., who caused the eighteen-minute gap in the Watergate tapes, or whether there will be a nuclear war within the next ten years) because they assign different weights to the various considerations involved. Thus, when I argue that, on the basis of the total evidence, it is reasonable to believe that mystical consciousness is a cognitive mode of experience, I am not claiming that it is unreasonable *not* to believe it, but only that someone who does believe this in the light of the kind of information we have been outlining is not violating any canons of rationality.

Fourth, as I have repeatedly indicated, nearly every introductory textbook in philosophy of religion contains some brief criticism of mysticism and religious experience as a possible source of support for religious beliefs, with different authors adopting different approaches to the question. Unfortunately, since few philosophers seem to take religious experience very seriously, these objections are often carelessly formulated, and it is not always clear how strong a conclusion a given author means to draw, whether he is trying to prove that religious experience should *not* be regarded as a "way of knowing," or merely criticizing particular attempts to show that it should.[4] All of this makes it more difficult to deal with such criticisms in a succinct and systematic way. To help meet this difficulty, the material in this chapter will be organized around certain general *patterns of argumentation*, rather than around the views of individual authors. Thus I will construct and respond to my own versions of the standard objections to the cognitive value of mystical and religious experience, versions which represent a synthesis of the views of many philosophers, but which may not correspond exactly with the way in which any of them actually presents his position.

Fifth, in the present context I will give these reconstructed arguments the strongest possible negative conclusion, regarding them as attempts by those who *doubt* the noetic significance of mystical and religious states to assume the burden of proof (i.e., as attempts to furnish a demonstration that it is *unreasonable* to regard such states as cognitive). We may find that these objections actually support the weaker conclusion that there are other data besides those mentioned in previous chapters which would tend to count in favor of hypotheses incompatible with H_1 (the supposition that mystical consciousness is a cognitive mode of experience). However, such a conclusion would simply mean that these additional facts are part of the data to be explained, and it could turn out that, given the importance of the data listed earlier and the presumption in favor of cognitivity implied by the principle of credulity, H_1 still provides at least as good an explanation of the *total* evidence as the alternatives it is reasonable to consider; indeed, this is what I hope to show. Here, therefore, I am interested in these arguments only insofar as they might raise considerations which would count *decisively* against the cognitive value of mysticism, and thus demonstrate that it is unreasonable to accept H_1 or to believe, in particular, that these states are encounters with the God of theism. Any less conclusive evidence which they may uncover will be dealt with in the sixth chapter.

Finally, a review of the literature on the subject quickly reveals that most philosophical criticisms of mysticism and religious experience as a potential source of knowledge take the form of an argument that such states lack certain features needed in order to be considered cognitive; moreover, the features mentioned usually have something to do with the issues of *testability* and *inter-subjective* agreement.[5] Thus many philosophers maintain that these states cannot be cognitive because they are not open to appropriate checks, or because there is disagreement between the experiences of the mystic and the non-mystic, or among the mystics themselves. Accordingly, the remainder of this chapter will be divided into three principal parts. In the first, I will discuss the various arguments based on claims about the agreement (or lack thereof) between mystics of different cultures, or between the mystic and the non-mystic. The second will deal with arguments based on the testability requirement in general. Finally, the third section will briefly consider some further criticisms which do not easily fit into the other two categories.

5.1. Objections Based on the Problem of Inter-Subjective Agreement

In popular works on mysticism it is often suggested that the existence of a "universal consensus" among mystics shows that they must be on to something, that their experiences must reveal at least part of the truth. But what this consensus comes to, and to what degree it actually obtains, is not always easy to determine. Nor is it entirely clear why such agreement should be so important in evaluating cognitivity. After all, there are mass delusions; and even though all schizophrenics, for example, might agree that they experience the the unreality of the world and themselves, we would hardly count such unanimity as evidence for the truth of *their* claims (but compare Scharfstein 1974, pp. 133-140). Some critics would argue that any mystical consensus should be treated in the same way. Still, under ordinary circumstances we do tend to give greater credence to unusual perceptual claims when the ostensible perceptions are shared by numerous witnesses whom we have no special reason to doubt. And this is surely why many defenders of mysticism are eager to prove that the mystics agree, and why their opponents are just as eager to call this alleged consensus into question.[6]

Now philosophers attempting to turn the issue of agreement against those who affirm that mystical and religious experiences are veridical seem to propose three main lines of objection, one having to do with the differences between the mystic and the non-mystic, and the other two having to do with disagreements among the mystics themselves. According to arguments of the first sort, the fact that so many people do *not* have such experiences counts strongly against their cognitivity. In the second type of objection, a similar negative conclusion is drawn from the observation that different mystics make incompatible claims on the basis of their experiences. Finally, some authors present a third line of reasoning which is similar to the second but involves the additional charge that the character of these states "seems to depend on the interests, background, and expectations of those who have them rather than upon anything separate and autonomous" (Flew 1966, p. 126). These three kinds of objection are most often directed against the assertion that mystical and religious experiences provide knowledge of the God of traditional theism, but they have also been used to imply that such states have no cognitive value whatsoever. Let us consider these three types of argument in order.

5.1.1. DISAGREEMENT BETWEEN MYSTICS AND NON-MYSTICS

Rem Edwards points out that veridical experiences must be "public," i.e., "capable of being shared, at least by normal qualified observers" (1972, p. 126). Bertrand Russell, in the quotation given at the beginning of this chapter, appears to be saying that while the "consensus of mankind" justifies our confidence in the deliverances of the senses, no such justification is available for mystical experiences. Another author maintains that :

...There is a big difference between saying, 'There is a fire in the fireplace,' and saying, 'I have had an experience of the divine.' The difference, of course, is that I can go and see for myself whether there is a fire in the fireplace, whereas there is no possible way to verify or confirm, say, mystical experience; such a claim is by its nature subjective and private. (Miller 1972, p. 115)

Finally, C. B. Martin, comparing the assertion, "I had a direct experience of God," with someone's claim to have seen a star, writes:

...If Jones wanted to know whether it was really a star that he saw, he could not only take photographs, look through a telescope, and the like but also ask others if they saw the star. If a large proportion of a large number of people denied seeing the star, Jones's claim about the star's existence would be weakened.... [Let] us now imagine that Jones does not make use of the tests and checking procedures (photographs and telescopes) but is left with the testimony of what he sees and the testimony of others concerning what they see. In this case, it is so much to the point if a large number of people deny seeing the star that Jones will be considered irrational or mad if he goes on asserting its existence....

The religious claim is similar to, though not identical with, the case above in certain important features. We have seen that there are no tests or checking procedures open to the believer to support his existential claim about God. Thus, he is left with the testimony of his own experience and the similar testimony of the experience of others. (Martin 1959, pp. 73-74; see also p. 82)

Though such remarks are somewhat obscure, they seem to suggest the following sort of argument against the cognitive value of mystical experiences: If we have nothing to go on in the evaluation of a perceptual claim except the testimony of the person making the claim and the experiences of others, then a large amount of disagreement with the claim counts decisively against its acceptance. Thus, in the absence of other evidence, if no one else sees the piece of blue paper which I claim to see on the desk, then it is reasonable to conclude that my experience is non-veridical. But while some contemplatives claim to have mystical encounters with the divine, the vast majority of people would deny that they have ever enjoyed such states; moreover, there are no other procedures available for testing the contemplatives' assertions. Consequently, it would be irrational to regard mystical experiences as cognitive.

This argument has a certain plausibility, but clearly requires some tightening up. In the first place, we must assume that all parties involved are reporting their experiences sincerely and accurately. If it seems to me that I am seeing Ursa Major, for example, the fact that others claim not to see it would not count against the veridicality of my ostensible perception if I had reason to believe that they were lying or did not understand how to identify this constellation. Now some defenders of mystical states would argue that such states are actually far more prevalent than might at first appear, but that many people do not admit having them either because they do not recognize them for what they are or because they are afraid of ridicule.[7] For the sake of the present argument, however, let us assume that both mystic and non-mystic are correctly describing their respective states.

Second, as Rem Edwards's comment suggests, the experiences of another person have a bearing on the evaluation of an ostensible perception only if the other person is a "qualified observer," i.e., someone whom we would reasonably expect to have an experience in accord with the ostensible perception if the latter were genuine. To be a "qualified observer" one must have the requisite perceptual capacities and skills, and be in a position to make the appropriate observation.[8] Suppose, for example, that it seems to me that I am tasting oolong tea. Even if many others report that it does not seem to them that they are tasting oolong tea, their testimony will cast doubt on the veridicality of my experience only if they are drinking the same liquid, have functioning taste buds, and are able to distinguish different kinds of tea by their flavor; otherwise, they would not be "qualified observers" with respect to my experience. Similarly, in order for the perceptual reports of non-mystics to count against the cognitivity of the mystic's contemplative awareness, the non-mystics must be regarded as "qualified observers" with respect to the mystic's states; in other words, we would have to assume that the non-mystics are in the right circumstances, with the necessary capacities and skills, so that they would probably have had an experience like the mystic's if the latter's experiences were veridical. As we shall shortly see, this is the weak point of this whole line of argument.

Expressed more formally, then, the objection would run more or less as follows:

(1) In the absence of other checking procedures, it is unreasonable to accept a reported ostensible perception as cognitive if it conflicts with the reported experiences of a majority of other qualified observers (i.e., those whose experiences we would otherwise expect to agree with the ostensible perception if it were valid).

(2) Some individuals (call them mystics) report experiences in which they seem to be aware of, and united with, a transcendent order of reality, or more specifically, God.

(3) However, a much greater number of other people (call them non-mystics) accurately report that they do not have such experiences.

(4) Moreover, these non-mystics can be regarded as "qualified observers" with respect to mystical states. That is, we would expect them to have similar experiences if the mystics' experiences were perceptions.

(5) There are no other checking procedures for evaluating the mystics' perceptual claims.

(6) Therefore, it is unreasonable to accept mystical experiences as cognitive.

I will assume, for the sake of discussion, that the argument is valid and that the first two premisses are true.[9] The truth of the third premiss is at least open to question; further research could conceivably reveal that at least half of the populace has had contemplative experiences, or something very much like them. However, let us grant the truth of this step as well. Then the soundness of the argument turns on the truth of steps (4) and (5), and both of these seem extremely dubious.

Looking first at (5), we can easily see its importance for this line of objection, since it is sometimes reasonable to continue trusting an ostensible perception in the face of widespread disagreement by qualified observers, when the former is confirmed by other tests and checking procedures. Thus, I may be the only one at the track who seems to see Jones cross the finish line ahead of Smith, but if photographs support the validity of my experience, it is rational for me to persist in believing it even though everyone else seemed to see Smith win the race. Likewise, if mystical states successfully pass other tests for veridicality, then it might be reasonable to regard them as genuine perceptions even if they were enjoyed by only a tiny minority of people. And indeed, despite what Martin supposes, the mystic and others employ a variety of criteria to determine the cognitive value of his experiences, including the coherence and orthodoxy of the claims he makes, the effects of these experiences on himself and others, their delicacy, depth, pleasurableness, and so on.[10] Whether or not these constitute suitable tests is a further issue we will discuss more fully in the second section of this chapter. Here I will simply note that (5) is highly controvertible as it stands.

Step (4) is obviously crucial to the whole argument, but it is not clear that the mystic or anyone else needs to accept it. After all, the defender of mysticism can presumably claim that non-mystics are not "qualified observers" because they have not undertaken the necessary course of asceticism and prayer which would put them in the right "situation" with the requisite perceptual skills, and that this, rather than the non-veridicality of mystical consciousness, explains their failure to enjoy the experiences in question. As I have shown in earlier chapters, John suggests that God is willing to communicate himself in different ways and degrees to everyone, but that it takes a certain amount of time and effort to overcome the moral, psychological, and spiritual impediments to contemplative awareness; if non-mystics make no serious attempt to surmount these obstacles and cooperate with the divine initiative, then their failure to have mystical experiences is hardly surprising, and does not count strongly against the cognitivity of these states.

To this the critic might have two responses. First, he could accuse the mystic's defender of redefining the requirements for being a qualified observer in terms of conditions which seem likely to produce misperceptions and illusions. Just as the habitual drunk is not allowed to save his ostensible perception of pink elephants from disconfirmation by claiming that the only qualified observers are those who have consumed large amounts of alcohol, so too it is illegitimate to try to save mystical consciousness by accepting as qualified observers only those who have undertaken spiritual disciplines which result in unusual mental states. But the obvious reply to this is that, apart from the question of mystical experiences themselves, these spiritual disciplines seem to increase rather than inhibit the ability to perceive accurately (cf. Murphy and Donovan 1988, pp. 33-39). Another reply would be to note the difference in the kinds of objects ostensibly perceived. A pink elephant is presumably supposed to be like any other elephant except for its color, so that there seems to be no reason why the imbibing of alcohol would be needed to see one if it were real. However, since spiritual beings, if they existed, would be very different from the normal objects of perception, it is not implausible to suppose that an unusual mental state might be required in order to perceive them (see Broad 1953, pp. 197-198; Rowe 1978, pp. 72-76).

The critic's second response might be to argue that the hypothesis that non-mystics fails to enjoy mystical experiences because they lack the appropriate dispositions is unacceptable because it is entirely *ad hoc* and not subject to independent checking. To illustrate the point with an example from another field, while scientists are not forced to abandon a good theory every time some experiment yields observations contrary to what it predicts, their explanation of why these unexpected results occur (e.g., because of faulty instruments, or impure chemicals) must be independently testable; that is to say, "the kind of saving hypothesis which is never allowable in science is the kind which is not corroborated by anything except the non-fulfillment of the predictions deduced from the theory which it is invoked to save" (Hudson 1974, p. 71; see Ibid., pp. 67-71; Matson 1965, pp. 26-29). By contrast, if non-mystics did undertake the recommended discipline and still failed to achieve mystical consciousness, the mystics would simply insist that, despite all appearances to the contrary, the non-mystics had not made a sincere effort, or were still held back by their moral, psychological, and spiritual handicaps; moreoever, their only evidence for this claim would be the fact that the experiences in question did not occur. Thus the defender of mysticism seems to be resorting to unfair tactics in a desperate attempt to protect the cognitive value of contemplative states.

Several points can be made in reply. First, contrary to what the scientific example may suggest, there appear to be many cases in ordinary life where we account for the non-occurrence of some experience by a hypothesis which is difficult to check independently. Suppose, for instance, that one day at the office the fire inspectors test a new alarm system which they believe is audible throughout the building; suppose also that I have acute hearing and the noise is very loud, but that I alone, out of hundreds of workers, fail to hear the alarm. I might explain this failure to the fire inspectors and myself by claiming that, although it had never happened before and may never happen again, I was on this occasion completely absorbed in my own thoughts. While this seems like an acceptable explanation, it is not obvious that there is much to corroborate my claim about the intensity of my concentration apart from the fact that I failed to hear and respond to the alarm.[11]

Second, even though a scientist's hypothesis that her experiment failed because, say, the voltmeter was broken is easier to check than the assertion that the non-mystic failed to achieve mystical consciousness because, say, her thoughts and desires were not yet sufficiently integrated and pacified, it is not clear that the latter kind of hypothesis is *totally* immune to testing. After all, we have various formal and informal ways of estimating the degree of someone's mental tension, moral maturity, psychological integration, obsessive-compulsive tendencies, and so on. Admittedly, the crite ria we use (e.g., psychological tests, general impressions based on observed behavior) are vague and fallible, which is perhaps why the defenders of mysticism do not immediately give up their position as soon as they meet an apparently well-rounded and mature non-mystic who has pursued the recommended spiritual exercises unsuccessfully; they may even conclude that God, for some mysterious divine reason, has simply chosen not to grant the non-mystic a contemplative experience at this time.[12] Still, the fact that the defenders of mysticism find such cases *puzzling* shows that the criteria we ordinarily use are at least relevant (if not decisive) in evaluating their position; and I think they would also have to concede that their position would be seriously undermined if a substantial number of checking procedures indicated a strong *negative* correlation between mystical states and moral and psychological maturity.

Third, in judging the cognitive value of an ostensible perception, it is the nature of what is ostensibly perceived which determines, in part, whether it is legitimate to restrict the class of qualified observers to those individuals satisfying a particular requirement. As noted above, only the most basic skills and conditions are usually needed to have veridical sensory experiences of ordinary physical objects. Given the nature of elephants, for example, we would naturally expect anyone in the pub with good eyesight and a clear view to be able to see a pink elephant dancing on the bar if there really were one there. Consequently, the drunk is not allowed to "save" his alcoholic vision of pink elephants by claiming that only the testimony of other wine-drinkers is relevant, for we have no reason to suppose here that wine-drinking would make a veridical perception more likely. One the other hand, if we were evaluating Lord Peter Wimsey's claim to have perceived by taste that wine from an otherwise unknown source was Chateau Rothschild 1935, then it might be reasonable to consult the testimony of other wine-tasting experts; in this case, we can see why wine-tasting might play a role in making someone a qualified observer.

Moving further afield, let us imagine that at some future time astronauts from earth land on a distant planet containing strange green creatures shaped like sea anemones, which are able to exert hypnotic control over the minds of those within visual range, and which protect themselves by making it seem to those in whom they detect aggression and hostility that there is no such object present, thus rendering themselves effectively imperceptible to potential enemies. Let us further suppose that during their explorations of the planet these astronauts come upon one of these creatures, and it seem to some of them that they are seeing something that looks like a large green sea anemone, while others (the more pugnacious individuals) deny seeing any such thing. One natural way of describing the situation is to say that the first group is perceiving the creature, while the second group is prevented from perceiving it by the creature's hypnotic powers. (Of course, this example needs to be filled out in various ways; perhaps the astronauts had already heard of such creatures on other planets or from other travelers, or perhaps the creature is somehow able to explain what is going on to those who seem to see it.) Now it might be argued that this hypothetical creature is so strange and so far removed from normal objects of perception that it *makes no sense* to speak of perceiving it, especially since the same distribution of experiences could be explained in other ways as well, e.g., by supposing that some totally different force was producing misperceptions in both groups. But this, I think, would be a mistake, since it would make the assertion that we have so far never knowingly encountered such a creature a *conceptual* truth, whereas we would ordinarily regard it as a statement of *empirical* fact.

It may also be argued that, as Flew says of God, "when this is the sort of thing which is supposedly involved it must become more rather than less necessary to provide some warrant for claims to have encountered it, or him" (1966, p. 138). But whatever this means, it is surely unreasonable to expect that a creature of the sort we have described will be as readily available for comparative observations as elephants, stars, or pieces of blue paper. Indeed, if we were evaluating an astronaut's ostensible perception of such a creature, we would presumably focus our attention on the experiences reported by other individuals with a phlegmatic or peaceable temperament, because these are the only subjects whom we would expect to have similar experiences if the alleged perception were veridical. If the majority of these subjects denied having similar experiences, then we would probably conclude that the ostensible perception was non-cognitive. Yet once again, because our ordinary criteria for distinguishing aggressive from non-aggressive individuals are vague and fallible, we would not necessarily draw this negative conclusion as soon as we came across some apparently peaceable individual who failed to see the creature, since we could also suppose that this person harbored some concealed aggressiveness which the creature was nonetheless able to detect. In any case, the interesting point here is that the class of qualified observers would seem to be limited to those whom the creature permits to perceive it.

Returning once again to contemplative experiences, we have seen that Christian mystics report that in many of these states it seems to them that they are encountering God. Part of what this means, I take it, is that in such states it seems to them that they encounter, and are united with, something (or someone) nonsensuous, holy, ultimate, personal, loving, powerful, and so on (where the feelings of a "personal" quality, etc. need not be *inferred* from more primordial impressions any more than we *infer* in a dream that the furniture seems "alive" or "malevolent"). Moreover, it also seems to them that this experience is not attained through their own unaided efforts, but that this "something" freely and graciously discloses itself. If these qualities are indeed part of the direct "felt" character of such contemplative experiences, as I believe they are, then we are dealing with ostensible perceptions of an object or reality which, like the creature in the previous example, can determine which individuals are able to perceive it, and therefore would not be generally available for comparative observations in the same way that ordinary physical objects are. Instead, the only people we could reasonably expect to have similiar experiences if the mystic's alleged encounter with God were veridical would be those to whom God freely granted a mystical revelation of himself.[13] Since it is not clear that, if there were an object of the sort Christian contemplatives claim to perceive (and which I am here calling "God"), it would so manifest itself to non-mystics, it is not clear that non-mystics should be regarded as qualified observers for the purposes of deciding whether mystical experiences are cognitive or not.

In light of all the foregoing considerations, then, the crucial fourth premiss remains extremely dubious, and the critics' argument therefore fails to establish (6), the conclusion that they want. That many people do not enjoy mystical experiences would prove that it is unreasonable to regard these states as cognitive only if we had very firm grounds for thinking that these states would be more widespread if they were veridical (i.e., if the object allegedly perceived by the mystics really existed). However, while the argument fails as a strict refutation of the cognitive value of mystical states, it does direct our attention to additional data which have a significant bearing on this issue. For although the actual distribution and relative infrequency of contemplative experiences is not *incompatible* with their being veridical, it is at least somewhat *surprising*, especially when we meet individuals who seem to fit all of the requirements specified by mystics (in terms of emotional balance, good will, and so on) and yet have never attained mystical consciousness. By themselves, such facts might be regarded as tending to count to some degree *against* the hypothesis that mystical awareness is not a cognitive mode of experience, though it is not clear how strongly. At any rate, these facts (which we may refer to as "E_{10}" following the symbolization of the previous chapter) should be included as part of the total evidence to be used in the explanatory inference of the next chapter.

5.1.2. DISAGREEMENT AMONG MYSTICS THEMSELVES

Since popular works on mysticism so often seem to suggest, at times rather incautiously, that the universal consensus of mystics demonstrates the validity of their experiences, it is hardly surprising that many philosophers of religion should view this alleged unanimity with a skeptical eye. These critics are quick to point out, for example, that not all mystics describe their experiences in Christian terms. Thus Walter Kaufmann asserts that the notion that "all the mystics agree on essentials,...is, on the face of it, patently false," and that "to the extent to which there is agreement, there is doubt about its significance" (1961, p. 315). Antony Flew, as we have seen, argues that "religious experiences are enormously varied, ostensibly authenticating innumerable beliefs many of which are in contradiction to one another or even themselves (1966, p. 126). C. H. Whitely states that "Christian, Mohammedan, Hindu, Buddhist mystics give similar accounts of the nature of their mystical experiences, and different accounts of the object of these experiences," concluding from this and other considerations that "we can hardly take the cognitive factors in religious experiences at their face value, as information about the nature of the supernatural" (Lewis & Whitely 1955, p. 89). And in response to those who would attempt to establish "cumulative evidence for the truth of claims to experience God" by "compiling records of numerous experiences of the same general kind," Hepburn writes:

Without doubt there is an impressive mass of such records within the Judeo-Christian tradition. Other religious traditions, however, can also produce their own very different records—of the various well-ordered phases in the quest for nirvana or for mystical union with a pantheistic object of worship.

Are these differences, however, real incompatibilities; do they correspond to genuinely different sorts of religious experience? Or are the experiences basically the same, though differently interpreted? On this it is extremely hard to give any confident answer.... What can be said is that any common elements must be very indeterminate in content and able to bear a great variety of interpretation.... But from such an experience alone one can hardly infer anything so definite as the God of theism. (Hepburn 1967b, 'Religious Experience, Argument for the Existence of God,' *Encyclopedia of Philosophy*, vol. 7, p. 166)[14]

Now all of these authors seem to be asserting that there is a certain amount of disagreement among mystics, and that this disagreement somehow limits the cognitive value of their experiences. As the above quotation from Hepburn suggests, however, they do not all locate the disagreement at the same level. Some philosophers, especially those who follow Stace, believe that mystical states are "everywhere the same," involving an apprehension of an ultimate non-sensuous unity which "remains neutral" with respect to the competing metaphysical and theological interpretations which mystics impose upon it. Others hold that these experiences themselves are of fundamentally diverse kinds. Again, several authors who question the legitimacy of the theistic interpretation of mystical states are nonetheless willing to grant that they might be to some extent cognitive, while another group reaches the far stronger negative conclusion that "the very variety of mystical interpretations [is] itself an argument against accepting the truth of any of them," even the less ramified ones (Penelhum 1977, p. 79).[15]

Yet despite these differences, I believe it is possible, by drawing upon suggestions found in the above quotations and by spelling out their implicit assumptions, to develop a single line of argument which philosophers like those we have cited would acknowledge as an acceptable presentation of their basic objection. The argument would run as follows: mystics of differ ent traditions and cultures make claims about their experiences which, at least superficially, seem to conflict. Some, for example, claim to encounter God, while others refuse to describe their contemplative consciousness in these terms. Now either these disagreements represent genuine differences in the "felt character" and ostensible object of the experiences themselves, or else the mystics are placing incompatible interpretations on what is essentially the same experience. If the first alternative is correct, then insofar as different mystical states have different ostensible objects (e.g., the God of Christianity versus the Void of Buddhism) which cannot all be simultaneously instantiated, at least some of them must be non-veridical. But since we have no way of determining which these are, it would be arbitrary to suppose that theistic rather than non-theistic experiences are veridical, and it seems more reasonable to reserve judgment on the cognitive value of contemplative consciousness in general. On the other hand, if mystical states are fundamentally the same, then the experience which the Christian mystic characterizes as an encounter with God is equally open to less ramified, non-theistic descriptions (e.g., those of the Theravadin Buddhist or philosophers such as Smart and Nielsen). This indicates that the former interpretation is not demanded by anything in the experience itself; moreover, there seem to be no other grounds for preferring it to less ramified accounts which make no mention of occult spiritual beings. Consequently, the claim that contemplative consciousness involves a perception of God is without foundation; at best, it could only be a veridical awareness of an ultimate, non-sensuous unity. Thus, whether mystical states are of distinctive kinds or all the same, it would be unreasonable to regard them as cognitive encounters with God, and perhaps also unreasonable to regard contemplative consciousness in general as a cognitive mode of experience.

A more formal version of this argument would be the following:

(1) Mystics of different traditions and backgrounds make apparently conflicting assertions on the basis of their contemplative states. In particular, while all of them claim to be aware of "Ultimate Truth" or "Reality" in these states, they describe the object of this awareness in contrasting terms.

(2) Either these mystics are describing fundamentally different types of mystical experience, or they are interpreting the same experience in different ways.

(3) Suppose that these mystics enjoy fundamentally different kinds of mystical experiences, with different ostensible objects.

   (3.1) Now the ostensible objects of these different experiences cannot all be simultaneously instantiated.

(3.2) Hence at least some of these experiences are non-veridical.

(3.3) But we have no way of differentiating the veridical from the non-veridical, and no grounds for thinking that one type of mystical awareness (e.g., the phenomenally theistic) is more likely to be veridical than any other.

(3.4) Therefore, it is better to reserve judgment on the cognitive value of mysticism.

(4) So if the mystics whose claims appear to be in conflict are actually having different kinds of experiences with different ostensible objects, then it would be unreasonable to regard any of these states as cognitive, much less as perceptions of God.

(5) Suppose, on the other hand, that mystical consciousness is everywhere the same, but that these mystics are simply interpreting the same experience in incompatible ways.

(5.1) Now this experience has been interpreted in an astounding variety of ways, and in both theistic and non-theistic terms.

(5.2) But any experience which can bear such a broad range of characterizations must be very indeterminate. In particular, nothing in the "felt character" of the experience itself would call for a theistic rather than a non-theistic interpretation.

(5.3) There are no other reasons for favoring a theistic interpretation of this state over other alternatives.

(5.4) Hence the claim that this state involves a veridical experience of God is without foundation.

(6) So if the mystics whose claims appear to be in conflict are simply placing different interpretations on what is essentially the same experience, then at the very least it is unreasonable to regard mystical consciousness as a perception of God.

(7) Therefore, it is unreasonable to think that mystical states ever involve a cognitive experience of God.

(8) Moreover, it is not clear that contemplative consciousness should be regarded as a cognitive mode of experience, even of a very restricted kind. At best, contemplative consciousness could involve cognition only of an extremely vague and indeterminate "ultimate unity."

Before I begin to examine this argument in greater detail, two points should be made. First, despite its somewhat disorganized appearance, which comes in part from the inclusion of steps left implicit by authors such as those we have cited above, the argument is formulated as carefully as possible. The cautious wording of (8), for example, is deliberate. It seems to me that the most a critic could legitimately hope to conclude from this argument is that mystical states should not be regarded as perceptions of God, because some mystics do not describe the object of their experiences in such terms. On the other hand, there seems to be much more widespread agreement among mystics that there is a transcendent order of reality or "Supreme Truth"; thus the Christian and Theravadin mystics, though they differ on the theistic character of their respective states, seem to be in greater accord with each other than either is with the positivist or materialist. If agreement counts for anything here, then it might be reasonable to regard mystical experiences, if not as perceptions of the God of Christianity, then at least as perceptions of this transcendent reality, which would still be an interesting and significant result. Many authors (with the notable exceptions of Stace and Broad) seem to think that if mystical experiences cannot support belief in God they are of no further philosophical interest. However, if one could show that the mystics unanimously testified to a supreme spiritual Reality beyond the play of phenomena, then whether this Reality was personal or impersonal would seem by comparison to be a secondary question, despite its importance.

Second, for a thorough treatment of this line of objection we would need a more precise account of the nature and seriousness of the disagreement between mystics of different traditions, something beyond the scope of this present study.[16] Nonetheless, it is possible to identify some of the weak points in the above argument, as I will now try to show.

Let us assume, for the sake of discussion, that premiss (1) is true, although it provides little information about the ways in which various mystical claims seem to conflict. Of course, there would be no problem if one could hold that these mystics were simply perceiving entirely different objects. But those against whom this argument is directed would not want to say this, since they want to appeal to the "unanimous" testimony of the mystics regarding the nature of "ultimate reality" as evidence for the veridicality of their experiences.

I am also willing to accept the second premiss, as long as it is understood in an inclusive sense. As noted earlier, it seems that the individual contemplative typically enjoys a whole spectrum of diverse mystical states; thus John, describing the mystical experiences of those who attain spiritual marriage, writes that, "there are many kinds of awakening which God effects in the soul, so many that we would never finish explaining them all" (F 4, iv). Given a pair of mystics from different religious backgrounds, then, I suspect that some of their contemplative experiences will be very similar, some will be quite dissimilar, and that in either case each will tend to interpret his or her experiences in terms of his or her own conceptual framework.

The strategy in the remainder of the argument is to show that either disjunct of (2) leads to a negative judgment regarding mysticism's cognitive value. Step (3) is simply the assumption that the first disjunct is true, i.e., that the mystics whose claims seem to be in conflict are actually enjoying different kinds of experiences, with different ostensible objects. From this (3.1) infers that not all of the ostensible objects of these different experiences can be instantiated together. The latter step has a certain intuitive appeal. Thus if it really seems to St. Teresa that she is encountering a personal God, and it really seems to a Buddhist mystic that he is conscious of an impersonal Void, we might be inclined to say that they are ostensibly perceiving incompatible "objects," since both God and the Void are supposed to be "ultimate," and the unique "ultimate" could not be simultaneously personal and impersonal. However, there are other ways of characterizing this situation. Given a sufficiently sophisticated notion of the ultimate (e.g., the God described by John of the Cross, containing an infinity of attributes which are never fully plumbed by the human mind), one could affirm that Teresa and the Buddhist mystic are perceiving different *aspects* of the same Reality.[17] As long as the experience of each did not seem to involve an *exhaustive* awareness of its object or to *exclude* the possible veridicality of the other's experience, this approach could perhaps be defended with some success.[18]

However, since it may not be possible to harmonize *all* contrasting (and sometimes apparently incompatible) contemplative apprehensions in this manner, for the sake of discussion let us grant the truth of (3.1), and therefore of (3.2), which follows from it. It seems to me, in any case, that the defender of mysticism can frankly admit that *some* mystical experiences are non-veridical.[19] As noted above, this by itself would no more show that mystical consciousness is not a cognitive mode of experience than the occurrence of hallucinations proves that sensory experience is without cognitive value.

Step (3.3), then, is obviously crucial for establishing the conclusion (3.4) of the subsidiary argument. As far as I can see, however, this premiss is altogether dubious. There clearly are, at least in principle, certain ways of determining which mystical experiences are more *likely* to be veridical. For example, besides the other "testing procedures" to be described in a later section, we can look at the inner coherence of the experiences themselves; if a mystical state somehow seemed to reveal that its ostensible object possessed fundamentally incompatible attributes, this would tend to show that the experience was non-veridical. We can also estimate the *frequency* of different types of mystical awareness; those which were extremely rare and idiosyncratic (e.g., alleged encounters where the divine seemed altogether bizarre or trivial) would appear to be more questionable.[20] And we can compare the different kinds of contemplative consciousness with the rest of our experiences; those which seemed most consistent with the totality of our religious experience would be the more promising candidates for veridicality. To illustrate this last point, suppose that some mystical states (call them "phenomenally theistic") seem to their recipients to be loving encounters with a powerful, personal Spirit, that others (call them "phenomenally monistic") involve the feeling that nothing exists but the transcendent, eternal "One" with which the subject is completely identified, and that these two kinds of experiences could not both be totally veridical. In such a case one could argue that, of the two types, the phenomenally monistic states are less likely to be cognitive, since, if they were, it would be difficult to explain the occurrence of numinous states, which constitute a major strand of humanity's religious experience; if, as the phenomenally monistic states seem to reveal, everything is already identical with the transcendent One, then it is not clear how there could ever be any sense of dread, fascination, and unworthiness in the face of the Wholly Other. The feeling of total identification with the changeless "One" also seems to be in conflict with another phenomenal feature of these states, i.e., their transitoriness. (On the other hand, if "phenomenally theistic" mystical experiences were cognitive and thus if God existed, it would nonetheless be easier to understand how an intense experience of union with God might sometimes be *felt* as a kind of monistic identification with the transcendent One, even though strict monism would be false.)

Premiss (3.3), then, is not evidently true. Without it, however, the first subsidiary argument fails, because (3.4) cannot be deduced from the remaining steps alone. For from the fact that *some* mystical experiences are non-veridical, it by no means follows that *all* of them might be, or that I have any grounds for thinking that the theistic ones in particular are.[21] Therefore, this attempt to infer a skeptical conclusion about the cognitive value of mysticism from the supposition that mystics of different traditions have fundamentally different kinds of experiences does not succeed.

The second subsidiary argument is based on the assumption, in (5), that mystical consciousness is "everywhere the same," a popular view which has been criticized at length in Chapter Four. But let us suppose for the moment that it is true, and that, as (5.1) affirms, mystics interpret this same mode of consciousness in an amazing variety of ways, and in both theistic and non-theistic terms. Given this diversity, many authors apparently believe that the proper method for determining the "essence" of mysticism is to uncover common elements in various descriptions of contemplative consciousness from different periods and traditions; they take it for granted that whatever is found in nearly all accounts must be part of the phenomenological core of the experience, whereas any assertions which are only made by those of a particular tradition, or about which the mystics themselves seem to be in disagreement, must be purely extraneous interpretation.[22] It is hardly surprising, then, that these authors should typically draw the conclusion expressed in (5.2), that any experience which can be so differently interpreted must be very indeterminate, and cannot contain anything which would call for a description in theistic terms.

However, both (5.2) and the assumptions on which it is based are open to serious question. It is certainly not the case, in general, that one can simply identify the phenomenal core of an ostensible perception with the "lowest common denominator" in the reports of those who share it. Thus if two people are looking at a tree in the yard, and one claims to see a maple while the other claims to see an oak, we would probably conclude that both were seeing the tree and that at least one of them was mistaken or confused about the kind of tree it was, but it would seem very odd to say that both are having the same vague "tree-experience" which is totally indeterminate with respect to the tree's genus. Again, modifying an example used in the last chapter, suppose that I and several other witnesses are being questioned in court, and I report that I clearly saw Smith shoot Jones with a Luger, while those who were standing beside me at the time and looking in the same direction report only that they saw one figure approaching another, followed by a loud noise. Now if the judge in the trial tries to establish what all of us "really" saw by employing the same methodology used by Stace and others to determine the "essence" of mystical consciousness, he will presumably conclude that our common experience was very indeterminate in content, that the reports of the other witnesses are closer to the ideal of pure description, but that my testimony involves a highly-ramified interpretation, since it assumes the existence of Smith, Jones and Lugers. Indeed, the judge's conclusion would be correct if it turned out that I likewise saw only vague figures, and that my references to Smith, Jones and the Luger were based on pure speculation. There is another possibility, however; it could be that the phenomenal character of the experience actually was as I have testified (i.e., seeming to see Smith shoot Jones with a Luger), but that for some reason the other witnesses offer a much vaguer description, perhaps because they do not know Smith and Jones, or have some prior reason for doubting that they could be perceiving what they seemed to see. (For example, the other witnesses may believe that Smith and Jones were away in China at the time, and consequently that they could not have been seeing the former shoot the latter, but must have only seen two figures; or perhaps the other witnesses do not know what guns are, and have no idea what it would seem like if one person shot another.) In this case the differences between our reports would be due, not so much to my "over-interpreting" a phenomenally neutral experience, as to the others "under-describing" an ostensible perception of a more determinate character.

Returning to the question at hand, then, even if mystics were interpreting the same experience in widely divergent ways, it would not necessarily follow that the content of the experience is extremely indeterminate. It might be instead that all contemplative states involve a certain feeling of loving encounter with a transcendent Spirit, however subtle this might be, but that some mystics do not describe their experiences in this way because they lack the conceptual categories to do so, or because the feeling is often so delicate that it is easily overlooked unless one is attending to it.[23] Since this possibility has not been ruled out, the truth of (5.2) remains in doubt.

Step (5.3) seems equally dubious, for reasons analogous to those presented in connection with (3.3). Thus even if mystical consciousness never involved anything more definite than an awareness of an ultimate, non-sensuous unity, it might still be appropriate to interpret the experience in theistic rather than monistic or pantheistic terms, on the grounds that the theistic interpretation is better able to account for the *totality* of our religious experience (cf. Smart 1970, pp. 141-145). Finally, since the conclusion (5.4) depends upon (5.2) and (5.3), this second subsidiary argument fails to prove that if mystics were simply interpreting the same experience in radically different ways, it would be unreasonable to regard mystical consciousness as a veridical experience of God.

In short, the two subsidiary arguments, each of which is based on one of the disjuncts of (2), do not succeed in justifying a negative judgment regarding mysticism's veridicality. Furthermore, because the truth of (4) and (6) has not been established, neither has the truth of (7), which is supposed to follow from (2), (4), and (6); that is to say, the argument as a whole does not prove that it is *unreasonable* to regard mystical states as cognitive experiences of God. Nor does it prove (8), that it is irrational to regard mystical consciousness as a cognitive mode of experience, which would still be in doubt even if (7) were true, as explained above.

Here again, however, though this argument fails to *demonstrate* that contemplative states are non-veridical, or that they should not be treated as cognitive experiences of God, it does bring out some further data with a significant bearing on the issue. For while the actual amount of disagreement between mystics of different traditions is not clearly *incompatible* with the veridicality of their experiences, it is at least somewhat surprising; even those who believe that contemplative consciousness involves a loving encounter with God seem to some extent puzzled that there is not a greater consensus among the mystics on this point (at least insofar as they feel some urge to explain the disagreement). Taken by itself, then, the actual disagreement among mystics of different traditions (symbolized as "E_{11}") can be regarded as tending to count *against* the hypothesis that mystical awareness is a cognitive mode of experience; how strongly it does so will have to be decided in the next chapter, and will depend on how extensive we judge the disagreement to be, and whether it can be accounted for in other ways. Thus insofar as this lack of consensus is more than merely apparent, it should be included as part of the total evidence on which an explanatory inference will be based.

5.1.3. THE ROLE OF THE MYSTICS' PRIOR BELIEFS IN SHAPING THEIR EXPERIENCES

The objection considered in the previous section was based simply on the apparent disagreement between mystics of different backgrounds, but the structure of the argument would have been the same even if it were the *Christian* contemplative who spoke of the "Void" and the *Theravadin* who described his states in theistic terms. There is a second version of this argument, however, in which the relationship between the mystics' reports and their religious tradition plays a much more crucial role. Thus Rem Edwards observes that "another standard objection to mysticism is that the Holy always seems to assume a localized form" (1972, p. 321), and Antony Flew, as we have already seen, asserts that the character of mystical and religious experiences "seems to depend on the interests, background, and expectations of those who have them rather than upon anything separate and autonomous" (1966, p. 126); Matson considers it "suspicious" that it is only the mystics "reared in theistic cultures" who agree that mystical states reveal "the existence of God" (1965, p. 23). Walter Kaufmann agrees that:

Mystical experiences are by no means always the same, and the differences are not reducible to the interpretations which the mystics offer afterward. The experiences themselves are molded by the personality and the prior beliefs and expectations of the mystic. Suzuki does not have the same experience as Santa Teresa. (1961, p. 328)

Finally, C. H. Whitely contends that:

...subjects are apt to perceive and learn what they are expecting to perceive and learn. These expectations will be affected both by their personal desires and by the religious doctrine with which they are familiar.... Now if the subject's notions of what it is he is apprehending are partly determined by his preconceived notions of what he is likely to apprehend, it would be rash to cite the evidence of religious experience in favour of the doctrines of any particular religious creed, or any particular theory of the nature of God. (Lewis & Whitely 1955, pp. 89-90)[24]

Though such remarks are somewhat obscure, they suggest the following sort of objection: the lack of agreement in the reports by mystics of different traditions indicates that their experiences are of fundamentally diverse kinds. Moreover, they seem to differ along strictly sectarian lines; for example, only Christians have trinitarian experiences, and only Hindus experience Brahman. In fact, since variations in the phenomenal content of mystical states are so closely correlated with variations in the subject's prior religious commitment, it seems likely that the latter, rather than anything external and autonomous, is responsible for the specific "felt character" of the experience. (Thus Christians would have had *theistic* experiences, and monists *monistic* experiences, even if none of these states were veridical.) But in ordinary cases we do not count an ostensible perception as genuine if its occurrence is caused by the expectations of the subject rather than by the object or state of affairs allegedly perceived. Hence it is rash to suppose that mystical states ever involve a veridical awareness of God. Furthermore, since we have no grounds for supposing that the mystical experiences of one tradition are more probably true than those of any other, it is unreasonable to regard contemplative consciousness in general as a cognitive mode of experience.

Before we evaluate this argument, two points should be made. First, this line of objection will not be open to authors such as Stace, Smart and Nielsen, who believe that contemplative states are everywhere the same. At most they could maintain, as Nielsen does, that the *characterization* which a mystic places on his experience "is largely a function of his own religious and theological tradition" (1971, p. 53). But even if, say, St. Teresa's prior beliefs cause her to interpret her experience in a certain way, this does nothing to show that her interpretation is *false*, especially if we have some other grounds for determining the adequacy of competing interpretations. The question then becomes whether we have any such grounds, an issue already touched on in the preceding section. (Similarly, Schrödinger's theory of wave mechanics would not be discredited even if we could show that it derived in part from his mysticism [cf. Scharfstein 1974, pp. 77-80]. Of course, one could hardly appeal, say, to the "unanimous testimony" of Christian mystics in arguing for the "phenomenally theistic" character of their experiences, if it could be shown that their use of theistic language was *solely* determined by prior religious beliefs and expectations. Such does not seem to be the case, however. For example, as shown above, both John and Teresa creatively adapted many of the descriptive phrases and categories they had inherited, invented others, and sometimes even characterized mystical states in terms contrary to what their religious convictions would have led them to expect.)

Second, the gist of the present objection is that the characteristics of different mystical states can be adequately accounted for without supposing that these experiences are veridical. In effect, then, the argument is suggesting that the facts can be explained at least as well by the hypothesis that the phenomenal content of these states is determined by the mystic's antecedent religious views; hence it might more properly be dealt with in the next chapter, when we discuss the alternative hypotheses in competition with H_1. However, since the argument is so closely related to the one we have just considered, it seems preferable to deal with it briefly here.

Expressed more formally, then, the argument would run roughly as follows:

(1) Contemplatives of different backgrounds have different kinds of mystical experiences, with different ostensible objects which cannot all be simultaneously instantiated. Therefore, some types of mystical awareness are non-veridical.

(2) Moreover, the ostensible objects of these diverse experiences inevitably correspond with what the antecedent religious views of their recipients lead them to expect. Thus, theistic mystics have theistic experiences, Theravadins have non-theistic experiences, monists have monistic experiences, and so on.

(3) Hence it seems probable that what the mystic seems to perceive (e.g., God, Brahman, the Void) is determined by his or her prior religious beliefs and expectations, rather than by anything separate and autonomous.

(4) But when an ostensible perception of X (where X is an object or state of affairs) is caused by something other than X, it should not be considered cognitive.

(5) Therefore it is unreasonable to regard phenomenally theistic mystical states as cognitive.

(6) In addition, since we have no other grounds for supposing that mystical experiences of any kind are veridical, it is unreasonable to regard contemplative consciousness as a cognitive mode of experience.

Once again, I have given the argument both a stronger and weaker conclusion, according to the range of influence which different philosophers ascribe to the mystic's background. Certain philosophers who admit that mysticism may have limited cognitive value hold that the mystic's prior beliefs determine, not the entire content of the experience, but only some of its characteristics, e.g., whether the Ultimate seems to the mystic to be personal rather than impersonal, theistic rather than non-theistic. (This is apparently the view of C. D. Broad, for example, who writes that the beliefs which mystics acquire from their background "in part determine the details of the experiences," but not "the features which are common to the religious experiences of persons of widely different times, races, and traditions" [1953, pp. 193-194]). Such authors would presumably accept (5) but reject (6).

Let us now examine the argument in closer detail. The first premiss includes what is presumably necessary to get the argument going. Thus, if there were distinct forms of mystical experience with different ostensible objects, but these ostensible objects could all coexist, then the defender of mysticism would be able to explain the apparent disagreement between mystics of different cultures and traditions by claiming that each is having a veridical experience of a different object or reality. As noted in the last section, I would tend to agree that mystical experiences are of many different kinds, though I am less sure of the extent to which these differences represent fundamental incompatibilities. Still, for the purposes of the present discussion let us grant the truth of (1).

Step (2) asserts that the ostensible objects of these diverse mystical experiences always correspond with what the mystics' prior beliefs lead them to anticipate. This claim is ambiguous, and can be understood in a stronger or weaker sense. According to the weak interpretation (2) is simply pointing out that mystics rarely have contemplative experiences whose ostensible object forms part of a religious belief system which they do not share; thus Christians do not seem to encounter Krishna, Jewish mystics do not have trinitarian experiences, and Theravadins do not feel that they are enjoying union with a personal, loving creator. Or course, this requires some qualification. For example, Ramakrishna was supposed to have had visions of Mohammed and Jesus; we are also familiar enough with dramatic conversions precipitated by intense religious experiences which are sometimes mystical in character.[25] Still, even in these cases the subject generally has some prior knowledge of the ostensible object of his contemplative state. We would be astounded to learn of someone experiencing explicit mystical union with Christ or the Trinity who had never heard of them before. In this weak sense, then (2) is probably true.

However, if (2) is understood as making the much stronger claim that there is a total congruence between the mystic's religious background and the character of his or her contemplative awareness, so that there is nothing in the experience which the mystic and those who share the same religious tradition find novel or surprising, then it is certainly false. For example, as we have seen above, St. Teresa was at first quite astonished by her apprehension of God's presence in all things, and the presence of the Trinity in her soul, since she had not previously known that such experiences were possible; indeed, an ignorant confessor had tried to convince her that the former experience could not be veridical, since God was only present in souls in the state of grace. St. John of the Cross likewise encountered some difficulty in trying to fit certain contemplative states into the categories of the scholastic theology of his day; moreover, he constantly teaches that one of the chief causes of spiritual stagnation is that pious souls often tend to resist new and deeper mystical communications because they do not understand and had not anticipated them.[26] And in general, mystics are by no means always extreme religious conformists; on the contrary, they are frequently major religious and ethical reformers, which is one reason why they are often regarded with suspicion by the official guardians of orthodoxy. In short, if (2) is true, it is true only in the weaker sense that mystics do not generally seem to encounter the divine beings or realities which constitute the central focus of religions they do not know of or accept, but instead tend to have mystical experiences which are roughly compatible with their own prior religious traditions and beliefs, if they have any.

Step (3) affirms the likelihood that what the mystics seem to perceive is *determined* by their prior beliefs and expectations. Once again, this claim is somewhat ambiguous. If it means only that the subject's antecedent beliefs shape and modify the phenomenal characteristics of his or her experience, this is undoubtedly true, just as it is true of sensory experience as well. But if (3) is suggesting that the character and ostensible object of mystical consciousness is determined *solely* by the subject's antecedent religious views, then the claim is almost certainly mistaken. Quite apart from whatever causal role is played by the object or reality ostensibly perceived, numerous other factors besides the mystic's background seem to be just as closely correlated with variations in the phenomenal properties of contemplative states. Thus, while Roman Catholic mystics share the same doctrinal commitments, their experiences are by no means always identical in content; the mystical states of the warm and affectionate St. Teresa seem to be marked by a much stronger personal tone than those of less emotional Christian mystics, whose experiences seem comparatively impersonal and abstract. Consequently, even if it were strictly true, as (2) asserts, that none but theistic mystics ever have experiences involving a clear sense of loving union with a personal deity, this would at most indicate that some prior belief in God is a *necessary* condition for explicitly theistic experiences, but would not prove that such a belief is by itself a *sufficient* cause of their theistic character; this character presumably has other causes as well, and the Christian mystic's antecedent faith may simply direct his or her attention to certain features of these states "which would otherwise remain at the margin of consciousness" (Moore 1978, p. 112).[27] In short, the mystics' religious beliefs and expectations are only one part of a complex set of conditions which influence the character of their experiences.

Step (4) states that when an ostensible perception of X (where X is an object or state of affairs) is cause by something other than X, it should not be considered as cognitive. This premiss is a rough attempt to capture the general epistemological principle which Flew and others seem to be taking for granted in proposing the line of objection we are currently considering. The principle itself is reasonably clear, though somewhat difficult to formulate precisely. Thus, if it seems to Smith that he is seeing a large green snake on top of the bar, but this ostensible perception is caused by his consuming too much alcohol rather than by the actual presence of a snake, we would not ordinarily count his experience as cognitive. The issue becomes more complex when an ostensible perception is causally overdetermined.

Imagine, for instance, that the circumstances are the same as in the case just mentioned, except that there really *is* a large green snake where Smith seems to see one. Would Smith then be perceiving the snake? If we are still supposing that its seeming to Smith that he is seeing a snake is caused by the alcohol *rather than* by the presence of a snake, my own inclination would be to answer in the negative. At any rate, here it will be assumed that an experience of X is not a perception of X if it is not in some way causally dependent on X.[28]

Now obviously Flew and his fellow critics require something like step (4) if they are to argue successfully that the theistic character of the Christian mystics' contemplative states can be adequately accounted for in terms of their prior beliefs, and that therefore it is unreasonable to regard these states as perceptions of God; indeed, such a premiss will no doubt be needed in any attempt to disprove the cognitive value of mystical experiences by providing a satisfactory natural explanation of their nature and occurrence. However, once we begin to add the necessary refinements to (4), it becomes less and less clear that it will give these authors what they want. For example, since (4) claims that an experience of X should not be regarded as a perception of X when it is caused "by something other than X," we need some further clarification of what is meant here by a cause "other than X." Now in typical cases of sensory perception, a perception of X is brought about, not by X alone, but by X in conjunction with other prerequisites which can each be called a partial cause of the experience; together with X, these prerequisites constitute a set of sufficient conditions for the occurrence of the ostensible perception. Thus, in order for me to perceive an amoeba through a microscope, it is necessary not only that there be an amoeba present on the microscope slide, but also that the microscope be functioning properly, that there be sufficient light, that I have reasonably good eyesight, and so on; all of these other conditions may also be called "causes" of the perception. But clearly it would not count against the validity of an ostensible perception of X that it has causes "other than X" of this sort, since these are only the other necessary conditions for the perception of X.

Suppose, then, that we try to eliminate this difficulty by replacing (4) with something like the following:

(4') An experience of X is not a perception of X if a set of causally sufficient conditions of the experience is present and in operation at the time it occurs, and X is not a member of the set.

Now the truth of this new version of the fourth step may still be open to doubt. The important point to notice, however, is that once the necessary qualifications are added, the premiss poses no special threat to the defender of mysticism. For if those who propose this argument are going to establish, in (5), that it is unreasonable to regard phenomenally theistic states as perceptions of God, then they will now have to prove that it is reasonable to suppose that there are sets of causally sufficient conditions of these experiences which do not include God and which are operative at the time these states occur. But it is not at all clear how they could show this, except by proving that God does not exist, since according to the traditional Christian notion of God, God's causal activity is a necessary condition for the occurrence of any experiences whatsoever.[29] And as I have tried to indicate above, the strongest conclusion one could legitimately draw from the preceding steps of the argument is that some prior belief in God is a *necessary* condition for having phenomenally theistic mystical experiences; Flew and his fellow critics have not shown that this prior belief is by itself a *sufficient* cause of such experiences, nor that God is not among the necessary conditions for their occurrence.

Since the argument fails to establish the weaker conclusion, in (5), that it is unreasonable to regard theistic mystical states as cognitive, it certainly fails to establish the stronger conclusion, in (6), that it is unreasonable to consider mystical awareness in general as a cognitive mode of experience. Though the content of contemplative states may indeed vary somewhat according to the subject's prior beliefs, this does not mean that they are all equally dubious, despite what (6) suggests; on the contrary, if (5) is false, then there might be grounds for claiming that phenomenally theistic experiences are more likely to be cognitive than certain other types, as noted earlier. Besides, even if (5) were true, it would not entail (6), for one could argue, as C. D. Broad apparently does, that quite apart from the theistic or non-theistic character of mystical states, there remain a sufficient number of features common to the experiences of all mystics, regardless of their background, that it is reasonable to ascribe some cognitive value to this mode of awareness (see above and Broad 1953, pp. 193-194).

In short, this argument does not succeed in demonstrating that it is unreasonable to think that mystical experiences are sometimes veridical, and sometimes involve perceptions of God. However, like the preceding objections, it does direct our attention to some curious data. For if we suppose that mystics of different backgrounds disagree about the nature of the Ultimate Reality they seem to experience, and if we also suppose that there *is* an Ultimate Reality with the nature ascribed to it by one of these competing religious belief-systems, it may nevertheless strike us as odd that this Reality should be accurately perceived only by mystics of that particular tradition. Thus even committed Christian contemplatives may wonder why the God they seem to encounter in their experiences does not manifest himself more clearly to Theravadins. By itself, then, the fact (if it is a fact) that what a subject seems to perceive in mystical experiences is generally not part of a belief system which he does not know or accept, but instead is broadly compatible with his prior religious views, might be regarded as counting *against* the cognitive value of mystical states in general, and theistic experiences in particular, though perhaps not very strongly (since the defender of mysticism has some fairly plausible ways of accounting for it). In any event, this correspondence between the content of mystical experiences and their recipient's prior beliefs and expectations can be symbolized for future reference as "E_{12}" and should be included among the evidence on which an explanatory inference might be based.

5.2. Objections Based on the Issue of Testability

One of the most common criticisms of mystical states as a "way of knowing" is that they fail to satisfy certain standards of testability which any experience must meet if it is to count as cognitive and be regarded as a perception. Thus Hepburn writes:

> If someone claims to have discovered, perceived, become aware of an ordinary sort of object, we usually know what to do about checking his claim. If we are told that there is a frog in the garden pond, we know what it will be like to confirm this or to find it untrue.... But when someone claims to have direct awareness of God, to encounter, see, or intuit the divine, we are not able to suggest a test performance of an even remotely analogous kind. The more developed and theologically sophisticated the concept of deity is, the more it eludes and resists any such check. (Hepburn 1967b, 'Religious Experience, Argument for the Existence of God,' *Encyclopedia of Philosophy*, vol. 7, p. 166; cf. Hepburn 1968, pp. 24-59)

According to A. J. Ayer, the fact that the mystic "cannot reveal what he 'knows,' or even himself devise an empirical test to validate his 'knowledge,' shows that his state of mystical intuition is not a genuinely cognitive state" (1946, p. 119). William Blackstone insists that the claim to have encountered God in mystical experience "cannot be classified as knowledge" because "there are no intersubjective testing procedures for checking such claims" (1963, pp. 141-142). Finally, in the most famous and influential presentation of this objection, C. B. Martin observes:

> Certainly, people have had special sorts of experiences which incline them to claim with the greatest confidence that their experiences are of God. But whether the experiences are or are not of God is not to be decided by describing or having those experiences.... The presence of a piece of blue paper is not to be read off from my experience as of a piece of blue paper. Other things are relevant: What would a photograph reveal? Can I touch it? What do others see? It is only when I admit the relevance of such checking procedures that I can lay claim to apprehending the paper, and, indeed, the admission of the relevance of such procedures is what gives meaning to the assertion that I am apprehending the paper. *What I apprehend is the sort of thing that can be photographed, touched, and seen by others....*
> It can be objected, "But God is different, and we never meant that our experience of God should be checked by procedures relevant to physical objects." Of course not, but what *sort* of checks are there then, so that we are left with more than the mere experiences

what *sort* of checks are there then, so that we are left with more than the mere experiences whose existence even the atheist need not deny. (1959, pp. 87-88; cf. Schmidt 1961, pp. 49-56, 97-101, 122-136; Gunderson in Hick 1964, pp. 57-58; and Hospers 1967, p. 447)

Before attempting a formal reconstruction of this line of argument, several comments are in order. In the first place, since one of the most common ways of checking an ostensible perception is by comparing it with the experience of others, the issue of testability is closely related to the issue of inter-subjective agreement just discussed. Part I of this chapter tried to show that *by itself* the apparent lack of accord between the mystic and the non-mystic, and between mystics of different traditions, does not provide decisive grounds for rejecting the cognitive value of contemplative consciousness. But in this section we are considering the issue of inter-subjective agreement only insofar as it constitutes one of the checking procedures for evaluating perceptual claims.

Second, as Hepburn notes, some critics point out "a disturbing resemblance between claims to experience God and a certain other range of statements that are not publicly testable—namely, psychological statements such as 'I seem to hear a buzzing noise,' or 'I seem to see a patch of purple,'" which "cannot be refuted, ...only because they make no assertions about what exists, beyond the experiences of the speaker at the moment he speaks" (Hepburn 1967, 'Religious Experience, Argument for the Existence of God,' *Encyclopedia of Philosophy,* vol. 7, p. 166; cf. Flew 1966, 124-139; Schmidt 1961, pp. 133-135; and, of course, Martin 1959, pp. 64-88). I am taking it for granted here, however, that no clear-thinking mystic will want to preserve his mystical claims from all possible disconfirmation at the cost of reducing them to mere reports about his subjective impressions. On the contrary, contemplative states typically have a strong noetic character, and seem to their recipients to reveal an ultimate order of reality or truth, in comparison with which "all natural and political knowledge of the world is ignorance" (**C** 26, xiii; cf. **A** I, 4, v).

I am also assuming, in the third place, that what it seems to mystics that they encounter in contemplative consciousness is not to be conceived in crudely anthropomorphic or physical terms.[30] If someone insisted that her religious experiences put her in touch with a divinity who lives on Mount Olympus and has a human body, we could in principle check her claim by exploring the mountain in question; if our explorations failed to turn up anything, we would presumably conclude that her experiences were not veridical. The testability requirement poses a special problem for the contemplative mode of awareness only insofar as its object is supposed to be immaterial, transcendent, and so on, and thus seems to elude the tests we ordinarily use in evaluating ostensible perceptions.

Fourth, a surprising number of critics flatly assert that there simply are no testing procedures for evaluating alleged mystical perceptions, and that "many theologians deny the possibility of any such test or tests" (Martin

1959, p. 67; see also Blackstone 1963, pp. 140-145). However, more careful writers question the *adequacy* rather than the *existence* of such checks, recognizing that mystics and mystical theologians do in fact employ a whole variety of criteria (which include both empirical tests and considerations of logic) in determining the veridicality of mystical states. Thus, as Wainwright points out, most Christian mystics would admit that their reports of mystical union with God would be discredited if it were proved that God did not exist or that the notion of God were incoherent (1973a, pp. 260-261; idem 1981, pp. 84-86).[31] We have likewise come across a number of other criteria in our study of the doctrine of St. John of the Cross. Thus John clearly teaches that the overall effect of authentic contemplative experiences upon their recipients must be positive, tending toward an increase in physical and psychological well-being, and in the virtues of wisdom, charity, humility, fortitude, and so on; in his view, states which seem to arise from "melancholia or some other humor" (N I, 9, iii), or which produce "spiritual dryness...and an inclination to self-esteem" (A II, 24, vii) are less likely to be valid mystical perceptions (see also, e.g., A II, 13, vi; 29, viii-xi; 30, iv). Contemplative communications which are truly of divine origin are likewise expected to have beneficial effects on others, and to involve a depth, sublimity, and delight which other states lack; one of the reasons John gives for a negative evaluation of the experiences of a certain Carmelite nun is that they lead her to make foolish assertions "about what she said to God and God said to her" ('Censure and Opinion on the Spirit and the Attitude in Prayer of a Discalced Carmelite Nun').[32] Another important criterion for John is conformity with Scripture, the doctrine of the Church, and the teaching and paradigmatic experiences of recognized authorities on the Christian spiritual life (e.g., Aquinas, Pseudo-Dionysius, Gregory the Great); he is inclined to doubt the veridicality of any religious experience which gives rise to claims which are not even roughly compatible with orthodoxy (see, e.g., A Prologue, ii; II, 22, v-xi; 24, i; 27, iv; 29, xii; C Prologue, i; iv; F Prologue, i; 2, xiii). In addition, John consistently maintains that an experience cannot be authentic contemplation if it involves particular images and ideas, as I have indicated earlier; this, however, may simply be part of the definition of a contemplative state for him. Finally, John gives a good deal of weight to the judgment of a qualified spiritual director, who has a sound theological background and is familiar with the states in question.

These, then, are the sorts of criteria which mystics like John use in distinguishing veridical from non-veridical mystical apprehensions. As noted, more careful writers do not deny that such checks are employed, but instead question their adequacy. They argue that procedures for testing ostensible perceptions must be *of a certain kind;* in particular, the tests must be relevant, and must be such that satisfaction of them tends to confirm claims based upon these experiences, rather than their contradictories (see especially Nielsen 1971, pp. 60-65; cf. Wainwright 1973a, pp. 269-270). An investigation determining the color of Smith's eyes, for example, would be an inappropriate checking procedure for evaluating his claim to see a tree, since the results have no bearing on the truth or falsity of his statement; on the other hand, a procedure which ascertained whether he had any eyes at all *would* be relevant. Now the problem with the criteria outlined above, according to the critics, is that they do nothing to establish the truth of mystical claims, because fundamentally incompatible states "are admitted by these criteria," and because the atheist can cheerfully concede that contemplative experiences cause good effects, are delightful, and so on, while denying their cognitive value (Hospers 1967, p. 447; cf. Schmidt 1961, pp. 54-55, 98-99; and Martin 1959, pp. 88-94). By contrast, satisfaction of the checking procedures ordinarily used in evaluating standard perceptual claims do tend to confirm their truth. Consequently, the critics would say, mystical experiences should not be considered cognitive, because they are not testable in the way that any experience must be if it is to be counted as a perception.

In light of the foregoing comments, this whole line of objection might be summarized as follows: mystics report experiences in which they seem to be aware of some transcendent order of reality, or to encounter God. Now in order for any ostensible perception to be counted as cognitive, it must be open to to relevant checking procedures; there must be possible tests the satisfaction of which would tend to count in favor of perceptual claims based on the experience, and against incompatible assertions. The mystics and their supporters maintain that the veridicality of contemplative states can be tested by their coherence, their effects on the recipient and others, their depth, sweetness, orthodoxy, and so on. However, these criteria are so general that they are fulfilled by fundamentally incompatible types of mystical consciousness (e.g., by both the theistic experiences of the Christian mystic and the non-theistic experiences of the Theravadin mystic). In addition, there is no inconsistency in admitting that these states are beneficial, coherent, and so on, while denying their veridicality. Thus, satisfaction of the checking procedures proposed by the mystics and their supporters does not tend to count in favor of the truth of claims based upon contemplative experiences, nor do there seem to be any other tests which would do the job. Consequently, it is unreasonable to regard contemplative consciousness as a cognitive mode of experience.

We can present the argument more formally as follows:

(1) Mystics claim that their contemplative experiences involve an awareness of God, or at least of some transcendent order of reality.

(2) Now it is unreasonable to regard alleged perceptions of X as cognitive unless the claim to have perceived X is subject in principle to appropri

ate checking procedures, the results of which have bearing on the issue of its truth or falsity.

(3) In particular, there must be some conceivable outcome of these tests which would not be equally compatible with the denial of the perceptual claim in question.

(4) Many mystics and mystical theologians insist that the veridicality of alleged mystical perceptions can be evaluated by checking whether the experience is coherent, whether its effects are beneficial for the recipient and others, whether it is profound, sublime, delightful, consistent with orthodoxy, approved by qualified spiritual authorities, and so on.

(5) However, the critic can consistently admit that a mystical experience meets such tests while denying that the experience is cognitive.

(6) In addition, these criteria are satisfied by fundamentally incompatible types of mystical awareness. For example, Teresa's assertion that she enjoyed mystical union with God, and the claim of an oriental mystic to have apprehended an impersonal Absolute, both satisfy these tests even though the latter entails the falsity of the former.

(7) Hence, the checking procedures proposed by mystics and mystical theologians for the evaluation of perceptual claims based on contemplative states have no possible outcome which is not equally compatible with the denial of these claims.

(8) Moreover, there seem to be no other tests which would meet the necessary requirements.

(9) Therefore, it is unreasonable to regard contemplative consciousness as a cognitive mode of experience.

Let us begin by granting the truth of the first premiss. Step (2) asserts that it is unreasonable to regard an ostensible perception of X as cognitive unless the claim to have perceived X is subject in principle to appropriate checking procedures, the results of which must have a bearing on the question of its truth or falsity. This premiss is slightly more controversial; perhaps we can imagine some creature so strange and unpredictable that no sighting of it could ever be tested. (Suppose, for example, that there were creatures which existed only for an instant, and appeared only to those who were alone, and then only rarely; if it is possible to speak of seeing such a creature, then we might have an instance of a perception which could never be tested.) However, let us assume here that (2) is true. Thus, to borrow an example from Martin, if someone "claims to see a blue piece of paper" imperceptible to anyone else, but refuses to acknowledge the relevance of any checking procedures because "it isn't the sort of thing that can be photographed, touched, or seen by others," we would be unwilling to count his experience as a perception of a blue piece of paper; even if he allowed that his claim could be tested by determining if the President of the United States is older than 65, our judgment would still be negative, since the results of such a test are not relevant to the cognitive status of ostensible perceptions of this sort (Martin 1959, p. 88).

Nevertheless (2) requires some further clarifications. First, the nature of what is ostensibly perceived "should (at least in part) determine the tests for its presence" (Wainwright 1981, p. 94). We do not reject claims to have seen a new star or to feel a sudden increase in the humidity simply because they are not amenable to the same simple checks we use in evaluating alleged sightings of trees and cars. Again, if we lived in a world where "mountains jumped about in a discontinuous fashion, randomly appeared and disappeared, and behaved in other lawless and unpredictable ways," we would naturally need to modify the procedures we now employ in determining the veridicality of ostensible mountain-experiences; testing would presumably become even more difficult with a being which has some control over whether it is perceived or not (Ibid.).

Second, the results of the checking procedures need only "have a bearing" on the truth or falsity of the perceptual claim in question; it is not necessary that some possible outcome of these tests *entail* the cognitivity of the experience. Using Martin's example, it is *appropriate* to test Smith's claim to see a blue piece of paper by taking photographs, trying to touch it, consulting the experiences of others, and so on, since the results would tend to confirm or disconfirm his assertion; however, it is logically *possible* that Smith's experience should fail to be cognitive even though all of the relevant tests are satisfied (perhaps everyone is being tricked by a demon, for example). Now it might be argued that, regardless of logical entailment, there comes a point in such cases where further doubt of the perceptual claim is no longer *reasonable*. However, while this may be true for standard experiences of familiar medium-size objects (e.g., cars, trees, pieces of paper), it is not clear that it is always true for more unusual ostensible perceptions. Thus suppose that a "chicken-sexer" with a 60% success rate claims to be able to perceive that this particular chick is female, although he cannot explain how he knows; even if the chick developed into a hen and the chicken-sexer's experience passed every other test we could think of (e.g., it occurred while he was sober, looking in the right direction, with good lighting), it would not be manifestly irrational to continue maintaining that, on this occasion, he just made a lucky guess.[33]

Third, it is not clear that the testing procedures need to involve an entirely different mode of experience than that of the ostensible perception being evaluated. As Wainwright notes, for example, there seem to be no checks of alleged "'tree experiences' (those complex experiences involving visual, tactual...elements, which reveal the presence of trees)" which "do not directly or indirectly rely on the tree experiences of ourselves and others" (1973, pp. 276). Consequently, if someone's doubt about the veridicality of an ostensible tree experience were based on skepticism about the cognitive value of tree experiences in general, we would not be able to allay his doubts by *independently* establishing the existence of trees at certain places and times and showing how these are correlated with the occurrence of tree experiences. Nevertheless, this inability by itself gives us no grounds for thinking that it is unreasonable to regard any tree experience as cognitive. Analogously, it may not be reasonable to demand that *religious* experiences be testable by *sensory* observations, as Ayer and Nielsen presumably hold; at least this demand requires further argument.

The point of these qualifications is to prevent us from simply reading a controversial world-view into the standards of testability we adopt. If the critics flatly insist, without further argument, that the only "appropriate checking procedures" for ostensible perceptions of *any* kind are those used in the evaluation of ordinary sensory experiences, then they are begging the question against the mystic; they are *stipulating*, rather than *proving*, that nonsensory mystical perceptions of the divine are impossible. On the other hand, step (2), properly clarified, expresses a principle which most mystics and their partisans would be willing to accept.

The wording of the third premiss is based on certain remarks by Nielsen. In *Contemporary Critiques of Religion*, he maintains that the assertion "God governs the world" as well as its denial, "It is not the case that God governs the world," are both "devoid of factual content" because "both statements...seem equally compatible with all actual or conceivable empirical phenomena" (1971, pp. 63-64).[34] Nielsen therefore would presumably endorse the idea, expressed in (3), that it is unreasonable to regard an ostensible perception of X as cognitive unless there are in principle some tests of the claim to have perceived X with a conceivable outcome which would not be "equally compatible" with its denial. Certain remarks in *Religious Belief* indicate that this premiss represents the views of Martin as well (1959, pp. 88-94; cf. Pletcher 1971, pp. 30-45).

Clearly, the problem with (3) lies in the ambiguity of the requirement that there be imaginable test results which are not "equally compatible" with both the claim to have perceived X and its denial. Insofar as this is simply another way of saying that these test results must "have a bearing" on the question of the truth or falsity of the perceptual claim, (3) is no more than a restatement of (2), and could therefore be willingly accepted by the mystics and their supporters, with the qualifications noted before. (Thus if Jones refuses to allow any checks on his alleged sighting of a new planet except for tests determining George Bush's age, weight, annual income, and so on, his perceptual claim could be dismissed on the basis of (3); here any outcome of the proposed tests is "equally compatible" with his claim or its denial, because such tests are completely *irrelevant* to the cognitive status of his experience.)

However, authors such as Nielsen and Martin would want to give the third premiss a much stronger interpretation. Judging from the passage cited above, Nielsen would apparently hold that the outcome of a checking procedure is "equally compatible" with a perceptual claim and its denial as long as the skeptic can admit that the test is satisfied while refusing to accept the claim in question. But when the third premiss is understood in this way, it becomes much less plausible, for reasons we have already seen; even for familiar sensory experiences, there is no *logical* inconsistency in rejecting the veridicality of an ostensible perception while acknowledging that it fulfulls all of the relevant tests. Nielsen might respond that he is only demanding conceivable test results which would put the truth or falsity of a putative perceptual claim beyond all *reasonable* doubt.[35] But while this requirement may be legitimate for *some* ostensible perceptions (e.g., ordinary experiences of trees, cars, houses) its legitimacy in *all* cases is by no means obvious (recall the chicken-sexer example mentioned above), nor is it altogether obvious that mystical experiences would be unable to meet this demand. Even if no *actual* outcome of current testing procedures puts the veridicality of mystical experiences beyond all reasonable doubt, it is not clear that no *possible* outcome could do this; thus if such experiences were far more widespread, mystical testimony far more unanimous, if there were support from miracles, voices from the heavens, etc., then the skeptic's position would presumably begin to seem like sheer stubbornness. But if Nielsen and Martin retreat to the assertion that "some kind of observation" must be "relevant" to the truth or falsity of a perceptual claim, then they are simply reiterating the principle already expressed in (2), which the mystic can adopt without difficulty, as we shall see.

Step (4) lists some of the checking procedures employed by mystics and mystical theologians to discern the authenticity of alleged mystical perceptions, and should be acceptable to both the defender and the critic of mysticism's cognitive value. Of course, the criteria mentioned here (for example, sublimity, beneficial effects, orthodoxy) are not the only ones used; those evaluating an experience may also ask whether it bears some of the other phenomenal "marks" discussed in the previous chapter, e.g., whether the experience was *passive*, whether its ostensible object seemed *holy* (cf. Clarke 1964, pp. 58-60). It should likewise be noted that such checks are generally employed, not in the context of philosophical debate, but rather in pastoral practice, as handy though fallible rules of thumb. Still, even the critic can recognize that many of these tests are in some sense *relevant* to the question of the truth or falsity of a mystic's claims. It seems unlikely, for example, that a contemplative could have been in mystical union with a compassionate God of love if the experience turned out to have overwhelm ingly destructive effects (cf. Wainwright 1981, pp. 97-98); by contrast, when we evaluate astronomers' claims to have seen new stars through their telescopes, we are not particularly concerned with the spiritual and psychological impact of their experiences, since we have no particular reason to suppose that a veridical visual experience of a new star is any more likely to produce beneficial psychological effects than a non-veridical one. Both the mystic and the critic could agree, then, that the failure to satisfy at least some of these criteria would tend to count *against* the veridicality of a contemplative experience.

I am willing to grant the truth of the fifth step, which says that the critic can consistently admit that a mystical experience meets the criteria proposed by mystics and mystical theologians while denying that the experience is cognitive. I have much stronger reservations about the assertion, in (6), that these criteria are satisfied by fundamentally incompatible types of mystical awareness. Thus it is not strictly true that a contemplative state which seemed to conflict with Christian mystical experiences would meet all of *John's* criteria; presumably it would not satisfy his orthodoxy requirement. However, since determining whether a given experience is broadly compatible with Christian doctrine would not be a *relevant* test unless we had other grounds for thinking that the doctrine is true, we may let this point pass. (It might be relevant, however, to see whether the experience is compatible with some religious tradition or other; if it turned out to be fundamentally incompatible with the mystical experiences of *every* tradition, this would make the experience more dubious, since it seems unlikely that this particular experience is veridical while all the others are not.)

A more important objection to (6) is that it is uncertain to what extent different kinds of contemplative consciousness are fundamentally incompatible. For example, Hospers (1967, p. 445) apparently believes that the Christian's experience of the Christian God and the Sufi's experience of Allah could not both be cognitive; however, given the historical relationship between Islam and Christianity this view appears doubtful, once proper allowance is made for differences in vocabulary and emphasis between the two religions. A more plausible example of fundamental incompatibility would be to suppose, as (6) suggests, that some eastern mystics have contemplative experiences which are decidedly *atheistic* in their implications, and seem to preclude the veridicality of Teresa's ostensible encounters with a loving, personal God. It is arguable whether eastern mystics ever have experiences of this sort, but let us assume that they sometimes do, and that these states have beneficial effects, are profound, sublime, delightful, roughly compatible with Buddhist doctrine, approved by qualified spiritual masters, and so on.

The seventh step, which many philosophers apparently believe is deducible from either (5) or (6), asserts that any possible outcome of the checking procedures employed by mystics and mystical theologians in evaluating contemplative claims is equally compatible with the denial of these claims. Step (3), on the other hand, has already state that it is unreasonable to count alleged perceptions of X as cognitive unless the claim to have perceived X is subject in principle to tests with conceivable results which would *not* be equally compatible with the denial of this perceptual claim. Now if any skeptical conclusion about the cognitive value of mysticism is to follow from the combination of (3) and (7), the expression "equally compatible" must be given the same meaning in both steps, presumably a meaning which gives (3) some likelihood of being true. But I have argued above that the third premiss is highly plausible only if the phrase is interpreted so as to make (3) equivalent to (2). In order to avoid the fallacy of equivocation, then, the seventh step must also be interpreted as saying that the results of the testing procedures employed by mystics and mystical theologians *have no bearing* on the issue of the truth or falsity of mystical claims. But when (7) is understood in this way, it no longer obviously follows from (5) or (6).

Thus, as noted above in the discussion of (2), the results of appropriate tests can *have a bearing* on a perceptual claim but still not entail its truth, nor even place it beyond all reasonable doubt. Consequently, from the assertion in (5) that the critic can consistently deny that the mystic's experience is cognitive while admitting that it satisfies all the proposed tests, one cannot necessarily infer that such tests have no bearing on the truth or falsity of the mystic's perceptual claims. Indeed, most of the criteria suggested are clearly *relevant* to the cognitive status of mystical experiences, given the nature of the object or reality ostensibly perceived; one need not believe in God, for example, to see that if a mystical encounter with God really did occur, it would presumably have positive effects for the recipient and others, lead to an increase in charity and humility, be profound, delightful, and so on. In this respect, the mystic's claims are better able than other religious statements to meet Nielsen's demand (1971, p. 60) that "some at least in principle observable state of affairs or happenings or series of happenings" count for or against its truth, since these criteria specify possible observations which would strongly *disconfirm* the veridicality of his contemplative state (cf. Mitchell 1981, pp. 11-14). And it seems fair to say that satisfaction of the proposed criteria counts to some extent *in favor* of the mystic's claim, just as the successful outcome of tests measuring the chicken-sexer's sobriety and visual acuity weakly confirms his claim to perceive that a given chick is female, without establishing the truth of his assertion. (In general, there seems to be no reason to deny that satisfaction of the criteria proposed for evaluating mystical experiences weakly confirms their veridicality, which would not also be a reason for denying that satisfaction of checks on a person's physical and emotional condition, sensory powers, and so on, weakly confirms the veridicality of his or her unusual sensory experiences.)

Nor is (7) implied by (6). To see this, let us return to our assumption above that certain eastern mystics have atheistic mystical experiences which they describe in terms of an impersonal Void, that Teresa enjoys theistic mystical states which she describes as encounters with God, and that both types of experience fully satisfy the proposed criteria, though both cannot be veridical. This presumably means that, insofar as the checking procedures used by mystics and mystical theologians confirm the veridicality of either sort of contemplative consciousness, they confirm both of them. It does not follow, however, that the outcome of these procedures *has no bearing* on the truth of Teresa's theistic claims, just because it also seems to support a contrary assertion. To see this, imagine that a detective is trying to determine who poisoned Harry at the party, and that the maid claims to have seen Dick slipping arsenic into his drink, that the butler asserts that he saw Tom do it, and that there are fifty others who were present and had a viable motive. Imagine also that by means of various checking procedures the detective is able to eliminate all other suspects except Tom and Dick; certainly the results of these tests count in favor of the veridicality of the maid's ostensible perception (and *a fortiori* have a bearing on her perceptual claim), even though they provide equal support for the butler's experience (cf. Swinburne 1979, p. 19). Similarly, tests determining the effects, depth, sublimity, etc. do *have a bearing* on the claims of Teresa and the eastern mystic to have apprehended and been mystically united with the "Absolute" (which the former describes in theistic and the latter in atheistic terms), for even if they cannot conclusively establish which of the two claims is true, they could conceivably show that both are false; indeed, the proposed criteria could theoretically have indicated that *all* alleged mystical perceptions were non-cognitive, because none of them were sufficiently sublime, had sufficiently good effects on the recipient and others, and so on. Perhaps the critic will insist that, in order for mystical experience to be regarded as cognitive, there must be checking procedures which could decide once and for all which type of contemplative consciousness is veridical; however, this requires further argument, since it is not clear that the critic is thereby making a reasonable demand.

In short, there appears to be no interpretation of the phrase "equally compatible" which would make steps (3) and (7) both acceptable. Even if they were true, however, step (8) would still remain doubtful, because there seem to be other possible, though unlikely, observations which could have a bearing on the truth of mystical claims. For example, if future research produced overwhelming evidence that Jesus had never existed and that the whole Bible was a tissue of lies, this would presumably tend to count against the veridicality of at least some of St. Teresa's contemplative experiences.

Thus the argument fails to establish the conclusion, in (9), that it is unreasonable to regard contemplative consciousness as a cognitive mode of experience. Moreover, the present objection, in contrast to those considered above, does not direct our attention to any additional puzzling data to be accounted for in an explanatory inference. As far as I can see, mystical experiences and claims are as checkable as we can reasonably expect them to be, given the nature of the ostensible object of these states. The only "fact" which might be regarded as puzzling in this context is that the relevant tests are not more often and more fully satisfied, i.e., that the number of mystical states with good effects, depth, and so on is not as great as one might initially expect if such states were veridical. And this has more to do with questioning the strength of the positive evidence listed in the second part of the preceding chapter, an issue that will be treated again below in connection with the "explanatory inference" I plan to develop.

5.3. Other Objections

The final portion of this chapter deals with a few additional objections which cannot be easily fitted under the headings of testability or intersubjective agreement. These are not as popular, and perhaps not as significant, as those we have already discussed, and can be handled rather briefly, without a formal reconstruction of each argument. Still, they merit at least passing consideration.

First of all, some authors defend a negative conclusion about the cognitive value of mystical experiences on the grounds that such states are not properly "objective." Thus Richard Gale writes:

Mere unanimity or agreement among observers is not a sufficient condition for objectivity. *Everybody* who presses his finger on his eyeball will see double,.... The true criterion for objectivity is the Kantian one: An experience is objective if its contents can be placed in a spatio-temporal order with other experiences in accordance with scientific laws. The objectivity of a sense experience means the verifiability of further possible sense experiences which are inferred from this experience in accordance with known scientific laws. In accordance with this criterion we would say that our sense experience of seeing things double when we press our fingers on our eyeball is subjective—a mere illusion—because the inferences we make from this sense experience to other possible sense experiences do not hold....

In accordance with this new criterion for objectivity we must classify mystical experiences as subjective because they represent a break in the temporal continuity of our experience. What we have in the case of mystical experience is a moment of eternity, i.e., phenomenological atemporality, suddenly appearing in the midst of a temporal sequence of events. When the mystic reports that during his experience all change and multiplicity were obliterated, we must, from the naturalistic standpoint, tell him that he was "seeing things." Because we cannot fit the content of mystical experiences into a temporal order with other experiences in accordance with scientific laws, we must call these experiences subjective. (Gale 1960, pp. 479-480; cf. Stace 1960a, pp. 139-146)

Now this argument seems to be open to several fatal objections. First, many experiences which Gale considers "illusions" would meet his criterion of objectivity. Thus the example of eyeball-pressing is poorly chosen, since we certainly can make predictions about our future experiences once we understand how this action affects our vision; I can know, for instance, that when I reach toward what appear to be two apples on the table before me, I will touch only one.

Second, I see no reason to deny that there might be truly objective experiences which nevertheless could not be fit into a spatio-temporal ordering, and do not provide grounds for future predictions. Thus, as Hepburn notes, "we may be quite properly convinced that certain phenomena are objective before we have assured ourselves of their orderliness, and they may indeed remain anomalous" (Hepburn 1967a, 'Mysticism, Nature and Assessment of,' *Encyclopedia of Philosophy,* vol. 5, p. 432).

Third, Gale ties objectivity too closely to our current state of scientific knowledge. An Amazonian tribesman who sees an eclipse may not be able to predict his future sensations "in accordance with known scientific laws," but his experience of the event is surely every bit as objective as our own. If Gale merely wants to claim that predictions of *some* sort must be possible, then it is no longer clear that mysticism would fail to meet such a weakened criterion of objectivity. According to John's teaching on spiritual development, for example, one *can* to some extent predict the course of future contemplative experiences on the basis of mystical states; one can predict, for example, that the "transitory unions" of spiritual espousal will eventually give way to the sense of permanent union in spiritual marriage, if all goes well. To sum up, then, Gale has not shown that mystical experiences are non-objective in an epistemically interesting sense.

A second line of objection is sometimes raised against those who would describe mystical consciousness as an encounter with God. Alasdair MacIntyre asks:

If God is infinite, how can he be manifest in any particular finite object or experience? The definition of God as infinite is intended precisely to distinguish between God and everything finite, but to take the divine out of the finite is to remove it from the entire world of human experience. The inexorable demands of religiously adequate language seem to make of experience of God a notion that is a contradiction in terms. (MacIntyre 1966, p. 256; cf. Whitely in Lewis & Whitely 1955, pp. 91-92)

Hepburn likewise observes that:

...if part of what we mean by "God" is "an infinitely and eternally loving Being," no conceivable experience or finite set of experiences could by itself entitle us to claim that we had experienced such a being. We might well report experiencing "a sense of immense benevolence toward us," "a sense of complete safety and well-being," but from their intensity alone one could not rigorously conclude, "Therefore I am in touch with an infinitely and eternally loving God." (Hepburn 1967b, 'Religious Experience, Argument for the Existence of God,' *Encyclopedia of Philosophy,* vol. 7, p. 167)

While MacIntyre and Hepburn are making slightly different points, both seem to agree that, given the definition of God as infinite, no finite human being could ever knowingly encounter God in a religious experience. To answer this charge adequately, we would need to furnish a general account of the relationship between religious language and human experience, something obviously beyond the scope of this study. Still, the following comments should be sufficient for present purposes.

In the first place, this line of objection, on the face of it, seems extremely odd. If a philosopher proposes an account of material objects according to which perceptions of tables, houses, rocks, trees and other such things are *logically impossible*, we naturally suspect, in lieu of further argument, that there is something wrong with the particular philosophical theory which leads to such radical results. Similarly, if MacIntyre could show that, according to a certain understanding of divine infinitude, the notion of an experience of God is "a contradiction in terms," the believer would presumably conclude, not that encounters with God are impossible, but rather that God is not "infinite" in this problematic sense. After all, the philosophical notion of divine infinitude from which MacIntyre is arguing is a relatively late development in the ongoing effort of Christian believers to articulate their faith. Philosophers sometimes insist that that anything which lacked this kind of infinitude would not be a "suitable object of worship," but such an assertion seems highly doubtful as it stands.

Second, this line of objection seems to involve a confusion about the meaning of the claim that all human experience is finite. It is undoubtedly true that the subjects who have these human experiences are all finite. From this it does not necessarily follow, however, that the *object* of such experiences must be finite, particularly if human beings have a certain capacity for experiencing the infinite, as St. John of the Cross claims (see, for example, F 3, xviii-xx). Certainly finite minds have the capacity to conceive infinite numbers, as mathematicians can testify. If there is some special logical difficulty with the notion of a finite subject *experiencing* the infinite, it needs to be further explained. (MacIntyre may share the common view of Locke, Hume, Kant and others that our perceptual faculties are constitutionally suited only to the apprehension and knowledge of finite realities, but whether or not such a view is correct is part of the question raised by the mystical data.)

Finally, even if the mystic "could not rigorously conclude" from the phenomenal features of his contemplative experience that its object possesses all of the properties attributed to God by orthodox Christian theologians, his theistic interpretation of the state is not wholly gratuitous. Thus, it is part of the "felt character" of many of the states reported by Teresa and John that their ostensible object is apprehended as nonsensuous, personal, loving, holy, and supremely valuable. At times the mystic seems to be aware of this "object" or reality present in all things, sustaining their existence, with its power apparently unlimited by anything external to itself. Moreover, this ostensible object of contemplative consciousness discloses a seemingly endless array of attributes and virtues all united in one single being (see, e.g., **F** 3, ii-vi). While these and other phenomenal properties might not *require* that contemplative states be characterized as encounters with the ubiquitous, omnipotent, infinitely good and loving God of tradition, such an interpretation is certainly reasonable, especially since, for John and Teresa, the categories of Christian orthodoxy seem to fit the experiences so well (cf. Becker 1971, pp. 66-67). In short, then, this argument appears unsuccessful in discredited theistic accounts of mystical consciousness.

According to a third line of objection, we could never be justified in regarding mystical awareness as cognitive except on the basis of a probability estimate which is impossible in principle to attain. Thus George Nakhnikian writes:

> The logic of the situation is very much like the one mapped out by Hume in the *Dialogues on Natural Religion*.... It is conceivable that our feelings of cosmic thankfulness and cosmic awe have a fitting recipient, but the mere fact of our having the feelings does not support the probability of the hypothesis. (Nakhnikian 1961, p. 160)

Similarly, John Hick's response to theologians who claim that "a theistic interpretation of the world is superior to its alternatives because it alone takes adequate account of man's moral and religious experience" is that "as David Hume points out in his discussion of analogical reasoning, the fact that there is only one universe precludes our making probable judgments about it" (1963, p. 29).[36] And Basil Mitchell asks, "How could one estimate the degree of probability that an experience represents a genuine encounter with God when one is not in a position to compare the experiences in question with others that are known to be experiences of God?" (1981, p. 31).[37] Such comments suggest the following sort of argument: in order to justify our confidence in the cognitive value of mysticism, we would need to show that mystical states are very likely to be veridical. But in order to show this, we need standards of comparison, either other contemplative states which are antecedently known to be cognitive, or else a set of other universes, in some of which mystical experiences are cognitive, and in some of which they are not. Since these standards are, of course, unavailable, it is unreasonable to regard contemplative awareness as a cognitive mode of experience.

This objection seems misguided for two reasons. First, it is not at all clear that probability judgments require a "plurality of cases," and that therefore no such judgment can be made with respect to the world or the mystical mode of consciousness as a whole; physical cosmologists, for example, obviously do "reach justified conclusions about such matters as the size, age, rate of expansion, and density of the universe as a whole" (Swinburne 1979, p. 117). Second, there seem to be other ways of defending the cognitive value of mysticism which do not rely on any questionable probability judgments. The defense by means of an explanatory inference is one such way, as I hope to show.

Finally, a number of critics challenge the view that mystical and religious experiences are cognitive, and involve encounters with God, on the grounds that this hypothesis fails to provide the only, or even the most adequate, explanation of the phenomena involved. Thus Hepburn remarks that:

...a skeptical critic may deny that the existence of God is the likeliest, or simplest, or most intelligible, explanation of the experiences. We cannot be intellectually compelled to posit God if more economical and naturalistic explanations can be found—psychoanalytic accounts, it might be, or accounts in terms of individual suggestibility or the influence of religious expectations or traditions. (Hepburn 1967b, 'Religious Experience, Argument for the Existence of God,' *Encyclopedia of Philosophy*, vol. 7, p. 164; see also Nakhnikian 1961, p. 160)

Shepherd also writes that:

...it seems possible to provide a naturalistic explanation of mystical experiences.... If a naturalistic explanation of mystical phenomena is available, however, the allegiance to Occam's razor should ensure that it is adopted; for it is then unnecessary to posit an extra entity or state such as God or Nirvana. Thus the basic principle of parsimony pre-empts the positive epistemological inference one might otherwise be tempted to draw from the unity of mystical experience. (1975, pp. 7-8)

Hick likewise commends that "any special event or experience which can be construed as manifesting the divine can also be construed in other ways, and accordingly cannot carry the weight of a proof of God's existence" (1963, p. 29).

Now as Hepburn evidently realizes, the mere fact that some naturalistic account of mystical experiences is *available* does not by itself show that it is a mistake to regard these states as veridical. The real question is instead whether the naturalistic account provides a better explanation of the evidence than the view that contemplative consciousness is a cognitive mode of experience. And the answer to this question will depend, in part, on what we expect of an explanation, and what we take to be the evidence. Thus the proper response to this objection is to argue in detail that the hypothesis (H_1) that contemplative awareness is cognitive offers at least as good an explanation of mystical phenomena as the naturalistic hypotheses which it is reasonable to consider. Developing such an argument is the task of the next chapter.

The preceding pages, then, have dealt with several standard philosophical objections to mysticism based on the issues of testability and agreement, and on other considerations. I have tried to show that none of these objections succeeds in proving *conclusively* that it is unreasonable to regard contemplative consciousness as a cognitive mode of experience, or as a way of knowing God. However, this does not mean that the veridicality of these states has been fully vindicated. On the contrary, even if the standard objections fail as strict refutations, they do point out some potentially embar rassing facts for the defender of H_1, e.g., the relative rarity of mystical experiences, and the nature and extent of the disagreement between mystics of different cultures. Accordingly, we must now ask which hypotheses best account for all the facts, and determine whether the cognitive value of mysticism can be defended by an explanatory inference based on the *total* evidence.

NOTES

[1] Here I will count mystical experiences as a subset of the larger class of religious experiences, since most philosophers clearly intend their objections to the cognitive value of the latter to apply to the former as well. However, I am not trying to settle the complex question of the relationship between mysticism and religion. I realize that some writers insist that "intrinsically and in itself mystical experience is not a religious phenomenon" (Stace 1960b, p. 23; cf. Stace 1960a, pp. 341-343; Staal 1975).

[2] Vague feelings of depression or happiness are often cited as examples of non-intentional states, though some philosophers might want to argue that *all* experiences are intentional in some sense. I am not interested here in settling this issue, except to say that if there *are* any non-intentional states, most mystical experiences are not among them.

[3] Again, this is only a necessary, rather than a sufficient, condition for cognitivity and would need to be spelled out in much greater detail if this were a study in the philosophy of perception. These comments, however, should suffice for present purposes.

[4] This is an important distinction, comparable to the difference between criticizing some proposed solution to skepticism about the external world and actually endorsing a skeptical position. Some authors seem to forget that refuting certain attempts to prove the cognitive value of religious experiences is not the same as proving that these states are not cognitive. Indeed, a few philosophers devote all their attention to showing that the occurrence of these experiences does not logically entail the existence of their object. But if this were the strongest conclusion warranted, it would scarcely pose any special threat to the defender of mysticism, since the same point could be made about sensory experience.

[5] Some authors regard comparison with the experience of others as one of the checking procedures for determining whether an experience is cognitive; in other words, they deal with *agreement* within the context of *testability*. However, because certain special considerations arise in connection with the question of agreement which are not raised by other checks, it will be useful to handle them separately.

[6] For a forceful defense of the notion that agreement among mystics provides strong support for the validity of their experiences, see Pletcher 1971 and idem 1972, pp. 5-15. Yet some critics argue that this very agreement provides grounds for skepticism about the mystics' reports, since the latter individuals are not disinterested observers but are already predisposed to receive and describe such states in the way they do; this objection is discussed in section 5.1.3 of this chapter.

[7] See again Greeley and McCready 1975, pp. 18-21. The authors note that when they first began reporting their findings on the prevalence of ecstatic experiences, many friends and colleagues simply dismissed the data or began searching for natural explanations of these states; a few, however, admitted privately to having such experiences, but explained their

reticence on the subject by noting that, "It just didn't seem to be the kind of thing people talk about" (p. 21).

[8] In many cases only very rudimentary perceptual skills are needed. Most percipients can tell that something is a car or a vine just by looking at it, but it takes greater expertise to identify poison ivy or a 1979 Datsun 280 ZX sports car on sight.

[9] Some might argue that certain experiences are so compelling that it is reasonable, at least for the person who has them, to go on believing in them in spite of overwhelming testimony to the contrary, and that mystical experiences are of this kind; William James seems to suggest a position like this (James 1936, pp. 414-415). I am willing to grant, however, that if the mystic's experience conflicted with the experience of the vast majority of qualified observers and failed to pass all other relevant tests, it would be unreasonable even for the mystic himself to go on believing that his experience was cognitive.

[10] After writing 'A Religious Way of Knowing,' Martin apparently came to realize that his original supposition was not altogether true, since in the corresponding chapter of *Religious Belief* he adds a final section criticizing the "tests" proposed by certain Christian mystics such as St. Teresa; compare Martin 1952, pp. 497-512 with the seventh chapter of Martin's *Religious Belief* (1959).

[11] There might be evidence that I was preoccupied at the time, but it is hard to see how one could independently establish that this preoccupation was *deep* enough to exclude hearing the alarm, and that I was not *deliberately* ignoring this raucous intrusion on my thoughts; for other examples, see Pletcher 1971, pp. 20-32.

[12] See, for example, John's comment in N I, 9, xix: "God does not bring to contemplation all those who purposely exercise themselves in the way of the spirit, nor even half. Why? He best knows." Christian mystics agree that while ascetical exercises may be helpful, they are neither necessary nor sufficient for attaining mystical awareness, which depends on God's initiative.

[13] Compare Mavrodes 1970, pp. 78-80. A Christian mystic like St. John would presumably claim that God antecedently wills to reveal himself in this way to everyone, but chooses not to do so in certain cases because, for example, he respects the individual's right to reject these communications, or recognizes that they might be harmful to him at this time.

[14] Compare Hospers 1967, pp. 445-446. Commenting on the apparent conflict between the religious experiences of believers from different backgrounds, Hospers asks: "Why not admit them all? Because, of course, they contradict each other and cannot all be true" (p. 445).

[15] Penelhum is articulating a skeptical position which he himself does not necessarily share. Both Stace and Broad attribute some cognitive value to mystical experiences, although they deny that these states support belief in God (Broad 1953, pp. 172-173; Stace 1960b, p. 27). In any case, those who wish to appeal to the consensus of mystics in support of Christian beliefs are faced with an apparent dilemma: if they maintain, with Stace and others, that contemplative consciousness is "everywhere the same," then they must also admit that it can be given a non-theistic interpretation, whereas, if they insist that the experiences of theistic mystics are fundamentally different from (and perhaps more "authentic" than) those of their non-theistic counterparts, then they substantially reduce the number of witnesses included in the theistic consensus. Any similar attempt to defend some controversial metaphysical or religious claim on the basis of mystical "unanimity" would seem to be confronted with the same difficulty.

[16] Some authors acquainted with various religions and cultures would argue that much of the disagreement between mystics of different traditions is merely apparent, maintaining, for example, that when eastern mystics deny encountering God in mystical states, they are using "God" in a different sense than Christian mystics use it. The question need not be settled here; I suspect that there really are some genuine differences in the experiences of mystics from different backgrounds, though I would hesitate to say how fundamental these are. Katz presents an extreme version of the pluralistic view of mystical states in Katz 1978, pp. 22-74.

[17] See, for example, C 7, vi-x; 14 & 15, viii; 36, x-xiii; 37, iii-viii. John Hick develops this sort of approach along broadly Kantian lines; see Hick 1977, pp. 47-52, where he suggests that "the infinite Spirit presses in all the time upon the multiplicity of finite human spirits, and yet always so that our finite awareness of this encompassing reality is filtered through a set of human religious concepts" (p. 52). Here the contrasting ostensible objects of mystical states would be the *aspects* under which the one infinite Spirit is experienced.

[18] Reacting to Hick, Penelhum argues that this approach is *possible* but not *preferable*, in Penelhum 1977, pp. 72-81. I suspect that this approach works best in explaining why, for example, some Christian mystics seem to experience the Trinity while others seem primarily to experience the divine unity.

[19] Admittedly, the defenders of mysticism would have much more difficulty affirming the cognitive value of such states if they were forced to concede that a very *sizeable* portion of them (e.g., all those of Eastern mystics) were non-veridical and delusive, since "no type of experience can be called cognitive if it typically induces those who have it to make false claims." In my opinion, however, none of the considerations raised by opponents require the defenders of mysticism to make this concession (cf. Wainwright 1981, p. 83).

[20] An example here might be Daniel Paul Schreber's psychotic experience of "nerve-filaments" leading "from God to his own brain and from there to all other souls, transmitting both voices and poisons," if this can be regarded as a mystical state (see Scharfstein 1974, pp. 134-136). Of course, *all* mystical experiences might be characterized as idiosyncratic by comparison with the everyday experiences of non-mystics. But my point is that we are naturally less inclined to regard X's mystical consciousness as veridical if its ostensible object bears little or no resemblance to that of other contemplative experiences, since to do so would seem to imply that all of these other experiences were non-cognitive, and that the "Ultimate" was manifested to X alone.

[21] Norman Malcolm makes a similar point with respect to ostensible perceptions in Malcolm 1963, p. 39. In the same essay ('The Verification Argument') he writes, "To argue that since some perceptual statements are false therefore it is not certain that any particular perceptual statement is true is unsound reasoning" (p. 49).

[22] Stace, for one, tends to favor this approach, as we have already shown (see 1960a, pp. 55-62; idem 1960b, pp. 14-15).

[23] As I have indicated in earlier chapters, John seems to believe that all contemplative experiences involve some obscure "loving knowledge" of God, although, especially at the beginning and during crisis periods, this delicate awareness may be almost drowned out by distractions and sufferings (see, e.g., A II, 13, vii; 14, viii; N II, 8, iii-v; F 1, xviii-xxvi).

[24] C. D. Broad notes that "when a set of religious beliefs has once been established, it no doubt tends to produce experiences which can plausibly be taken as evidence for it," but he does not feel that this completely undermines mysticism's cognitive value (1953, p.

193). Compare Bertrand Russell's comment that "Catholics, but not Protestants, may have visions in which the Virgin appears; Christians and Mohammedans, but not Buddhists, may have great truths revealed to them by the Archangel Gabriel; the Chinese mystics of the Tao tell us, as a direct result of their central doctrine, that all government is bad, whereas most Europeans and Mohammedan mystics, with equal confidence, urge submission to constituted authority" (1961, p. 180).

[25] St. Paul is the obvious example of a dramatic conversion, though it is not clear to what extent his experience on the road to Damascus should be regarded as mystical. William James describes a number of interesting cases, such as the conversion of M. Alphonse Ratisbonne, "a free-thinking Jew" (1936, pp. 186-253).

[26] See pp. 81-82 and 114-115 above, as well as A Prologue, iii-vii; II, 14, iv; N I, 8, iii; 10, i-vi; II, 2, ii-v; and so on. John also maintains that contemplation involves an increasingly more profound penetration of the divine mysteries (see, e.g., C 7, ix; 37, iv).

[27] Moore's whole article contains a good discussion of this point; see also Katz's 'Language, Epistemology, and Mysticism' on pp. 22-74 of the same volume (Katz 1978). Of course, the critic may wish to counter this reply here by proposing a more sophisticated third step (3'), according to which it seems probable that what the mystic seems to perceive is determined not only by his or her prior religious beliefs and expectations, but also by his or her personality, desires, emotional and physical state, and so on. However, the truth of (3') is no easier to defend without some clearer information about the degree of influence exerted by each of these factors. And in any case, for mystics such as Teresa and John, the reality seemingly encountered never *exactly* corresponds with what a prior knowledge of these factors would lead one to expect.

[28] If I understand him correctly, Wainwright apparently doubts that this assumption is true, and seems uncertain whether or not to call Smith's experience in the second case a perception of the snake (see Wainwright 1973b, p. 98; idem 1981, pp. 69-73). It seems to me, however, that our answer will depend on which factors are playing the decisive causal role in the production of this experience. Thus, suppose that there actually is a snake on the bar, but that, instead of drinking, Smith has taken a drug which causes ostensible perceptions of green snakes only when none are present. In this case, we would probably regard Smith's experience as a perception of a snake, even though the experience would still have occurred even if the snake were not present.

[29] Throughout this section I am indebted to Wainwright 1973b, pp. 98-101; see also Swinburne 1979, pp. 269-270. Granted, God's causal relationship to human experiences is generally different from that of other necessary conditions, insofar as it involves primary rather than secondary causality. Nevertheless, this would not seem to affect the validity of the point made here.

[30] Recall John's constant teaching that all "creatures, earthly or heavenly, and all distinct ideas and images, ...are incomparable and uproportioned to God's being" (A III, 12, i). I make this point in light of Flew's observation that if ordinary empirical checks *were* admitted as relevant to the truth of claims based on religious experience, "the question would by common consent be accounted settled, and in the negative" (1966, p. 139).

[31] Wainwright's discussion of the issues treated in this section is extremely helpful, and I am following his general categories in listing some of the criteria used by John. Although he does not say much about considerations of logic, John would presumably acknowledge their importance, since he insists that matters of faith transcend, but are not contrary to, reason (see A II, 22, xiii).

[32] Among the other reasons John mentions in this opuscule are that the nun involved is overly possessive and self-confident, eager to convince others of the validity of her experiences, and lacking in humility. See also **A** II, 26, v-vi; **N** I, 2, i-viii; **C** 29, i-iii; 36, iv; 39, iii-x.

[33] This example is adapted from Pletcher 1971, pp. 20-21; he discusses many of the issues dealt with here, though his approach is somewhat different. Within a few days of hatching, while "the appropriate organs are as yet indiscernable," accomplished chicken-sexers are able to tell with a high degree of accuracy whether chicks are male or female, even though "there are no features at all which are ever consciously employed in the decision-making process" (Ibid.).

[34] Nielsen's evidence that both statements are equally compatible with all conceivable empirical phenomena is apparently that the non-believer can grant the occurrence of any phenomena which the believer might invoke in defense of his claim, while continuing to deny that God governs the world. His position is not entirely clear, however, since he has earlier said that a "statement is a factual statement only if some kind of observation is relevant to its truth or falsity" (p. 60), which he regards as a defensible version of the principle of verification.

[35] Nielsen's position is unclear. However, since he does say that he is not demanding that some "finite and consistent set of observation statements" entail the affirmation or denial of a factual statement, perhaps the force of noting that the non-believer can persist in his denial despite any possible empirical phenomena is not that such a denial is logically possible, but that it is not unreasonable.

[36] Actually, Hick's discussion is somewhat more sophisticated than this quotation indicates, since he recognizes that there are different theories of probability.

[37] Nonetheless, Mitchell does want to grant religious experience some evidential value.

CHAPTER SIX

MYSTICISM AND THE EXPLANATORY MODE OF INFERENCE

Philosophers who doubt the cognitive value of mysticism will perhaps have felt a growing dissatisfaction with the handling of the issues in the previous chapter, and at this point may want to lodge a general protest against the approach taken in the present study. They might charge that the strength of the critic's case has been seriously underestimated by blithely assuming (according to the all-too-aptly named "principle of credulity") that there is a presumption in favor of the validity of contemplative awareness, and then proceeding to dismiss the standard objections to mysticism's cognitive value because they do not conclusively disconfirm the veridicality of these experiences. For surely when the object of a experience is very strange or unusual, as the object of mystical states certainly is, then the assumption in favor of validity is substantially reduced, and the question of what others observe and what tests reveal becomes crucial. In this respect (they might argue), mystical experiences are more appropriately compared with Linus's reported encounters with the Great Pumpkin (in the comic strip "Peanuts") than with the perceptions of the wine-connoisseur or chicken-sexer.[1] Like the mystic, Linus has ways of explaining why others fail to have similar experiences (e.g., their pumpkin patches are not "sincere"); yet we would reject his alleged perceptions on the basis of considerations like those considered in the fifth chapter. If the force of the standard objections is denied, then, we seem to be opening the floodgates to all sorts of bizarre "perceptions" which can claim as much validity as mystical experiences.

In response, let me hasten to agree that any approach which required us to admit indiscriminately all putative perceptions of Great Pumpkins, gremlins, little green men from outer space, and so on, would for that very reason be highly suspect. I do not believe, however, that the approach taken here has such implausible consequences. I am willing to say, for example, that if it seems to Linus that he is encountering the Great Pumpkin, this gives him and ourselves at least prima facie grounds for thinking that he is.[2] However, the weight of this presumption is more than offset by the fact that Linus's experiences are less successful than mystical states in turning aside the standard objections. Thus, unlike the mystic, Linus stands *completely* alone in his ostensible perception, and offers no plausible reason why the Great Pumpkin should never have appeared before. Moreover, the very notion of a "Great Pumpkin" seems hopelessly confused; is it a pumpkin or a person, material or spiritual, or (*per impossibile*) all of these at once? If Linus holds that it is something like a physical pumpkin, and that he saw it with his own eyes, then his critics can point out that any such thing ought to show up in photographs, on radar, etc., and ought to be visible to others; that is, any normal percipient (e.g., Sally or Charlie Brown) in the same place at the same time would count as a "qualified observer" with respect to Linus's experiences. On the other hand, if Linus tries to avoid this challenge by claiming that the Great Pumpkin has the power to conceal himself even from cameras, and only reveals himself to those who cultivate "sincere" pumpkin patches, then his critics can ask why anything of this sort should be called a Great *Pumpkin,* and rightly insist on some further account of the capabilities and motives of such a being. Indeed, Linus's "saving hypothesis" looks entirely *ad hoc;* he seems to be modifying his perceptual claims after the fact, solely to avoid disconfirmation. By contrast, a mystic like St. Teresa maintains from the beginning that her experiences seemed to be encounters with something nonsensuous, holy, personal, loving, and able to manifest itself at will; we have argued that these features in some way belong to the phenomenal character of the original experience, and are not merely invoked after the fact to explain why others do not enjoy similar states.

But the decisive consideration in rejecting Linus's perceptual claims is that we have a much better explanation of the facts than the one he proposes. In particular, it seems fairly evident that the whole notion of the Great Pumpkin is nothing more than a young boy's garbled version of the Santa Claus legend, and that, like other children with active imaginations, Linus is simply "seeing things." This hypothesis accounts for all the data, some of which might otherwise remain unexplained, and does so in terms of everyday processes with which we are all familiar. Can mystical experiences also be rejected on similar grounds? As we saw at the end of the last chapter, a number of authors believe that they can. The following pages will attempt to show that this belief is mistaken.

The present chapter, then contains a defense of the cognitive value of mysticism by means of an explanatory inference. In other words, I will argue that, given a plausible view of the facts involved, it is reasonable to regard contemplative consciousness as a cognitive mode of experience, because the supposition that it is (i.e., H_1) provides at least as good an explanation of the evidence as the competing hypotheses that it is reasonable to consider. Before reconstructing such an explanatory inference, however, it seems appropriate to say something about what an explanation is, and what criteria we use in deciding whether an explanation is good or bad, and whether one explanation is better than another. Obviously these involve complicated philosophical questions which cannot be fully treated here, but the following considerations, derived mainly from Peter Achinstein, should suffice for present purposes.

6.1. Explanations and the Explanatory Mode of Inference

In the fourth chapter of his *Law and Explanation* (1971), Achinstein develops a lengthy and elaborate account of explanation, which he views primarily as a matter of trying to furnish adequate answers to questions. Roughly speaking, he suggests that E (e.g., "one of several events, facts, phenomena, states of affairs, propositions") is classifiable as an explanation of q (that which is to be explained) if and only if person A could attempt to render q understandable to those in a particular situation S by citing E as providing what he or she believes is or might be a correct answer to their question regarding q (Ibid., pp. 61-78).[3] We need not delve any further at this point into the complexities of Achinstein's theory, except to note that it clearly brings out the contextual nature of explanation. As he emphasizes, "the notion of *someone* attempting to explain something *to someone else* is central for a definition of explanation," and therefore the adequacy of a proposed explanation will depend in part on the "knowledge and concerns" of those to whom it is offered (Ibid., p. 67; see also pp. 61-62).[4] For example, when Mrs. Brown asks her family at breakfast why the milk is sour, she is presumably not looking for the same kind of answer that Louis Pasteur was seeking; given her interests, she would regard the "deeper" answer in terms of the chemical processes of fermentation as less satisfactory than the simple explanation that one of her children left the milk out overnight, or that it was already sour when the milkman delivered it.

But how do we decide whether a proposed explanation should be counted as good or satisfactory in a given context? In a later section of the same chapter (Ibid., pp.79-80), Achinstein mentions six considerations which play a role in making this judgment: relevance, correctness, depth, completeness, unification, and manner of presentation. A proposed explanation E satisfies the criterion of *relevance* to the extent that it renders q "understandable...in respects that are or might be of concern" to those in a particular situation; thus the theory of fermentation furnishes a relevant answer to Pasteur's question, but not to Mrs. Brown's. *Correctness* has to do with the accuracy and precision of answers provided by E; Achinstein observes that "in some cases approximations, simplifications, idealizations are in order, in others not," and also notes that correctness is closely related to "evidential support and simplicity" (though he does not indicate in what way). An explanation may be regarded as "superficial" and lacking in *depth* "if we think that more fundamental considerations should have been adduced"; for example, "although one can explain why gases at constant pressure expand by citing a temperature increase, a deeper answer would appeal to the molecular constitution of gases." *Completeness* is a matter of how fully E answers the questions that those in specific circumstances might raise about q; although someone "may attempt to answer questions about pressure at the microscopic level, instead of the macroscopic (thermodynamic) level, his answers at the more fundamental level may be quite sketchy." An explanation may be given "high marks" with respect to *unification* if by means of a "few ideas" it brings together "a wide range of items, relationships among which would otherwise be unknown or not considered." The sixth consideration Achinstein mentions is whether or not E has a "sufficiently clear, simple, and organized" *manner of presentation*, "so as to be more likely to render q understandable."

Of course, these are not necessarily the only considerations employed in evaluating explanations, nor the only way in which they can be presented. Paul Thagard lists consilience, simplicity and analogy as "three important criteria for determining the best explanation" in the scientific arena (Thagard 1978, p. 79). Roughly speaking, one theory has greater *consilience* than another "if it explains more classes of facts than the other does"; this seems to be closely related to Achinstein's criterion of unification.[5] The most significant constraint on consilience is *simplicity*, which keeps us from maximizing the range of a theory by merely tacking on *ad hoc* hypotheses; Thagard suggests that the simplicity of a theory can be regarded as "a function of the size and nature" of the set of auxiliary hypotheses invoked to explain the facts, though he admits that this important notion is notoriously difficult to pin down (Ibid., pp. 85-86). Finally, the criterion of *analogy* has to do with whether an explanatory hypothesis is similar to others with which we are already acquainted. "Explanations afforded by a theory are better explanations if the theory is familiar, that is, introduces mechanisms, entities, or concepts that are used in established explanations"; for example, according to Thagard "explanations in terms of the kinetic theory of gases benefit from the mechanical model of billiard balls" (Ibid., p. 91).

Now as Achinstein points out, there is no automatic procedure for the application of these various criteria, since the standards we demand of an explanation will vary according to our knowledge and concerns. In many situations, for example, the relevance, depth, consilience, and simplicity of a theory will be of much greater importance than its manner of presentation, provided that the latter is not unduly obscure. Taking the contextual nature of explanation into account, then, we may say, with Achinstein, that "E is, on the whole, a good or satisfactory explanation of q" within a particular situation if and only if, on the whole E satisfies the criteria of evaluation appropriate to that situation (Achinstein 1971, p. 81). It is much more difficult, however, to specify what makes one explanatory hypothesis better than another. Certainly we can say that E provides a better explanation of q than an alternative if the former is vastly more successful that the latter in meeting each of the criteria at the appropriate level. Frequently, though, a hypothesis will rank higher than its alternative with respect to certain criteria, and lower with respect to others. Then it becomes a matter of deciding which considerations are most significant in the given context, and on this point reasonable individuals may differ, though all arrive at their conclusions rationally. Thus two Biblical scholars who share the same evidence and the same methodological principles may adopt opposing theories regarding the composition of the Pentateuch or the Pauline authorship of Ephesians and Colossians; though both arrive at their choices through a rational process, each picks the theory which has the advantages he or she regards as most important.

Having made these remarks, we are now in a position to give a general characterization of what Achinstein calls "the explanatory mode of inference." Though the name may be unfamiliar, the pattern of reasoning is one that we use all the time. When a judge rules that a purported will of Howard Hughes is a clever forgery because of certain peculiarities in the handwriting and content, when a teacher suspects a usually poor student of cheating on an exam because his answers match those of the better student beside whom he is sitting, when a woman concludes that her husband is having an affair from the lipstick on his collar and his changed behavior, each is employing the explanatory mode of inference; that is, they reason that a hypothesis is plausible on the grounds that it would explain the evidence better than the alternatives. C. S. Peirce describes this pattern of reasoning, which he also terms "abduction" or "retroduction," in the following terms:

> Every inquiry whatsoever takes its rise in the observation,...of some surprising phenomenon, some experience which either disappoints an expectation, or breaks in upon some habit of expectation.... The inquiry begins with pondering these phenomena in all their aspects, in the search of some point of view whence the wonder shall be resolved. At length a conjecture arises that furnishes a possible Explanation, by which I mean a syllogism exhibiting the surprising fact as necessarily consequent upon the circumstances of its occurrence together with the truth of the credible conjecture, as premisses. On account of this Explanation, the inquirer is led to regard his conjecture, or hypothesis, with favor. (Peirce 1958, p. 367)[6]

Commenting on Peirce's and Hanson's treatment of retroduction, and on the further refinements introduced by Gilbert Harman in what the latter calls "the inference to the best explanation," Achinstein makes several important observations. First, "from the fact that a hypothesis H, if true, would explain the data it does not in general follow that there is reason to think that H is true," since these facts could be inferred from the truth of any number of crazy suppositions; for example, while the supposition that the CIA stole my missing pencil would explain its loss, this gives me no particular grounds for thinking that they did. What gives H its plausibility is that, "*in the light of everything else we know or take for granted*," it accounts for the data more successfully than other hypotheses (Achinstein 1971, pp. 118-120). Second, the conclusion of an abductive inference is not always that H provides the *best* explanation and is therefore true, but sometimes simply that H seems to offer "an explanation that is as good as, or at least not markedly inferior to, other competing ones," and is therefore plausible (Ibid., p. 121). Third, the answers to questions about the facts to be explained "are supplied typically not by a single hypothesis H but by that hypothesis in conjunction with others which form part of the background information" (Ibid., p. 122); in other words, the hypothesis alone may not explain a great deal until it is conjoined with other reasonable hypotheses. Finally, we do not compare H with "all possible competitors," but only "with hypotheses that can be deemed reasonable to consider as alternatives given the evidence...and background information" (Ibid., p. 121).

Achinstein then sets out his formal reconstruction of the explanatory mode of inference (Ibid., p. 123):

Premiss 1: Evidence E is obtained in the light of background information B. (Or: Facts E are assumed in the light of background information B.)

Premiss 2: H, possibly in conjunction with certain other assumptions, is capable of providing a set of answers S to questions concerning facts F which may be part of E or B. (Incompatible competing hypotheses $H_2,...,H_n$ that it is reasonable to consider, given E and B, when conjoined with auxiliary hypotheses are capable of providing sets of answers $S_2,...,S_n$ to questions concerning F, or, in some cases, no answers at all.)

Conclusion 1: It is plausible to suppose that H, when conjoined with certain other assumptions, is capable of offering what in certain situations can be counted as a good explanation of the facts F. (This conclusion warranted provided that (a) the answers H is capable of supplying could be given in the situations in question in order to render F understandable in those situations; (b) within these situations the answers H is capable of supplying satisfy to a reasonable extent the criteria of evaluation for explanations at a level appropriate to those situations; they satisfy such criteria on the whole better than, or at least not significantly less well than, answers supplied by $H_2,..., H_n$; (c) any other hypotheses that it is reasonable to consider, given E and B, supply answers that are inferior to those supplied by H, or at least not superior.)

Conclusion 2: H is plausible.

Now an important feature of the explanatory mode of reasoning, which partly accounts for its recent applications to some perennial metaphysical and epistemological questions, is that it does not necessarily "presuppose the possibility of using the inductive mode" (Ibid., p. 136).[7] To deny this, says Achinstein:

...is to deny the existence of some of the most interesting sorts of theoretical reasoning. I mean reasoning in situations in which observations of F's that are G's have not been made but where nevertheless the scientist infers that all F's are G's on the ground that this hypothesis offers a good explanation of other facts which have been observed or established. (Ibid., p. 136)

It seems legitimate to suppose, therefore, that retroduction is also applicable in the philosophical analysis of mysticism, and in developing a defense of H_1 (the hypothesis that contemplative consciousness is a cognitive mode of experience) according to Achinstein's model for an explanatory inference. As in other cases, it may not be possible to assign an exact value to each of the variables in his schema. Moreover, since the limited scope of this study precludes any attempt at an exhaustive specification of *all* possible criteria used in evaluating hypotheses, for example, or of *all* our background information, certain simplifying assumptions and clarifications must be made at the outset for the sake of space; while not beyond dispute, these assumptions nonetheless seem reasonable in the light of our discussion in the preceding chapters. The following comments, then, should enable us to see how such an explanatory inference might work.

First, I am assuming for the purposes of the present discussion that the criteria referred to in conclusion 1 of the schema include at least those mentioned earlier, and that the latter are sufficient for an overall evaluation of the adequacy of H_1 and its competitors; in other words, while there may be many other relevant criteria, I am supposing that they would not essentially change the verdict reached on the basis of considerations of simplicity, depth, unification, and so on. Second, "H_1" should be substituted for *"H"* in the above schema, and "It is reasonable to accept H_1" for "*H* is plausible" in conclusion 2. As Achinstein notes:

...the degree of plausibility assigned...to *H*, will depend upon the extent to which the answers supplied by *H* satisfy the criteria of evaluation and how much difference exists, with respect to the satisfaction of these criteria, in the answers supplied by *H* and those supplied by competitors. (Ibid., p. 124)

I am taking it for granted, in other words, that it is *reasonable* for individuals to regard mystical awareness as a cognitive mode of experience if they believe reasonably that H_1 (the hypothesis that it is), in conjunction with certain other hypotheses, furnishes an explanation of the evidence which is on the whole better than, or at least not clearly inferior to, that provided by the alternatives.

Third, there seems to be no sharp dividing line between the evidence E and the background information B in the light of which it is obtained, and thus our apportionment of the data between these two categories is to some extent an arbitrary matter. In the context of the present inference I will let

"*E*" represent, roughly, all that we have discovered or assumed about mystical phenomena, and will let "*B*" stand for everything else we already know or believe, including our acquaintance with the practice of describing one's experiences, our understanding of the process of moral and psychological growth, and so on.

In the fourth place, I am assuming that the facts F, "which may be part of E or B" and which H_1 is supposed to explain, include at least the data E_1 through E_{12} described in the last part of chapter four and the first part of chapter five. Since this is perhaps the most controversial assumption, let us review what these "facts" are (see above, pp. 117-120, 137, 145-146, 152-153):

E_1: There are certain intentional, perception-like states, commonly called contemplative or mystical experiences, in which it seems to subjects that they are aware of something ultimate which nonetheless cannot be seen, heard, tasted, touched, smelled, etc.

E_2: In addition to their strong noetic or perception-like quality, these experiences typically involve a sense of blessedness, joy, satisfaction and a feeling of the supreme value and holiness of what is apprehended. Among mystics from theistic religious traditions the intentional object of such states is usually experienced as personal, loving, creative, powerful, transcendent and so on.

E_3: Given the cooperation of the subject, mystical states typically grow in depth, duration, frequency, clarity and the degree of joy, peace and satisfaction obtained, according to a recognizable general pattern of successive stages with identifiable crisis points.

E_4: The "phenomenally theistic" features of the experience of many Christian mystics (and perhaps of contemplatives from theistic religions in general) become more pronounced as the subjects advance through the stages of spiritual development.

E_5: Progress in contemplation is generally associated with positive developments in other areas of life, with mystics gradually advancing from an initial state of psychological disequilibrium to a condition in which their capacities, emotions and desires are harmoniously integrated. Thus:

$E_{5.1}$: There seems to be a correlation between spiritual and psychological growth when viewed over the whole course of a mystic's life (toward a more realistic self-image, less emotional distortion in ordinary perceptions, greater clarity of judgment in normal affairs, etc.).

$E_{5.2}$: Progress in mystical awareness is likewise broadly associated with an increase in moral character and in the virtues of charity, humility, courage and so on.

$E_{5.3}$: In addition, over the long run spiritual growth often seems to be connected with an increased sense of physical well-being.

E_6: The capacity for contemplative consciousness appears to be innate in human nature (rather than requiring some special "organ of mystical perception" which only few possess), but is often left unactualized for one reason or another.

E_7: Mystical experience is generally passive. That is, it seems to the subject that the experience is not attained solely through his or her own efforts; indeed, the recipient may be surprised by its nature and occurrence, and later struggle unsuccessfully to reproduce the experience.

E_8: Generally, mystics are by no means altogether credulous about contemplative states. They appear at least as capable as anyone else of distinguishing between reality and illusion in the ordinary realm, and make the same distinctions with respect to mystical experiences. In addition, their religious faith, tested through fierce trials and struggles, is rarely naive and immature.

E_9: At least to the typical Christian mystic, the whole pattern of events and experiences that constitute mystical development seems to involve participation in a developing love-relationship with the good, holy and gracious divine partner encountered in contemplative states.

E_{10}: On the other hand, a significant number of individuals claim never to have had mystical experiences, and among these are many whose psychological and moral maturity can scarcely be impugned.

E_{11}: There likewise appears to be a fair amount of disagreement among mystics of different backgrounds in the description of their experiences.

E_{12}: Moreover, this disagreement tends to occur along sectarian lines. That is to say, in those areas where their claims seem to conflict, the assertions of each mystic seem to be more or less in accord with his or her own prior religious beliefs and expectations.

Now as we acknowledged earlier, not everyone will agree that these *are* among the facts about mysticism. Thus the recipient of mystical experiences will presumably be more firmly convinced than the outside observer of their morally and psychologically beneficial consequences, and will therefore find my explanatory inference more compelling, whereas the person who is already skeptical of the cognitive value of such states will be more inclined to doubt, say, E_3 through E_9.[8] However, it is not necessary that one already believe in the veridicality of such states in order to be persuaded of the truth of these statements; often a sympathetic reading of the mystical literature and some acquaintance with practicing contemplatives suffices. Thus psychologists such as Maslow and Ornstein apparently accept the majority of the claims in E_1 through E_{12}, while reserving judgment on the cognitive value of mystical states (see Maslow 1973; Ornstein 1972; Naranjo and Ornstein 1971). In any case, as I hope to show, all that is needed for a successful explanatory inference here is that it be *reasonable* for an intelligent individual who has studied the subject to accept a sufficient number of E_1 through E_{12}, and this, it seems to me, the skeptics can grant even if they do not themselves accept all of these claims.

In the fifth place, though the *situation* referred to in conclusion 1 is difficult to specify precisely, and will presumably vary from person to person, I will assume in general that those whose inquiries H_1 is intended to answer are interested in the possible veridicality of alleged contemplative perceptions, and approach the question with an open mind. Rational atheists would scarcely be moved by a retroductive defense of mysticism if they are convinced that they already have independent and conclusive grounds for disbelief in the existence of a supreme being or reality of the sort mystics claim to encounter. This means that the background information B must not include, for example, a successful argument from evil, or a valid proof that the notion of God or "the Transcendent" is totally inconsistent. It also means, in case there were any doubt, that an explanatory inference of the kind I am proposing cannot by itself provide a *comprehensive* apologetic for religious belief.

Sixth, as the previous paragraph suggests, I am supposing that the "questions concerning facts F" (e.g., "Why do mystical experiences occur?" "Why do they have the properties indicated by E_1 through E_{12}?") principally have to do with the cognitive value of mysticism, and are of an "existential" or "religious" character. In other words, the inquirer here is approaching mysticism, not, say, as a disinterested neurologist solely concerned with the physiological processes accompanying contemplation, but rather as someone wanting to know whether these states reveal anything about the nature of reality or the existence of God which might call for a personal response in terms of one's fundamental attitudes and behavior (possible responses might include faith in God or its opposite, cultivation of contemplative awareness or unremitting opposition to it, and so on). Thus an explanatory hypothesis which satisfies the neurologist would not necessarily furnish *relevant* answers to the questions of our inquirer.

In the seventh place, $H_2,\ldots, H_n$ represent "competing hypotheses" which are supposed to be "incompatible" with H_1; consequently, not just any alternative explanation of mysticism will do. For example, a psychological account of the emotional dynamics involved in contemplative states which leaves open the question of their veridicality would not be a *competing* hypothesis, since it might still be true that mystical awareness is a cognitive mode of experience. As I see it, then, the only hypotheses with which H_1 needs to be compared in this explanatory inference are reductive, naturalistic explanations of mysticism, which purportedly account better for all the data without presuming that these states are cognitive. Moreover, the only reductive explanations which it seems "reasonable to consider" in the present context are those currently "in the field." We now turn to an examination of some of these hypotheses.

6.2. Competing Explanations of Mysticism

In reconstructing an explanatory inference in defense of mysticism we need to outline the various sets of answers provided by H_1 and its competitors, and determine to what extent they meet the criteria of evaluation at the appropriate level, given the "existential" concerns of the inquirer. Let us first deal with H_1, and then discuss four major types of reductive explanations in turn.

6.2.1. THE HYPOTHESIS THAT MYSTICISM IS A COGNITIVE MODE OF EXPERIENCE

By itself, H_1 has *some* limited explanatory power, since it satisfies the inquirer's main "existential" concern with the assurance that mystical consciousness is indeed a cognitive mode of experience (as the hypothesis itself states). Analogously, it provides *some* answer to questions about alleged sightings of the Loch Ness monster to say that the experiences were veridical, i.e., that the subjects really were seeing what they thought they were seeing. Still, H_1 offers a more complete explanation of the mystical data "in conjunction with certain other assumptions" about the nature of this data, and in particular about the ostensible object of mystical states. For example, if H_1 were combined with Stace's claim that *all* such states involve an apprehension of an ultimate nonsensuous unity, it could perhaps account for their strong noetic quality and the mystic's conviction of their supreme value. Now throughout this study I have been presuming that John's writings contain a reasonably accurate description of the contemplative experiences of a least a vast number of Christian contemplatives, and have tried to show that these experiences are generally theistic in their implications, especially as they become more profound and clear. That is, it actually seems to mystics such as John and Teresa that they perceive, and are lovingly united with, something nonsensuous, transcendent, good, holy, divine, personal, loving, vastly powerful, creative, and so on, which takes the initiative in this relationship, and which appears to correspond to the deity of which Scripture and orthodoxy speaks. We may express this more succinctly by saying, as John presumably would, that it actually seems to the mystic that he or she is encountering *God*. (The use of the word "God" here is not crucial, however; if skeptics are uncomfortable with it on the grounds that orthodoxy attributes to God certain properties which do not show up in mystical experiences, then in the following paragraphs they may substitute for "God" the more cumbersome locution, "something non-sensuous, transcendent, holy, etc.")

In conjunction with the assertion that Christian mystics seem to perceive God, then, the hypothesis that contemplative consciousness is a cognitive mode of experience has a great deal of explanatory power, for it implies that God exists and is both cause and object of authentic mystical awareness; the doctrine of St. John of the Cross furnishes a very clear illustration of how most of the phenomena mentioned in E_1 through E_9 can be accounted for on this basis, as I have tried to show. Thus, the supposition that these experiences involve the self-disclosure of that divine benevolent "something" which Christian mystics apprehend explains the occurrence and passivity of such states, their phenomenally theistic features, and the feelings of insight, joy, blessedness, peace, and satisfaction which they bring; we would expect cognitive experiences of God to have such effects. This supposition, along with further assumptions about human nature, likewise explains the relationship between spiritual progress and progress in other areas, as well as the arduousness of the developmental process; it suggests that this loving God, out of compassion for human beings and a desire to communicate himself to them, gradually raises them from a harmful condition of psychological and moral disequilibrium which impedes awareness of himself. Granted, all of this needs much more spelling out in order to achieve maximum explanatory force (a task which theologians have typically undertaken). Still, it seems undeniable that H_1 in conjunction with the assumptions mentioned above does provide real answers to our inquirer's "existential" questions about the significance of the phenomena, by presenting the entire mystical life as an ongoing love-relationship between a divine and human partner. That these answers are often felt to be satisfying is indicated by the number of inquirers who have found consolation in the explanations given by someone like John of the Cross.

To the objection that these "answers" are not really explanatory because they have no testable consequences, the defender of mysticism can ask whether testable consequences are always necessary in an explanatory inference. Besides, as we noted in the last chapter, even if the hypothesis that God is the cause and object of these experiences cannot be checked by the methods we use in evaluating ostensible sense perceptions, and does not predict an observable outcome with as much precision as a scientific theory, it does not follow that it has no testable consequences whatsoever. Rather, such a hypothesis might be "confirmed" more informally by the fact that it seems to "work out" in practice; the belief of Christian mystics that they are encountering God gives them certain general expectations about the overall course of their spiritual lives which appear in the long run to be borne out, and enables them to cope with these states in an intelligent, purposeful way.

What about E_{10}, E_{11}, and E_{12}? I have noted earlier that the relative infrequency of mystical experiences and the apparent disagreement among the mystics themselves pose a certain problem for the hypothesis that mystical states involve perceptions of God, insofar as one could legitimately anticipate a greater consensus if these experiences really were what John and other Christian mystics believe them to be. However, while this problem should not be completely glossed over, it is hard to determine just how serious it is. After all, the hypothesis that mystical states involve perceptions of God is able to accommodate E_{10}, E_{11} and E_{12} to *some* degree by explaining that God is free to manifest himself as he wishes, that in certain cases God may decide not to communicate mystically because such communications would be harmful at this time or would override the individual's freedom in the matter, and that in other cases where God does manifest himself, the recipients lack the proper categories for articulating their experiences in theistic terms. Moreover, the extent to which apparently conflicting mystical claims represent genuinely incompatible mystical experiences is still, I think, an open question; likewise, the ratio of mystics to non-mystics in the general populace is not well-established, and (as we have seen) the limited empirical evidence available suggests that such experiences are far more common than is usually supposed (cf. Greeley and McCready 1975; Hay and Morisy 1978). And in any case, as I have tried to show in the last chapter, the differences between the mystic and the non-mystic, and among the mystics themselves, are not by themselves sufficient to *prove conclusively* that it is unreasonable to regard mystical experiences as cognitive, and as perceptions of God. It seems, then, that E_{10}, E_{11}, and E_{12} represent only one part of the data on which the explanatory inference is based, and that our inquirers must make their evaluations of the hypothesis we are discussing on the basis of how well it accounts for the evidence *as a whole;* their judgments will therefore depend on how *much* importance they attach to a theory's ability to explain E_{10} through E_{12} convincingly, and whether they believe that other incompatible hypotheses are better able to explain these particular facts. And I suspect that many inquirers trying to make a fair and rational decision here will nonetheless feel that the hypothesis that mystical states are cognitive experiences of God fits the rest of the evidence so impressively that they need not be overly concerned about the apparent disagreement between mystic and non-mystic, or among the mystics themselves, especially since these differences can be accommodated by the hypothesis.

Before turning to an examination of competing hypotheses, let us briefly consider how well the answers supplied by H_1 (in conjunction with the assumption that Christian mystics seem to perceive God) satisfy the criteria of evaluation at a level appropriate to the situation. It goes without saying, I think, that H_1 provides our inquirers with *relevant* answers which render mystical experiences understandable "in respects that are or might be of concern" to them. The *correctness* of these answers is precisely the point at issue, though we can say that H_1 is at least not demonstrably false. The question of *depth* is more problematic. In some respects the answers supplied by H_1 seem relatively shallow, since they make no reference to underlying "secondary" causal processes (e.g., neurochemical changes in the brain); on the other hand, the explanation that these experiences are caused by God is *metaphysically* as deep as it could be. It would seem that someone with a "religious" interest in the possible veridicality of theistic mystical consciousness will assume that, if these experiences *are* cognitive, then their divine object has the power to bring such experiences about however he wishes; hence the question of the secondary processes involved would be of less concern. In any case, given the inquirer's "existential" interest in the significance of mystical states, the hypothesis that such states are cognitive is presumably as deep as the situation demands.

While the answers which H_1 furnishes to "existential" questions are fairly complete, this *completeness* is definitely limited by the appeal to God's motives and intentions, which remain mysterious. Thus H_1 will not be able to explain in full why a particular mystical experience was granted to this particular person at this particular time; still, it is not clear that our inquirer expects more of H_1 than the response that such matters are governed by divine providence. H_1 seems to provide an appropriate amount of *unification,* employing the model of human love and friendship to bring together a wide variety of mystical and religious phenomena. This *analogy* "enhances the explanatory value" of H_1 by introducing notions with which we are all familiar, and which are often "used in established explanations." I take it that H_1 would have a fair degree of *consilience* if the hypothesis that God exists and causes mystical experiences also explains other "classes of facts" (e.g., other kinds of religious experience, the existence of something rather than nothing); though I believe that it does, I will not now argue the point, since our main interest here is in mysticism itself.

To what extent does H_1 satisfy the crucial criterion of *simplicity*? On the one hand, the supposition that God is responsible for contemplative awareness is ontologically less economical than reductive naturalistic explanations, since it postulates the existence of an additional "entity," God. But on the other hand, ontological economy is not an absolute and unqualified *desideratum* (or we would all presumably be monists). As Thagard points out, "Occam's razor counsels us only not to multiply entities *beyond necessity*," and "necessity is a function of the range of facts to be explained without the use of a lot of auxiliary assumptions" (Thagard 1978, p. 89). If the postulation of one more entity and the addition of relatively few auxiliary assumptions enables a hypothesis to account far more easily for a broad range of facts, as seems true in this case, then the decrease in ontological economy is more than offset by an enormous increase in explanatory power. If the reductive explanations of mysticism turn out to be extremely *complex,* and to depend on far more auxiliary hypotheses to account for the data, then we may still decide that H_1 is in some sense more simple than its competitors. And it seems most inquirers would admit that H_1 offers a relatively simple explanation for what is going on in mystical consciousness.

While the foregoing considerations do not prove that H_1 offers the best possible (or "ideal") explanation of the facts F about mysticism (cf. Achinstein 1971, p. 81), they do suggest that H_1 fulfills some of the conditions which would warrant the first conclusion in Achinstein's schema; in particular, H_1, when conjoined with other assumptions, seems capable of supplying answers which "could be given in the situations in question in order to render F understandable in those situations," and these answers "satisfy to a reasonable extent the criteria of evaluation for explanations at a level appropriate to those situations" (Ibid., p. 123). However, before drawing the conclusion that H_1 "is capable of offering what in certain situations can be counted as a good explanation of the facts," we must also show that the answers provided by H_1 "satisfy such criteria on the whole better than, or at least not significantly less well than, answers supplied" by incompatible competing hypotheses.

Let us consider, then, several reductive accounts of mysticism currently "in the field," which for the sake of clarity I have organized into four main categories: psychoanalytical, psychological, physiological, and sociological or anthropological.[9] As we shall see, there are often non-reductive versions of such theories, some of which may in fact be true. But since we are concerned in what follows with possible competitors to H_1, I will generally interpret the theories treated here as attempts to furnish an alternative causal explanation of the nature and occurrence of mystic states, preferable to the view that these experiences are cognitive. This, at any rate, is how most of the following hypotheses were understood by those who initially proposed them.

6.2.2. REDUCTIVE PSYCHOANALYTICAL ACCOUNTS OF MYSTICISM

A number of philosophers challenge the presumption that mystical and religious experiences involve contact with God on the grounds that psychoanalytic theory provides an alternative (and apparently preferable) explanation of these same states. In a passage cited at the end of the preceding chapter, for example, Ronald Hepburn argues that "we cannot be intellectually compelled to posit God if more economical and naturalistic explanations [of religious experiences] can be found," and mentions "psychoanalytic accounts" as plausible candidates for this role (Hepburn 1967b, 'Religious Experience, Argument for the Existence of God,'

Encyclopedia of Philosophy, vol. 7, p. 164). Similarly, George Nakhnikian maintains that "the mere fact of our having" feelings of cosmic thankfulness and awe "does not support the probability of the hypothesis" that these feelings have "a fitting recipient," since "the occurrence of the cosmic feelings can be explained in more than one plausible way," adding that "Freud's is one way" (Nakhnikian 1961, p. 160).

As we can see, and as is typical in such discussions, here Hepburn and Nakhnikian merely invoke the authority of Freudian psychoanalytic theory without actually examining the preferable "naturalistic" explanations it is alleged to provide. When one begins to look more closely at the Freudian account of mysticism, however, its advantages over H_1 become far less obvious.

Freud's general views on religion and the human personality are widely known, and have been thoroughly discussed and evaluated by other commentators[10]. For present purposes, we need only review a few of his key claims, as background to the Freudian analysis of mysticism and religious experience.

In works such as *Totem and Taboo, Moses and Monotheism* and *The Future of an Illusion,* Freud attempts to explain the origins of religion in society and the life of the individual, along the lines of his celebrated analysis of the Oedipus complex. In terms of historical development, he adopts the hypothesis that human beings "originally lived in small hordes," and that "each of the hordes stood under the rule of an older male, who governed by brute force, appropriated all the females, and belaboured or killed all the young males, including his own sons" (Freud 1939, p. 168). Eventually these brothers:

...joined forces, slew and ate the father, and thus put an end to the father horde....
...They hated the father who stood so powerfully in the way of their sexual demands and their desire for power, but they also loved and admired him. After they had satisfied their hate by his removal and had carried out their wish for identification with him, the suppressed tender impulses had to assert themselves. This took place in the form of remorse, a sense of guilt was formed which coincided here with the remorse generally felt. (Freud [1918] 1946, pp. 183-185)

Totemism (in which the totem serves as a father substitute, with corresponding taboos against the killing of the totem animal except in ritual contexts) arose as a means of expiating guilt feelings for this primitive patricide.

In this connexion some features were formed which henceforth determined the character of every religion. The totem religion had issued from the sense of guilt of the sons as an attempt to palliate this feeling and to conciliate the injured father through subsequent obedience. All later religions prove to be attempts to solve the same problem, varying only in accordance with the stage of culture in which they are attempted and according to the paths which they take.... (Freud [1918] 1946, p. 187)

As speculation about the historical development of human society, Freud's theory has few followers today and rests on little supporting evidence. Much more influential, however, has been his proposal that religion arises in the life of the individual through an analogous process, as a way of resolving Oedipal conflicts.

...Psychoanalytic investigation of the individual teaches with especial emphasis that god is in every case modelled after the father and that our personal relation to god is dependent upon our relation to our physical father, fluctuating and changing with him, and that god at bottom is nothing but an exalted father. (Freud [1918] 1946, p. 190)

In *The Future of an Illusion,* Freud explores the similarities between the infant's helplessness and humanity's experience of helplessness and dependency in the face of a seemingly indifferent and sometimes hostile universe. Both infant and adult are threatened by various dangers and in need of protection.

In this function [of protection] the mother is soon replaced by the stronger father, who retains that position for the rest of childhood. But the child's attitude to its father is coloured by a peculiar ambivalence. The father himself constitutes a danger for the child, perhaps because of its earlier relation to its mother. Thus it fears him no less than it longs for him and admires him. The indications of this ambivalence in the attitude to the father are deeply imprinted in every religion.... When the growing individual finds that he is destined to remain a child for ever, that he can never do without protection against strange superior powers, he lends those powers the features belonging to the figure of his father; he creates for himself the gods whom he dreads, whom he seeks to propitiate, and whom he nevertheless entrusts with his own protection. (Freud 1964b, pp. 34-35)

...Thus the benevolent rule of a divine Providence allays our fear of the dangers of life; the establishment of a moral world-order ensures the fulfillment of the demands of justice...; and the prolongation of earthly existence in a future life provides the local and temporal framework in which these wish-fulfillments shall take place.... It is an enormous relief to the individual psyche if the conflicts of its childhood arising from the father-complex—conflicts which it has never wholly overcome—are removed from it and brought to a solution which is universally accepted. (Ibid., pp. 47-48)

For Freud, then, religious belief serves both the individual and society, by alleviating the individual's emotional conflicts while at the same time coercing and compensating members of civilization in the necessary renunciation of their antisocial drives. Yet religious belief is an "illusion," because "wish-fulfilment is a prominent factor in its motivation," with little regard for the question of its truth or verification (Ibid., pp. 48-49). Human beings believe in a God primarily as a way of resolving certain deep-seated conflicts, needs and anxieties, not because they have any evidence for their beliefs. Religion can therefore be considered in certain respects as the "universal obsessional neurosis of humanity," comparable to infantile neuroses; "like the obsessional neuroses of children, it arose out of the Oedipus complex, out of the relation to the father" (Ibid., p. 71).

This psychoanalytic account of religion obviously raises many important questions. As has often been observed, it is a difficult theory to test, since if religion is both a *product of* and a *solution to* psychological conflicts, it is unclear whether to expect that religious believers will be more neurotic and unhappy than their unbelieving counterparts, or less so (cf. Hay and Morisy 1978, p. 256). Again, by grounding religion in the Oedipal tensions between father and son, Freud's theory seems to offer little explanation for the development of the idea of God among *women*, thereby neglecting over half of the world's population (and the majority of the active membership in most churches). More generally, one wonders whether the Oedipus complex can actually bear the explanatory weight which Freud places upon it; might there not be other factors and relationships (pre-oedipal or otherwise) which enter into the formation of the God-concept, as the object-relations theorists now suggest (see McDargh 1984)?

Whatever the answer to such questions, and whatever our ultimate evaluation of psychoanalytic theory as a whole, there is no doubt that it has become an important dialogue partner in modern discussions of religion. A number of contemporary theologians influenced by the hermeneutical tradition, for example, hail Freud as a master of the "hermeneutics of suspicion" (along with other "masters of suspicion" such as Marx and Nietzsche), helping to "unmask" the projection and alienation underlying much religious behavior and belief (cf. Ricoeur 1970; Buckley 1979).

But what does all of this have to do with mysticism as such, the focus of our study? So far, at least, we have seen little in psychoanalytic theory that touches directly upon mystical experience, or would give us any particular reason to doubt its veridicality. In fact, although Freud has much to say about religion in general, his comments on mystic states are surprisingly few. In the thirty-first of his *New Introductory Lectures on Psychoanalysis* (1965), for example, Freud first provides an outline of his tripartite "dissection of the psychical personality," into the *id* (the "dark, inaccessible part of our personality," a "cauldron full of seething expectations" and "instinctual needs" [Ibid., p. 73]); the *super-ego* (which internalizes and "takes over the power, function and even the methods of the parental agency" [Ibid., p. 62]); and the *ego* (which mediates among the demands of id, super-ego, and perceived world [see Ibid., p. 77]). Then, in his closing lines, Freud comments that:

In thinking of this division of the personality into an ego, a super-ego and an id, you will not, of course, have pictured sharp frontiers like the artificial ones drawn in political geography.... It is highly probable that the development of these divisions is subject to great variations in different individuals; it is possible that in the course of actual functioning they may change and go through a temporary phase of involution.... It is easy to imagine, too, that certain mystical practices may succeed in upsetting the normal relations between the different regions of the mind, so that, for instance, perception may be able to grasp happenings in the depths of the ego and in the id which were otherwise inaccessible to it. It may be safely doubted, however, whether this road will lead us to the ultimate truths from which salvation is to be expected. Nevertheless it may be admitted that the therapeutic efforts of psycho-analysis have chosen a similar line of approach. (Ibid., pp. 79-80)

Elsewhere, he observes cryptically that "mysticism is the obscure self-perception of the realm outside the ego, the id" (Freud 1964a, p. 300).

But the *locus classicus* for Freud's views on mysticism, and the text which has most influenced Freud's followers in their analysis of mystical states, is the opening section of *Civilization and Its Discontents*. Here he takes up the suggestion of his friend Romain Rolland that "the true source of religious sentiments" lies not in the Oedipal situation but in a peculiar "feeling which he would like to call a sensation of 'eternity', a feeling as of something limitless, unbounded—as it were, 'oceanic'" (Freud 1962, p. 11). Freud himself is inclined to doubt that such sensations are the "*fons et origo* of the whole need for religion" (Ibid., p. 12), preferring instead the hypotheses already presented in his own work, *The Future of an Illusion*, outlined above. Nevertheless, he is moved to make the following observations:

The idea of men's receiving an intimation of their connection with the world around them through an immediate feeling which is from the outset directed to that purpose sounds so strange and fits in so badly with the fabric of our psychology that one is justified in attempting to discover a psychoanalytic—that is, a genetic—explanation of such a feeling. The following line of thought suggests itself. Normally, there is nothing of which we are more aware than the feeling of our self, of our own ego. This ego appears to us as something autonomous and unitary, marked off distinctly from everything else....
Further reflection tells us that the adult's ego-feeling cannot have been the same from the beginning. It must have gone through a process of development, which cannot, of course, be demonstrated but which admits of being constructed with a fair degree of probability. An infant at the breast does not as yet distinguish his ego from the external world as the source of the sensations flowing in upon him. He gradually learns to do so, in response to various promptings....
...Our present ego-feeling is, therefore, only a shrunken residue of a much more inclusive—indeed, an all-embracing—feeling which corresponded to a more intimate bond between the ego and the world around it. If we may assume that there are many people in whose mental life this primary ego-feeling has persisted to a greater or lesser degree, it would exist in them side by side with the narrower and more sharply demarcated ego-feeling of maturity, like a kind of counterpart to it. In that case, the ideational contents appropriate to it would be precisely those of limitlessness and of a bond with the universe—the same ideas with which my friend elucidated the 'oceanic' feeling. (Ibid., pp. 12-15)

Though Freud does not use the word 'mysticism' in this context, subsequent commentators have generally assumed that mystic states are included among (if not identical with) the "oceanic feelings" he discusses here. If so, then the Freudian theory (which in various modified forms still enjoys fairly widespread acceptance) is that mystical experience involves a *regression* to the undifferentiated awareness of the nursling as a "way of disclaiming the danger which the ego recognizes as threatening it from the external world" (Ibid., p. 19).[11] Freud presumably chooses this infantile state as the one to which the mystic returns because he detects a similarity between mystical reports of ineffable joy, satisfaction and union, and the conjectured infantile feeling of "symbiotic union with the all-good, all-giving, all-nurturing maternal breast" (Meissner 1977, p. 56; cf. Meissner 1984, p. 151). Later authors influenced by Freud have often elaborated on this theory:

It would therefore not be surprising to discover that mystics are so troubled by the world of their maturity that they tend to retreat toward the omnipotence of infancy and its undifferentiated pleasure....
The state that is attained by a mystic is a state of euphoria or ecstasy in which the outer world seems to vanish and the self to stretch out, lose its boundaries, and engulf everything. This is simultaneously a projection of the self into the whole environment and an introjection of the whole environment into the self. It is a return to what some psychoanalysts call the "oceanic reunion," the world of the fed, satisfied baby on the delicious edge of sleep. All one's pleasure impulses are withdrawn from external objects and located inside oneself. And the variegated responses of the mind are narrowed and merged until they approximate the semiconscious, slumbrous, undifferentiated pleasure of the baby immersed in the uniform ocean of his feeling. It is a state of both omnipotence and dependence, and often the mystic feels his absorption to be a happy helplessness in which a force that is greater than himself but includes himself handles him as a parent handles the little child....
...But whether we retreat inward or expand outward, it is ourselves we have found and our own breathing to which the world keeps time. (Ostow and Scharfstein 1954, pp. 118-125)

Now in evaluating such an account of mysticism, we should note, first of all, that it seems relatively independent of Freud's general theory of religion. Instead of interpreting "oceanic feelings" as an attempted resolution of the Oedipal conflicts underlying religion through union with a divine *father,* Freud speaks instead of regression to the *maternal* breast. This explains in part why Freud is so reluctant to make oceanic experiences the "fons et origo" of religion, since that would mean effectively abandoning his position in *The Future of an Illusion.* As Van Herik notes:

In denying psychological primacy to the oceanic feeling, Freud was in effect repeating his earlier claim that the psychically central mother was soon replaced by the "stronger father." Whatever else the oceanic feeling might be, it is surely, in Freudian terms, pre-oedipal. Freud's insistence on this point underlines both the tenacity with which he granted paternal authority a privileged place in mental life and the psychological importance he placed on the paternal character of the religious object. (Van Herik 1982, p. 157)

This suggests that to a large extent the Freudian theory of mysticism stands or falls on its own merits; since it is not dependent on his general theory of religion, one could accept the latter without in any way committing oneself to the truth of the former, and the plausibility of one does not automatically carry over to the other. Too often, philosophical authors seem to assume that the respect enjoyed by psychoanalytic theory as a whole (where it is esteemed) can be simply transferred to all of its particular components.

It is important to note, as well, that Freud's starting point in this discussion is obviously different from that of our imaginary inquirer, or even of philosophers such as Hepburn and Nakhnikian. Freud is *not* comparing his theory with H_1 (the hypothesis that mysticism is a cognitive mode of experience) in terms of their respective abilities to explain the mystical data. Instead, he simply *assumes* at the outset for independent reasons (e.g., because the contrary hypothesis "fits in so badly with the fabric of our psychology") that "oceanic feelings" are unlikely to be cognitive experiences of reality, and that therefore he is justified in proposing "a psychoanalytic—that is, a genetic—explanation of such a feeling." And certainly if an inquirer had sufficient independent grounds for doubting the veridicality of mystic states, then his task would be different from the one we are pursuing in this chapter; with H_1 presumed to be out of the running, he would simply need to discover the most adequate alternative (and presumably naturalistic) explanatory hypothesis. In such a context, any weaknesses discovered in the psychoanalytic account would imply, not that mystical experiences are cognitive, but only that a better alternative explanation was needed.

By contrast, however, philosophical critics of mysticism's cognitivity who invoke Freud tend to pose the problem differently, and in keeping with our line of argument in this chapter. That is to say, with the Freudian account of "oceanic feelings" now "in the field," these authors typically interpret it as a causal account of the sufficient conditions for the occurrence and nature of mystical states, and (like Hepburn and Nakhnikian above) *do* compare it to H_1 in terms of explanatory power, arguing that the psychoanalytic explanation is preferable. The clear implication of the Freudian account, on this interpretation, is that contemplative states cannot be cognitive, since what the mystic regards as a perception of God or ultimate reality is only an apparently pathological replay of the original nursing experience, representing "something like the restoration of limitless narcissism" (Freud 1964b, p. 19) in the face of some threat or need.[12] (The allegedly pathological nature of the mystic's regression would presumably make his ostensible perceptions even more suspect, since pathology often produces systematically misleading experiences.)

Let us designate this reductive psychoanalytical account of mysticism along Freudian lines as H_2. How well do the answers which H_2 supplies meet the criteria of evaluation at a level appropriate to the situation of our inquirer? Certainly these answers are *relevant* to his concerns about the significance of mysticism, insofar as they suggest that mysticism is "merely a regression" to the infantile experience of the maternal breast. They may lack a certain *depth* to the extent that our inquirer demands an account of how this "regression" is accomplished in terms of more fundamental processes, but we can let this pass. A Freudian theory would seem to be *consilient* insofar as the concept of regression can be used to explain other psychological disorders as well.[13] Moreover, H_2 enjoys a certain plausibility (at least among philosophical critics of mysticism), perhaps in part because of its vivid *manner of presentation*, its *simplicity,* and its introduction of the nursing *analogy* and of mechanisms familiar from established psychoanalytical explanations.

Yet even in the foregoing areas it is by no means clear that the answers provided by H_2 meet such criteria of evaluation better than those supplied by H_1. One might argue, for example, that Freud's theory is more ontologically economical because it does not assume the existence of God, but the defender of mysticism could respond that H_2 requires us to postulate psychoanalytic entities and processes which are almost as problematic (e.g., the ego, the unconscious). Moreover, with respect to the remaining criteria besides simplicity, H_2 seems to fare much more poorly that H_1. Freud's theory offers less *completeness* and *unification,* since it explains only relatively few of the facts about mysticism (e.g., why mystical experiences occur, and why they involve feelings of contentment, peace, limitlessness and so on), and even then furnishes only a very sketchy account of them. Moreover, without further elaboration (which would diminish its simplicity), the Freudian account based on regression to the preeminently sensuous nursing experience provides *no* answers to questions about the theistic and nonsensuous character of Christian mystical states, the possibility of a continuous mystical awareness at the highest stage of spiritual development, or the reason for the disagreement between mystics of incompatible religious backgrounds. (Freud might want to deny, for example, that mystical experiences are entirely nonsensuous, but it is not clear what evidence he could provide independently of his theory to justify this denial.) Particularly hard to explain on the Freudian account is why so many mystics customarily use nuptial rather than infantile imagery to describe their experiences, and picture the divine partner with which they are mystically united in male rather than female terms.

Another way of stating the problem is that H_2 suffers from a serious lack of the *evidential support* that one should reasonably expect from a hypothesis of this sort, proposed as a more enlightened and scientific alternative to H_1. In general, it would seem that reductive accounts of mysticism *ought* to be more directly accessible than H_1 to empirical testing, because they purport to explain mystical experiences in terms of purely natural processes, and therefore should be open in principle to the same kinds of test we use in evaluating other empirical claims. Yet insofar as the original Freudian theory of mysticism is testable at all, it seems to be disconfirmed. Thus, if contemplative states really did involve a regression to the primordial awareness of the maternal breast comparable to psychotic regression, we might naturally anticipate that these experiences would have pathological consequences, that the mystic would exhibit a greater degree of infantile narcissism or more poorly defined ego-boundaries than the non-mystic, for example, and that such difficulties would become *more* severe as the mystic advanced in the spiritual life. But on the contrary, what many researchers today are finding is that "authentic mystical experience (as distinguished from pseudomystical types of experience or their psychotic substitutes) not only does not undermine or destroy identity, but it in fact has a powerful capacity to stabilize, reinforce, sustain, and enrich identity" (Meissner 1977, p, 56). Moreover, these states often lead to an extraordinary altruism, and the actualization of previously untapped talents and abilities. As Deikman observes:

The fact is, we know practically nothing about the actual experience of the infant, except that whatever it is, it is not that of a small adult. No one who has read carefully the accounts of "enlightenment" can accept this glib equation of mystical = infantile. An infant mind could hardly have had the experience [described in mystical texts]. (Deikman 1979, p. 192)

As a result, some recent authors in the psychoanalytic tradition now describe mysticism and meditation (in the eastern, non-discursive sense) somewhat more favorably as "regression in service of the ego," a temporary "return to an earlier level of functioning" for the purposes of "rejuvenation and rebirth" (Prince and Savage 1972, pp. 118-119).[14]

According to this view, the meditation experience offers the opportunity to ego-synotically reexperience and reexamine unresolved conflicts and desires embodied in material that unfolds through the practice of meditation.... These "adaptive" regressive states have been differentiated from pathological regressive states by virtue of their transitory, quickly reversible nature and their ability to increase self-esteem.... In this view, meditation can be seen as an arena in which to uncover primitive material, with side effects resulting when ego strength is not sufficient to withstand the force of such material. (Wilber et al. 1986)

If this is the kind of "regression" involved in mysticism, however, it no longer bears any clear negative implications regarding the cognitive value of mystic states; after all, scientists and artists often undergo a similar "regression in service of the ego" before producing their most brilliant insights and creations. Once it is admitted that mystical experiences may involve more than *just* a pathological replay of the primordial nursing experience, then some further argument is needed to show why these states should be any more suspect than those involved in other positive and therapeutic forms of "regression" whose cognitive value we accept.

In fact, apart from reverence for Freud, there may be little reason to continue using such a tendentious term as "regression" in this context, especially since the features Freud attributes to the infant's awareness of the maternal breast are also clearly exhibited in many other states, not all of which are clearly "regressive" in the same sense. Thus, as Freud admits in the same section of *Civilization and Its Discontents,* the ordinary "boundary between ego and object" likewise "threatens to melt away" in the unusual but non-pathological experience of love (Freud 1962, p. 13). In light of the emphasis he elsewhere places upon the sexual instinct, and the prominence of erotic imagery in some traditional mystical literature, it is rather surprising that Freud *avoids* explaining mystical states in terms of the dynamics of love and sexuality.[15] One reason may be that for him to do so might involve an implicit concession that such states are perhaps non-pathological, and therefore might possibly be cognitive. In fact, the recent development of object-relations theory within the psychoanalytic tradition seems to have redirected Freudian thought in precisely this direction, maintaining that "what motivates human beings from the very beginning" is not "the satisfaction of this or that primary instinctual drive," but "the hunger for a relationship that will confirm and affirm the self as loving and beloved for its own sake" (McDargh 1984, p. 352). And insofar as this new approach acknowledges the relationships "which actually do (or fail to) obtain" (and which may be far more complex and varied than Freud's stereotyped Oedipal situation or nursing memory suggest), it opens up psychoanalytic theory:

to an acceptance of the possible effect of the reality of objects as encountered, even when those objects have been mentally constructed into a replication of earlier experience. It follows that it would be impossible on psychoanalytic grounds alone to exclude the possibility that God is a source of the sense of God: however much a sense of God may be constructed through, and as a consequence of, the replication of infantile experience, and however much the characterization of God may replicate parental relationships, the possibility cannot be excluded that there may be x in reality which has in the past sustained those replications and which has reinforced the continuity of such terms as 'god'. (Bowker 1973, p. 129-131)

Actually, this is what we might have expected all along from a careful reading of Freud's original proposal. In *Civilization and Its Discontents,* Freud attributes to his reconstruction of early ego-development only "a fair degree of probability," and admits that it is difficult to identify in particular cases the precise causes which would trigger regression to the "unlimited narcissism" of the nursing experience (Freud 1962, pp. 13-20). After all, every person was at one time presumably fed at the maternal breast, and experiences many of the same instinctive drives, needs and anxieties, yet only a few attain to contemplative awareness. Obviously, then, the Freudian theory in its original form is incomplete if intended as a naturalistic causal explanation of the occurrence and character of mystic states. And if other factors also play a causal role, it seems arbitrary to rule out in advance the possibility that one of these factors might be the impingement of God (or some ultimate dimension of reality) on the subject's awareness, however much the experience may draw upon primitive psychological material for its phenomenal contours.

In short, the Freudian theory of mysticism seems to be in competition with H_1 only insofar as it is interpreted (according to our definition of H_2) as an attempt at a psychoanalytic explanation of the sufficient causal conditions for the occurrence and nature of mystic states. And it may be true that "a successful explanation of certain mystical experiences in terms of purely natural factors would enable us to disallow claims that in these experiences one is directly apprehending God" (Alston 1964, p. 90). This is apparently what some philosophical commentators assume that psychoanalytic theory provides. At best, however, the classic Freudian account identifies only *some* of the causal factors involved, and even for these the evidence seems shaky. Far from the "regression to limitless narcissism" that Freud's theory would lead us to expect, what one generally finds in the lives of mystics is a high degree of altruism, other-directedness and healthy ego-boundaries. There seems to be little evidence to support a purely reductive psychoanalytic account of mysticism, and consequently its *correctness,* which is surely a primary concern of our inquirer, appears highly doubtful. It seems fair to say, then, that the answers provided by H_1 satisfy the criteria of evaluation "on the whole better than, or at least not significantly less well than," the answers supplied by H_2. Of course, H_2 can be (and has been) modified in various ways in order to accommodate the data more adequately; but once these modifications are added, the Freudian account either begins to lose the simplicity which constituted much of its original appeal, or becomes no longer clearly incompatible with H_1. Moreover, there do not appear to be any recent attempts at an explanation of mysticism from within the psychoanalytic tradition which are both clearly reductive and have a better chance of success than H_2. Therefore, while psychoanalytic theory may have much to offer in other respects in the analysis of religion, there seem to be no psychoanalytic theories of mysticism now "in the field" which are incompatible with H_1 and do a significantly better job of explaining the facts about mysticism.

6.2.3. REDUCTIVE PSYCHOLOGICAL ACCOUNTS OF MYSTICISM

As we saw at the end of the previous chapter, John Shepherd challenges attempts to infer the existence of God from contemplative states on the grounds that "it seems possible to provide a naturalistic explanation of mystical experiences" (Shepherd 1975, p. 7). However, contrary to what one might expect, the naturalistic account Shepherd has in mind is not the

Freudian theory of mysticism but a curious proposal (reminiscent of Stace's) presented by Ronald Hepburn in the following passage:

> When concepts are withdrawn and fundamental distinctions are obliterated, it is understandable that our ordinary sense of limits and boundaries between thing and thing, person and person, should also temporarily disappear. In this we may have an important clue to the mystic's claims about the overcoming of finite individuality, the cessation of the subject-object relation, and mergings and meltings into the infinite. Because our normal sense of our powers and their limits is fostered by the utilitarian and practical view of the world, when that view is suppressed, there can come a sense of exhilarating expansion or liberation that is often described in the mystical literature.
> Similarly, if the practical orientation is suspended and, with it, the related conceptual framework of normal experience, we may lose awareness of the passage of time. In introvertive mystical experience the awareness of space is also obliterated, for there is a still more thoroughgoing withdrawal from perception and even from sensation. (Hepburn 1967a, 'Mysticism, Nature and Assessment of," *Encyclopedia of Philosophy*, vol. 5, p. 433)

Thus Hepburn seems to be endorsing at least one element in Stace's analysis of mysticism as discussed in the fourth chapter: namely, that experiences of the sort described by mystics can be expected as a matter of course once familiar distinctions and categories of everyday life are temporarily suppressed. (Indeed, as we shall see in a moment, it is just such a conviction that seems to undergird much of the recent psychological research on "sensory deprivation" and "deautomatization," in which Stace is frequently cited.)

Now Hepburn and Shepherd evidently regard this proposal as a *reductive naturalistic* account of mysticism, but it is not entirely clear why they do so. After all, despite the apparent absence of particular ideas and images in mystical states, their recipients remain convinced that these experiences are cognitive, a conviction which Hepburn here fails to explain. Admittedly, the suspension of one's practical orientation can produce illusions and errors of judgment, but at the same time, our ordinary conceptual framework can itself lead to systematic misperceptions of reality (as, for example, in experiments where subjects shown a red ace of spades will consistently describe it, and actually "see" it, as an ace of hearts).[16] In fact, many poets, artists and scientists will deliberately strive at times to set aside their ordinary way of looking at a subject precisely in order to attain fresh and more accurate insights. A mystic like St. John of the Cross would presumably reply to Hepburn that the temporary obliteration of concepts and distinctions enables us to perceive a transcendent order of reality usually obscured by our preoccupation with mundane interests.

At least in its bare outlines, then, Hepburn's proposal seems compatible with H_1. There are similar theories, however, which are not. One of the more popular is Arthur J. Deikman's account of mystical phenomena in terms of "deautomatization," which for our purposes can be treated as fairly representative of the most common reductive psychological accounts of mysticism.

Deikman's view that meditation techniques bring about contemplative experiences by temporarily dismantling "the normal construction of consciousness" was initially worked out in two widely-anthologized and often quoted articles, 'Experimental Meditation' (Deikman 1972), and 'Deautomatization and the Mystic Experience' (Deikman 1980). In the former, he hypothesizes that "many of the phenomena described in mystic accounts can be regarded as the consequence of a partial deautomatization of the psychic structures that organize and interpret perceptual stimuli," and goes on to explain that:

...automatization is assumed to be a basic process in which the repeated exercise of an action or of a perception results in the disappearance from consciousness of its intermediate steps. Deautomatization is the undoing of automatization, presumably by reinvestment of actions and percepts with attention. (Deikman 1972, p. 208)

In order to test his hypothesis, Deikman arranged an experiment in which four subjects meditated on a blue vase in comfortable surroundings for twelve sessions, averaging around fifteen minutes in length. The results of the experiment were intriguing. All four subjects reported various alterations in their perceptions of the vase; it sometimes seemed to change shape, move, or lose its perceptual boundaries, and appeared "more vivid" and "luminous" (Ibid., p. 208). The meditation periods seemed shorter to the subjects than they actually were, and they found it hard to describe their experiences consistently, though all agreed that the sessions were pleasurable and worthwhile. One subject reported a sense of "merging" with the vase, while another experienced difficulty in reorganizing his visual field after a period of meditation, and on one occasion noted that the outside landscape viewed from a window seemed "transfigured."

According to Deikman, these and other results are enough like reported mystical phenomena to suggest that similar processes are involved in both cases, especially since the concentration exercise with the blue vase resembles certain traditional meditation techniques. Deikman likewise correlates his results with those obtained in sensory deprivation experiments (Ibid., p. 220-221).[17] He concludes that "through contemplative meditation deautomatization occurs and permits a different perceptual and cognitive experience," thus enabling "the adult to attain a new, fresh perception of the world by freeing him from a stereotyped organization built up over the years" (Ibid., p. 222). So far, all of this implies a rather positive assessment of mysticism perfectly compatible with H_1, and indeed he rejects the view that mystical states are "regressive" in the strict Freudian sense (Deikman 1980, pp. 250-251).[18]

Deikman's account becomes more clearly reductive in the second article, however, where he attempts "to explain five principle features of the mystic experience: (a) intense realness, (b) unusual sensations, (c) unity, (d) ineffability, and (e) trans-sensate phenomena," and concludes finally that:

> Such an explanation says nothing conclusive about the source of "transcendent" stimuli.... There is no evidence...that God or a transcendent reality exists (as affirmed by Western religions). The available scientific evidence tends to support the view that the mystic experience is one of internal perception, an experience that can be ecstatic, profound, or therapeutic for purely internal reasons. (Ibid., pp. 252 and 259)

Though he does not indicate what this "available scientific evidence" is, Deikman is presumably thinking of his own research and the few studies he mentions in the course of presenting his own account. Briefly, Deikman's reductive hypothesis is that mystical states are simply unusual experiences of the subject's own natural psychological processes, rather than perceptions of God or ultimate reality. Let us now see how he employs this theory to explain the five features mentioned above.

First, Deikman suggests that the contemplative experiences involve a sense of *intense realness* because meditative techniques cause "a profound disruption of the subject's normal psychological relationship with the world"; as a result, the feeling of "realness" ordinarily attached to external objects is displaced onto the "particular sensations and ideas that enter awareness during periods of...deautomatization" (Ibid., p. 252-253). Second, he attributes the *unusual sensations* sometimes accompanying contemplation (e.g., "perceptions of encompassing light, infinite energy, ineffable visions, and incommunicable knowledge") to the process of "sensory translation," described as "the perception of psychic *action* (conflict, repression, problem solving, attentiveness, and so forth) via the relatively unstructured sensations of light, color, movement, force, sound, smell, or taste" (Ibid., pp. 253-254). Thus Deikman conjectures that the ubiquitous references to "light" and "illumination" in mystical literature "may be derived from an actual sensory experience occurring when in the cognitive act of unification, a liberation of energy takes place" (Ibid., p. 254).

In the third place, while Deikman admits the logical possibility that the *unity* experienced by mystics "may in fact be a property of the real world that becomes perceptible via the techniques of meditation and renunciation," he seems to favor an alternative explanation of this feature.

> It is a commonplace that we do not experience the world directly. Instead, we have an experience of sensation and associated memories from which we infer the nature of the stimulating object. As far as anyone can tell, the actual *substance* of the perception is the electrochemical activity that constitutes perception and thinking. From this point of view, the contents of awareness are homogeneous.... If awareness were turned back upon itself, as postulated for sensory translation, this fundamental homogeneity (unity) of perceived reality—the electrochemical activity—might itself be experienced as the truth about the outer world, rather than the inner one. (Ibid., pp. 255-256)

Fourth, he indicates that different contemplative experiences may be *ineffable* for different reasons, some because they are "probably based on primitive memories and related to phantasies of a preverbal (infantile) or nonverbal sensory experience," others because they are "too complex to be verbalized" (Ibid., p. 257). Finally, Deikman recognizes that certain advanced mystical experiences involve *trans-sensate phenomena* which go beyond the unusual sensory phenomena already mentioned, and he suggests that such phenomena "are the result of the operation of a new perceptual capacity responsive to dimensions of the stimulus array previously ignored or blocked from awareness" (Ibid., p. 258).

As we can see, Deikman's account would not necessarily rule out a theistic interpretation of mystical states if we suppose that *God* is part of the "stimulus array previously ignored or blocked." However, Deikman himself apparently believes that the new perceptual capacities awakened by deautomatization are responsive to purely natural aspects of the environment which had previously escaped notice. If we combine the latter view with his explanation of other features of mysticism in terms of "sensory translation," the "displacement of reality feeling," and direct awareness of the uniform neurochemical basis of perception, the result is a reductive hypothesis which seems genuinely incompatible with H_1. We may designate this reductive version of Deikman's theory of mysticism as H_3, and try to determine how well it meets the criteria of evaluation at the appropriate level.

The answers supplied by H_3 are obviously *relevant* to our inquirer's questions about the cognitive value of contemplative awareness (insofar as they indicate that such awareness is *not* what it seems to the recipient to be, and does *not* involve perception of a transcendent order of reality). These answers likewise seem *deeper* than those provided by H_2, since they refer to the more fundamental psychological mechanisms which presumably underlie the processes described by Freudian psychoanalysis. H_3 is also *consilient* insofar as the same mechanisms can be used to explain other experiences brought about by sensory deprivation, hypnosis, hallucinogenic drugs, and so on. Indeed, it seems that much of the current popularity of Deikman's hypothesis is due to the *analogy* he draws between mysticism and other "altered states of consciousness," which are still in vogue among many psychologists. In addition, certain components of H_3 (e.g., the assertion that meditation exercises cause alterations in the perception of reality) can lay claim to a degree of *evidential support* which the Freudian theory lacks (cf. Murphy and Donovan 1988).

With respect to other criteria, however, this hypothesis offers no obvious advantages over H_1 or H_2. In the first place, perhaps because of an inadequate *manner of presentation*, some parts of Deikman's theory remain extremely puzzling and obscure. Notice the host of unexamined epistemological assumptions in his treatment of unity, for example, where he regards it as a "commonplace" that we perceive the world indirectly by *inferring* "the nature of the stimulating object" from a more primordial experience of "sensations and associated memories," the substance of which is homogeneous neurochemical activity, and where he suggests that in mystic states this awareness is "turned back upon itself" to perceive its own homogeneity. But what exactly can this mean? Our inquirer's reaction might well be that the notion of experiencing God, however problematic, seems no more bizarre than the notion of electrochemical activity directly perceiving *itself* and *mistaking* this awareness for an experience of God. Furthermore, there appears to be no way of testing this proposal, as there should be if H_3 is intended as a *scientific* alternative to H_1. (How could one determine, for example, whether the feeling of unity involves a perception of the homogeneity of electrochemical activity rather than, say, the uniformly organic character of the neurons?)

Second, even though this hypothesis does not postulate the existence of God, it seems as a whole to have far less *simplicity* than H_1; for each of the five features of mysticism he discusses, Deikman introduces a new psychological concept or mechanism (e.g., "sensory translation," "displacement of reality feeling") often as obscure as the phenomena it is meant to explain, and he offers few clues as to how all of these mysterious processes interconnect in mystic states. It is unclear, for instance, how "awareness" could simultaneously perceive both its own homogeneous electrochemical character and also the unusual percepts (e.g., light, ineffable revelations and visions) caused by "sensory translations."

In the third place, H_3 is not particularly *complete*, since its responses to inquiries about the significance of contemplative consciousness are quite sketchy, and raise as many questions as they answer. Finally, H_1 evidently satisfies the criterion of *unification* more adequately in this context than Deikman's theory, since it manages to handle a broader range of facts with fewer ideas; H_3, on the other hand, fails to account for spontaneous mystical states, phenomenally theistic mystical states, or the apparent conflict between mystics of different backgrounds, and its explanation for the contrasting experiences of the mystic and non-mystic is essentially the same as the one given by St. John of the Cross (i.e., that the non-mystic's preoccupation with the ordinary concepts and categories of everyday existence impedes mystical awareness).

On the basis of such considerations, then, one might reasonably conclude that the answers provided by H_1 satisfy the criteria of evaluation "on the whole better than, or at least not significantly less well than," those supplied by H_3. This is not to deny Deikman's claim that traditional meditation techniques can bring about a certain "deautomatization" of stereotyped perceptual patterns and enable us to become aware of previously unnoticed aspects of reality; however, as indicated above, such a claim does not rule out the possible veridicality of mystical states, since God may be among the new aspects of reality which deautomatization allows us to experience.

Furthermore, while there are other psychological accounts of contemplative consciousness, at least those with which I am familiar are either compatible with H_1 or seem less plausible than H_3. If this is correct, then, there are no reductive psychological theories of mysticism currently "in the field" which do a significantly better job of explaining mystical phenomena than H_1. In short, contrary to what is sometimes asserted by modern philosophers, the findings of contemporary psychology have not "explained mysticism away" or provided any compelling reasons for doubting its cognitive value.

6.2.4. REDUCTIVE PHYSIOLOGICAL ACCOUNTS OF MYSTICISM

According to a third class of naturalistic hypotheses, the occurrence and character of mystical states are due solely to physiological and neurological changes known to produce misperceptions in other contexts. Such hypotheses will be dealt with only briefly here, because although the defender of mysticism's cognitivity may be willing to grant that a detailed and reductive physiological account could in principle provide a better explanation of the facts about mysticism than H_1, no account of this sort seems to be available (or even likely).

In recent years the relationship between drugs, mysticism and schizophrenia has been widely discussed, and some authors, intrigued by certain similarities in the reports of mystics, psychotics and drug-users, have wondered whether all of these experiences might have a similar chemical basis, especially since drugs such as LSD and mescaline are known to have a chemical structure analogous to that of epinephrine, serotonin and other neurohumors which "chemically transmit impulses across synapses between two neurons, or nerve cells, or between a neuron and an effector such as a muscle cell" (Barron, Jarvik and Bunnell 1964, p. 32; see also Mandell et al. 1972, pp. 68-72). One hypothesis is that substances resembling the hallucinogens occur naturally in the brain of the schizophrenic, and can be produced in the brain of the mystic through fasting, vigils, intense concentration, self-flagellation, sexual abstinence, poor health and so on (see Mandell, et al. 1972, p. 71; Masters and Huston 1966, pp. 248-249). It would presumably follow from this that mystical states, like the strange experiences of the psychotic and drug-user, are simply the result of an imbalance in the neurohumors, transmitting impulses between neurons in the brain which do not ordinarily interact in this way.

What can we say about such a hypothesis? Certainly an account of mystical experiences in terms of underlying neurological processes would be *deeper* and more *consilient* that H_2 or H_3. But would it necessarily be incompatible with H_1? This is a more difficult question to answer. Obviously the claim that mystical experiences involve neurochemical activity would not by itself imply that such experiences are non-cognitive, since ordinary sense perceptions have a chemical basis as well. Moreover, the defender of mysticism could argue that the unusual impulse transmission in the mystic's brain does not cause misperceptions, but merely accompanies or triggers an unusual cognitive experience of God.

Now perhaps if scientists were able to develop a simple and straightforward explanation of the occurrence and phenomenological features of contemplative states in terms of some well-understood and fairly uncomplicated neurological process which in every other context is known to produce illusions and misperceptions, then we might have a genuine competitor to H_1, not because this theory would definitely prove that mystical states are non-cognitive, but rather because it would offer a simpler, deeper, more unified and complete account of the data without assuming that these experiences are actual perceptions.[19] Let us call this hypothetical competitor H_4. The problem is, however, that no hypothesis of this kind has any significant *evidential support*. Thus, while there are admittedly certain similarities between mystical and psychotic or psychedelic experiences, there are ordinarily important dissimilarities as well. For example, schizophrenic and drug-induced states are often accompanied by "complex auditory hallucinations as well as visual ones" (Barron, Jarvik and Bunnell 1964, p. 35), whereas in the highest states of mystical consciousness all sensual imagery is excluded. Also, while mystics are convinced that their experiences are perceptions of ultimate reality, someone under the influence of a hallucinogen can usually "distinguish his visions from reality, and even when they seem quite compelling he is able to attribute them to the action of the drug" (Ibid., p. 29); indeed, he can often exert some degree of conscious control over the course of his experience. Again, the brain-wave patterns of hallucinogenic drug-users generally seem to be different from those of advanced contemplatives (compare Ibid., p. 35; Mallory 1977, pp. 75-88; Wallace and Benson 1972, pp. 85-90).

But even if the chemical bases of some mystical and psychedelic experiences *were* similar, this would not necessarily mean that the drugs or neurohumors involved are the *sole* cause of their respective states. As Barron, Jarvik and Bunnell point out:

...in all the hallucinogen-produced experiences it is never the drug alone at work. As in the case of alcohol, the effects vary widely depending on when the drug is taken, where, in the presence of whom, in what dosage and—perhaps most important of all—by whom. What happens to the individual after he takes the drug, and his changing relations to the setting and the people in it during the episode, will further influence his experience. (Barron, Jarvik and Bunnell 1964, p. 35)

Thus LSD, mescaline and their analogues interact with the brain and with other environmental factors in extremely complex ways.

In short, even though a physiological account of contemplative states of the kind designated H_4 would offer a better explanation of the facts than H_1, no such account is currently available, nor is there any reason to expect that one ever will be. One might reasonably conclude, then, that there seems to be no physiological theory of mysticism currently "in the field" which is clearly incompatible with H_1 and does a better job of explaining the facts about mysticism.

6.2.5. REDUCTIVE SOCIOLOGICAL OR ANTHROPOLOGICAL ACCOUNTS OF MYSTICISM

With the rise of the social sciences in modern times has come a corresponding development in sociological and anthropological accounts of religion. Marx's analysis of religion as an ideological reflection of the current economic order, or Durkheim's more detailed presentation of religion as "before all, ...a system of ideas with which the individuals represent to themselves the society of which they are members, and the obscure but intimate relations which they have to it" (Durkheim 1947, p. 225), are only among the better known examples in a large field of contenders. Both approaches are often understood as, in some sense, reductive explanations of religious phenomena (though Durkheim in particular stresses the indispensible value of religion, even if its practitioners misidentify the source of its power).

Now it is not immediately evident that such theories have much to offer in response to our questions here about the epistemic value of mystical experiences (except insofar as they undermine confidence in the truth of religious claims in general). According to John Hick, for example, "Durkheim's theory has nothing to say about the phenomenon of mysticism, which is often highly individualistic" (Hick 1989, p. 117). Similarly, authors sympathetic to liberation theology have emphasized the *affinities* between Marxist analysis and the doctrines of certain Christian mystics.[20] Conceivably, reductive accounts of religion in its organized social manifestations might leave mysticism relatively unscathed.

Still, attempts are occasionally made to "explain" mysticism in terms of the social purposes it serves. Durkheim himself notes that the "moral forces" of society which are collectively represented in religion are in themselves powerful enough to plunge members of the society "into a state that may be called *ecstatic*" (Durkheim 1947, p. 227). It seems easy enough to extend to the analysis of mystical phenomena what Durkheim says of cultic practices: i.e., "By the mere fact that their apparent function is to strengthen the bonds attaching the believer to his god, they at the same time really strengthen the bonds attaching the individual to the society of which he is a member, since the god is only a figurative expression of the society" (Ibid., p. 226).

Thus, sociologists and anthropologists may argue, for example, that the "trance-states" of the shaman and mystic not only satisfy their own personal needs, but also have a positive function within the larger tribe or group as well (see, e.g., Lewis 1971). While such accounts are seldom worked out in any detail, they deserve at least passing mention, if only for the sake of completeness.

As a brief illustration of this kind of approach, consider Arnold M. Ludwig's remarks on the social function of "altered states of consciousness," using spirit possession as a paradigm:

From the individual's vantage point, possession by one of the tribal or local deities or Holy Spirit during a religious ceremony would allow him to attain high status through fulfilling his cult role, gain a temporary freedom of responsibility for his actions and pronouncements, or enable him to act out in a socially sanctioned way his aggression and sexual conflicts or desires....

From society's standpoint, the needs of the tribe or group are met through its vicarious identification with the entranced person who not only derives individual satisfaction from divine possession but also acts out certain ritualized group conflicts and aspirations, such as the theme of death and resurrection, cultural taboos, and so on. Moreover, the dramatic behavioral manifestations of spirit possession serve to convince the participants of the continued personal interest of their gods, reaffirm their local beliefs, allow them to exert some control over the unknown, enhance group cohesion and identification, and endow the utterances of the entranced shaman, or priest with an importance they might otherwise not have if spoken in an ordinary setting. In general, the existence of such practices represents an excellent example of how society creates modes of reducing frustration, stress and loneliness through group action. (Ludwig 1966, p. 232).

Now obviously not everything said here about spirit possession is equally applicable to mysticism, but we can see fairly clearly how these comments might be adapted to handle contemplative states. A skeptical theorist following Ludwig's lead could presumably claim that mystical experiences not only aid their recipients, but also fulfill the needs of the larger religious community to which the mystic belongs by reaffirming its beliefs, convincing the members of the continued interest of the divine, reinforcing group cohesion and the *status quo* (e.g., by redirecting the energies of the oppressed away from fundamental social reforms and toward mystical escape) and so on.

What can we say about an explanatory hypothesis of this sort? Let us grant, for the sake of argument, that it would be sufficiently *deep*, given the interests of our inquirer (though not as deep as a physiological explanation), and that it would be *consilient* insofar as other group phenomena could be similarly explained. The problem, however, is that social theories of mysticism in general are not necessarily incompatible with H_1. After all, sense perception also serves certain social purposes, but this scarcely counts against its cognitive value. Likewise, whether mystical awareness is cognitive or not, we will always be able to find *some* communal needs it satisfies by discovering whatever positive effects it may have on the group in question. (The mystics would be the first to admit that their experiences have good social effects, since they produce a high degree of altruism, and direct people toward the union with God for which they were intended.) In short, the mere fact that a mode of experience serves a positive social function does nothing, by itself, to show that it is non-cognitive.

On the other hand, if social scientists could develop a relatively simple theory of mysticism showing an almost exact correspondence between the characteristics of contemplative experiences and a set of independently identifiable social needs, and were also able to establish that no other variables played a significant role in evoking such states, then we might have a serious competitor to H_1, not because it would strictly imply that mystical consciousness is non-cognitive, but rather because it would offer a sufficiently deep, simple, complete, unified, and consilient account of all the facts without postulating the existence of God or some transcendent order of reality. Let us call this hypothetical theory H_5. One of the obvious virtues of H_5 is that it would explain the apparent conflicts between mystics of different backgrounds and traditions more adequately and completely than any of the other hypotheses we have examined so far; indeed, some of the philosophers who challenge the cognitivity of mystical consciousness on the basis of this apparent conflict may perhaps do so because they assume that an alternative such as H_5 is available.

Here again, however, no simple hypothesis of this kind seems to have any significant *evidential support;* the social consequences of mysticism are much too complex, and affected by too many other factors. As Andrew Greeley notes:

Ecstasy may well reduce frustration, stress, and loneliness; it may dissipate fears and tensions and generate a new sense of spiritual security and confidence; it may ease the despair and hopelessness of a marginal existence. But it does not follow that this is what ecstasy is all about either for the ecstatic himself or for those with whom he interacts. Much less is it reasonable to assume, as functional analysis frequently does, that the ecstatic and his fellows are somehow or other conspiring to arrive at socially adaptive functions. The mystic may be up to something else altogether, and the general reaction of those who have one on their hands is not to know what the hell to do with him. Efficiently administered families, schools, and congregations are hard put to cope with a mystic. (Greeley 1974, p. 43)

Mystics may be rich or poor, liberal or conservative, hermits or social activists, critics or supporters of the current political and religious order. Their impact on society varies widely; there is no single set of social needs and pressures that could reasonably be regarded as *the* cause which evokes their mystical experiences. As a result, there seems to be no naturalistic sociological or anthropological account of contemplative states which poses a serious challenge to their alleged cognitivity; to deal adequately with the enormously complex interrelationships between mysticism and society, any such account would have to sacrifice the very simplicity which could make it an attractive and plausible competitor to H_1. This is not to deny that the social sciences have much light to shed on religion in general, and mysticism in particular. As far as can be determined here, however, there is no social theory of mysticism currently "in the field" which is incompatible with H_1 and better able to explain the full range of mystical data.

6.3. The Reasonableness of Accepting Mysticism as a Cognitive Mode of Experience

These last pages have dealt with the various sets of answers which certain psychoanalytical, psychological, physiological and social theories are capable of providing to our hypothetical inquirer's "existential" questions about the significance of mysticism. Unfortunately, limitations of space make it necessary to treat such theories in a more summary (and perhaps superficial) manner than they might otherwise have deserved. Nevertheless, perhaps what has been said is sufficient to establish that, given a reasonable conviction that the mystical data are roughly as I have indicated and include at least a substantial portion of E_1 through E_{12}, the answers provided by the kinds of theories discussed above are no more adequate *on the whole* than those furnished by H_1. Thus the Freudian account of mystical consciousness in terms of pathological regression, though simple and (to some) appealing, is largely contradicted by the empirical evidence, and by itself is no more able than H_1 to explain such features as the apparent lack of consensus among mystics of different religious backgrounds. Again, Deikman's attempts to develop a reductive explanation of the phenomenal features of contemplative states only make his "deautomatization" hypothesis more obscure, complex and problematic. Furthermore, there appear to be no current physiological or social theories of mysticism which adequately fit the available data and at the same time are simple and clear enough to be plausibly regarded as true competitors to H_1. In short, an overall assessment on the basis of the foregoing considerations is that simple reductive accounts of contemplative consciousness generally lack any serious evidential support, and that insofar as such theories are further elaborated in order to deal more adequately with the evidence, they lose much of the simplicity which originally recommended them, or become less clearly incompatible with H_1.

At this point, then, let us return to our retroductive defense of H_1 according to Achinstein's schema, which can now be quickly completed. I have already indicated that *some* of the conditions warranting the first conclusion are satisfied. In particular, I have argued that the answers H_1 "is capable of supplying could be given in the situations in question in order to render [the mystical data] understandable" to our inquirer, and likewise that these answers "satisfy to a reasonable extent the criteria of evaluation at a level appropriate" to his situation of "existential" concern, though without entirely removing his puzzlement at the apparent disagreements between mystic and non-mystic (E_{10}), or among the mystics themselves (E_{11} and E_{12}). We can now see that the remaining conditions are also met. Thus the answers supplied by H_1 seem to "satisfy such criteria on the whole better than, or at least not significantly less well than, answers supplied by" H_2, H_3, H_4 and H_5; this position, at any rate, could be justifiably adopted in light of the kinds of considerations raised above. Furthermore, every other competitor to H_1 with which I am acquainted seems either less promising than the reductive theories of mysticism already treated, or could be handled in essentially the same way. Therefore, it seems legitimate to say that "any other hypotheses that it is reasonable to consider," given the evidence and background information, "supply answers that are inferior..., or at least not superior," to those furnished by H_1. Since Achinstein's three conditions are satisfied, then, we may conclude that "it is plausible to suppose that" H_1, "when conjoined with certain other assumptions, is capable of offering what in certain situations can be counted as a good explanation of the facts" about mysticism, and thus that H_1 "is plausible."

Indeed, I believe an even stronger assumption is warranted. As Achinstein notes, the degree of plausibility we assign to H_1 here will depend upon how much difference exists between H_1 and its competitors with respect to the criteria of evaluation. Now if others have rational grounds for accepting my assessment of the facts about mysticism and the alternatives to H_1, as I certainly think they might, then presumably they also have rational grounds for agreeing that H_1 on the whole does a *significantly* better job of meeting these criteria than other incompatible hypotheses. They would consequently be justified in concluding, it seems, that H_1 is not just barely plausible but also fairly probable. That is, it would be reasonable for them to accept contemplative consciousness as a cognitive mode of experience. Moreover, insofar as they likewise agree about the phenomenally theistic character of many Christian mystical states, it would be reasonable for them to regard contemplation as a cognitive experience of God.

The following example may help to clarify how an individual might justifiably arrive at such a position. Imagine, then, an open-minded, rational inquirer (call her Mary Smith) who takes a serious interest in the possible cognitive value of contemplative consciousness, and begins to study both classic mystical texts (such as those of St. Teresa and St. John of the Cross) as well as contemporary critiques of mysticism, while at the same time consulting some practicing contemplatives and pondering whatever personal experience she may have in this area. Suppose, too, that Smith's careful reflections gradually and legitimately lead her to the conviction that an author such as St. John of the Cross presents a fairly reliable picture of the phenomena associated with mysticism, and thus that these phenomena include at least a substantial portion of E_1 through E_{12}. She decides, for example, that mystical experiences cannot be casually dismissed as "mere feeling states" or the product of pious wish fulfillment, since they typically have a strong perception-like quality, and since their occurrence and phenomenal character are often different from what their recipients expected, impinging on them powerfully, as if "from beyond." Smith's investigations also convince her that not all contemplative states are properly described as an awareness of "pure undifferentiated unity," but that many involve a sense of loving union with something ultimate, nonsensuous, powerful, personal, loving, etc., and that for Christian mystics this "phenomenally theistic" character generally grows stronger as they advance in contemplation. Smith likewise notes that, far from being the pathologically unbalanced individuals she would have expected from reading Freud and Leuba, contemplatives ordinarily seem to manifest a greater than average degree of psychological and moral maturity, which becomes increasingly evident in those who have progressed furthest along the mystic path. Moreover, she is particularly struck by the close correspondence, at least in the case of Christian contemplatives, between the virtues seemingly imparted to recipients through their mystical states (e.g., charity, strength, mercy, justice, wisdom), and those attributed to the ostensible object of those experiences.

Eventually, Smith comes to recognize that such intriguing and otherwise puzzling phenomena can be largely explained by supposing that contemplative consciousness is in fact what the Christian mystic takes it to be, since these are the kinds of effects one might reasonably expect from a cognitive mode of experience involving mystical union with a loving God. She is somewhat perplexed by E_{10} through E_{12} (i.e., the apparent lack of consensus between mystic and non-mystic, and among mystics of different backgrounds), and wonders why, if the experiences of Christian mystics are veridical, the God they claim to encounter does not reveal himself more widely and more powerfully. Yet she is not altogether sure that this is a serious problem, since it may be that God has good reasons for temporarily withholding (or allowing human subjects to resist) such divine communications, and since it is unclear just how fundamental the disagreement between mystics of various religious traditions actually is; perhaps the experiences of the Theravadin, for example, sometimes do contain phenomenal elements which are theistic in their implications, but that such elements are overlooked either because Theravadin mystics do not explicitly attend to them, or because they describe their experiences using a different conceptual framework.

At the same time, Smith finds, in keeping with the considerations raised earlier, that reductive theories of mysticism seldom offer a substantially different and more serious explanation of E_{10}, E_{11} and E_{12}, and that those which do are generally inadequate in other respects. She notices, for example, that reductive accounts in terms of pathological regression, deautomatization or unusual brain chemistry make no particular attempt to explain any lack of consensus among the mystics, since they generally take it for granted that the same basic processes are involved in all cases. She notes, too, that the reasons offered by Deikman for the contrasting experiences of the mystic and non-mystic (i.e., that our ordinary preoccupations and thought patterns impede contemplative awareness) are essentially the same as those proposed by St. John of the Cross. She further observes that although E_{10} might indeed be explained by theories attributing to the mystic either poorly defined ego boundaries or a neurochemical disorder known to be a regular cause of misperceptions, such theories do not seem to be borne out by the facts; similarly, the view that the occurrence and character of contemplative states are determined by the needs of the mystic's social group could admittedly account for E_{11} and E_{12}, but fails to do justice to the evident complexity of the relationship between mystic and society.

On the basis of reflections such as these, then, our imaginary inquirer legitimately concludes that, when conjoined with certain other assumptions, H_1 on the whole offers a better explanation of the mystical data in its entirety than the best known reductive theories of mysticism, or any other alternatives which is reasonable to consider. Among other things, she sees that H_1 accounts for a broad range of phenomena by means of a few simple ideas, and enables those who so choose to respond intelligently and constructively to mystical states, by situating these experiences within the larger context of an ongoing relationship to a personal God analogous to familiar human love relationships. And because she recognizes the enormous explanatory power of H_1 in other respects, our inquirer is no longer unduly disturbed by E_{10}, E_{11} and E_{12}, but is willing to grant that these puzzling facts may simply be part of the mystery of divine providence. Thus, through a rational mode of retroductive inference, such an individual finally reaches the conclusion (which it has been the goal of this study to elucidate) that it is reasonable to regard contemplative consciousness as a cognitive mode of experience, and indeed as a way of experiencing God.

NOTES

[1] My "Great Pumpkin" example here should not be confused with what Alvin Plantinga dubs "the Great Pumpkin objection" to his views on "Reformed epistemology" in an unrelated discussion brought to my attention after this section had been written. Plantinga's article, 'Reason and Belief in God,' is concerned with a different issue, namely, which beliefs can be considered "properly basic" (see Plantinga 1983, pp. 74-78).

[2] Swinburne mentions four considerations that would limit the application of the principle of credulity to an alleged perception of x: 1) "one may show that the apparent perception was made under conditions or by a subject found in the past to be unreliable"; 2) "one may show that the perceptual claim was to have perceived an object of a certain kind in circumstances where similar perceptual claims have proved false"; 3) one may show that "on background evidence it is probable that x was not present"; and 4) one may show that "even if x was present, it probably did not cause the experience of its seeming that x was present" (Swinburne 1979, pp. 260-264). It is not clear, however, that these are of much use in distinguishing between the experience of Linus and the mystic.

[3] According to Achinstein's symbolization, q is actually an *oratio obliqua* form of the question Q raised by those to whom the explanation is offered; thus E is meant to provide an answer to the question Q.

[4] Achinstein also notes that whether E is classifiable as an explanation likewise depends on the context. Thus the Babylonian creation myth might count as an explanation of the origin of the universe in the context of the comparative study of religions, but presumably not in the context of scientific cosmology.

[5] Thus Thagard observes that "the general theory of relativity proved to be more consilient" than Newtonian mechanics "by explaining the perihelion of Mercury, the bending of light in a gravitational field, and the red shifts of spectral lines in an intense gravitational field" (Thagard 1978, pp. 81-82).

[6] The "neglected argument for the existence of God" which Peirce describes in this essay seems to be a retroductive inference, with affinities to my project in this study (compare Shepherd 1975, pp. 146-152). Norwood Russell Hanson discusses this mode of reasoning in *Patterns of Discovery* (1958), as does Gilbert Harman in 'The Inference to the Best Explanation' (1965) and the more recent *Thought* (1973).

[7] Compare, for example, Hilary Putnam's modified use of the "inference to the best explanation" with respect to skepticism about the external world and the existence of other minds, in Putnam's 'Other Minds' (Putnam 1972, pp. 80-86, 95-99), and Thagard's remark that "arguments concerning the best explanation are relevant to problems concerning scientific realism, other minds, the external world, and the existence of God" (Thagard 1978, p. 92).

[8] This is perhaps the truth behind James's assertion that "mystical states, ...have the right to be, absolutely authoritative over the individuals to whom they come," but not "for those who stand outside of them" (James 1936, p. 414). Since mystics presumably know their own moral character better than we do, they are in a better position to estimate how strongly they are affected. Yet their evidence for $E_{5.1}$, $E_{5.2}$, $E_{5.3}$ and so on is not purely private, since moral and psychological improvement should be manifested in one's behavior, and to some extent observable by others. Thus the mystics' convictions about the beneficial effects of their experiences would presumably be unjustified if everyone else noted a marked change for the worse.

[9] Compare the similar organization of John Bowker's *The Sense of God: Sociological, Anthropological and Psychological Approaches to the Origin of the Sense of God* (1973), which came to my attention as this section was being revised.

[10] For illuminating discussions of some of the issues in epistemology and philosophy of religion raised by psychoanalytic theory, see, for example, Alston 1964 and Bowker 1973, pp. 116-134.

[11] For a more recent variation on this kind of theory, see Prince and Savage 1972, pp. 114-134.

[12] In *Civilization and Its Discontents*, Freud seems to make a point of comparing "oceanic feelings" with pathological states; see Freud 1964b, p. 13.

[13] For a comparison of mysticism with pathological states likewise involving regression, see, for example, Wapnick 1972, pp. 153-174.

[14] For criticisms of this concept of "regression in service of the ego" analogous to my own, see Owens 1972, pp. 135-152. Alexander Maven even goes so far as to suggest that mystical experiences involve a return to the moment of conception as experienced "by the ovum, by the sperm, and by both together," a theory which, in my view, represents the

reductio ad absurdum of attempts to explain mystical states in terms of regression (see Maven 1972, pp. 429-435). Compare Greeley's objections to this whole approach in Greeley 1974, pp. 38-40.

[15] Leuba, on the other hand, claims that "many of the curious phenomena to which most great mystics owe in part their fame or notoriety are due to perturbations of the sex function consequent upon its repression," and that "the virgins and unsatisfied wives who undergo the repeated 'love-assaults of God'...suffer from nothing else than intense attacks of erotomania, induced by their organic need and the worship of the God of love" (Leuba 1929, pp. 119-120, 151). But this theory at best only accounts for certain ecstatic experiences, and is no better supported by the evidence than Freudian views (see the critique of Leuba in Laski 1968, pp. 143-153).

[16] See Ornstein's discussion of this point in chapter 2 of Naranjo and Ornstein 1971. The same point is made in a different context in Kuhn's *The Structure of Scientific Revolutions* (Kuhn 1970, pp. 62-65).

[17] For reports of some interesting research in these areas, see, for example, Huston and Masters (1972, pp. 303-321), and the extensive bibliography in Ludwig (1966).

[18] He notes that the "undoing of automatic perceptual and cognitive structures" might be called "regressive in the developmental sense, but the actual experience is probably not within the psychological scope of any child" (Deikman 1980, p. 251).

[19] In addition, the occurrence of ostensible mystical perceptions "under conditions...found in the past to be unreliable" would give us reason to limit the application of the principle of credulity here (see Swinburne 1979, p. 260).

[20] See, for example, Matthew Fox's 'Meister Eckhart and Karl Marx: The Mystic as Political Theologian,' (Fox 1980, pp. 541-563). For a more recent attempt to establish a Durkheimian theory of the origin of religion, see Swanson 1960. An extended critique of Swanson's thesis can be found in the second chapter of Bowker 1973.

CHAPTER SEVEN

CONCLUSIONS

As we have often observed in the preceding pages, philosophers have little difficulty disposing of mystical states as a possible source of support for religious beliefs when these states are understood in a fairly unsophisticated way and treated solely within the context of traditional "arguments from religious experience." Once we begin to take a closer look at the evidence and the issues involved, however, the task no longer seems as easy as it at first appeared. In this study I have offered a defense of the cognitive value of mysticism by analyzing in detail the testimony of one major mystical author, St. John of the Cross, and using the results of this analysis as the basis for an explanatory inference to the conclusion that it is reasonable to regard contemplative consciousness as a cognitive mode of experience. My work, then, has been divided into two main sections: Chapters One through Three, dealing with the life and teachings of St. John of the Cross, and Chapters Four through Six, dealing more directly with some of the major philosophical issues raised by mysticism.

The first chapter contained essential background information on the life, writings, intellectual milieu, and influence of St. John of the Cross, whom I imagined would be unfamiliar to many readers; I pointed out that he is an intelligent and careful author who is today recognized, by Christians and non-Christians alike, as one of the foremost authorities on mysticism, and that therefore his works can be regarded as a reliable account of a broad range of contemplative phenomena. In the second chapter I outlined John's notion of the fundamental structure of the human person, which generally follows the scholastic psychology of his day, but with certain significant modifications. There I tried to show that many of the popular interpretations of Sanjuanist mysticism as harshly dualistic and anticognitive rest on a misunderstanding of his doctrine; for John, contemplation involves the human being as a whole, and is not simply an acquired state of mental blankness, but a passive experience with a positive, though non-sensory, content.

Chapter Three traced the successive stages of spiritual development according to the Sanjuanist account, noting that, at least for John, there is no such thing as *the* mystical experience; instead, contemplation begins as a vague, transitory, almost imperceptible sense of peaceful recollection, and gradually develops in intensity through definite stages and crisis points, culminating in a state of almost continual mystical consciousness which, in the case of Christian mystics, generally has a phenomenally theistic character. Moreover, John indicates that progress in contemplation is associated, over the course of the spiritual life, with moral and psychological development as well; if he is correct, then it is difficult to dismiss mysticism as a purely pathological phenomenon.

In Chapter Four I used my findings to criticize certain popular accounts of the nature and common features of mystical states, especially those presented by James and Stace, and tried to show that, while the characteristics they list pertain to *some* contemplative experiences, they do not pertain to all of them; in particular, I argued against Stace's claim that all introvertive states consist only of an undifferentiated awareness of pure unity, contending instead that at least many Christian mystical experiences involve an apprehension of something personal, loving, powerful, and so on. The fourth chapter closed with a summary of the evidence gleaned from John's writing, for use in the retroductive defense of the cognitive value of mysticism in Chapter Six.

Clearly my explanatory inference would have no chance of success if the falsity of its conclusion could be established in advance. In Chapter Five, therefore, I discussed various attempts to prove conclusively that it is unreasonable to regard contemplative awareness as a cognitive mode of experience, concentrating in particular on certain standard objections having to do with the issues of testability and inter-subjective agreement (between mystic and non-mystic, and among the mystics themselves). There I maintained that while none of these objections are completely successful, they do point to additional data (e.g., the large number of mature non-mystics, and the apparent disagreement between mystics of different traditions) which are part of the total evidence, and potentially more difficult for the defender of mysticism to explain.

Chapter Six began with a general description of the explanatory mode of inference, followed by my application of this pattern of reasoning to the case of mysticism, in which I compared the explanatory power of the hypothesis that contemplation is a cognitive mode of experience with that of reductive accounts of mysticism in terms of regression, deautomatization, neurological disturbances in the brain, and so on. My conclusion was that, given a justified conviction that the facts about mysticism are more or less as described in earlier chapters, the former hypothesis provides at least as good an explanation of these facts as any alternative it is reasonable to consider, and that therefore it is reasonable for someone with such a conviction to accept contemplative awareness as a cognitive mode of experience, and even as a way of knowing God.

Now several points are worth noting about these results. First, in contrast to most other religious claims, my evaluation of the mystic's perceptual claims depends to a greater extent on the empirical evidence. Thus, if we were to discover that mystical experiences generally lead to moral turpitude and infantilism, or that they are triggered in a simple way by a process known to cause misperceptions, then it might no longer be reasonable to regard contemplation as cognitive, since the facts could be better explained in other ways. Similarly, it seems to me that if it could be shown that the vast majority of mystical experiences are phenomenally atheistic, then we would no longer be justified in believing that Christian mystics are encountering God; consequently, my project here needs to be supplemented by further research in comparative mysticism, to determine just how deep and extensive the disagreement is between mystics of different traditions.

Second, if it is rational for someone to regard contemplation as cognitive, and also rational for him to think that it seems to many mystics that they are experiencing God, then it is presumably rational for him to believe that God exists. In this way, the explanatory inference outlined above can be used in defending the reasonableness of religious belief, even though it involves neither a deductive or inductive proof of God's existence; this approach, in other words, apparently circumvents some of the difficulties associated with the traditional "proofs."

But the most obvious advantage of my explanatory inference, in the third place, is that it seems to be only a more formal version of the reasoning process which the mystics and their followers use in arriving at their beliefs in the veridicality of contemplative awareness. One of the problems with the ontological argument, for example, is that even if the argument were successful, it would not show that the average Christian's belief is rational, because his belief is not founded on the proof. On the other hand, many mystics and students of mysticism become convinced that contemplative states are cognitive simply because no other explanation seems to them to fit the facts as well. Provided their views about the facts are justified, then, the considerations of the last chapter would indicate that such a conviction is reasonable.

Fourth, while I have argued that, given certain justified convictions about the facts, it is reasonable to believe that mystical awareness is a cognitive mode of experience, I have not claimed that it is irrational *not* to do so. A person's judgment here depends on the relative importance he or she assigns to the merits and demerits of competing explanatory hypotheses, and on this point different individuals may reach different conclusions without either of them being obviously unreasonable. To see this more clearly, let us briefly consider how those in different epistemic situations with respect to mysticism (in particular, the Christian mystic, the Christian non-mystic, the non-Christian mystic, the agnostic, and the atheist) might respond to the kinds of considerations presented in this book.

First of all, let us imagine a modern-day St. Teresa, who begins to have experience during prayer in which it seems to her that she encounters something nonsensuous, personal, loving, divine, powerful, good, holy, and so on, roughly corresponding with what she already has been told and believes about God; yet despite her irresistible conviction *during* these experiences that she is encountering God, she wonders afterward whether she is perhaps merely mentally unbalanced or deceived by the devil. In such circumstances, after reflecting on the passive and utterly compelling nature of these states, their overwhelmingly beneficial effects (which are noted by others as well and seem to surpass everything attainable through her own efforts), and their congruity with her prior faith, she might reasonably conclude that these experiences are indeed veridical, since she finds it altogether implausible to suppose that psychopathological or demonic states could have such consequences.

Christian non-mystics (among whom I would include myself) would be in an analogous position, except that their knowledge of the effects and phenomenal characteristics of contemplative awareness would be more indirect and more open to challenge. Thus we might imagine a Christian believer who has read philosophers such as Martin, Nielsen, and Stace, and begins to wonder how anyone, on earth or in heaven, could ever be confident that he was really experiencing God; he might also be disturbed by the discovery that some mystics of other traditions do not describe their experiences in theistic terms. Still, after reflecting on the philosophical issues, studying the mystical literature, becoming acquainted with some practicing Christian contemplatives, and pondering his own faith experience, he might be reasonably persuaded that an author like St. John of the Cross presents a more or less accurate picture of human nature and the range of mystical phenomena, and that therefore Christian mystical experiences are probably cognitive, especially since it remains unclear to what extent these experiences are fundamentally incompatible with those of other mystics of non-theistic traditions.

Non-Christian mystics, on the basis of their own prior religious convictions, may believe that the phenomenal characteristics of mystical consciousness, at least in its highest stages, are generally more in conformity with the doctrine of their own tradition, and may therefore tend to doubt that phenomenally theistic contemplative states are as widespread or as important as I have suggested in this study. Thus, using the explanatory mode of inference, they might reasonably conclude that contemplative awareness is a cognitive mode of experience, but be less certain that it involves an encounter with God. Still, both the Christian and the non-Christian mystic would presumably want to consult each other to find out how different their experiences really are; perhaps they would discover that their respective states are basically complementary.

It seems unlikely that many agnostics will be persuaded by my explanatory inference, even if they approach the evidence with an open mind, since some of the assumptions and claims about mysticism are open to legitimate dispute; thus an agnostic may doubt that growth in contemplation is generally associated with psychological and moral development, or may feel that the extent of evil in the world makes it far less plausible to suppose that Christian mystics are encountering God. Still, it can and does happen that a sympathetic agnostic becomes convinced of the validity of Christian mystic experiences at least partly because the testimony of Teresa and others has such a powerful "ring of truth," and cannot easily be explained away as the product of wish-fulfillment, regression, deautomatization, mental confusion, or other purely natural causes. Such a conviction, it seems to me, may be justified.

Finally, atheists would not be compelled to change their position by anything said in this work if they remain confident that they have conclusive independent grounds for denying the existence of God or "ultimate reality." Still, they would presumably have to concede that the belief of other intelligent and informed individuals in the cognitive value of mysticism is not clearly irrational, as they might have previously supposed.

These may seem to be extremely modest conclusions for a study of this length, for, in a certain sense, they leave all parties secure in their respective positions, provided of course that their background convictions are justified. Still, I think we have shown that, given the satisfaction of certain conditions which many believers probably meet, it is reasonable to accept contemplative awareness as cognitive mode of experience. And this, it seems to me, is as much support as faith can legitimately expect of philosophy here: not a conclusive demonstration that belief in the cognitive value of mystical states is true, but only a solid argument that this belief is not contrary to reason. For as St. John of the Cross says, "all matters must be regulated by reason save those of faith, which though not contrary to reason, transcend it" (A II, 22, xiii).

BIBLIOGRAPHY

Achinstein, Peter: 1971, *Law and Explanation: An Essay in the Philosophy of Science*, Clarendon Press, Oxford.
Adams, Douglas: 1988, *The Long Dark Tea-Time of the Soul*, Simon & Schuster, New York.
Ahern, Barnabas: 1952, 'The Use of Scripture in the Spiritual Theology of St. John of the Cross,' *Catholic Biblical Quarterly* 14, 6-17.
Alberto de la Virgen del Carmen: 1947, *Historia de la Filosofía Carmelitana*, Manuales del Colegio Filosófico de "La Santa," Avila, Spain.
Alston, William P.: 1956, 'Ineffability,' *Philosophical Review* 65, 506-522.
Alston, William P.: 1964, 'Psychoanalytic Theory and Theistic Belief,' in John Hick (ed.), *Faith and the Philosophers*, Macmillan & Co., London, pp. 63-110.
Ansen, David, with Huck, Janet: 1982, 'When You Wish Upon a "TRON",' *Newsweek* (5 July 1982), 64-68.
Aristotle: 1941, *The Basic Works of Aristotle*, edited with introduction by Richard McKeon, Random House, New York.
Augustine. *De Trinitate*.
Ayer, A. J.: 1946, *Language, Truth and Logic*, 2d ed., Dover Publications, New York.
Baillie, John: 1959, *Our Knowledge of God*, Charles Scribner's Sons, New York.
Baker, Augustin: 1876, *Holy Wisdom*, edited by Serenus Cressy, re-edited by Abbot Sweeney, Burns & Oates, London.
Ballestero, Manuel: 1977, *Juan de la Cruz: de la angustia al olvido*, Historia/Sciencia/Sociedad Series, no. 138, Ediciones Península, Barcelona, Spain.
Barbour, Ian: 1974, *Myths, Models and Paradigms: A Comparative Study in Science and Religion*, Harper & Row, New York.
Barron, Frank, Jarvik, Murray E., and Bunnell, Sterling, Jr.: 1964, 'The Hallucinogenic Drugs,' *Scientific American* 210, 29-37.
Baruzi, Jean: 1924, *Saint Jean de la Croix et le Problème de l'Expérience Mystique*, Felix Alcan, Paris.
Baruzi, Jean: 1947, 'Saint Jean de la Croix,' in Maxime Gorce and Raoul Mortier (eds.), *Histoire Générale des Religions*, vol. 4, 188-191, 517-518, Librarie Aristide Quillet, Paris.
Baum, Gregory: 1970, *Man Becoming: God in Secular Experience*, Herder & Herder, New York.
Becker, Lawrence C.: 1971, 'A Note on Religious Experience Arguments,' *Religious Studies* 7, 63-68.
Bendick, Johannes: 1972, 'God and World in John of the Cross,' *Philosophy Today* 16, 281-294.
A Benedictine of Stanbrook Abbey: 1954, *Mediaeval Mystical Tradition and Saint John of the Cross*, Newman Press, Westminster, Maryland.
Bernardo María de la Cruz: 1966-1967, 'San Juan de la Cruz y la fenomenología husserliana,' *Revista de Espiritualidad*, 25, 62-74, and 26, 171-186.

Berrigan, Daniel: 1971, *The Dark Night of Resistance*, Doubleday, Garden City, New York.
Blackstone, William T.: 1963, *The Problem of Religious Knowledge: The Impact of Philosophical Analysis on the Question of Religious Knowledge*, Prentice-Hall, Englewood Cliffs, New Jersey.
Blondel, Maurice: 1925, 'Le Probléme de la Mystique,' *Cahiers de la Nouvelle Journée* (Paris) **3**, 2-63.
Boler, John: 1982, 'Intuitive and Abstractive Cognition,' in Norman Kretzmann, et al. (eds.), *The Cambridge History of Later Medieval Philosophy*, Cambridge University Press, Cambridge, pp. 460-478.
Bord, André: 1971, *Mémoire et Espérance chez Jean de la Croix*, Bibliothèque de Spiritualité, no. 8, Beauchesne, Paris.
Bouyer, Louis: 1961, *Introduction to Spirituality*, translated by Mary Perkins Ryan, Desclée Co., New York.
Bouyer, Louis, Leclerq, Jean, Vandenbroucke, François, and Cognet, Louis: 1969, *A History of Christian Spirituality*, Vol. 3: *Orthodox Spirituality and Protestant and Anglican Spirituality*, by Louis Bouyer, Seabury, New York.
Bowker, John: 1973, *The Sense of God: Sociological, Anthropological and Psychological Approaches to the Origin of the Sense of God*, Clarendon Press, Oxford.
Brenan, Gerald: 1973, *St. John of the Cross: His Life and Poetry*, with a translation of his poetry by Lynda Nicholson, Cambridge University Press, Cambridge.
Broad, C. D.: 1953, *Religion, Philosophy and Psychical Research: Selected Essays*, Routledge & Kegan Paul, London.
Bruno de Jésus- Marie: 1932, *Saint John of the Cross*, edited by Benedict Zimmerman, Sheed & Ward, New York.
Bucke, Richard Maurice: 1901, *Cosmic Consciousness: A Study in the Evolution of the Human Mind*, Innes & Sons, Philadelphia. (Reprint edition, Causeway Books, New York, 1974.)
Buckley, Michael: 1979, 'Atheism and Contemplation,' *Theological Studies* **40**, 680-699.
Burrell, David B.: 1967, 'Understanding St. John of the Cross,' *Cross and Crown* **19**, 399-414.
Casteneda, Carlos: 1974, *Tales of Power*, Simon & Schuster, New York.
Chapman, John: 1935, *Spiritual Letters*, Sheed & Ward, London. (New Ark Library, 1959.)
Chevalier, Jacques: 1959, *Entretiens avec Bergson*, Librarie Plon, Paris.
Chevallier, Philippe: 1922, 'Le "Cantique spirituel" de saint Jean de la Croix a-t-il été interpolé?' *Bulletin hispanique* **24**, 307-342.
Chevallier, Philippe: 1930, *Le 'Cantique Spirituel' de saint Jean de la Croix*, Desclée de Brouwer & Cie., Bruges, Belgium.
Clark, L. D.: 1964, *The Dark Night of the Body: D. H. Lawrence's "The Plumed Serpent,"* University of Texas Press, Austin, Texas.
Clark, Orville: 1972, 'The Optics of Nothingness,' *Philosophy Today* **16**, 243-253.
Clarke, Norris: 1964, 'Some Criteria Offered,' in John Hick (ed.), *Faith and the Philosophers*, Macmillan & Co., London, pp. 58-60.
Cognet, Louis: 1959, *Post-Reformation Spirituality*, translated by P. Hepburn Scott, Vol. 41 of The Twentieth Century Encyclopedia of Catholicism Series, Hawthorn Books, New York.

Copleston, Frederick C.:1950, *A History of Philosophy*, Vol. 2, *Medieval Philosophy: Augustine to Scotus*, Newman Press, Westminster, Maryland.
Copleston, Frederick C.: 1952, 'David Hume and St. John of the Cross,' *The Month* 8, pp. 69-81.
Copleston, Frederick C.: 1955, *Aquinas*, Penguin Books, Baltimore, Maryland.
Coward, Harold, and Penelhum, Terence (eds.): 1977, *Mystics and Scholars: The Calgary Conference on Mysticism 1976*, SR Supplements, no. 3, Wilfrid Laurier University Press, Waterloo, Ontario.
Crisógono de Jesús Sacramentado: 1929, *San Juan de la Cruz, su obra científica y su obra literaria*, 2 vols., Mensajero de Santa Teresa y de San Juan de la Cruz, Madrid.
Crisógono de Jesús Sacramentado: 1932, 'Maitre Jean Baconthorpe,' *Revue néoscholastique de philosophie*, 34, 341-365.
Crisógono de Jesús Sacramentado: 1958, *The Life of St. John of the Cross*, translated by Kathleen Pond, Longmans, Green & Co., London.
Crisógono de Jesús Sacramentado: 1973, 'Vida de San Juan de la Cruz,' revised and enlarged by Matías de Niño Jesús, in Lucinio Ruano (ed.), *Vida y Obras de San Juan de la Cruz*, 7th ed., Biblioteca de Autores Cristianos, Madrid.
Cugno, Alain: 1982, *Saint John of the Cross: Reflections on Mystical Experience*, translated by Barbara Wall, Seabury Press, New York.
Culligan, Kevin G.: 1972, 'William James and *The Varieties of Religious Experience*: The Birthday of a Classic,' *Spiritual Life* 18, 15-23.
Culligan, Kevin G.: 1979, 'Towards a Model of Spiritual Direction Based on the Writings of Saint John of the Cross and Carl R. Rogers: An Exploratory Study,' Ph.D. Dissertation, Boston University.
Cupitt, Don: 1981, *Taking Leave of God*, Crossroad, New York.
Dalton, Canon (trans.): 1863, *The Spirit of St. John of the Cross: Consisting of his maxims, sayings and spiritual advice on various subjects*, n.p., London.
Deikman, Arthur J.: 1972, 'Experimental Meditation,' in Charles Tart (ed.), *Altered States of Consciousness*, Doubleday & Co., Anchor Books, Garden City, New York.
Deikman, Arthur J.: 1979, 'Comments on the GAP Report on Mysticism,' in Daniel Goleman and Richard J. Davidson (eds.), *Consciousness: Brain, States of Awareness, and Mysticism*, Harper & Row, New York, pp. 191-194.
Deikman, Arthur J.: 1980, 'Deautomatization and the Mystic Experience,' in Richard Woods (ed.), *Understanding Mysticism*, Doubleday & Co., Image Books, Garden City, New York.
Delaye, Alain: 1975, *La Foi selon Jean de la Croix*, Sentiers pour l'Esprit, no. 5, Editions du Carmel, Avrillé, France.
de Mille, Richard: 1977, *Castenada's Journey*, Capra Press, Santa Barbara, California.
Dewart, Leslie: 1966, *The Future of Belief: Theism in a World Come of Age*, Herder & Herder, New York.
Dicken, E. W. Trueman: 1963, *The Crucible of Love: A Study of the Mysticism of St. Teresa of Jesus and St. John of the Cross*, Sheed & Ward, New York.
Donceel, Joseph F.: 1967, 'Knowledge, Process of,' in *New Catholic Encyclopedia*, McGraw-Hill, New York, vol. 8, pp. 230-232.
Dupré, Louis: 1980, 'The Mystical Experience of the Self and Its Philosophical Significance,' in Richard Woods (ed.), *Understanding Mysticism*, Doubleday & Co., Image Books, Garden City, New York, pp. 449-466.
Durkheim, Émile: 1947, *The Elementary Forms of Religious Life: A Study in Religious Sociology*, translated by Joseph Ward Swain, Free Press, Glencoe, Illinois.

Duvivier, Roger: 1971, *La Genèse de "Cantique spirituel" de saint Jean de la Croix*, Les Belles Artes, Paris.
Edwards, Rem B.: 1972, *Reason and Religion: An Introduction to the Philosophy of Religion*, Harcourt Brace Jovanovich, New York.
Emeterio del Sagrado Corazón: 1959, 'La noche pasiva del espíritu del San Juan de la Cruz,' *Revista de Espiritualidad* 18, 5-49.
Eulogio de la Virgen del Carmen: 1958 & 1960, 'La clave exegética del "Cántico Espiritual",' *Ephemerides Carmeliticae* 9, 307-337 and 11, 312-351.
Eulogio de la Virgen del Carmen: 1961, 'La antropologia Sanjuanistica,' *El Monte Carmelo* 69, 47-70.
Eulogio de la Virgen del Carmen: 1967, *El Cántico Espiritual: trayectoria historica del texto*, Teresianum, Rome.
Eulogio de la Virgen del Carmen: 1969, *San Juan de la Cruz y sus escritos*, Ediciones Cristianidad, Madrid.
Eulogio de la Virgen del Carmen: 1976, 'El "Cántico Espiritual" retocado,' *Ephemerides Carmeliticae* 27, 382-452.
Eulogio de San Juan de la Cruz: 1963, *La Transformación total del alma en Dios según San Juan de la Cruz*, Editorial de Espiritualidad, Madrid.
Farmer, H. H.:1942, *Towards Belief in God*, SCM Press, London.
Fenton, Joseph C.: 1938, 'The Theology of Meditation,' *American Ecclesiastical Review* 98, 209-222, 323-333.
Ferraro, Joseph: 1971, 'Sanjuanist Doctrine on the Human Mode of Operation of the Theological Virtue of Faith,' *Ephemerides Carmeliticae* 22, 250-294.
Ferré, Frederick: 1967, *Basic Modern Philosophy of Religion*, Charles Scribner's Sons, New York.
FitzGerald, Constance: 1984, 'Impasse and Dark Night,' in Tilden H. Edwards (ed.), *Living With Apocalypse: Spiritual Resources for Social Compassion*, Harper & Row, San Francisco, pp. 93-116.
Fitzgerald, Marie Christine: 1948, 'The Influence of St. John of the Cross on Several Poets of the Victorian Era,' M.A. Thesis, Catholic University of America, Washington, DC.
Flew, Antony: 1966, *God and Philosophy*, Dell Publishing, Delta Book, New York.
Flew, Antony, and MacIntyre, Alasdair (eds.): 1966, *New Essays in Philosophical Theology*, Macmillan Co., New York.
Forest, Aimé: 1942, 'La Doctrine de saint Jean de la Croix et la pensée contemporaine,' in *Saint Jean de la Croix et la pensée contemporaine*, Les Editions du Carmel, Petit-Castelet, Tarascon, pp. 31-51.
Fox, Matthew: 1980, 'Meister Eckhart and Karl Marx: The Mystic as Political Theologian,' in Richard Woods (ed.), *Understanding Mysticism*, Doubleday & Co., Image Books, Garden City, New York, pp. 541-563.
Freud, Sigmund: 1918, *Totem and Taboo: Resemblances between the psychic lives of savages and neurotics*, authorized translation with an introduction by A. A. Brill, Vintage Books, Random House, New York.
Freud, Sigmund: 1939 [1967], *Moses and Monotheism*, translated from the German by Katherine Jones, Vintage Books, Random House, New York.
Freud, Sigmund: 1962, *Civilization and Its Discontents*, translated and edited by James Strachey, W. W. Norton & Co., New York.
Freud, Sigmund: 1964a, 'Findings, Ideas, Problems,' in *The Standard Edition of the Complete Psychological Works of Sigmund Freud*, Vol. 23 (1937-1939), *Moses and*

Monotheism, An Outline of Psycho-Analysis and Other Works, translated from the German under the General Editorship of James Strachey, in collaboration with Anna Freud, assisted by Alix Strachey and Alan Tyson, Hogarth Press, London.

Freud, Sigmund: 1964b, *The Future of an Illusion,* translated by W. D. Robson-Scott, revised and newly edited by James Strachey, Doubleday & Co., Anchor Books, New York.

Freud, Sigmund: 1965, *New Introductory Lectures on Psychoanalysis,* newly translated and edited by James Strachey, W. W. Norton & Co., New York.

Frost, Bede: 1937, *Saint John of the Cross: An Introduction to His Philosophy, Theology and Spirituality,* Harper & Bros., New York.

Gale, Richard M.: 1960, 'Mysticism and Philosophy,' *Journal of Philosophy* 57, 471-481.

Galilea, Segundo: 1985, *The Future of Our Past: The Spanish Mystics Speak to Contemporary Spirituality,* Ave Maria Press, Notre Dame, Indiana.

Garaudy, Roger: 1966, Remarks on St. John of the Cross quoted in 'Geliebter Feind,' *Der Spiegel* 47, 157-159. Cited in Lucinio Ruano (ed.), *Vida y Obras de San Juan de la Cruz,* 7th ed., Editorial de Espiritualidad, Madrid, p. xxx.

Garrigou-Lagrange, Reginald: 1937, *Christian Perfection and Contemplation according to St. Thomas Aquinas and St. John of the Cross,* translated by M. Timothea Doyle, B. Herder Book Co., St. Louis, Missouri.

Gibbs, Benjamin: 1976, 'Mysticism and the Soul,' *Monist* 59, 532-550.

Giles, Mary: 1986, *The Poetics of Love: Meditations with John of the Cross,* American University Studies, Series VII: Theology and Religion, Vol. 18, Peter Lang, New York.

Gimello, Robert M.: 1978, 'Mysticism and Meditation,' in Steven T. Katz (ed.), *Mysticism and Philosophical Analysis,* Oxford University Press, New York, pp. 170-199.

Gosse, Edmund W.: 1883, *Seventeenth Century Studies,* Kegan, Paul, Trench, & Co., London.

Greeley, Andrew M.: 1974, *Ecstasy: A Way of Knowing,* Prentice-Hall, Englewood Cliffs, New Jersey.

Greeley, Andrew M., and McCready, William C.: 1975, 'Are We a Nation of Mystics?' *New York Times Magazine,* 26 January 1975, pp. 12-25.

Group for the Advancement of Psychiatry: 1979, 'What Mysticism Is,' in Daniel Goleman and Richard J. Davidson (eds.), *Consciousness: Brain, States of Awareness, and Mysticism,* Harper & Row, New York, pp. 187-190.

Guillet, Louis: 1971, *L'Éveil de l'Aurore: Introduction à saint Jean de la Croix,* Mame, Paris.

Gunderson, Keith: 1964, 'Are there Criteria for "Encountering God"?' in John Hick (ed.), *Faith and the Philosophers,* Macmillan & Co., London, pp. 57-58.

Hanson, Norwood Russell: 1958, *Patterns of Discovery: an inquiry into the conceptual foundations of science,* Cambridge University Press, Cambridge.

Happold, F. C.: 1970, *Mysticism: A Study and an Anthology,* rev. ed., Penguin Books, Baltimore, Maryland.

Hardy, Richard P.: 1978a, 'Early Biographical Documentation on Juan de la Cruz,' *Science et Esprit* 30, 313-323.

Hardy, Richard P.: 1978b, 'Fray Juan de la Cruz (1542-1591): A Personality Sketch,' *Ephemerides Carmeliticae* 29, 507-518.

Hardy, Richard P.: 1982, *Search for Nothing: The Life of John of the Cross,* Crossroad, New York.

Harkness, Georgia: 1945, *The Dark Night of the Soul*, Abingdon Press, Nashville, Tennessee.
Harman, Gilbert:1965, 'The Inference to the Best Explanation,' *Philosophical Review* 64, 88-95.
Harman, Gilbert: 1973, *Thought*, Princeton University Press, Princeton, New Jersey.
Hay, David, and Morisy, Ann: 1978, 'Reports of Ecstatic, Paranormal, or Religious Experience in Great Britain and the United States—A Comparison of Trends,' *Journal for the Scientific Study of Religion* 17, pp. 255-268.
Hepburn, Ronald W.: 1968, *Christianity and Paradox: Critical Studies in Twentieth-Century Theology*, Pegasus, New York.
Hepburn, Ronald W.: 1967a, 'Mysticism, Nature and Assessment of,' in Paul Edwards (ed.), *Encyclopedia of Philosophy*, Macmillan, New York, vol. 5, pp. 429-434.
Hepburn, Ronald W.: 1967b, 'Religious Experience, Argument for the Existence of God,' in Paul Edwards (ed.), *Encyclopedia of Philosophy*, Macmillan, New York, vol. 7, pp. 163-168.
Herrera, Robert A.: 1968, *St. John of the Cross: Introductory Studies*, Editorial de Espiritualidad, Madrid.
Herrera, Robert A.: 1977, 'Mysticism: St. John of the Cross,' in Sebastian A. Matczak (ed.), *God and Contemporary Thought: A Philosophical Perspective*, Learned Publications, New York, pp. 573-585.
Hick, John: 1963, *Philosophy of Religion*, Prentice-Hall, Englewood Cliffs, New Jersey.
Hick, John: 1977, 'Mystical Experience as Cognition,' in Harold Coward and Terence Penelhum (eds.), *Mystics and Scholars: The Calgary Conference on Mysticism 1976*, SR Supplements, no. 3, Wilfrid Laurier University Press, Waterloo, Ontario.
Hick, John: 1989, *An Interpretation of Religion: Human Responses to the Transcendent*, Yale University Press, New Haven, Connecticut.
Hippolyte de Sainte-Famille: 1946, 'Le conflit Doria-Gratien avec un présentation du P. Bruno,' *Etudes Carmelitaines*, 189-273.
Hirst, Désirée: 1964, *Hidden Riches: Traditional Symbolism from the Renaissance to Blake*, Barnes & Noble, New York.
Hocking, William Ernest: 1928, *The Meaning of God in Human Experience: A Philosophical Study of Religion*, Yale University Press, New Haven, Connecticut.
Hood, Ralph W., Jr.: 1975, 'The Construction and Preliminary Validation of a Measure of Reported Mystical Experience,' *Journal for the Scientific Study of Religion* 14, pp. 29-41.
Horne, James R.: 1978, *Beyond Mysticism*, Wilfrid Laurier University Press, Waterloo, Ontario.
Horsburgh, H. J. N.: 1972, 'The Claims of Religious Experience,' in John Donnelly (ed.), *Logical Analysis and Contemporary Theism*, Fordham University Press, New York, pp. 58-75.
Hospers, John: 1967, *An Introduction to Philosophical Analysis*, 2d ed., Prentice-Hall, Englewood Cliffs, New Jersey.
Hudson, W. Donald: 1974, *A Philosophical Approach to Religion*, Macmillan, London.
Huot de Longchamp, Max: 1981, *Lectures de Jean de la Croix: Essai d'Anthropologie Mystique*, Théologie Historique, no. 62, Beauchesne, Paris.
Huston, Jean, and Masters, Robert E. L.: 'The Experimental Induction of Religious Type Experiences,' in John White (ed.), *The Highest State of Consciousness*, Doubleday & Co., Anchor Books, Garden City, New York, pp. 303-321.

Inge, William Ralph: 1956, *Christian Mysticism*, Meridian Books, Living Age Books, New York.
Institutum Historicum Teresianum, eds.: 1973-, *Documenta Primigenia*, Teresianum, Rome.
James, William: 1936, *The Varieties of Religious Experience: A Study in Human Nature, Being the Gifford Lectures on Natural Religion Delivered at Edinburgh in 1901-1902*, Modern Library, New York.
John of the Cross: 1864, *The Complete Works of St. John of the Cross*, translated by David Lewis, edited by the Oblate Fathers of St. Charles, with a preface by Cardinal Wiseman, 2 vols., Thomas Baker, London.
John of the Cross: 1953, *The Complete Works of Saint John of the Cross*, translated and edited by E. Allison Peers, from the critical edition of P. Silverio de Santa Teresa, new ed., rev., 3 vols., Newman Press, Westminster, Maryland.
John of the Cross: 1957, *The Dark Night of the Soul*, translated, abridged and edited by Kurt F. Reinhardt, Frederick Ungar Publishing Co., New York.
John of the Cross: 1973, *Vida y Obras de San Juan de la Cruz*, edited with notes and appendices by Lucinio Ruano, with a biography by Crisógono de Jesús Sacramentado, rev. and enlarged by Matías del Niño Jesús, 7th ed., Biblioteca de Autores Cristianos, Madrid.
John of the Cross: 1979, *The Collected Works of St. John of the Cross*, translated by Kieran Kavanaugh and Otilio Rodriguez, 2d ed., ICS Publications, Washington, DC.
Johnston, William: 1971, *The Still Point: Reflections on Zen and Christian Mysticism*, Harper & Row, Perennial Library, San Francisco.
Juan de Jesús María: 1943, 'El díptico Subida-Noche,' in Theological Faculty of the Discalced Carmelites (eds.), *Sanjuanistica*, Collegium Internationale Sanctorum Teresiae a Jesu et Johannis a Cruce (Teresianum), Rome, pp. 27-83.
Juan de Jesús María: 1955: 'La amará tanto como es amada,' *Ephemerides Carmeliticae* 6, 3-103.
Katz, Steven T.: 1978, 'Language, Epistemology, and Mysticism,' in Steven T. Katz (ed.), *Mysticism and Philosophical Analysis*, Oxford University Press, New York.
Kaufmann, Walter: 1961, *Critique of Religion and Philosophy*, Doubleday & Co., Anchor Books, Garden City, New York.
Kellenberger, James: 1979, 'The Ineffabilities of Mysticism,' *American Philosophical Quarterly* 16, 307-315.
Kennick, William E.: 1962, Review of *Mysticism and Philosophy*, by W. T. Stace, *Philosophical Review* 71, 387-390.
Kenny, Anthony: 1976, 'Intellect and Imagination in Aquinas,' in Anthony Kenny (ed.), *Aquinas: A Collection of Critical Essays*, University of Notre Dame Press, Notre Dame, Indiana.
Knowles, David: 1961, *The English Mystical Tradition*, Harper & Bros., New York.
Knudsen, Christian: 1982, 'Intentions and Impositions,' in Norman Kretzmann et al. (eds.), *The Cambridge History of Later Medieval Philosophy*, Cambridge University Press, Cambridge, pp. 479-495.
Krynen, Jean: 1948, *Le "Cantique Spirituel" de saint Jean de la Croix commenté et réfondu au xviie siècle: un regard sur l'histoire de l'exégèse du Cantique de Jaen*, Universidad de Salamanca, Salamanca, Spain.
Kuhn, Thomas: 1970, *The Structure of Scientific Revolutions*, 2d ed., enlarged, University of Chicago Press, Chicago.

Lane, Dermot: 1981, *The Experience of God: An Invitation to Do Theology*, Paulist Press, Ramsey, New Jersey.
Larkin, Ernest E.: 1967, 'Ways, the Three Spiritual,' in *New Catholic Encyclopedia*, McGraw-Hill, New York, vol. 14, pp. 835-836.
Laski, Marghanita: 1968, *Ecstasy: A Study of Some Secular and Religious Experiences*, Greenwood Press, New York.
Le Brun, Jacques: 1964, 'France: VI. Le Grand Siécle de la Spiritualité Français et ses Lendemains,' in *Dictionnaire de Spiritualité, Ascétique et Mystique, Doctrine et Histoire*, Beauchesne, Paris, tome V, cols. 921-923.
Leuba, James: 1929, *The Psychology of Religious Mysticism*, rev. ed., Kegan Paul, Trench, Trübner & Co., London.
Lewis, H. D., and Whitely, C. H.: 1955, 'The Cognitive Factor in Religious Experience,' *Proceedings of the Aristotelian Society*, Supplementary Volume 29, 59-92.
Lewis, I. M.: 1971, *Ecstatic Religion: An Anthropological Study of Spirit Possession and Shamanism*, Penguin Books, Baltimore, Maryland.
Locke, John: 1964, *An Essay Concerning Human Understanding*, rev. ed. with an introduction by John W. Yolton, 2 vols., Dent, Everyman's Library, London.
Lucien-Marie de Saint-Joseph: 1974, 'Jean de la Croix (Saint),' in *Dictionnaire de Spiritualité, Ascétique et Mystique, Doctrine et Histoire*, Beauchesne, Paris, tome VIII, cols. 408-447.
Ludwig, Arnold M.: 1966, 'Altered States of Consciousness,' *Archives of General Psychiatry* 15, 225-234.
Luis de San José: 1948, *Concordancias de las Obras y Escritos del Doctor de la Iglesia San Juan de la Cruz*, El Monte Carmelo, Burgos, Spain.
Maas, Frans: 1977, 'A Personal or Impersonal God—An Old Problem of Western Mysticism?' in Edward Schillebeeckx and Bas van Iersal (eds.), *A Personal God?* Concilium Series, vol. 103, Seabury Press, Crossroad Book, New York.
McCann, Leonard A.: 1955, *The Doctrine of the Void: The Doctrine of the Void as Propounded by St. John of the Cross in his Major Prose Works and as Viewed in the Light of Thomistic Principles*, Basilian Press, Toronto.
McCready, William S.: 1974, 'A Survey of Mystical Experiences: A Research Note,' *Listening* 9, 55-70.
McDargh, John: 1984, 'The Life of the Self in Christian Spirituality and Contemporary Psychoanalysis,' *Horizons* 11, pp. 344-360.
McInnes, Neil: 1967, 'Spanish Philosophy,' in Paul Edwards (ed.), *Encyclopedia of Philosophy*, Macmillan, New York, vol. 7, pp. 511-516.
MacIntyre, Alasdair: 1966, 'Visions,' in Antony Flew and Alasdair MacIntyre (eds.), *New Essays in Philosophical Theology*, Macmillan Co., New York, pp. 254-260.
Maio, Eugene A.: 1973, *St. John of the Cross: The Imagery of Eros*, Playor, Madrid.
Malcolm, Norman: 1963, *Knowledge and Certainty: Essays and Lectures*, Prentice-Hall, Englewood Cliffs, New Jersey.
Mallory, Marilyn May: 1977, *Christian Mysticism: Transcending Techniques: A Theological Reflection on the Empirical Testing of the Teaching of St. John of the Cross*, Van Gorcum Assen, Amsterdam.
Mandell, Arnold J., Segal, David S., Kuczenski, Ronald T., and Knapp, Suzanne: 1972, 'The Search for the Schizococcus,' *Psychology Today* 6, 68-72.
Marcelo del Niño Jesús: 1930, *El Tomismo de San Juan de la Cruz*, El Monte Carmelo, Burgos, Spain.

Maritain, Jacques: 1959, *Distinguish to Unite, or The Degrees of Knowledge*, newly translated from the 4th French edition under direction of Gerald B. Phelan, Charles Scribner's Sons, New York.
Martin, C. B.: 1959, *Religious Belief*, Cornell University Press, Ithaca, New York.
Martin, C. B.: 1966, 'A Religious Way of Knowing,' in Antony Flew and Alasdair MacIntyre (eds.), *New Essays in Philosophical Theology*, Macmillan Co., New York, pp. 76-95.
Mascall, E. L.: 1943, *He Who Is: A Study in Traditional Theism*, Longmans, Green & Co., London.
Maslow, Abraham H.: 1972, *Religions, Values, and Peak Experiences*, Viking Press, New York.
Masters, Robert E. L., and Huston, Jean: 1966, *The Varieties of Psychedelic Experience*, Holt, Rinehart & Winston, New York.
Matson, Wallace I.: 1965, *The Existence of God*, Cornell University Press, Ithaca, New York.
Maurer, Armand A.: 1967, 'John Baconthorp,' in *New Catholic Encyclopedia*, McGraw-Hill, New York, vol. 7, pp. 1029-1030.
Maven, Alexander: 'The Mystical Union: A Suggested Biological Interpretation,' in John White (ed.), *The Highest State of Consciousness*, Doubleday & Co., Anchor Books, Garden City, New York, pp. 429-435.
Mavrodes, George I.: 1970, *Belief in God: A Study in the Epistemology of Religion*, Random House, New York.
Mavrodes, George I.: 1978, 'Real v. Deceptive Mystical Experiences,' in Steven T. Katz (ed.), *Mysticism and Philosophical Analysis*, Oxford University Press, New York, pp. 235-258.
Meadow, Mary Jo, and Kahoe, Richard D.: 1984, *Psychology of Religion: Religion in Individual Lives*, Harper & Row, New York.
Meissner, W. W.: 1977, 'The Psychology of Religious Experience,' *Communio* 4, 36-59.
Meissner, W. W.: 1984, *Psychoanalysis and Religious Experience*, Yale University Press, New Have, Connecticut.
Merlan, Philip: 1969, *Monopsychism Mysticism Metaconsciousness: Problems of the Soul in the Neoaristotelian and Neoplatonic Traditions*, International Archives of the History of Ideas, no. 2, Martinus Nijhoff, The Hague.
Merton, Thomas: 1951, *The Ascent to Truth*, Harcourt, Brace & Co., New York.
Miller, Ed. L.: 1972, *God and Reason: A Historical Approach to Philosophical Theology*, Macmillan Co., New York.
Mitchell, Basil: 1981, *The Justification of Religious Belief*, Oxford University Press, New York.
Moore, Peter G.: 1973, 'Recent Studies of Mysticism: A Critical Survey,' *Religion* 3, 146-156.
Moore, Peter G.: 1978, 'Mystical Experience, Mystical Doctrine, Mystical Technique,' in Steven T. Katz (ed.), *Mysticism and Philosophical Analysis*, Oxford University Press, New York, pp. 101-131.
Morel, Georges: 1960-1961, *Le sens de l'Existence selon S. Jean de la Croix*, Vol. 1: *Problématique;* Vol. 2: *Logique;* Vol. 3: *Symbolique*, Editions Montaigne, Aubier, Paris.

Morel, Georges: 1970, 'Sur Nietzsche et Jean de la Croix,' in Lucien-Marie and Jacques Marie Petit (eds.), *Actualité de Jean de la Croix*, Desclée de Brouwer, Tournai, Belgium.
Moriones, Ildefonso: 1968, *Ana de Jesús y la herencia teresiana: ¿Humanismo cristiano o rigor primitivo?* Teresianum, Rome.
Moriones, Ildefonso: 1972, *The Teresian Charism: A Study of the Origins*, translated by Christopher O'Mahoney, Teresianum, Rome.
Mouroux, Jean: 1964, *The Mystery of Time: A Theological Inquiry*, Desclée, New York.
Murphy, Michael, and Donovan, Steven: 1988, *The Physical and Psychological Effects of Meditation: A Review of Contemporary Meditation Research, With a Comprehensive Bibliography 1931-1988*, Esalen Institute Study of Exceptional Functioning, San Rafael, California.
'Mystic Moods Move the British,' *Boston Pilot* (17 June 1977), p. 5.
Nakhnikian, George: 1961, 'On the Cognitive Import of Certain Conscious States,' in Sidney Hook (ed.), *Religious Experience and Truth: A Symposium*, New York University Press, New York, pp. 156-164.
Naranjo, Claudio, and Ornstein, Robert E.: 1971, *On the Psychology of Meditation*, Viking Press, New York.
Nielsen, Kai: 1971, *Contemporary Critiques of Religion*, Herder & Herder, New York.
Nieto, José: 1979, *Mystic, Rebel, Saint: A Study of St. John of the Cross*, Librarie Droz, Geneva, Switzerland.
Orcibal, Jean: 1959, *La Recontre du Carmel Thérésian avec les Mystiques du Nord*, Presses Universitaires de France, Paris.
Orcibal, Jean: 1963, 'Le Role de L'Intellect Possible chez Jean de la Croix: ses Sources Scolastiques et Nordiques,' in Phillipe Dollinger et al. (eds.), *La Mystique Rhenane: Colloque de Strasbourg 16-19 mai 1961*, Presses Universitaires de France, Paris.
Orcibal, Jean: 1966, *Saint Jean de la Croix et les mystiques rhéno-flamands*, Desclée de Brouwer, Bruges, Belgium.
Ornstein, Robert E.: 1972, *The Psychology of Consciousness*, Viking Press, New York.
Ostow, Mortimer, and Scharfstein, Ben-Ami: 1954, *The Need to Believe: The Psychology of Religion*, International Universities Press, New York.
Otto, Rudolf: 1958, *The Idea of the Holy: An Inquiry into the non-rational factor in the idea of the divine and its relation to the rational*, translated by John W. Harvey, Oxford University Press paperback, New York.
Owen, H. P.: 1969, *The Christian Knowledge of God*, University of London, Athlone Press, London.
Owen, H. P.: 1971, 'Christian Mysticism: A Study in Walter Hilton's The Ladder of Perfection,' *Religious Studies* 7, 31-42.
Owens, Clair Myers: 1972, 'The Mystical Experience: Facts and Values,' in John White (ed.), *The Highest State of Consciousness*, Doubleday & Co., Anchor Books, Garden City, pp. 135-152.
Owens, Joseph: 1982, 'Faith, Ideas, Illumination, and Experience,' in Norman Kretzmann et al. (eds.), *The Cambridge History of Later Medieval Philosophy*, Cambridge University Press, Cambridge, pp. 440-459.
Pahnke, Walter N.: 1966, 'Drugs and Mysticism,' *International Journal of Parapsychology* 8, 295-320.
Pahnke, Walter N.: 1967, 'LSD and Religious Experiences,' in R. C. Debold and R. C. Leaf (eds.), *LSD, Man and Society*, Wesleyan University Press, Middleton, Connecticut, pp. 60-84.

Panakal, Justin: 1969, *The Theology of Private Revelations According to St. John of the Cross*, Piusnagar, Kerala, India.
Paton, H. J.: 1962, *The Modern Predicament: A Study in the Philosophy of Religion*, Collier Books, New York.
Payne, Steven: 1978, 'Eros and Contemplation,' *Spiritual Life* 24, 126-136.
Payne, Steven: 1979, 'To Ask God the Right Questions,' *Spiritual Life* 25, 204-214.
Payne, Steven: 1990, 'The Relationship Between Public Revelation and Private Revelations in the Theology of Saint John of the Cross,' *Teresianum* (forthcoming).
Peers, E. Allison: 1944, *Spirit of Flame: A Study of St. John of the Cross*, Morehouse-Goreham Co., New York.
Peers, E. Allison: 1946, *St. John of the Cross*, Faber & Faber, London.
Peirce, Charles Sanders: 1958, 'A Neglected Argument for the Existence of God,' in Philip P. Wiener (ed.),*Values in a Universe of Chance: Selected Writings of Charles S. Peirce (1839-1914)*, Stanford University Press, Stanford, California, pp. 358-379.
Penelhum, Terence: 1977, 'Unity and Diversity in the Interpretation of Mysticism,' in Harold Coward and Terence Penelhum (eds.), *Mystics and Scholars: The Calgary Conference on Mysticism 1976*, SR Supplements, no. 3, Wilfrid Laurier University Press, Waterloo, Ontario, pp. 71-81.
Pike, Nelson: 1967, 'Comments,' in W. H. Capitan and D. D. Merrill (eds.), *Art, Mind, and Religion: Proceedings of the 1965 Oberlin Colloquium in Philosophy*, University of Pittsburgh Press, Pittsburgh, Pennsylvania, pp. 144-150.
Pike, Nelson: 1986, 'John of the Cross on the Epistemic Value of Mystic Visions,' in Robert Audi and William J. Wainwright (eds.), *Rationality, Religious Belief, and Moral Commitment: New Essays in the Philosophy of Religion*, Cornell University Press, Ithaca, New York, pp. 15-37.
Plantinga, Alvin: 1983, 'Reason and Belief in God,' in Alvin Plantinga and Nicholas Wolterstorff (eds.), *Faith and Rationality: Reason and Belief in God*, University of Notre Dame Press, Notre Dame, Indiana, pp. 16-93.
Pletcher, Galen K.: 1971, 'Mysticism and Knowledge,' Ph.D. Dissertation, University of Michigan.
Pletcher, Galen K.: 1972, 'Agreement Among Mystics,' *Sophia* 11, 5-15.
Polkowski, William Allen: 1971, 'The Evidential Value of Religious Experiences for the Existence of God,' Ph.D. Dissertation, University of Michigan.
Poulain, Auguste: 1911, *The Graces of Interior Prayer: A Treatise on Mystical Theology*, translated by Leonora L. Yorke Smith, Kegan Paul, Trench, Trübner & Co., London.
Preller, Victor: 1967, *Divine Science and the Science of God: A Reformulation of Thomas Aquinas*, Princeton University Press, Princeton, New Jersey.
Prince, Raymond H.: 1980, 'Cocoon Work: An Interpretation of the Concern of Contemporary Youth with the Mystical,' in Richard Woods (ed.), *Understanding Mysticism*, Doubleday & Co., Image Books, Garden City, New York, pp. 338-354.
Prince, Raymond H., and Savage, Charles: 1972, 'Mystical States and the Concept of Regression,' in John White (ed.), *The Highest State of Consciousness*, Doubleday & Co., Anchor Books, Garden City, New York, pp. 114-134.
Pringle-Pattison, Andrew Seth: 1910-1911, 'Mysticism,' in *Encyclopedia Brittanica*, 11th ed., Encyclopedia Brittanica Co., New York, vol. 19, pp. 123-128.
Proudfoot, Wayne: 1985, *Religious Experience*, University of California Press, Berkeley, California.

Putnam, Hilary: 1972, 'Other Minds,' in Richard Rudner and Israel Scheffler (eds.), *Logic and Art: Essays in Honor of Nelson Goodman*, Bobbs-Merrill Co., New York, New York, pp. 78-99.
Rahner, Karl: 1963, *Visions and Prophecies*, Quaestiones Disputatae, no. 10, Herder & Herder, New York.
Rahner, Karl: 1966a, 'The Concept of Mystery in Catholic Theology,' in *Theological Investigations, Vol. 4: More Recent Writings*, translated by Kevin Smyth, Helicon Press, Baltimore, Maryland, pp. 36-73.
Rahner, Karl: 1966b, 'Nature and Grace,' in *Theological Investigations, Vol. 4: More Recent Writings*, translated by Kevin Smyth, Helicon Press, Baltimore, Maryland, pp. 165-188.
Rahner, Karl: 1966c, 'Remarks on the Dogmatic Treatise "De Trinitate",' in *Theological Investigations, Vol. 4: More Recent Writings*, translated by Kevin Smyth, Helicon Press, Baltimore, Maryland, pp. 77-102.
Rahner, Karl: 1978, *Foundations of Christian Faith: An Introduction to the Idea of Christianity*, translated by William V. Dych, Seabury Press, Crossroad Book, New York.
Ricoeur, Paul: 1970, *Freud and Philosophy: An Essay on Interpretation*, Yale University Press, New Haven, Connecticut.
Rohrbach, Peter-Thomas: 1966, *Journey to Carith: The Story of the Carmelite Order*, Doubleday & Co., Garden City, New York.
Rowe, William L.: 1978, *Philosophy of Religion: An Introduction*, Wadsworth Publishing Co., Belmont, California.
Ruiz Salvador, Federico: 1968, *Introducción a Juan de la Cruz: El hombre, los escritos, el sistema*, Biblioteca de Autores Cristianos, Madrid.
Russell, Bertrand: 1957, 'Mysticism and Logic,' in *Mysticism and Logic*, Doubleday & Co., Doubleday Anchor Books, Garden City, New York, pp. 1-31.
Russell, Bertrand: 1961, *Religion and Science*, Oxford University Press, Galaxy Book, New York.
Russell, Bertrand, and Copleston, Frederick C.: 1964, 'A Debate on the Existence of God,' in John Hick (ed.), *The Existence of God: Readings Selected, Edited and Furnished with an Introductory Essay*, Macmillan, New York, pp. 167-191.
Sanchez de Murillo, José: 1976, 'Der Strukturgedanke in de mystischen Purifikation bei Johannes vom Kreuz: Versuch einer Interpretation,' *Philosophisches Jahrbuch* 83, 266-292.
Sanson, Henri: 1953a, *L'esprit humain selon Saint Jean de la Croix*, Presses Universitaires de France, Paris.
Sanson, Henri: 1953b, *Saint Jean de la Croix entre Bossuet et Fénelon*, Presses Universitaires de France, Paris.
Scharfstein, Ben-Ami: 1974, *Mystical Experience*, Penguin Books, Baltimore, Maryland.
Schillebeeckx, Edward: 1981, *Christ: The Experience of Jesus as Lord*, translated by John Bowden, Crossroad, New York.
Schmidt, Paul F.: 1961, *Religious Knowledge*, Free Press of Glencoe, Glencoe, Illinois.
Sheehan, Peter: 1976, 'Aquinas on Intentionality,' in Anthony Kenny (ed.), *Aquinas: A Collection of Critical Essays*, University of Notre Dame Press, Notre Dame, Indiana, pp. 307-321.
Shepherd, John J.: 1975, *Experience, Inference and God*, Barnes & Noble, New York.

Silverio de Santa Teresa: 1937, *Historia del Carmen Descalzo en España, Portugal y America*, Vol. 6, *Fr. Jeronimo Gracián (1545-1614)—Fr. Nicolas Doria (1539-1594)*, El Monte Carmelo, Burgos, Spain.
Smart, Ninian: 1958, *Reasons and Faiths: An Investigation of Religious Discourse, Christian and Non-Christian*, Routledge & Kegan Paul, London.
Smart, Ninian: 1965, 'Interpretation and Mystical Experience,' *Religious Studies* 1, 75-87.
Smart, Ninian: 1967a, 'John of the Cross, St.,' in Paul Edwards (ed.), *Encyclopedia of Philosophy*, Macmillan, New York, vol. 3, p. 286.
Smart, Ninian: 1967b, 'Mystical Experience,' in W. H. Capitan and D. D. Merrill (eds.), *Art, Mind and Religion: Proceedings of the 1965 Oberlin Colloquium in Philosophy*, University of Pittsburgh Press, Pittsburgh, Pennsylvania, pp. 133-143.
Smart, Ninian: 1967c, 'Mysticism, History of,' in Paul Edwards (ed.), *Encyclopedia of Philosophy*, Macmillan, New York, vol. 5, pp. 419-429..
Smart, Ninian: 1967d, 'Sankara,' in Paul Edwards (ed.), *Encyclopedia of Philosophy*, Macmillan, New York, vol. 7, pp. 280-282.
Smart, Ninian: 1970, *Philosophers and Religious Truth*, Macmillan, New York.
Smart, Ninian: 1978, 'Understanding Religious Experience,' in Steven T. Katz (ed.), *Mysticism and Philosophical Analysis*, Oxford University Press, New York, pp. 10-21.
Staal, Frits: 1975, *Exploring Mysticism: A Methodological Essay*, University of California Press, Berkeley, California.
Stace, Walter T.: 1960a, *Mysticism and Philosophy*, Macmillan, London.
Stace, Walter T.: 1960b, *The Teachings of the Mystics*, New American Library, Mentor Books, New York.
Stein, Edith: 1960, *The Science of the Cross: A Study of St. John of the Cross*, edited by Lucy Gelber and Romaeus Leuven, translated by Hilda Graef, Henry Regnery Co., Chicago, Illinois.
Stock, Michael Edward: 1967, 'Appetite,' in *New Catholic Encyclopedia*, McGraw-Hill, New York, vol. 1, pp. 703-706.
Swanson, Guy E.: 1960,*The Birth of the Gods: The Origin of Primitive Beliefs*, University of Michigan Press, Ann Arbor, Michigan.
Swinburne, Richard: 1979, *The Existence of God*, Clarendon Press, Oxford.
Tavard, George H.: 1988, *Poetry and Contemplation in St. John of the Cross*, Ohio University Press, Athens, Ohio.
Teresa of Jesus: 1972, *The Complete Works of St. Teresa of Jesus*, translated and edited by E. Allison Peers, from the critical edition of P. Silverio de Santa Teresa, 3 vols., Sheed & Ward, London.
Teresa of Jesus: 1976-1987, *The Collected Works of St. Teresa of Avila*, translated by Kieran Kavanaugh and Otilio Rodriguez, 3 vols., ICS Publications, Washington, DC.
Thagard, Paul R.: 1978, 'The Best Explanation: Criteria for Theory Choice,' *Journal of Philosophy* 75, 76-92.
Thibon, Gustave: 1957, *Nietzsche und der heilige Johannes vom Kreuz: Eine charakterologische Studie*, Verlag Ferdinand Schöningh, Paderborn.
Thomas Aquinas: *Quaestio Disputata de Anima*.
Thomas Aquinas: 1947-1948, *Summa Theologica*, translated by the Fathers of the English Dominican Province, 3 vols., Benziger Bros., New York.

Thomas Aquinas: 1952-1954, *Truth* (translation of *Quaestiones Disputatae de Veritate*), translated by R. W. Mulligan, J. V. McGlynn, and R. W. Schmidt, 3 vols., Henry Regnery, Chicago, Illinois.

Thomas Aquinas: 1955-1957, *On the Truth of the Catholic Faith: Summa Contra Gentiles*, translated by Anton C. Pegis et al., 5 vols., Doubleday & Co., Image Books, New York, New York.

Thomas, George F.: 1967, *Philosophy and Religious Belief*, Charles Scribner's Sons, New York.

Thompson, Colin P.: 1977, *The Poet and the Mystic: A Study of the Cántico Espiritual of San Juan de la Cruz*, Oxford University Press, Oxford.

Thompson, William M.: 1987, *Fire and Light: On Consulting the Saints, Mystics, and Martyrs in Theology*, Paulist Press, Mahwah, New Jersey.

Tracy, David: 1975, *Blessed Rage for Order: The New Pluralism in Theology*, Seabury Press, New York.

Trethowan, Illtyd: 1975a, Introduction to Walter Hilton, *The Scale of Perfection*, translated by Leo Sherley-Price, new abridged ed., Abbey Press, St. Meinrad, Indiana.

Trethowan, Illtyd: 1975b, *Mysticism and Theology: An Essay in Christian Metaphysics*, Geoffrey Chapman, London.

Tyrell, Thomas J.: 1980, *Urgent Longings: Reflections on the Experience of Infatuation, Human Intimacy, and Contemplative Love*, Affirmation Books, Whitinsville, Massachusetts.

Underhill, Evelyn: 1955, *Mysticism: A Study in the Nature and Development of Man's Spiritual Consciousness*, Noonday Press, Meridian Books, New York.

Van Herik, Judith: 1982, *Freud on Femininity and Faith*, University of California Press, Berkeley, California.

Vaughan, Robert Alfred: 1893, *Hours With the Mystics: A Contribution to the History of Religious Opinion*, 6th ed., 2 vols. in one, Charles Scribner's Sons, New York.

Vilnet, Jean: 1949, *Bible et mystique chez Saint Jean de la Croix*, Desclée de Brouwer, Bruges, Belgium.

Vilnet, Jean: 1958, 'Écriture Saint et Vie Spirituelle, Part III, L'Écriture el les mystiques,' in *Dictionnaire de Spiritualité, Ascétique et Mystique, Doctrine et Histoire*, Beauchesne, Paris, tome IV, part 1, cols. 248-253.

Vogelgesang, Sandy: 1974, *The Long Dark Night of the Soul: The American Intellectual Left and the Vietnam War*, Harper & Row, New York.

von Balthasar, Hans Urs: 1986, *The Glory of the Lord: A Theological Aesthetics*, Vol. III: *Studies in Theological Style: Lay Styles*, translated by Andrew Louth et al., Ignatius Press, San Francisco.

Wainwright, William J.: 1970, 'Stace and Mysticism,' *Journal of Religion* 50, 139-154.

Wainwright, William J.: 1973a, 'Mysticism and Sense Perception,' *Religious Studies* 9, 257-278.

Wainwright, William J.: 1973b, 'Natural Explanations and Religious Experience,' *Ratio* 15, 98-101.

Wainwright, William J.: 1975, 'Two Theories of Mysticism: Gilson & Maritain,' *Modern Schoolman* 52, 405-426.

Wainwright, William J.: 1977, 'Interpretation, Description, and Mystical Consciousness,' *Journal of the American Academy of Religion* 45, Supplement, 989-1010.

Wainwright, William J.: 1978, *Philosophy of Religion: An Annotated Bibliography of Twentieth Century Writings in English*, Garland Publishing, New York.

Wainwright, William J: 1981, *Mysticism: A Study of its Nature, Cognitive Value and Moral Implications*, University of Wisconsin Press, Madison, Wisconsin.

Wallace, Robert Keith, and Benson, Herbert: 1972, 'The Physiology of Meditation,' *Scientific American* **226**, pp. 85-90.

Wallace, William: 1977, *The Elements of Philosophy*, Alba House, Staten Island, New York.

Wapnick, Kenneth: 1972, 'Mysticism and Schizophrenia,' in John White (ed.), *The Highest State of Consciousness*, Doubleday & Co., Anchor Books, Garden City, New York, pp. 153-174.

Werblowsky, R. J. Zwi: 1966, 'On the Mystical Rejection of Mystical Illuminations: A Note on St. John of the Cross,' *Religious Studies* **1**, 177-184.

White, John (ed.): 1972, *The Highest State of Consciousness*, Doubleday & Co., Anchor Books, Garden City, New York.

Whitson, Robley Edward: 1966, *Mysticism and Ecumenism*, Sheed & Ward, New York.

Wilber, Ken, Engler, Jack, and Brown, Daniel P.: 1986, *Transformations of Consciousness: Conventional and Contemplative Perspectives on Development*, with chapters by John Chirban, Mark Epstein, and Jonathan Lieff, Shambhala, Boston.

Wilhelmsen, Elizabeth: 1985, *Cognition and Communication in John of the Cross*, European University Studies, Series 23: Theology, Vol. 246, Peter Lang, New York.

Wittgenstein, Ludwig: 1958, *Philosophical Investigations*, 2d ed., translated by G. E. M. Anscombe, Macmillan, New York.

Wojtyla, Karol: 1981, *Faith According to Saint John of the Cross*, translated by Jordan Aumann, Ignatius Press, San Francisco.

Wolfe, Tom: 1973, 'Post Orbital Remorse, Part III: The Dark Night of the Ego,' *Rolling Stone* (15 February 1973).

Woods, Richard (ed.): 1980, *Understanding Mysticism*, Doubleday & Co., Image Books, Garden City, New York.

Zabalza, Laureano de la Inmaculada: 1963, *El Desposorio Espiritual según San Juan de la Cruz*, El Monte Carmelo, Burgos, Spain.

Zaehner, R. C.: 1961, *Mysticism: Sacred and Profane: An Inquiry into Some Varieties of Praeternatural Experience*, Oxford University Press, New York.

Zaehner, R. C.: 1970, *Concordant Discord: The Interdependence of Faiths, Being the Gifford Lectures on Natural Religion Delivered at St. Andrews in 1967-1969 by R. C. Zaehner*, Clarendon Press, Oxford.

INDEX OF NAMES

Achinstein, Peter, xii-xiii, 175-184, 188, 209-210, 213
Adams, Douglas, 1
Ahern, Barnabas, 14
Alberto de la Virgen del Carmen, 4, 20
Al-Ghazali, 20
Al-Hallaj, 116
Alston, William P., 100, 198, 213
Ana de Jesús, 7, 9, 15
Ana de Peñalosa, 9, 55
Ansen, David, 1
Aquinas, *see* Thomas Aquinas, St.
Aristotle, 5, 14, 20-21, 25, 29, 31, 45-46
Augustine, St. 14, 23, 38, 40, 43, 49
 Pseudo-Augustine, 14
Aurobindo, Sri, 122
Averröes, 20
Avicenna, 21
Ayer, A. J., xii, 100, 153, 159

Bacon, Francis, 10
Baconthorpe, John, 4, 20
Baillie, John, ix
Baker, Augustine, 1, 13
Ballestero, Manuel, 13
Barbour, Ian, 121
Barron, Frank, 204-205
Baruzi, Jean, 1, 11-14, 38, 85, 88
Baum, Gregory, xvi
Becker, Lawrence C., 167
Bendick, Johannes, 17, 37, 85
Benedictine of Stanbrook Abbey, 14
Benson, Herbert, 205
Berger, Peter, ix
Bergson, Henri, 13
Bernard of Clairvaux, St., 14
Bernardo María de la Cruz, 49
Berrigan, Daniel, 1
Blackstone, William T., 153, 155
Blondel, Maurice, 13
Boethius, 14, 35
Boler, John, 26

Bonaventure, St., 23
Bord, André, 20-22, 38-40, 44, 46, 49, 86
Boscan, 14
Bossuet, Jacques Bénigne, 13
Bouyer, Louis, 13, 46
Bowker, John, 197, 213-214
Brenan, Gerald, 14-15
Broad, C. D., 127, 134, 141, 148, 152, 170-172
Bruno de Jésus-Marie, 13-14
Bucke, Richard Maurice, 2
Buckley, Michael, 88, 191
Buddha, 93, 116
Bunnell, Sterling, Jr., 204-205
Burrell, David B., 45, 48

Casteneda, Carlos, 1
Catherine of Siena, St., 23
Cervantes, Miguel, 10
Chapman, John, 75, 85
Chevallier, Philippe, 11, 13, 15
Clark, Orville, 59, 88
Clarke, Norris, 160
Cognet, Louis, 11
Copleston, Frederick C., 24-25, 45-46
Crashaw, Richard, 1, 13
Crisógono de Jesús Sacramentado, 4-7, 13-15, 49, 86
Culligan, Kevin G., 3, 16, 34
Cupitt, Don, 33

Dalton, Canon, 2
Deikman, Arthur J., 87, 196, 199-203, 211, 214
Delaye, Alain, 70, 87
Descartes, René, 10
Dewart, Leslie, 88
Dicken, E. W. Trueman, 3, 16, 43-45, 49, 64, 85-88
Dionysius the Areopagite (Pseudo), 14, 47, 102, 122-123, 155
Donceel, Joseph F., 26

Donovan, Steven, 76, 124, 202
Doria, Nicolás, 6-7, 11, 14
Duns Scotus, John, 5, 9
Dupré, Louis, 49
Durandus of Saint-Pourçain, 5
Durkheim, Émile, 206, 214
Duvivier, Roger, 15

Eckhart, Meister, xiii, 3, 93, 105, 110-111, 113, 116, 123, 214
Edwards, Rem B., 93, 122, 130, 146
Emeterio del Sagrado Corazón, 86
Erasmus, Desiderius, 10
Eulogio de la Virgen del Carmen, 6-7, 14-15, 45, 85
Eulogio de San Juan de la Cruz, 53, 78

Farmer, H. H., ix
Fénelon, François, 13
Fenton, Joseph C., 46
Ferraro, Joseph, 71
Ferré, Frederick, 121
FitzGerald, Constance, 88
Fitzgerald, Marie Christine, 2
Flew, Antony, 126, 130, 136-137, 146, 150-152, 154, 172
Forest, Aimé, 13
Fox, Matthew, 214
Freud, Sigmund, 188-198, 200, 202, 211, 213-214
Frost, Bede, 44, 49

Gale, Richard M., 164-165
Garaudy, Roger, 3
Garrigou-Lagrange, Reginald, 44
Gassendi, Pierre, 10
Gibbs, Benjamin, 31, 43, 49
Gimello, Robert M., 88
Gosse, Edmund W., 13
Gracián, Jeronimo, 6-7, 14
Grajal, Gaspar de, 5
Greeley, Andrew M., 124, , 169, 186, 208, 214
Gregory the Great, St., 14, 155
Guillet, Louis, 34
Gunderson, Keith, 154
Guyon, Madame, 13

Hakuin, xiv

Hanson, Norwood Russell, 178, 213
Happold, F. C., 3
Hardy, Richard P., 4
Harman, Gilbert, 178, 213
Hay, David, 186, 191
Hegel, G. W. F., 73, 88
Heidegger, Martin, 88
Hepburn, Ronald W., ix, 99, 138, 153-154, 165-166, 168, 188-189, 194, 199
Herrera, Robert A., 17
Hick, John, 127, 167-168, 171, 173, 206
Hippolyte de Sainte-Famille, 14
Hirst, Désirée, 13
Hobbes, Thomas, 10
Hocking, William Ernest, 93
Horne, James R., 92, 121
Horsburgh, H. J. N., 65, 86
Hospers, John, 154, 156, 161, 170
Huck, Janet, 1
Hudson, W. Donald, 134
Hume, David, 166-167
Huston, Jean, 121, 204, 214

Ignatius of Loyola, St., 46
Inge, William Ralph, 2-3, 11, 13, 32, 59, 71

James, William, 2-3, 13, 86, 93-98, 104-107, 115-116, 121, 123, 170, 172, 213, 216
Jarvik, Murray E., 204-205
Jeffries, Richard, 116
Jeremiah, 121
John of the Cross, St., *passim*
Johnston, William, 87
Juan de Jesús María, 14, 59, 85-86
Juan de la Cruz, St., *see* John of the Cross, St.
Jung, Carl G., ix

Kant, Immanuel, 105, 110-111, 164, 166, 171
Katz, Steven T., 107, 171-172
Kaufmann, Walter, 137, 146
Kavanaugh, Kieran, 7-8, 43, 49
Kellenberger, James, 33, 103
Kennick, William E., 92
Kenny, Anthony, 26, 46-47
Knapp, Suzanne, 204

INDEX OF NAMES

Knowles, David, 13
Knudsen, Christian, 46
Krynen, Jean, 15
Kuczenski, Ronald T., 204
Kuhn, Thomas, 214

Lane, Dermot, x
Laredo, Bernardino de 14, 23
Larkin, Ernest E., 55
Laski, Marghanita, 214
Law, William, 1, 13
Lawrence, D. H., 1
Le Brun, Jacques, 13
Leibniz, Gottfried Wilhelm von, 13
Leuba, James, 211, 214
Lewis, I. M., 207
Locke, John, 44-45, 166
Lucien-Marie de Saint-Joseph, 13
Ludwig, Arnold M., 207, 214
Luis de Leon, 5
Luis de San José, 34

McCann, Leonard A., 44
McCready, William S., 124, 169, 186
McDargh, John, 191, 197
McInnes, Neil, 10
MacIntyre, Alasdair, 165-166
Maine de Biran, 13
Maio, Eugene A., 17
Malcolm, Norman, 171
Mallory, Marilyn May, 17, 37, 124, 205
Mandell, Arnold J., 204
Marcelo del Niño Jesús, 44
Maritain, Jacques, 44, 83-84, 90
Martin, C. B, 122, 126, 130-131, 133, 153-160, 170, 218
Marx, Karl, 191, 206, 214
Mascall, E. L., 87
Maslow, Abraham H., ix, 183
Masters, Robert E. L., 121, 204, 214
Matson, Wallace I., 93, 134, 146
Maurer, Armand A., 4
Maven, Alexander, 213
Mavrodes, George I., 123, 170
Meissner, W. W., 193, 196
Merlan, Philip, 29
Merton, Thomas, 44
Michael of Bologna, 4
Miller, Ed. L., 130

Mitchell, Basil, 162, 167, 173
Montaigne, Michel de 10
Moore, Peter G., 107, 122, 150, 172
Morel, Georges, 14, 44, 63, 86, 88
Moriones, Ildefonso, 4
Morisy, Ann, 186, 191
Mouroux, Jean, 87-88
Murphy, Michael, 76, 124, 202

Nakhnikian, George, 167-168, 189, 194
Nielsen, Kai, 87, 121, 139, 147, 156, 159, 160, 162, 173, 218
Nieto, José, 14
Nietzsche, Friedrich, 88, 191

Orcibal, Jean, 13-14, 29, 43, 49, 86
Ornstein, Robert E., ix, 183, 214
Ostow, Mortimer, 193
Osuna, Francisco de, 14
Otto, Rudolf, 74-75
Owens, Clair Myers, 213
Owens, Joseph, 46

Pacho, Eulogio, see Eulogio de la Virgen del Carmen
Pahnke, Walter N., 121
Panakal, Justin, 68
Paton, H. J., 37
Paul, St. 18, 47, 84, 92, 172
Payne, Steven, 38, 68, 75, 124
Peers, E. Allison, 2-3, 12-13, 15, 86
Peirce, Charles Sanders, 178, 213
Penelhum, Terence, 138, 170-171
Peter Lombard, 47
Pike, Nelson, 123
Pius XI (Pope), 1
Plantinga, Alvin, 212
Plato, 29
Pletcher, Galen K., 92, 159, 169-170, 173
Plotinus, 88, 93, 116
Poiret, Pierre, 13
Polkowski, William Allen, 127
Poulain, Auguste, 49
Preller, Victor, 26
Prince, Raymond H., 121, 196, 213
Pseudo-Dionysius, see Dionysius the Areopagite (Pseudo)
Putnam, Hilary, 213

Quiroga, José de Jesús María, 14, 28-29

Rahner, Karl, 85, 87, 89-90, 114
Rainaldo da Piperno, 47
Ramakrishna, 149
Reinhardt, Kurt, 105, 122
Ricoeur, Paul, 191
Rodriguez, Otilio, 49
Rohrbach, Peter-Thomas, 14
Rolland, Romain, 192
Rous, Francis, 1, 13
Rowe, William L., 98, 134
Ruiz Salvador, Federico, 7, 14, 34, 44-45, 85-86
Rumi, Jalal-ud-din, xiv
Russell, Bertrand, 122, 126, 130, 172
Ruysbroeck, Jan van, 3, 14, 23, 110, 113, 123

Sanchez de Murillo, José, 75, 85, 88
Sankara, 93, 116
Sanson, Henri, 13, 45, 49, 85
Savage, Charles, 196, 213
Scharfstein, Ben-Ami, 129, 147, 171, 193
Schillebeeckx, Edward, x
Schmidt, Paul F., 122, 154, 156
Schreber, Daniel Paul, 171
Schrödinger, Erwin, 147
Scotus, *see* Duns Scotus, John
Segal, David S., 204
Sheehan, Peter, 26
Shepherd, John J., 87, 168, 198-199, 213
Silverio de Santa Teresa, 14
Smart, Ninian, 37, 55, 88, 93, 121, 123, 139, 145, 147
Staal, Frits, 169
Stace, W. T., 3, 11, 30, 37, 77, 81, 87, 89, 92-116, 121-122, 138, 141, 144, 147, 169-171, 184, 199, 216, 218
Stein, Edith, 49, 85
Stock, Michael Edward, 34, 45
Suárez, Francisco, 10
Swanson, Guy E., 214
Swinburne, Richard, 127, 163, 167, 172, 212, 214
Symonds, J. A., 110

Tauler, Johannes, 14
Pseudo-Tauler, 29, 86
Teilhard de Chardin, Pierre, 122
Teresa of Avila, St., 1, 3-4, 6, 8, 11, 13-15, 23, 48-49, 56, 86-87, 105-106, 110-114, 122-123, 142, 146-147, 149-150, 157, 161-163, 170, 172, 218-219
Thagard, Paul R., 177, 187, 213
Thibon, Gustave, 88
Thomas Aquinas, St., 4, 5, 9, 14, 17, 20-21, 23, 25-29, 34, 38, 40, 44-47, 49, 90, 155
Pseudo-Thomas, 14
Thomas, George F., 113
Thompson, Colin P., 12, 15
Tracy, David, xvi
Trethowan, Illtyd, 33
Tyrell, Thomas J., 64

Underhill, Evelyn, 2, 87-88, 92

Van Herik, Judith, 193
Vaughan, Robert Alfred, 2-3, 13, 59
Victorines, 14
Vilnet, Jean, 14-15
Vogelgesang, Sandy, 13
von Balthasar, Hans Urs, 31

Wainwright, William J., 37, 90, 93, 97-99, 106, 121-124, 127, 155-156, 158-159, 161, 171-172
Wallace, Robert Keith, 205
Wallace, William, 27, 34
Wapnick, Kenneth, 213
Werblowsky, R. J. Zwi, 3, 26, 31, 71
Whitely, C. H., 138, 146, 165
Whitson, Robley Edward, xiii
Wilber, Ken, 196
Wilhelmsen, Elizabeth, 44
Wittgenstein, Ludwig, 121
Wolfe, Tom, 1

Zabalza, Laureano de la Inmaculada, 59-60, 77, 86, 88-89
Zaehner, R. C., 37, 107

INDEX OF SUBJECTS

Adam, 29, 47, 51, 79
Affectivity, 20, 34, 37
Agreement, inter-subjective, xi, xiv, 126, 129-154, 169, 170-171, 174, 182, 211, 216
   among mystics themselves, 126, 137-146, 182, 186, 195, 203, 208-209, 210-211, 217-218
   between mystic and non-mystic, 130-137, 182, 186, 203
   role of mystic's prior beliefs, 126, 146-153, 171-172, 182, 186, 208, 210-211
Analogy, 177, 187, 195, 202
Anthropological Accounts of Mysticism, Reductive, *see* Sociological Accounts of Mysticism, Reductive
Appetites, 20, 33-35, 37-38, 45, 47-48, 51-52, 54, 61-63, 66, 79, 85
   mortification of, 51, 54, 57-62
Aridity/Dryness, 64-66, 69, 73
Ascent of Mount Carmel, 7, 9, 12, 14
   organization of *Ascent-Dark Night*, 14, 21, 24, 39, 56-59
Atheists/Atheism, xiv, 183, 217, 219

Beatitude/Beatific Vision, 47, 82-85, 90
Beginners (in the spiritual life), 55-66, 72, 86, 100, 105, 118
Best Explanation, Argument to, *see* Explanatory Inference
Bible, *see* Scripture
Body, 17-19, 45, 82, 89, 119
Buddhism/The Buddha, 93, 116, 138-139, 141-142, 146, 148-149, 152, 161, 172, 211

Carmelites, 4-6, 12
Central Sense (*sensus communis*), 20-21, 40-44, 49
Charity, *see* Love

Christ/Jesus, 63, 81-82, 87, 114, 149, 163
Cognitive Mode of Experience, Hypothesis that Mysticism is, xv, 175, 180-181, 184-188, 194, 198, 202, 205-210, 212
'Common Core' Hypothesis (that mysticism is 'everywhere the same'), xii, xiii, 92, 96, 106-116, 123, 129, 138-139, 143-144, 147, 152, 170
Completeness, 176-177, 187, 195, 203, 205, 208
Concepts, *see* Intelligible Species
'Consciousness Without Content'/Awareness of 'Pure Undifferentiated Unity,' xii, xiii, 30, 99, 105, 106-116, 123, 211, 216, *see also* Unity, Mystical
Consilience, 177, 187, 195, 202, 204, 207-208, 213
Consolations, 61, 65, 88
Contemplation/Contemplative Awareness, 65-67, 72, 74-75, 84, 90, 96-97, 105, 116, 118, 139
   continuity throughout stages of spiritual life, 64-65, 72, 75-76, 84-85
Correctness, 176, 187, 198
Creatures, contemplative awareness of, 67, 77, 80-81, 87, 89, 97, 106, 117, 172, *see also* Extrovertive Mysticism
Credulity, Principle of, 127-128, 174, 212, 214

Dark Night of the Soul, 9, 12, 14, 56
Deautomatization, 199-203, 209, 211, 216, 219
Depth, 176-177, 187, 195, 202, 204-205, 207, 208
Devil/Evil Spirits, 42, 67, 85, 87, 89, 100, 113, 123, 158, 218
Director, Spiritual, 8
Discalced Carmelites, 6-8, 12

INDEX OF SUBJECTS

Disequilibrium/Disharmony/Disorder, 51-54
Divinization, 29-30, 81-82, 89
Drugs and Mysticism, 202, 204-205
Dualism
  between body and soul, 17-18, 215
  between mystic and God, 11-12, 76, 111, 215, *see also* Monism *and* Theistic Interpretation of Mystical Experience

Ecstasy, *see* Extraordinary Phenomena
Empiricism, 19-20, 33, 44-45
  empiricist theory of meaning, 103
Espousal, Spiritual, 56, 59-60, 77-78, 88-89, 95-96, 165
  distinguished from day of espousal, 77
  relation to passive night of spirit, 77-78, 88-89
Evidence/Mystical Data to be Explained, xiv, 116-121, 124, 128-129, 137, 145-146, 152-153, 164, 168, 178-179, 180-183, 185-186, 209-211, 216-217
Evidential Support, 176, 195-196, 202, 208-209
Evil, Argument from, 183, 218
Experience vs. Interpretation (in reports of mystical states), xii, 81-82, 85, 106-116, 123, 138, 143-144
  'low-level' vs. 'high-level' interpretations, 107-108
Explanation, 175-177, 179
Explanatory Inference, ix, xii-xv, 10, 91, 116-117, 126, 168, 175, 177-213, 216-217
Extraordinary Phenomena (visions, raptures, etc.), 19, 22, 29, 45, 47, 56-57, 67-69, 72, 80, 87, 89, 95, 105, 112, 118-119
Extrovertive Mystical Experiences, 77, 81, 87, 89, 94-95, 97, 106, 121

Faith, 58, 70-73, 75, 87-88, 182, 219
  as cognitive, 71-72
  as continuous with contemplation, 72
  trials of, 75, 120, 182
Fall/Original Sin, 19, 29, 51, 61, *see also* Adam

French Spirituality, Influence of John on, 1, 13

God, Ways of Knowing, 18-19, 23, 26-30, 47-48
  known through attributes, 81, 115, 118, 122-123
  mystical knowledge of God, 65, 104, 139
Grace/Gratuity, 52-53, 90, 104, 106, 115, 136, 149
  mystic confirmed in grace, 79

Heaven, *see* Beatitude
Hinduism, 110-112, 123, 138, 146, 149, 156
Holy/Sacred, 95, 98, 116-117, 123, 136, 160, 181, 217
Hope, 41, 58, 70, 72
Humility/Self-Knowledge, 65, 74, 76, 162, 173, 182

Illumination (of faith), 72
Illuminative Way, 55, 57, 60, 66-78, 89, 96
Imagination, 20-25, 38, 46, 49, *see also* Interior Senses
Incarnation, 71, 81-82, 90, *see also* Christ, Jesus
Induction/Plurality of Cases, xii-xiii, 167, 179-180, 217
Ineffability, xi-xii, 32-33, 94-96, 99-104, 115, 122, 201-202
Infantile State/Nursing Experience, Regression to, 192-198, 202, 217
Infinitude (of object of mystical experiences), 165-167
Inquisition, 8, 10-12, 15, 111-113
Integration (of human person), 19, 22, 52, 75, 76, 181, 196
Intellect, 17, 24-33, 42, 46, 48, 58, 77, 79, 85-86
  active vs. passive, 25-30, 36, 38, 46, 77
  relation to memory, 39
  relation to will, 24, 33-37, 48
Intention/Intentional Object of Experience, 25-26, 47, 98, 127, 169, 181

INDEX OF SUBJECTS

Introvertive Mystical Experiences, 81, 87, 94-95, 97, 106-116, 121
Islam/Mohammed, 138, 149, 161, 172

Jewish Mysticism, 149
John of the Cross, St., *passim*
  influence of, 1-3
  life of, 4-7, 13-14
  writings of, 10-15

Knowledge, Connatural (through virtues), 79, 89-90
Knowledge, Habitual vs. Occurent, 31-32, 72, 80
Knowledge, Mystical, 65-66, 69, 77, 80, 84
  general, 65, 69, 72
  loving, 65, 68, 116
  obscure, 48, 65, 69

Living Flame of Love, 8-9, 11-12, 59
Logic, x, 99, 101, 103, 155, 158, 166, 172, *see also* Reason/Rationality
Love, 36-37, 48, 53, 58, 70, 72, 79, 83-84, 115, 162, 182, 197, 211
  of neighbor, 66

Manner of Presentation, 176-177, 195, 202
Marriage, Spiritual, 47, 55-56, 59-60, 76, 78-84, 88-90, 95-97, 104-105, 113, 114-116, 118, 141, 165
'Mediated'/'Unmediated' Experience, 83-85, 201-203
Meditation/Discursive Prayer, 22-23, 46, 61-65, 72, 86, 105
  discontinuing meditation (signs for), 64-65, 86-87
Memory, 17, 20-24, 38-42, 49, 58, 79, 86
Monism, 108, 111, 143, 147-148
  compared to religious dualism, 76, 111, 143, 145
Morality/Moral Progress, Mysticism and, 52, 54-55, 65-66, 76, 78-79, 119-120, 123-124, 135, 155, 182, 185, 211, 213, 216-218
  moral disorder, 65, 78, 82, 85

Mortification, *see* Appetites
Moses, 47
Mystical Theology, 14, 69, 87
Mysticism, Problem of Defining, xi, 91-93, 116, 121

Night of Sense, Active, 57, 60-63, 85-86
Night of Sense, Passive, 55, 57, 60, 64-65, 85-88, 97-98, 105
Night of Spirit, Active, 57, 60, 70-73, 85-86
Night of Spirit, Passive, 55, 57, 60, 68, 73-78, 85-86, 88-89, 96-98, 105, 119-120
Nights, Number of (in John's doctrine), 57-60, 85-86, 88
  three reasons for calling journey 'night,' 50, 58-59, 71, 82
  two kinds, each with active and passive component, 57-59
Noetic Quality (of mystical states), xi, 28, 30-31, 37, 65, 77, 85, 91, 94, 97-98, 115-117, 122, 126-128, 154, 181, 184, 199, 211
Nominalism, 5
Numinous, xi, 74-76, 88, 121

Object-Relations Theory, 191, 197
Objectivity, 95, 97, 164-165, *see also* Noetic Quality
Occam's Razor, 168, 187, *see also* Simplicity
'Oceanic Feeling,' 192-195, 213
Oedipal Origins of Religion, Freud's Theory of, 189-193, 197
Orthodoxy, 149-150, 155-157, 160-161, 166-167, 185

Paradoxicality, 95, 98-99, 122
Passions, 34-38, 48
Passivity, 30, 47, 94, 104-106, 115, 119-120, 136, 160, 182, 185, 211, 218
Pathology, 119, 194, 196, 211, 213, 216, 218
Perception, 20-23, 39, 43, 127
  causal theory of, 150-152, 172, 212
Perception-like, Mystical Experiences as, *see* Noetic Quality

INDEX OF SUBJECTS

Perfect, 55-60, 78-82, 84, see also Unitive Way
Phantasy, 20-25, 40, 46
Physical Health of Mystic, 65, 76, 119, 155, 182
Physiological Accounts of Mysticism, Reductive, xv, 188, 204-206, 209, 211-212
Presence, 52-54, 85
Probability, see Induction
Proficients, 55-60, 66-78, 88, 95, see also Illuminative Way
 their imperfections, 56, 69-70, 72-74, 88
Psychoanalytic Theory, 74, 188-189, 198, 202, 213
Psychoanalytical Accounts of Mysticism, Reductive, xv, 168, 188-198, 202, 209, 211-212
Psychological Accounts of Mysticism, Reductive, xv, 188, 198-204, 209, 211-212
Psychological Maturity, Mysticism and, 52, 54-55, 76, 79, 118-120, 123-124, 135, 155, 160-162, 181, 185, 211, 213, 216, 218
 psychological disorder, 65, 79, 82, 85, 118, 181, 185
Purgatory/Hell, 82, 88
Purgative Way, 55, 57, 61-66, see also Beginners

Qualified Observer, 130-137, 175

Raptures, see Extraordinary Phenomena
Reason/Rationality, 32, 38, 49, 72, 128, 172, 219
Regression, 191-198, 200, 209, 211, 213-214, 216, 219
 in service of the ego, 196-197, 213
Relevance, 176-177, 187, 194-195, 202

Schizophrenia, Mysticism and, 204-205
Scholasticism/Scholastic Philosophy, 5, 8-10, 16-17, 20, 24-26, 29, 33-34, 37-38, 43, 45-46, 48, 50, 67, 70, 83, 89, 114, 149, 215, see also Thomas Aquinas, St.
Scripture, 5, 8, 155, 163, 177-178, 185

Self-Knowledge, see Humility
Sense Perception/Sensation/Sensory Experience, xii, 108, 127, 135, 144, 150, 156, 158-160, 166, 169, 204-205, 207
Sense/Spirit Dichotomy, 17-18, 45, 57, 85
Senses, Exterior, 17, 19, 24, 42, 67
Senses, Interior, 17, 20-23, 67
Senses, Spiritual, 19-20, 41-44, 49
Sensory Part of the Soul, 17-23, 45, 57
Sexuality, Mysticism and, 63, 119, 197, 214
Simplicity, 176-177, 187, 195, 198, 203, 205, 208-209
Sociological Accounts of Mysticism, Reductive, xv, 188, 206-209, 212
Soul, 17-18, 45, 82
Spain, 10, 75
Species, Intelligible, 20-22, 24-28, 38-39, 45-48, 83, 100, 122
Species, Sensible, 21-27, 39-40, 44, 46-47, 89, 100
Spiritual Canticle, 7-9, 14, 56, 59
 Cántico A vs. *Cántico B*, 10-12, 15, 56, 85, 88
Spiritual Part of the Soul, 17-18, 23-45, see also Sense/Spirit Dichotomy
Spiritual Marriage, see Marriage, Spiritual
Stages of Spiritual Development, 50, 55-82, 117-118, 181, 215-216
Substance of Soul, 31, 41-44, 49
 substantial knowledge, 30-31, 47-48, 62
 substantial touch, 43, 49, 77, 87, 89, 100
 substantial union, 53, 80, 85
Sufism, see Islam/Mohammed

Testability, xi, 65, 69, 126, 129, 131-133, 142-143, 153-164, 169-170, 172-173, 185-186, 203, 216
Theistic Interpretation of Mystical Experience, xi-xii, xiv, 76, 81-82, 97, 106-118, 120, 123, 136-140, 143-153, 166, 170, 181-182, 184-186, 195, 202-203, 210-211, 216, 218
Timelessness/Spacelessness, 94, 98, 113, 122, 164, 199
Transformation, see Divinization

INDEX OF SUBJECTS

Transiency, 94, 98, 115, 122
Trinity, 23, 46, 71-72, 81-82, 90, 114-115, 118, 147, 149, 171

Unconscious, 39, 67
Unification, 176-177, 187, 195, 203, 205, 208
Union, Mystical, 36, 53-54, 68, 77, 80, 85, 91, 110-114, 116, 123, 193
 different kinds, 52-54, 97-98
 habitual union, 80, 97, 118
 touch of union, 67, 77, 80, 84, 96, 105
 union of wills, 33, 36, 52-54
Union with God, Natural, 52-54, 85
Unitive Way, 55, 57, 60, 76, 78-82, 89, 96, 97, 118

Unity, Mystical Experience of, xii, 94, 96, 103, 106-116, 123, 139-140, 171, 201-203
Unity of Human Person, 18
Universality of Capacity for Mystical Experience, xii, 54, 120, 123, 131-133, 182
Upanishads, *see* Hinduism

Vision of God, Direct, *see* Beatitude
Visions, *see* Extraordinary Phenomena
Voluntarism, 33

Ways, Three, 55, 57, 59-60, 88
Will, 17, 33-38, 42, 45, 48, 58, 79, 86

Synthese Historical Library
Texts and Studies in the History of Logic and Philosophy

Series Editor: Norman Kretzmann (Cornell University)

1. M.T. Beonio-Brocchieri Fumagalli: *The Logic of Abelard*. Translated from Italian by S. Pleasance. 1969 ISBN 90-277-0068-0
2. G. W. Leibniz: *Philosophical Papers and Letters*. A Selection, translated and edited, with an Introduction, by L. E. Loemker. 2nd ed., 2nd printing. 1976
ISBN 90-277-0008-8
3. E. Mally: *Logische Schriften*. Grosses Logikfragment – Grundgesetze des Sollens. Herausgegeben von K. Wolf und P. Weingartner. 1971 ISBN 90-277-0174-1
4. L. W. Beck (ed.): *Proceedings of the Third International Kant Congress*. 1972
ISBN 90-277-0188-1
5. B. Bolzano: *Theory of Science*. A Selection with an Introduction by J. Berg. Translated from German by B. Terrell. 1973 ISBN 90-277-0248-9
6. J. M. E. Moravcsik (ed.): *Patterns in Plato's Thought*. 1973 ISBN 90-277-0286-1
7. Avicenna: *The Propositional Logic*. A Translation from *Al-Shifā': al-Qiyās*, with Introduction, Commentary and Glossary by N. Shehaby. 1973 ISBN 90-277-0360-4
8. D. P. Henry: *Commentary on* De Grammatico. *The Historical-Logical Dimensions of a Dialogue of St. Anselms's*. 1974 ISBN 90-277-0382-5
9. J. Corcoran (ed.): *Ancient Logic and its Modern Interpretations*. 1974
ISBN 90-277-0395-7
10. E. M. Barth: *The Logic of the Articles in Traditional Philosophy*. A Contribution to the Study of Conceptual Structures. 1974 ISBN 90-277-0350-7
11. J. Hintikka: *Knowledge and the Known*. Historical Perspectives in Epistemology. 1974
ISBN 90-277-0455-4
12. E. J. Ashworth: *Language and Logic in the Post-Medieval Period*. 1974
ISBN 90-277-0464-3
13. Aristotle: *The Nicomachean Ethics*. Translation with Commentaries and Glossary by H. G. Apostle. 1974 ISBN 90-277-0569-0
14. R. M. Dancy: *Sense and Contradiction*. A Study in Aristotle. 1975
ISBN 90-277-0565-8
15. W. R. Knorr: *The Evolution of the Euclidean Elements*. A Study of the Theory of Incommensurable Magnitudes and its Significance for Early Greek Geometry. 1975
ISBN 90-277-0509-7
16. Augustine: *De Dialectica*. Translated with Introduction and Notes by B. D. Jackson from the Text newly edited by J. Pinborg. 1975 ISBN 90-277-0538-9
17. Á. Szabó: *The Beginnings of Greek Mathematics*. Translated from German. 1978
ISBN 90-277-0819-3
18. Juan Luis Vives: *Against the Pseudodialecticians*. A Humanist Attack on Medieval Logic. Texts (in Latin), with Translation, Introduction and Notes by R. Guerlac. 1979
ISBN 90-277-0900-9
19. Peter of Ailly: *Concepts and Insolubles*. An Annotated Translation (from Latin) by P. V. Spade. 1980 ISBN 90-277-1079-1
20. S. Knuuttila (ed.): *Reforging the Great Chain of Being*. Studies of the History of Modal Theories. 1981 ISBN 90-277-1125-9
21. J. V. Buroker: *Space and Incongruence*. The Origin of Kant's Idealism. 1981
ISBN 90-277-1203-4

Synthese Historical Library
Texts and Studies in the History of Logic and Philosophy

22. Marsilius of Inghen: *Treatises on the Properties of Terms*. A First Critical Edition of the *Suppositiones, Ampliationes, Appellationes, Restrictiones* and *Alienationes* with Introduction, Translation, Notes and Appendices by E. P. Bos. 1983
ISBN 90-277-1343-X
23. W. R. de Jong: *The Semantics of John Stuart Mill*. 1982   ISBN 90-277-1408-8
24. René Descartes: *Principles of Philosophy*. Translation with Explanatory Notes by V. R. Miller and R. P. Miller. 1983   ISBN 90-277-1451-7
25. T. Rudavsky (ed.): *Divine Omniscience and Omnipotence in Medieval Philosophy*. Islamic, Jewish and Christian Perspectives. 1985   ISBN 90-277-1750-8
26. William Heytesbury: *On Maxima and Minima*. Chapter V of *Rules for Solving Sophismata*, with an Anonymous 14th-century Discussion. Translation from Latin with an Introduction and Study by J. Longeway. 1984   ISBN 90-277-1868-7
27. Jean Buridan's *Logic. The Treatise on Supposition. The Treatise on Consequences*. Translation from Latin with a Philosophical Introduction by P. King. 1985
ISBN 90-277-1918-7
28. S. Knuuttila and J. Hintikka (eds.): *The Logic of Being*. Historical Studies. 1986
ISBN 90-277-2019-3
29. E. Sosa (ed.): *Essays on the Philosophy of George Berkeley*. 1987
ISBN 90-277-2405-9
30. B. Brundell: *Pierre Gassendi: From Aristotelianism to a New Natural Philosophy*. 1987   ISBN 90-277-2428-8
31. Adam de Wodeham: *Tractatus de indivisibilibus*. A Critical Edition with Introduction, Translation, and Textual Notes by R. Wood. 1988   ISBN 90-277-2424-5
32. N. Kretzmann (ed.): *Meaning and Inference in Medieval Philosophy*. Studies in Memory of J. Pinborg (1937–1982). 1988   ISBN 90-277-2577-2
33. S. Knuuttila (ed.): *Modern Modalities*. Studies of the History of Modal Theories from Medieval Nominalism to Logical Positivism. 1988   ISBN 90-277-2678-7
34. G. F. Scarre: *Logic and Reality in the Philosophy of John Stuart Mill*. 1988
ISBN 90-277-2739-2
35. J. van Rijen: *Aspects of Aristotle's Logic of Modalities*. 1989   ISBN 0-7923-0048-3
36. L. Baudry: *The Quarrel over Future Contingents (Louvain 1465–1475)*. Unpublished Latin Texts collected and translated in French by L. Baudry. Translated from French by R. Guerlac. 1989   ISBN 0-7923-0454-3

THE NEW SYNTHESE HISTORICAL LIBRARY
Texts and Studies in the History of Philosophy

37. S. Payne: *John of the Cross and the Cognitive Value of Mysticism*. An Analysis of Sanjuanist Teaching and its Philosophical Implications for Contemporary Discussions of Mystical Experience. 1990   ISBN 0-7923-0707-0

Kluwer Academic Publishers – Dordrecht / Boston / London